r

MANY FACES, ONE VOICE

"Greg Williams's powerful documentary, *The Anonymous People*, helped change the public's view of the world of people in recovery and those who love them, opening the doors to a new understanding of the usually hidden process of recovering from addiction. The new book, *Many Faces, One Voice*, takes the messages of that film to the next level, with even more powerful testimony and insight from an incredible group of brave, open souls. A moving, challenging, and revealing portrait of the world of recovery today—and tomorrow."

PATRICK KENNEDY
Former Congressman
Primary sponsor of the Mental Health Parity and Addictions Equity Act
Founder, The Kennedy Forum

"*Many Faces, One Voice* is a collection of inspirational stories of remarkable people who not only prove that recovery from addiction is possible, but with recovery comes a life people once thought was impossible—one characterized by love, accomplishment, and joy. In America, we often talk about the millions of people suffering the devastating illness of addiction but too often forget that it's treatable. There are twenty-three million reminders in America: People in recovery who, until recently, stayed hidden because of shame, guilt, and prejudice that accompany this disease. People are tired of hiding in the shadows. The documentary *The Anonymous People* celebrated the profoundness of recovery. The celebration continues in the moving stories collected in *Many Faces, One Voice*."

DAVID SHEFF
Author of *Beautiful Boy* and *Clean*

"Once in a while, a game-changing documentary revolutionizes the way people think about a subject, launching a movement in its wake. Greg Williams's

The Anonymous People did just that, cracking open the world of recovery for thousands of viewers. *Many Faces, One Voice* takes us deep inside that world once again. Profoundly real and moving, it's a must-read for anyone interested in the world of recovery from addiction."

ANN DOWSETT JOHNSTON

Author of *Drink: The Intimate Relationship Between Women and Alcohol*

"*Many Faces, One Voice* is a paradigm shifter! Like the film, *The Anonymous People*, the book changes the conversation from the sensationalized problems of addiction to the real solutions of recovery. It shows how important it is for people in recovery, with their wisdom and strength, to stand up and be public about the transformative and productive lives they live—not just to help others deal with this illness, but to help the world out of some of the other messes it's gotten itself into! *Many Faces, One Voice* points to a truly revolutionary idea: a World of Recovery."

CHRISTOPHER KENNEDY LAWFORD

Author, Actor, Advocate

"Several years ago I began to advocate for a young woman inmate who was addicted to crack cocaine in her early teens. She would shoplift, get arrested, get released, shoplift, get arrested, and get released. All during those many years there was no treatment available to her. It is clearly obvious, a lot of heartache could have been avoided for her and her young children if there were services in place to address her addiction and stop that all-too-common cycle of human destruction. There must be!

"Bud Mikhitarian has written an important book. There are lessons described here that are crucial to follow . . . if we want to see ourselves as a civilized country."

CHARLES GRODIN

CBS News Commentator

Winner of the William Kunstler Award for Racial Justice

MANY FACES
ONE VOICE

khitarian

MANY FACES ONE VOICE

Secrets from
THE ANONYMOUS PEOPLE

CRP
CENTRAL RECOVERY PRESS

LAS VEGAS

CENTRAL RECOVERY PRESS (CRP) is committed to publishing exceptional materials addressing addiction treatment, recovery, and behavioral healthcare topics, including original and quality books, audio/visual communications, and web-based new media. Through a diverse selection of titles, we seek to contribute a broad range of unique resources for professionals, recovering individuals and their families, and the general public.

For more information, visit www.centralrecoverypress.com.

Publisher: Central Recovery Press
3321 N. Buffalo Drive
Las Vegas, NV 89129

20 19 18 17 16 15   1 2 3 4 5

ISBN: 978-1-937612-93-1 (paper)
978-1-937612-94-8 (e-book)

PUBLISHER'S NOTE: Our books represent the experiences and opinions of their authors only. Every effort has been made to ensure that events, institutions, and statistics presented in our books as facts are accurate and up-to-date.

This book contains general information about addiction and addiction treatment and recovery. The information is not medical advice, and should not be treated as such.

Central Recovery Press makes no representations or warranties in relation to the medical information in this book; this book is not an alternative to medical advice from your doctor or other professional healthcare provider. If you have any specific questions about any medical matter related to the disease of addiction and/or treatment modalities for addiction, you should consult your doctor or other professional healthcare provider.

If you think you or someone close to you may be suffering from addiction or any other medical condition, you should seek immediate medical attention. You should never delay seeking medical advice, disregard medical advice, or discontinue medical treatment because of information in this or any book.   ·

Cover design and interior by Marisa Jackson

TABLE OF CONTENTS

FOREWORD

My name is Greg Williams and I am person in long-term recovery from addiction to alcohol and other drugs since age seventeen. My recovery was "established" in 2001. As a result of my personal freedom from addiction, not only have I stayed alive in the face of the most deadly health problem facing young people in America today, but I have thrived. I have been blessed with incredible opportunities to learn, chase dreams, and live a life full of purpose.

The Anonymous People became one of my dreams fulfilled and it continues to live on with purpose, thanks to the support and collaboration of many talented and resourceful people. One of those was Bud Mikhitarian. As the man behind the sound recording for every interview we conducted across the country, and as a person not in long-term recovery, Bud is the only person on the planet who could write a book about the making of the film with such depth and perspective.

Words cannot adequately express my deep gratitude to Bud, not only for his initiative and hard work putting together this book, but also for his incredible talent as a storyteller. I hope that when people see *The Anonymous People* and read this book, they will connect with the powerful stories we have captured and share these stories with others.

We must keep shining a light on what recovery gives back to our communities. We must keep pushing the agenda of the new recovery advocacy movement forward.

Sadly, more than four decades after the groundbreaking United States Senate hearings of 1969 hosted by Senator Harold Hughes, where Academy Award-winning actress Mercedes McCambridge and cofounder of Alcoholics Anonymous, Bill Wilson—both in long-term recovery—spoke candidly to our national elected representatives about the public stigmatization of alcoholics, discrimination still persists. People with addiction are still blamed and shamed by their so-called moral weaknesses.

The Anonymous People—and now this book—aim to be a part of the solution that erodes a bit of this perpetual, insidious stigma. People in recovery from addiction, our families, and allies have a duty to respond to the ignorance, prejudice, and injustice that continue to pervade our culture. Lives depend on it. In spite of a broken system and failed community response, many of us have been given the gift of recovery and that can have profound cultural, political, healthcare, criminal justice, and economic implications.

Bill White says, "We will shape the future of recovery with a detached silence or with a passionate voice."

The voices of recovery come from people of many different colors, ages, and backgrounds, but our message is pretty simple. We are a group of people who have battled (individually or collectively) and survived arguably the most devastating health problem of our time and now live dynamic, productive lives just like people who are managing diabetes, heart disease, or cancer.

Too few people are aware that through recovery more than twenty-three million of us have gotten well, families have been reunited, and our communities have been the ultimate beneficiary. Congress does not believe we exist in such significant numbers (yet), and the media continues to ignore this giant facet of the addiction story. It is our duty to share our stories with a unified message to a new audience so that future generations can live free from the greatest barriers to recovery—stigma, shame, and discrimination.

No matter how addiction has touched your life, I invite you to read the inspiring stories in this book and to consider becoming one of the many faces sharing your own story in harmony with a growing chorus of revolutionaries.

GREG WILLIAMS • Director of *The Anonymous People*

PROLOGUE

There are many faces in this book. They are all beautiful. Look at them closely. You will see truth in their eyes, as they share what they have seen. You may not have had experiences exactly like theirs, but they are yours now, if you embrace and absorb them.

These faces, they are you.

Next, listen to their voices. When you read the words that came from their hearts, imagine they are speaking to you—because they are. Intimately and honestly, they share secrets and wisdom for you.

These voices, as one, are yours.

INTRODUCTION

Hi. My name is Bud Mikhitarian and I'm a person in long-term . . . discovery.

And for me that means, while I've been fortunate not to have a problem with alcohol or other drugs, I have, nevertheless, been blessed with discovering the miracles of recovery. And what a journey that has been.

I say this with apologies to the twenty-three million Americans who are in long-term recovery from addiction to alcohol or other drugs, who will recognize that I am paraphrasing the heartfelt introduction many of them now use to self-identify:

> "My name is [name] and I'm a person in long-term recovery, and I haven't had a drink or other drug in [number] years. And for me that means . . ."

And then they go on to briefly state the personal benefit of not using and the consequential positive impacts their recovery has had on their family, community, and society.

You can hardly imagine how important this language is. I didn't, at first. But now I do. Simply stated, the message de-emphasizes the addiction experience and highlights the success of recovery. But do not be deceived, this is not a simple idea; it has profound, far-reaching, and no less than revolutionary ramifications. Thus, my introduction/greeting is not meant to detract from the power of the recovering person's affirmation, rather, it is meant to illuminate it and promote it. That is the thrust of this book, which I was motivated to write because of the transformative experience—and privilege—of working on *The Anonymous People*, the groundbreaking film about addiction and recovery, produced and directed by Greg Williams.

In January of 2012, three of us—Greg, Craig Mikhitarian, Director of Photography (my younger, smarter brother), and me (I was capturing sound and listening really hard)—jumped into Greg's Honda Pilot (borrowed from his family), crammed it with half a ton of film equipment, a case of water, and a box of granola bars, and then set out on a jam-packed journey that took us 10,000 miles through twenty states, and to every other Wawa along the way to refuel with gas and Red Bull.

We weren't always sure where we were going or what we would find when we got there, but through fate, generosity, and not a little of Greg's design, we discovered people and uncovered stories that would change our lives. For example, one of our trips was to Richmond, Virginia, where we met John Shinholser, a Renaissance man, if ever there was one. Much more about him later. He opened his house to us. He opened his BBQ pit to us. And he opened our hearts. As exceptional a person as he is, along with his wife and cause lobbyist, Carol McDaid, we soon found out that they are typical, though all in unique ways, of the many faces and voices of recovery we met throughout this country. These are the people who are part of the new recovery advocacy movement and who are, quite literally, changing the world.

In our journey, we talked with hundreds of people involved in this movement, from all walks of life, and we recorded nearly 120 hours of exclusive video. Add to that another eighty hours or so, of archival footage that Greg acquired and you have an accumulation of about 200 hours of images and sound that Greg and his talented film editor, Jeff Reilly, boiled down to the eighty-four-minute miracle that is *The Anonymous People*. But, let me tell you, the stuff left on the cutting room floor, which, for the simple reason of time didn't make it into the film, well, those stories, those people, and those outtakes are just as compelling and inspiring as anything in the finished film.

As I sat one day in the editing room with Greg, Craig, and Jeff reviewing an early rough cut, the discussions kept going to "What about . . . ? You can't leave him out!" or "You're cutting that? That's my favorite scene!" And so on. The frustration in the room over what had to be cut from the film was thick. From day one, we all had our precious scenes in mind, which we each felt must be included. But, among the four of us, we had over 100 years of professional experience in telling stories on film, and we all knew the old adage well, "Sometimes, you just have to kill your darlings." That cruel hyperbole attempts to describe the pain of recognizing that a glorious shot or a pithy interview, preconceived as once indispensible to the story, now no longer fits. Hit "Delete." Ouch!

The gems on the cutting room floor were piling up fast. Insightful interviews. Illuminating stories.

I said to Greg, "I want to write a book about this." Greg responded without hesitation. His exact words, I believe, were "Go for it!"

So, with Greg's encouragement, generous support, and quite a bit of patience, here finally is the book about the making of *The Anonymous People*, and about our journey to discover and celebrate the people of the recovery advocacy movement. There are so many stories from so many people to share that are not only inspiring but also contain useful information about how to achieve, maintain, and advocate for recovery. I hope it is a worthy complement to Greg's beautiful film.

This is not intended to be a scholarly book; it is observational. For books that carry the weight of authority, diligent research, and wisdom, I cannot direct you to better sources than *Slaying the Dragon: The History of Addiction Treatment and Recovery in America* or *Let's Go Make Some History: Chronicles of the New Addiction Recovery Advocacy Movement* both by William L. White. These, and so many more books by other titans in addiction and recovery, stand as bibles in the field and remain inspirations to me, and certainly were to Greg as he made *The Anonymous People*.

The real wisdom in this book lies in the words of all our interviewees, people whose stories could each be a book or a film of their own. If read individually at random, these interviews are like little story islands that both inspire and inform.

Some of them are just downright entertaining. They can be funny, poignant, moving, and smart. Collectively, all these voices combine to create an insight into what the new recovery advocacy movement is and what it could become.

A note about these interviews: They are as nearly verbatim as I could leave them; however, I did edit them. Our process of filming was informal, and what we recorded was more conversational than interrogatory. Greg put everyone at ease and gave everyone the opportunity to stop and start and say what they wanted to say in the way they wanted to say it. As a result, there was considerable repetition and veering off point, as relaxed conversation always is. Thus, in editing these interviews, I sometimes reordered the questions and responses to provide better logical flow to the content, just to make it easier to read. I also took care, as Greg did in his film editing, to protect any inadvertent breach of anonymity as it relates to a person's membership in an anonymous mutual aid fellowship, by respecting and adhering to the Eleventh Tradition of AA, which seeks to maintain anonymity at the level of press, radio, and films. Lastly, I took the liberty of improving spoken grammar, but only on those occasions when the incorrect form would mislead or cloud clarity. I never made an edit, no matter what, if I thought the edit would compromise the intent or character of the speaker.

The interviews, then, comprise the bulk of this book. But the story is also about my personal discovery, which came about with each new face and voice we met. It was like the search for a national treasure; clue by clue, people revealed secrets and knowledge that led to an epiphany. This journey is about what I have been blessed to learn by meeting Greg, hearing him tell his story, and exposing me to a powerful community of people in recovery. It is anecdotal and honest, and likely not without some controversy. While those of you in recovery will relate to the people and their stories, you may well find some of my insights obvious at times, because through your own addiction and recovery you have already had your hearts and minds opened to the light of spirit and knowledge such experience brings. What I hope is that you will take my comments, as an outside observer, to be both an appreciation of what you have endured and an affirmation of what you have accomplished. This book of stories may even help you in validating the path you are on, or perhaps, it will show you another. I hope that possibility alone will inspire you to act on your higher calling in life with new ideas and do even better. In any case, every word I have written in this book comes with a clap of my hands; collect them all at the end, and the resulting sound of applause is for you.

For those of you suffering and yet to experience the benefit and blessing of recovery, I hope you will be inspired, too. In addition to the estimated twenty-three million people in this country living in successful recovery, there are another twenty-two million people like you who are currently experiencing some form of active addiction, people who are in need of immediate counsel and treatment, but for a variety of reasons that we explore, cannot find the help. This book and the film are for you, too. If you are in the problem stage, know that recovery is the solution. Both the film and this book show what that solution looks like. It is hopeful. It is real.

For all the rest of us who are untouched by this affliction, or simply uniformed, be advised—we are not immune to addiction and its effects. Consequently, recovery means more to us than you might think. The profound changes that recovery brings to people's lives are worth examining and contemplating because the experience, the values, and the solutions of recovery from addiction are applicable to any individual or community problem. That's why this book is for everyone. What I learned and what we can all learn will wake you and shake you. People in long-term successful recovery are changing the world. They do this in incremental ways.

One: On an individual level, the peer-to-peer sharing of successful recovery stories gives help and hope to those suffering from addiction to alcohol and/or other drugs—right now, when they need it. That's how change of any kind starts—small, one-to-one. A life is saved and the ripple effect begins.

Two: On a larger scale, sharing recovery gives everyone in the same recovery boat the strength to maintain and sustain recovery for life. I have come to believe that long-term recovery represents a virtual cure from addiction. That's my opinion. Scientists can debate the idea of "cure," but practically speaking, one can recover from addiction—for life. That's a "cure" in my book of common parlance, and it is language we shouldn't be afraid to use. "When do I get 'well'?" the great recovery advocate, Senator Harold Hughes asked rhetorically as he challenged the notion that even after "fifty god-damn years" of sobriety one is still called a "happily recovering alcoholic." This book is filled with recovery stories that prove language alters perception. If your recovery story helps the wider community to believe there is a solution to addiction—a cure, if you will—and that recovery is real, then the conversation changes. Can you imagine the power of that positive perception? For a start, stigma turns to compassion; hopelessness to optimism.

And three: Globally, for all the rest of us, when twenty-three million Americans choose to tell their recovery stories, it should grab our attention and transform our lives. People in recovery teach us about change, at all levels. Simply put, recovery shows us how to live our own lives better, how to look out for each other, how to strengthen our communities, and how to build a society that embraces *everyone* with values common to our humanity. I think we can all buy into change like that.

These are not new thoughts. Men and women wiser than me have been expressing these ideas forever. What is new here is the realization that each of us is more directly touched by the destructive forces of addiction in our society than ever before; hence, it is more relevant than ever to catch the current of restorative change that flows from the concepts of recovery. In these pages, you will encounter some of the wisest of our contemporaries; they eloquently and intimately articulate the models of change we must embrace. They are people you know, and people unknown. All of them, at some point, lived with a secret and most lived anonymously, until they chose to go public and become advocates to help others. Now, here they are for all the world to see and hear, whether shining up there on the silver screen in Greg's film or illuminating these pages. How grateful we are.

It is Greg's hope, and mine now, that all the sages and soldiers of recovery who have gone before, all who are now marching forward one day at a time, and all those who are about to join ranks, can stand together on the platforms of our media and be a little louder, a little clearer, and a lot more powerful than a single voice in a dark and deaf world. That is how knowledge is transferred to the many and how change spreads.

So thank you, Greg, for helping me to become a person in long-term *discovery*. I see the world, and myself, differently now, thanks to you and your brothers and sisters in recovery. I hope those of you who have seen the film now feel the same. Likewise, I hope all who dip into this compendium of recovery experiences will gain new perspectives on life and see the enriching pathways that are ahead for your choosing.

Learn. Then, as William White might say, "Go out and make some history!"

(left to right) Greg Williams, Craig Mikhitarian, and Bud Mikhitarian on location in Belle Island, Detroit, Michigan, getting ready to shoot the National Recovery Month march and rally in September of 2012 for the film, THE ANONYMOUS PEOPLE.

Chapter One

JOURNEY OF DISCOVERY

Looks are deceiving.

I first met Greg Williams in 2010 when my brother Craig and I hired him to be a production assistant on a film we were producing for a major US corporation. It was an important project for us, and we needed an experienced crew to run the production as smoothly and expertly as our client expected. When Greg showed up on the first day I thought, *Who is this young fellow? He doesn't look like a seasoned pro.*

He had a boyish, innocent-looking face, opened by wide eyes and an easy smile. Would he have the professionalism we required to negotiate the multiple locations and set-ups we had planned for an intense schedule over several days?

As I learned throughout our production—and similarly during the making of his documentary, *The Anonymous People*—Greg is instinctive and resourceful well beyond his apparent youth and genuine modesty. Beneath his calm, effortless manner is a roiling current of competence, stirred by enthusiasm, intelligence, and impressive multitasking capabilities.

Without hesitation, Greg jumped in and did the work of three crew people. He was everywhere, not just doing, but anticipating our shoot's every need. He did this all cheerfully, with quiet assurance and efficiency. He made us look good. I told Craig this guy ought to be a producer. Little did I know.

And I never knew until some time later that he had once suffered from addiction and was in long-term, successful recovery.

You can't judge a book by ... well, you know the saying. Of course, we all know what an "addict" looks like, right? It's the down-and-out bum in smelly clothes sleeping it off under a bridge while holding an empty bottle of Muscatel like a teddy bear. It's not the guy in the immaculate dress shirt, who works in the next cubicle to yours, or the sweet soccer mom who lives next door, or your daughter's high school friend who's on the honor roll, or your doctor. That's not what an "addict" looks like. Oh no? Well, with twenty-two million people who suffer from substance use disorder in this country, you must know they're not *all* sleeping under bridges.

And that's the thing about people who are in long-term, successful recovery from addiction. Usually, you don't know who they are. Why should you? Most people in recovery remain anonymous to the rest of us. There are signs— not always, but often. If you need help, people in recovery will do whatever they can for you, without any expectations. I saw this time after time on our journey. Individuals in the recovery community were always there for us, guiding and providing, happy for a simple hug in return, as if they were the ones expressing gratitude for the opportunity to help. There is a serenity that comes with recovery and you can sometimes see it, if you are aware. There's positive energy and initiative evident, but with a mien of modesty that can disarm.

I guess the modesty or humility comes from a journey most of us cannot imagine—a descent into the black void of near-death and back again into the light of all-around wellness. It's a trip that would tend to change one's perspective on life and likely create a grateful demeanor. I saw all this in Greg and came to realize that he had seen something I had never seen, and knew something I cannot know. He and his brothers and sisters in recovery understand that those of us in the benighted masses cannot fully comprehend such a transformative experience. Perhaps the only way to comfortably share such a transformation is to serve others, and by example, show a trace of what it means to be saved, as they were, by some helping hand—human or providential.

People in recovery do not just give back, they give their all. They are selfless; yet, it is all about self. Contradictory as that sounds, I have learned that people who are successful in overcoming addiction become well again, in part, by strengthening the self through service to others. By helping a fellow sufferer, or anyone else for that matter, and giving everything they've got to lift the burden off another person, they change themselves and those around them.

I see it as an intriguing paradox: People in recovery are blessed by surrendering to their own powerlessness, which in turn, empowers them to change the world.

I once said to Greg, "Addicts can change the world!" I even suggested he make that the title of his film. If he didn't, then I was going to write a book and use it for my title. The look he gave me was classic—patient composure with a little tolerance thrown in. His expression unnerved me, and I thought, what was wrong with saying, "Addicts can change the world"? I thought the idea was profound. Greg understood my intention and, while he agreed with its implication, he hastened to object. He said that such a title was sensational, but not in a good sense, and he began to open my eyes to the power of the word "addict" to define and harm people. Thus began my understanding. It was not an easy start.

LANGUAGE

> "The limits of my language are the limits of my mind. All I know is what I have words for." —Ludwig Wittgenstein

As a writer, I have an appreciation of, if not an obsession with, words. I am sensitive to the impact of words on communication and their effects on understanding, feelings, and behavior.

If you are struggling with your recovery, or you are a former alcohol or other drug user living in successful long-term recovery, and you are uncomfortable with, or even offended by my use of the word addict, I sincerely apologize. But, let's be honest, we 268 million so-called non-addicted Americans think that is the term to use for the forty-six million people with addiction experience. Can't help it. It is the common vernacular, like it or not. There are certainly many derogatory terms in use out there: "Junkie," "Crack-Head," "Wino," "Drunk," and more. Unfortunately, we conflate the useful term addict with these and other pejoratives. Over time, however, terms loaded with stigma can be neutralized. I remember my father, a medical professional, describing a family friend's illness to my mother. "He's got C," he said, avoiding the word "cancer." Nobody ever committed suicide in my town (though we knew); instead, they died of "natural causes." Thank God we have socially (and morally) evolved to accept and say out loud words once whispered. Breast cancer. Epileptic. Gay.

Fascinating, this language of ours. It carries such power. Until it changes. And it is always changing. Ever since the comedians Lenny Bruce ("I was arrested for nine words.") and George Carlin ("Seven Words You Can Never Say on Television") opened our minds to the absurdity of censoring certain expressions, we have recently and quite quickly grown more comfortable with taboo words and subjects. Whether it's the "F-word" or the "C-word," just by daring to speak such words freely has made them more acceptable and even brought larger concepts out of the shadows of shame. This can happen with *addict*, too. So, what I say is, just say it. Addict. You want to erase stigma? Use the word; change the connotation. Associate the word with all the positive attributes of recovery and watch the sting come out of it. It won't be easy, but in the evolution of language, if we use the word openly, wrap it in care, empathy, and understanding, we can change the negative impact of the word. And we will be doing one small thing to break down the barriers of prejudice that language reinforces.

Greg doesn't entirely agree with my position. We argued about whether I would even use the word addict in this book. He preferred I didn't because it dehumanizes the individual. Addicts are people, he says, "persons" with disorders or problems, who then become "persons" in recovery. Labeling the sufferers of a disease with a pejorative term defines people in a limited way. He's right, of course. And I respect his position wholeheartedly. No person should be defined in one way. And certainly, it is unfair to label anyone in a degrading way. Greg's choice of language shows tenderness and sympathy to those who are suffering, and shows respect to those who are succeeding in recovery. Faces & Voices of

Recovery, a national organization for recovery advocacy, conducts intensive courses on the use and power of language. (See Aaron Kucharski's interview later in the book for more on this subject.) And I agree with their stance that by changing language, one can change perception. In the current state of public perception, addict does have a bad connotation. I just think we should change that. If we don't, addict will always be a bad word. And guess what, addicts are not bad people.

When Stacia Murphy, William Cope Moyers, and others in this book used the "a-word," the meaning of the word changed for me. When they said it, they humanized the word. They are such extraordinary people—smart, kind, successful, and good-humored. Their addiction does not dominate their identities. It was just a part of their experience. Clearly, addiction was a major and seminal event in the continuum of their lives, but addict no longer defines them. Addiction is part of their make-up, not their whole being. How's this for irony: Being addicts has made them better people. Their transformation from active addiction to successful recovery is cause for celebration. When these admirable and esteemed people embraced the word, I felt like embracing them and, in a weird way, absolutely no disrespect intended, I'm thankful they once lived in active addiction, given their contributions (as recovering individuals) to society today.

I like the idea that addicts can change the world. It challenges my preconceptions and shakes off my prejudice. It makes me care for addicts. It gives me hope.

In the United States alone, there are over forty-five million people who are directly affected by addiction to alcohol and/or other drugs. Twenty-three million of them are living in recovery. The other twenty-two million are suffering to one degree or another and are in immediate need of treatment and recovery services. By sheer numbers alone, that is a force to be reckoned with should such a large group mobilize for a cause. It is just that, maybe, the language I'm using predates the revolution to come.

And, by the way, this is not a new idea; Bill White put that bug in my ear (in better language than mine) in his brilliant *Let's Go Make Some History*, which was the first book I read when I came back from production. The experiences I had in the field, combined with Bill White's insights were gradually inducing an epiphany, as I confronted the reality of addiction and the power of recovery. I was realizing that the addiction experience is not limited to alcohol and/or other drugs, but is part of all of us, and thus, so is recovery a part of us. I faced a question: Who, exactly, are the addicts? My discoveries throughout the process of making the film, as you will see, explain why my use of the word addict is not denigrating, and not meant to be hurtful. It is healing. And it has universal meaning.

Anyone who can stay in recovery from addiction has acquired a transformative power unlike any other human capability to change. No other spiritual awakening compares. Recovery from addiction is not only an all-encompassing personal transformation involving the fundamental Freudian *troika* (Id, Ego, and Super Ego), along with physicality, intellect, spirituality, and socialization, among others, but the change also directly affects the entire world outside the individual. From the immediate circle of a person's family and friends to the whole of society, there are benefits that ripple outward: relief from pain and suffering, clear minds and open hearts, even significant economic gains. So when addicts change themselves, they change the world, theirs and ours. Recovery is revolutionary at all levels.

And, as I learned on our miraculous journey, we all have the power (often with words) to become recovery revolutionaries.

PERCEPTION

I want to be honest and confess something here. I had another difficulty, besides language, to overcome.

This is me when I first started working on the film, engaging with people in recovery, and learning that you can't know what recovery truly is, if you don't know what addiction truly is:

> Okay. I haven't been there. I have not lived in the hell that is addiction. So what do I know? I'm not qualified to truly understand recovery. I get that.

So lacking knowledge, I generalized. People in recovery have a kind and tolerant look in their eyes as you try to be empathetic. I feel them saying, "This guy has no idea." It's a patient look, not exactly patronizing, but off-putting, at times. They belong to a club you'll never be a member of, unless you pay your dues in hell. Their look is appreciative, and you can tell they respect you for trying. And they definitely want you on their side. But don't try to be one of them. You can carry the water, but you can't wear the uniform.

I felt like an outsider. I occasionally caught an uncomfortable cult-like vibe. I was afraid to even try to penetrate it. There was a framework and a language that was an obstacle to my understanding, a barrier even to inquiry. It was a bond between people that, no matter how hard I tried, I could not cultivate. That bond was closed to me because of experience or lack thereof.

This was all on me. It was my perception, born of ignorance. I'm embarrassed to reveal what I think I was feeling. I was projecting elements of my own bias onto others. It was prejudice. It was stigma. A little bit of fear thrown in. It was similar to any feeling of alienation one feels about a group that is unlike oneself.

What is it like, I wanted to know, to go out with "normal" people and not be able to celebrate an occasion, such as a birthday or a wedding, because you dare not put the volatile C_2H_5OH molecule near your nose or lips? Occasion? Hell, what about just hanging out with friends who might be having a beer? You can't do that anymore? You have to choose not doing that anymore? You have to limit your socialization to those with the same experience and self-restrictions as you? That puts you in a group, all right. And if you have rules, it's a club. And if you exclude others or keep your rules secret, it's a cult. As an outsider, I can't know your experience. And I am afraid to offend. I surely do not want to help you break your vow. I wanted to truly understand people in recovery, but I couldn't.

I guess you could say I grew up in a Norman Rockwell painting. I barely made it outside the frame of that idealized world of small-town goodness and safety. My upstate New York life was Main Street—two lanes, lined with trees, mom-and-pop shops and regulated by one traffic light, or sometimes by an actual policeman, who was overweight and stood in the middle of the intersection of

Main and Thompson directing traffic that wasn't much there. I could start at one end of that quaint thoroughfare and walk from Joe's Barbershop to my father's pharmacy at the other end in less than five minutes, unless I stopped along the way at Newberry's Department Store to buy the latest Superman comic book, or suck up a chocolate float at the Mayflower Shoppe soda fountain, or gaze at the gaudy one-sheets outside the Community Theatre, or spend two minutes and twenty-eight seconds auditioning Fats Domino's new 45 in Wishingrad's Record Store, or sit on my hands atop the sidewalk wall of the County Court House idly kicking my feet, where I could see the daily Greyhound bus arrive in front of Jimmy's Luncheonette across the street to pick up passengers bound for destinations that were fantasy to me. But if I did any of those things, they might make me late for my duty to help Dad unpack his precious delivery of pharmaceuticals and stock his shelves. Really, it's the only time I ever handled drugs. Yes, those innocent small town distractions and occasional tardiness were among my most serious transgressions. Comic books, ice cream sodas, popular records, and wanderlust were my escapes. Addiction? I didn't even know the word. Unless it applied to Milk Duds and Saturday matinees, neither of which I could live without.

How can I possibly understand what people in recovery have experienced? Because it ain't Norman Rockwell; it's more like Edvard Munch. This is what people in recovery must remember: We, the un-wakened masses need to hear the screams, too. Just as many of them do in anonymous, church-basement testimony. We all need to relate. Recovery advocates rightly protest that the media is obsessed with telling one-sided addiction stories, the salacious and lurid accounts of celebs and others who do those forbidden things that fascinate us so, the train wrecks from which we cannot avert our eyes. Again, people in recovery are right; the media is guilty of exploiting the suffering. But, to an extent, we all need those stories, balanced, of course, with the sensational stories of recovery. How can you understand and find that road to Damascus if you don't know what led Saul to his redemptive path?

It is a fine line we cross when we navigate our being from the past into the present. We are a product of our past, but we live in the present creating our past, moment to moment. In that sense, we are never far from what we were, but we are always capable of putting our past behind us, living fully in the now. People in recovery do that so well, constantly renewing themselves every day, every moment, and making their addictive history seem less and less relevant. I want to know the whole story, from the darkness of addiction to the glory and hope of recovery. With complete knowledge, fear disappears. Prejudice is expunged. And stigma is erased.

Walk into a pitch-black room. Find your way about, uncomfortable, stumbling and bumping into things, until you find that light switch. Flip the switch and you are in the light. The darkness has gone, and your world is brighter now. Better than it was, because by definition you can make the comparison.

I wanted to experience that transformation from dark to light, vicariously, of course. And who better than our fearless leader, Greg Williams, who could take us into those dark rooms, guide us around a bit, face the darkness, then turn on the light, so we could appreciate it even more.

Let's start by first unlocking the room, with the key-keeper himself.

GREG WILLIAMS

"You see the light go on in somebody the second they realize that recovery is possible."

Greg doesn't drive a car so much as he wills it. He's usually too busy talking on the phone, punching in an address on the GPS, debating with Craig over which codec to use in the edit, eating cheese doodles, and quaffing a Red Bull, usually all at the same time, to bother with actually steering the car. As we began our journey, this amazing multitasking worried me at first. After all, we were traveling in strange places, often at night, sometimes in foul weather, and always at high speeds. Ten thousand miles of this cavalier motoring would surely test my mettle. I did note that he seemed to keep his eyes on the road ahead without wavering, but I wondered if it were something else he was actually seeing. It was also some cause for worry that his hands were rarely on the wheel.

Once, after I reluctantly yielded my position of relative safety in the backseat to Craig, I rode shotgun for a spell and observed at close hand how Greg managed his magical, distracted navigation. First, he steered with his knees. He guided the car primarily with the top of his lower left thigh, the wheel snugged firmly against the area just above the knee. In this way he became one with the steering column, allowing it to respond both to the contours of the roadway and to his subtle nudges.

The whole time, Greg was entirely relaxed, alert, and confident; calm in the way a Zen Master would approve. It was as if everything else in the natural world hurtling by us at seventy-five miles per hour was appearing to him in slow motion. It is said that baseball Hall of Famer Ted Williams was such a great hitter because, among other things, as he stood in the batter's box with a ninety-mile an hour baseball flying his way, he perceived the ball at a slower speed than other players did and clearly saw its telltale rotation. So it was with our own MVP Williams, who now sat behind the wheel and, with great vision, was poised to hit the ball out of the park with *The Anonymous People*. And, even though his driving methods were a great source of teasing and fun in our claustrophobic cabin, he did, after all, drive us safely home.

Getting to know Greg was the first important step in my journey. Along the way, even as we sought out the stories of others, he told us his. The following interview I did with Greg includes information from several rambling car conversations we had throughout production, but most of it comes from four hours of private interview sessions I recorded with him after production and just after the film was released. Here you have the benefit of meeting him before, during, and after the making of the film. What he reveals will be amplified by all the stories of the faces and voices of recovery to follow.

BUD. What led you to conclude that *The Anonymous People* was a film that needed to be made now?

GREG. Addiction is the leading cause of death for young people. It is an epidemic, and people don't want to talk about it.

The system is broken. It's failing our communities. It's failing our families, and we allow people to shame individuals for a broken system. It's not fair when people are dealing with a health problem they didn't choose to have and to be discriminated against because of it. That is at the core of it.

If you study social health movements—smoking, women with breast cancer, people with HIV/AIDS, even the disability movement—they all require individuals, families, and allies who were impacted directly with those illnesses to step forward and tell their stories in order to advance the response to those issues.

We have roughly 100 million people in America who are directly impacted by addiction. Twenty-two million who are suffering, and twenty-two million in recovery, plus their families. We don't talk about it, and so it's time we talk.

B. Let's talk about your story first. John Shinholser says in the film that recovery stories are sensational. Yours certainly is. Let me start by asking you the same question you asked of just about every one of the amazing people in your film: Tell us about your journey to recovery. Where were you in your addiction that led to finding your recovery?

G. Alcohol and marijuana started the ball rolling when I was thirteen. I got addicted to pharmaceutical drugs, such as Xanax, Percocet, and Oxycontin as early as sixteen. I moved out of my house when I was seventeen and lived in what was basically a flop house with a friend of mine whose mother was never home, and we partied all the time. I got a job selling cell phones; I got paid on Friday, and I was broke by Friday night. There would be a bag of pills, a bag of pot, a liter of vodka, and once I picked up, I just really didn't have that shut-off switch. I'd wake up Saturday morning thinking somebody robbed me because I blacked out. I was sixteen when the blackouts and amnesia started. I'd wake up the next day and people would tell me we went here, we drank there, we all had a good time. I didn't remember any of it. I thought that was fun. I thought that's what life was about.

B. **What do you think led to your addiction?**

G. In hindsight, I was egocentric, fear-driven, and insecure. I had acceptance issues, being too short, not making the baseball team, and not knowing who I was. I see that in adolescents today who become addicted, a lot of identity and self-esteem issues. While that's a normal, human part of growing up, why did I and others become addicted and others not? In my case, I had a family history of mental health and addiction problems, I was diagnosed with ADD, and my age of first use was young. So, with my early developing brain, these things compiled and made me more susceptible to addiction.

B. **What does addiction feel like when you are fourteen or fifteen years old?**

G. I didn't have the emotional maturity to think much about feelings or consequences. I didn't analyze all that stuff then; I thought I just liked to party. I liked the feeling of escape; I liked the acceptance it gave me among a certain set of peers. When you're the one selling and bringing drugs to the party, you're *somebody*. I became a chameleon. I could party with the jocks. I could party with the Goth kids, the skateboarding kids—it didn't matter. I could put on any face you wanted. If I could bring something to the party that no one else could, I would be invited. I would be somebody; I would be accepted. The substances numbed all my feelings of inadequacy. Without any knowledge of family history, without any knowledge of addictive disorders, I had no context for my behavior. It was just about having fun, being accepted, ego-inflation, and doing something I thought everybody else was doing.

Then, by the time I was sixteen or seventeen, I was addicted. That's when the isolation, the loneliness, and the real pain started to set in. I was confronted with depression and physical withdrawal and feeling that my family and others around me didn't understand. That's when the real desperate emotions started to trickle in.

B. When did you first start experimenting with drugs?

G. Now that's a word I wish we could get rid of in our culture. Today, with what we now know about addiction, using the word "experimenting" when talking about alcohol or other drug use is playing with fire. We can't allow people to conjure up images of themselves as rational folks in white lab coats in laboratories standing over Bunsen burners as they test the effects of smoking marijuana or drinking alcohol. That's not what trying out these substances at fourteen years old is all about. It's playing with something much more detrimental to one's health than most realize. If you're not armed with the facts about your family history as related to addiction, then "experimenting" seems like a harmless idea, which obviously it is not. More importantly, it causes community denial to persist around this pediatric health issue.

B. That denial is really born out of the ignorance we all have about addiction, don't you think?

G. If we have learned one thing that can change the course of addiction in our society, it is that addiction is a pediatric health epidemic. Ninety percent of people who become addicted started using when they were adolescents.

When you start talking about it with the facts and with conviction, it changes everything. You can dismiss or lock up the fifty-year-old homeless person who has overdosed on the street who, by the way, started using when he was a teenager, but you certainly cannot dismiss the children—the fifteen-, sixteen-, seventeen-year olds—who are overdosing in epidemic proportion. This is the great mystery of why we are still where we are with addiction so rampant in our society. We ignore the facts, deny the issue: 10 percent of those who drink alcohol become addicted, 90 percent don't. The 90 percent who don't become addicted don't understand why those who are addicted can't choose to just stop. The denial persists that addiction is real.

We accept that some people can eat cake; others can't because they have Type II diabetes. And that's okay, because we understand it's part of a health condition; or heart disease, I can empathize and understand the facts behind that chronic illness. I can eat a cheeseburger, but some people can't. Does that mean if you have had a genetic predisposition, high cholesterol, and two previous heart procedures and you still decide to eat cheeseburgers that health insurance companies are going to withhold a third surgery from you and just let you die? That is what we do with addiction today. We discriminate against people because of a chronic health problem. Yes, their individual lifestyles, which, by the way, is largely influenced by our youth-driven, addiction-selling culture, plays a part in the progression of the illness, but no, people with addiction did not *choose* to become addicted anymore than a person with heart disease chooses to have heart failure.

Culturally we're not there yet with addiction, like we are with other chronic health problems. People just need to get over the fact that some people can drink and use other drugs, and some people can't.

B. I've heard people say addiction is the only disease that lies to you and that for the individual who is suffering, even he or she doesn't recognize addiction as being something real. Was that true for you? Didn't you understand that what you were putting into your body was not good for you, that it had bad consequences?

G. I think I was able to deny and tell big lies to myself. One of the huge components of addiction is denial. I was in denial about the trajectory of my life and the level of my chemical dependency. At sixteen, seventeen . . . I didn't see it. I thought I just liked to party, and it was cool. It's just a phase I was going through. It's what everyone does kind-of-a-thing.

And, it was always about looking at somebody who was worse than me, or looking at what I thought addiction was, or somebody with the brown bag, or with a needle in his arm on the side of the street. That's an addict. I'm not an addict because I'm using something doctors gave me. So, I continually told those lies to myself; I used that to justify and rationalize the continuation of my use.

I think we condone alcohol and other drug use as a right of passage for adolescents and young adults because we think these kids are having a blast, and it's cool. Until somebody gets addicted or dies. Then it's "Oh, bad kid," or "That family must have done something wrong." It is far easier to point the finger at the victims and deny our collective responsibility than to assess our own part in the system and our cultural failure when it results in someone's addiction.

B. **How did your parents handle your addiction?**

G. At first, my family was in the dark, and they really pushed it under the rug and denied it, similar to many families. You never want to believe that your thirteen-, fourteen-, fifteen-year-old kid is using drugs and alcohol in a harmful way.

We're a typical family. My father was like, "Oh, he's just going through a phase," whenever he or my mom found a bong or a pipe. They didn't address it with great urgency early on. But, then things got bad. Money started missing out of their wallets; I wrecked cars; and my circle of friends changed. The fighting, the manipulating, the lying, and all of that stuff started to come out in a dysfunctional way. My sister asking what's going on, my friends telling me I had a problem. Meanwhile, I kept lying and crashing cars. By the time I was seventeen they became more and more worried and really stepped in. They took away my keys, set boundaries, and sought outside help. They started drug testing me. They brought me to therapists. They brought me to outpatient programs to try to push me to confront the issue. But I always thought my problem was *them*. I was in denial and didn't want to believe that I was addicted.

B. Was there a time when you came to a tipping point?

G. It was a series of things, really. It was those external forces that first really began to make me cognizant of the reality of my addiction, such as people placing consequences on me, like drug tests and curfews and when I could and couldn't drive.

In April of 2001, I was at this family party and everybody knew I was having problems. My grandfather came over to me and said, "You know, I was eighteen once and had a good time. You just have to do it in moderation." And he put this glass of wine in front of me. Little did he know that I had just eaten a couple of Xanax bars. Two hours later, my parents find me behind the banquet hall, passed out, with two empty bottles of wine. They scoop me up and put me in the car, embarrassed for their son. They couldn't wake me up when they got home and the next morning they put me into an outpatient treatment program. At this program, I was in this circle with other young people, and they used the words "alcoholic and addict" in relation to me. I wasn't homeless; I didn't have a brown bag; I didn't have a needle sticking in my arm, so I didn't identify with those words. But I realized that Oxycontin might be a problem because I certainly spent a lot of money on it. I did a lot of things I was not proud of, like breaking and entering into houses and stealing from my family. There were certainly a lot of repercussions in my life as a result of this drug, but smoking pot and drinking beer, well, I didn't see that as a problem.

Then I went to my first twelve-step meeting and I'll never forget it. My friend Brian volunteered to go with me, but I was terrified to walk into a meeting that first time. I was seventeen years old; I couldn't be an alcoholic or an addict. I was sitting in a corner with Brian and all these people were sharing about multiple DUIs, and losing their kids, and their divorces. There were a couple of young people in the room, but I wasn't ready to share. There's only ten minutes left and all I wanted to do was get my paper signed for the treatment program, when Brian decides to raise his hand and said, "I'm Brian and I'm not an addict, but my friend Greg here is," and then he starts sharing about his guilt for using with me and playing a part in facilitating my addiction. And, for the first time in my life, I had this feeling in the pit of my stomach that I was wrong, that all the lies I had been telling myself, the rationalizing and the denial, and the story I had been internalizing for such a long time about my alcohol and other drug use were wrong. I'm not sure I knew it at that moment, but the heavy feeling in the pit of my stomach told me something, and I broke down in tears as I listened to my friend share.

That was my first moment, but I didn't stay sober that night. I still thought I could smoke pot and drink beer, but that was like the first time I realized the lies I was telling myself were actually lies. Nevertheless, I still talked a good game. All I wanted to do was get my papers signed, get through the treatment program, get my parents off my back, and get to college. I knew everything would be okay once I got to college and on my own—that all my pain would go away because everybody else in my life was the problem. I wasn't the problem. All of you were the problem.

B. **So despite the flash of insight you had at the meeting that exposed your self-denial, you still continued to use alcohol and other drugs?**

G. Well, I went to another twelve-step meeting, and I'll never forget this: There were these three young local guys who were celebrating two years of recovery, all of them on the same night. They were nineteen years old, they all got into recovery at seventeen, and they all told a harrowing story. They all ODed on the same night together and nearly died together in a car crash. They were literally pronounced dead at the scene of the accident, but they all came back to life at the hospital and made a pact together to get into recovery and not use. They showed me that recovery at a young age is possible. And living a life of recovery is actually a cool and attractive thing. It's an amazing story and it impacted me on such a deep level to understand that I'm not too young to identify as a person with addiction, and I'm not too young to seek recovery.

But I left thinking again, *Okay, Oxycontin is a problem for me and I'm not going to do that anymore; but I'm still going to drink beer and smoke pot and you're not going to tell me anything different.* So, I tried that, and within a week I was back to the pills and overdosing and blacking out.

B. **Then there was that one major event you talk about in the film—the car accident. Was that the turning point?**

G. On July 14, 2001, I got in a near-fatal car accident. We show the car wreck in the beginning of the film with blood all over the inside of the car. I ended up leaving the scene of the accident at two o'clock in the morning and going to the center of town. I was bloody from the accident. The police picked me up there and brought me to the scene of the accident where my mother was. I said to her, "Mom, sign me out. Sign me out." She had signed me out of a few ambulances before, but she looked at me and said, "Not this time." And I couldn't sign myself out, because I was under eighteen.

That was what really turned the tide in my recovery because it was the end for my parents. They were done with co-signing my BS. I woke up in the hospital, and they told me I needed to go to inpatient because I was driving under the influence. They put me in a treatment program, and it was there I opened the door to complete recovery. July 15, 2001, two months before my eighteenth birthday. I lucked out. I should be dead. I'm a product of relatively early-age intervention, a good adolescent addiction treatment program, a halfway house, and involvement in strong mutual support. Most young people don't get those opportunities.

B. We heard one gentleman say—he's in the film—that putting it down is the easy part. Maintaining is the hard part. What was your early recovery like?

G. It's a process. Peeling away the layers of the onion takes time. I remember I was in treatment, and my counselor looked at me and said, "You're going to leave here in twenty-eight days and you're going to go live in a college dorm at the University of Colorado and you're going to stay sober?" And I looked back at her and said, "Yeah, no problem." I walked out of her office and sat down on my bed and I got that feeling in the pit of my stomach again. I just knew I was wrong. I just knew there was no chance in hell I was going to leave treatment after twenty-eight days, go to live in a college dorm and stay sober and not use. I had no idea how to do that. I could tell you how to sell drugs; I could show how to do hits on gravity bongs; I could tell you the imprint codes on every narcotic medication there was, but I had no idea how to stay sober or live without alcohol and other drugs. It took the support of others before it became clear I couldn't get myself out of this one alone.

So this kid who was in treatment with me said, "Why don't you get your life together first? College will always be there." For the second time in my life I had that feeling in the pit of my stomach that I was wrong. It wasn't my will, something much bigger than me was at play, but I went back to my counselor's office and told her I wanted to look into that halfway house idea she had told me about, and that I'd put off college for a year. That moment changed everything. At that moment, I developed the desire to remain abstinent. And I developed a willingness to take direction and learn from the wisdom of other people's life experience. I realized people weren't trying to fight me; they were trying to help me. And I still do that to this day; I accept guidance from people because I don't have all the answers. I am forever grateful to have become teachable. And I don't need all the answers because there are so many more people far wiser than me who can help.

B. What was your experience like at the halfway house?

G. I labored for masons for three months, $6.50 an hour building a Staples in Pennsylvania, waking up at 5:00 A.M. with my body hurting at the end of the day, really having a humbling experience, living with other men in early recovery and learning from them. I owe my life to Scott, a guy who worked at that halfway house. Scott broke me down, in a good way, and therapeutically pulled me apart in a safe place and then put me back together.

There were moments I'll never forget. Three days out of treatment, I was in one of my first outside meetings and it was in a big smoke-filled gymnasium in a Catholic school. I raised my hand and introduced myself, "I'm Greg and I'm an alcoholic and a drug addict and this is a wonderful life of recovery and I'm thirty days sober and if we all just follow these principles and follow this lifestyle, we will get to live this amazing life, and if only the rest of the world knew about this, everybody would be at peace." And I put my hand down and thought to myself, *Wow, I just saved some people's lives.* I thought it was probably the best share at the meeting. And, I'll never forget, this old timer with many years of recovery, who was well-respected at the meeting, who everyone wanted to talk to, comes over to me and says, "Hey, kid, you know what? You probably shouldn't share for a year." I was mortified. I was devastated because I had convinced myself I had just saved people's lives.

So I go back to my halfway house and I tell Scott that this old guy told me I shouldn't share for a year. And he listens to me rant and rave for ten minutes. Then he says, "You know what? He's right. You need to listen for a long time." By then, I had grown to trust Scott and so I did that. It was one of the hardest things I ever did. Over the next year I didn't share about solutions, except when I was having a problem staying away from alcohol or other drugs. Because, really, I didn't know how to stay sober and not pick up and use. I had to listen to the wisdom of all those people in recovery. Realizing that I didn't have all the answers was the beginning of taking direction and learning from other people.

B. One of the takeaways from your story of finding recovery is how influential some of your peers were—young people your age who were in recovery and were role models who helped you. How important is peer support in demonstrating that recovery is possible?

G. That's the story of twelve-step recovery, non–twelve-step recovery, and the recovery movement itself. People with this shared life experience stand up and say, "I've had that experience. I don't experience life that way anymore. There is hope. You can have this way of life, too."

In this country, 90 percent of people with addiction don't get treatment for addiction. The number one reason so many don't get treatment is not because of access to care or the failures of the system, that's certainly a big part of it. But for most, it's because they think they don't need help. If we could tackle *that*, the floodgates will open for the possibilities of recovery.

The cultural story of making recovery visible is powerful. We're not going to move the public health piece of this until society sees, and accepts, that people from all walks of life can and do recover.

B. That's the thing we heard over and over again, "Recovery is possible. Recovery works." And what's amazing is how many people don't know this. Your recovery is solid, but you still work at it. Have you had any relapses?

G. I haven't had any relapses since July 15, 2001. I've certainly had my ups and downs during my recovery particularly with emotional serenity and emotional growth. It certainly was a challenge in early recovery. When I was faced with frustration, or whatever, I would often feel like resorting to the only coping mechanism I had known previously: Drinking or drugging, whether I was happy, mad, sad, or glad. In active addiction, when it was my birthday, I'd drink. A funeral, I'd get high. I used over resentments. I drank at my anger. Drugs would numb the fear. In early recovery, every little emotion I felt triggered my desire to get high. That had been my coping mechanism. Being able to go through the process of recovery in a safe environment, such as a halfway house, certainly gave me a foundation to succeed. It's about how to get through those kinds of trigger moments and build a foundation to reach bigger things.

B. What replaces that coping mechanism you used in your active addiction?

G. For me, I found the tools I needed in the Twelve Steps. A big one is spirituality, for example. Others find it in different places like church, Smart Recovery, yoga, and a number of other pathways.

B. But, in the moment, what specifically do you do to get through a difficult emotion, one that might cause you to think about reverting to your old coping mechanism?

G. Peer support. Call somebody. Spirituality. Belief in something bigger than me. The group dynamic is really powerful and supportive in recovery. It's the power of sharing. When I have a problem, and I share it, it gets cut in half. It's the secrets that kill us. It's the internalization of those emotions without having a mechanism to expunge them. The big missing link in our society is an outlet for sharing, talking about the things that ail us and doing that in a safe supportive environment. That's the gift—having that unique shared, lived experience where I feel good about sharing. I'll say, I'm mad or resentful and I want to get high. And somebody will say why don't you instead try a nature walk, or read this book, or try this prayer, or listen to some music, or why don't you go help somebody else. Those are the keys to the castle. Those are the coping mechanisms that now exist in my life and in the lives of many people who are in recovery.

B. Bill Wilson, the cofounder of AA, found that helping others was key to helping him sustain his own recovery. Do you experience that?

G. That is the greatest gift; that is the greatest high I've ever experienced. Paying recovery forward is an amazing, powerful solution. Then, immediately, my own individual struggles and challenges don't seem that big. My problems don't seem that insurmountable when I'm out there helping somebody find something to eat or find a place to live or get into treatment or trying to repair a relationship with their family. All of a sudden, the guy who cut me off on the highway is not so significant. It puts it all in perspective.

B. It's still a mystery to me how choosing a piece of music or saying a prayer or sharing an emotion can overcome the power of addiction and the chemical need it creates.

G. Again, it's a process. It's not an overnight journey of awakening. In early recovery, when I was close to that chemical use, it was much more challenging. But, over time, I was able to build a new lifestyle. The power of collective good is the antidote. Self-centeredness comes with addiction, and helping others is my antidote to my self-centeredness.

B. When you have a craving for a drug, can't you just choose not to? Don't you always have that choice?

G. No. Today in recovery, fully removed physically from my chemical addiction, I have the freedom and the choice around alcohol and other drugs. But that choice was not always present. With the developing brain and the social dynamics of adolescence and the onset of addiction, you can't tell me it's really a rational choice for fifteen-year-old kids. They don't know, nor do they expect that if they pick up a drink or a drug that they're going to become addicted. We don't give people the facts to make that choice. Once the progression of that illness starts, particularly for people with substance use disorders, it is no longer a choice. People who become addicted didn't choose to become addicted.

B. Isn't it true that to beat your addiction and to recover, you have to want to do it?

G. You can't want something if you don't know it even exists. There's a saying in recovery: "We don't come into recovery on the wings of victory."

We can expose more people to the reality of recovery by stepping into the light and simply telling them that they can have this life, too.

Nearly every woman in this country understands she should get a mammogram at a certain age, thanks to awareness that has been raised by breast cancer survivors coming out and telling their stories over the years. It has become culturally acceptable and visible.

We can do the same thing. Uncover the greatest secret in our communities. That can be more powerful than any policy shift or treatment innovation. Stripping away that community denial is the number one thing that will promote recovery transformation. And we have to do it at many different levels of culture.

B. **Unfortunately, our culture gives the strong opposite impression, at least in the mass media. Drinking, even drugging, is glorified and held up as a popular model of behavior in entertainment, news, and advertising everywhere.**

G. I watch football on Sundays and I am sold addiction constantly; drinking beer is equated with having fun. I'm not saying we need to take alcohol away from people, but we have to get honest. The fact is that one out of ten people who drink alcohol is going to become addicted to it. If we are going to aggressively sell addictive substances as a fabric of our culture, we are going to have a massive addiction problem. And we have to stop blaming the individual for becoming addicted. We have to get honest about the facts and hold our culture and our society accountable.

B. **There's no way we're going to curtail beer advertising. What can we do to get an alternative message out there, one with the facts that can inform people about the truth of addiction?**

G. Why not? We are one of the only developed countries that still allow this kind of advertising on television, billboards, and magazines without warning labels that tell of alcohol's addictive properties.

It's about education, changing social perception, and social behavior. We've done it with smoking. Smoking is one of the great public health success stories of recent times. Cigarettes are not illegal, but we've implemented aggressive public health measures to combat their harmful effects. We've made incredible strides reducing smoking rates in the last twenty years because we no longer allow people to deny the fact that smoking is hazardous to our health. You cannot tell me this stuff doesn't work.

B. What about drugs? Do you see a similar trend in our culture that fuels an acceptance of, or even encourages the use of, addictive drugs?

G. Kristen Johnston is in a war right now with people selling T-shirts in California that say, "Xanax," "Vicodin," "I Love Methadone," and other addiction-glorifying merchandise. I mean, in this country, prescription drug overdose is the number one cause of death of young people. Why isn't there more community outrage over this cultural popularization of a killer of our children? Kristen is a lone warrior out there fighting it. It's baffling to me that people give Kristen flack for taking this on. God bless her soul. It is wrong. I want those marketers to look into the eyes of the families who lost their children to drug overdoses and tell me they're not doing something that directly puts blood on their hands. How many wakes of young people who have died of these drugs have they gone to? And now they're going to make money off the idea?

B. On a personal level, you were lucky to have supportive parents who could counteract some of those harmful societal influences. Tell us more about the role your parents played in your recovery.

G. I wouldn't be alive today without my family. They certainly had a lot of shame and denial during my active addiction and during the early stages of my recovery. They worried about what they could have done differently. But, they entered a family education program and when I came home, they helped me a lot. Importantly, they defined and set certain boundaries, and they got very involved in supporting my recovery.

We had a better relationship once I started to take on some independence in my recovery. I moved out of the house after about eight months; I wanted to live on my own, do my own thing, and go to college. Certainly we've had some bumps along the road, but without a doubt I wouldn't be alive or sober today without their intervening assertively in my life.

Look, this is a pediatric health epidemic. I work with a lot of young people who don't come from families of support. Sometimes they come from families with active addiction in their house. I was blessed. We didn't have active addiction in our house other than me. I know that is not the case for many, many young people, so I know how important family support is in helping young people stay in recovery.

B. And then, once you were well into your recovery, how did your parents feel about you going public with your story?

G. I had six years of recovery when I decided to start speaking out, so I had to talk with them to make sure it was okay to speak publicly about my recovery. It was an important conversation because it obviously affected them in some way, shape, or form. They were proud of my recovery and they gave me permission to do it.

Today, they live with a great deal of pride about my recovery and not much shame about what happened during my active addiction. My father is on the Board of Directors of the nonprofit in Connecticut where we work on youth and family addiction issues. They talk publicly about their son who had an addiction problem. They are a resource for other families who are seeking help, so they get called all the time for friends, colleagues, and people in their community whose children are going through the same challenges I had when I was in my active addiction. And, of course, they were incredible supporters of the film project.

B. Let's talk about making your film, *The Anonymous People*. It is a groundbreaking film, and its success proves that people are hungry for the information and insights you have presented. Other than

trying to change the world—and I'm being only half facetious about that—what inspired you to make this movie?

G. My own personal recovery and involvement in recovery advocacy work were certainly the drivers in my personal passion around this film project. When I got into recovery at seventeen, I got very active with young people in mutual support groups. I did my best to help other people and their families find recovery. We struggled. It's not an easy illness to navigate; it is not an easy system to navigate. I got denied a lot of treatment beds because of health insurance discrimination. I wrote a lot of letters to friends of mine in jail who were getting sicker behind bars. I went to a lot of wakes.

My friends and I would complain about the barriers and the problematic system that we have, the frustration with it, but none of us would ever do anything about it. We didn't think we could. We didn't think we had a voice. Eventually I got more and more angry at the system, and became more and more engaged.

About three years into my recovery, my mentor, Donna Aligata and I started a nonprofit organization, Connecticut Turning to Youth and Families. Donna introduced me to Bill White's work and to Pat Taylor at Faces & Voices of Recovery in Washington, DC. I learned more. People brought me along and showed me there was this organized movement that had been in its infancy stages of growth over the last ten to twelve years. There were people in recovery who were beginning to really step out and put a face and a voice on recovery, and energizing the birth of a new recovery advocacy movement. They were trying to address the discriminatory barriers and the public perception that drives problematic addiction policy. I met a lot of these people who have been the leaders in this movement and who really inspired me to want to tell their story. Many of them are in the film.

Pat Taylor brought me down to Washington, DC, for recovery message training. Sitting through that training with Tom Coderre and Betty

Currier gave me a new language to tell my recovery story. That day, I told Pat Taylor and Tom that I wanted to make a movie about this stuff. Because this "stuff" is powerful. It is a transforming experience for a typically marginalized recovering person to be given a language of empowerment.

When I was introduced to that language and movement my recovery went from shame to pride, as Aaron Kucharski says. Prior to that I was living my life in recovery just like I lived my life in addiction—I had two separate lives. In addiction, I had a face for the cops and for my parents; then, I had another face for my friends at the keg party or alone in my room. I got into recovery, and I still had two separate lives. I had all these stories about why I don't drink or why I wouldn't go to a bar with friends. I had all this confusion around my status as a person in recovery from addiction. And it's all bound up in secrecy and shame and anonymity. And that's what this film is all about—shame to pride.

B. **What was the shame you felt in your recovery that drove you to want to make a film?**

G. Well, I'll give you one example. I worked in the dub room of a media production company as a young college grad, working the midnight shift, building up my resume. I worked with a bunch of other twenty-year-olds and nobody knew I was in recovery. One of the shows we duplicated was *Intervention*, and we would watch the shows and they would laugh at the sensational, humiliating things the camera would follow those people doing. I would watch that show through the eyes of other younger people who weren't addicted, who go out to bars, drinking and enjoying their lives. I would watch them laugh at the humiliating experiences of people on the show. I was demoralized by that. If they only knew that I was one of those people. What would they think of me? They'll never treat me the same. That's where I really internalized my own shame at a deep level, and not wanting to talk about my recovery. It was that fuel of watching reality television that fired me up to tell the other side of the story. Look, the intervention story has validity, the addiction story has validity, but we have run that into the ground. I mean, we have told that story for years. The American public is hungry for a different story around addiction. And that story is out there, but people haven't felt good about telling the story. People haven't had the language and they haven't been empowered to tell that story, or understand the necessity of taking their recovery experience outside the context in which they live it, as Dan Griffin says.

B. **It's not surprising that people are reluctant to tell their stories when you consider the way the media depicts addiction and contributes to the shame and stigma of the disease. You, personally, had some bad experiences with the media, didn't you?**

G. *ABC World News* did a feature story on prescription drugs and addiction. It was basically a fear-mongering story about locking your medicine cabinets. They interviewed me for forty-five minutes about my active addiction, treatment, and recovery, and took just one sound bite for the segment: "I used to call myself 'Pharmacist.'" That was it. There was nothing about my recovery.

Then there was the "Greg W" story in the *Hartford Courant* newspaper. I've told that story a lot. I went to testify at the Connecticut State legislature, talking about getting into recovery and I was interviewed afterward by a reporter from the newspaper. I indicated to him at the time that I preferred not to use my last name because I didn't think I was supposed to. So, the next day, when the story comes out in the paper, it makes a point of saying that Greg W didn't want to disclose his last name. Donna Aligata called me and spoke to me afterward. She said, "If I don't understand addiction and recovery or anonymity, what does that imply to the readers of the article?" That I'm ashamed of my recovery? I wasn't ashamed of my recovery. I was proud of it; that's why I testified in the first place, and decided to lend my story to the article.

That's the great thing about recovery message training. It teaches you how to frame the messaging and language of your story, so you can talk publicly about recovery, not violate any traditions of anonymity, and have some control over how your story is told by the media.

B. **When we shot the film, you took us to meet literally hundreds of people who advocate for recovery. Each of them has an incredible story of redemption and service. With so many ways to tell this complex story of recovery, how did you come to make your story such an important part of the film?**

G. You know better than anyone; I really struggled with being present in the film at all—thinking it should be a fly-on-the-wall type of documentary. It took you and Craig and Jeff and a great deal of prodding to get me to want to tell this story from a personal perspective. It was a big journey for me in making this film because I didn't know how I wanted to tell this story. I mean, at the deep level, this film wasn't about me. It was about people who blazed this trail, who had awakened me to this idea of advocacy, who awakened me to realize that taking my recovery experience and harnessing that personal power of recovery is relevant to the collective. It is with deep purpose and responsibility that I share my recovery story publicly because it is not about Greg Williams. It is about saving lives.

B. **But why film? It is such a huge undertaking to make a feature film. What led you to choose that path to tell your story?**

G. I got interested in movie-making in high school, about the same time I got interested in alcohol and other drugs. Then, after I was in recovery, I got a four-year degree in media production at Quinnipiac University. Editing was my strong interest. I didn't like production and shooting, but I liked working with footage to tell a story. There was one class I took and we had to make a short documentary. My professor said the best way to make a documentary is to choose a charismatic subject, so I picked my friend who, at sixteen, was in recovery for five years. I shot his story on a little hand-held camera and showed it to the class and I got an "A." My professor asked how I was able to get the subject to talk about his personal experience with such depth, and I realized how being able to access those powerful stories, because I was in recovery, too, was unique. And it allowed me to access stories that were largely untold.

Later, when I got into the media production world, I worked on a lot of powerful stories about sports, and at the same time, I was hearing these powerful redemption stories from friends in recovery that weren't being told. So, Craig shot a TV pilot for me called, *Halfway Home*, a tremendous documentary story about young people in recovery, about kids who should be dead, who are now vigilantes saving the lives of other young people. It was going to follow a group living in a house, living in recovery, and would capture the power of peer-lived experience that brings young people along the journey to want this lifestyle of recovery. This is an amazing untold story of recovery. Not of addiction, but of recovery. It was a great pilot, with great characters. I started pitching reality television. I pitched MTV. But, as in most industries, timing is everything, and it wasn't my time. Funny, but *The Anonymous People* would probably never have existed if that reality show had gotten picked up.

That experience of trying to market solution-focused entertainment in the reality TV business got me more interested in the nonprofit, filmmaking world, where there is a bigger opportunity to tell stories independently. *The Anonymous People* might not get as much viewership as *Celebrity Rehab* did, but the way we told the story with integrity makes me feel better when I look in the mirror.

B. What was most difficult thing about making the film?

G. The personal sacrifice. God bless my wife. You always hear directors and artists thanking their families at award shows, and I always thought that was just a nice thing to do. But I never really understood, until now, how much your passion for something makes you sacrifice other areas of your life. I'm glad I went through the process and have done something for the greater good, but I have certainly taxed other areas of my life.

And without a doubt, for a first-time filmmaker, one of the hardest parts is fundraising. It's impossible. Then, there's breaking into the entertainment industry itself; I just assumed that with such a transformative story like this, with a unique angle, that there would be an entertainment entity that would pick it up and want to run it. But, it's a business that's only about who you know. And luck plays a huge role in success.

It's baffling to me. The entertainment industry didn't believe how big the recovery audience is. Then, we became one of the highest grossing Theatrical-On-Demand films of all time—without a marketing budget. Now they believe it.

B. **Did you ever feel like you were not going to be able to find the support you needed to make the film?**

G. After making a huge personal investment, the scariest moment was putting together the promo after we shot the first phase of production. I wrote six grants for funding and didn't get a hit. If you're a first-timer and you're up against experienced Emmy and Academy Award-winning filmmakers, even with a good product, a funder is not going to take a risk on you. I'm twenty-seven years old. I never made a feature film before. Is this kid going to finish this film? A lot of people believed in me, but the recovery advocacy movement never had a film before, so it put those people in a new place. "How do I, or should I, support it?"

Our second production phase scheduled for Recovery Month in September was getting closer and closer, and I knew that was a really important visual for the story because of all its rallies and events. So I asked you guys to help me put together a Kickstarter promo. The page got a lot of compliments about how the story was being told, and it showed a lot of experience, which you have to have because we were asking for a lot of money. We were going for $45,000. On the very first day it launched, John Shinholser put in a big donation and by the end of the week we had a few thousand dollars and momentum was starting to build. Everyone could see how the recovery community was coming together, believing in it and supporting it. We passed our goal with over a week to spare and ended up with over $70,000 in funds. We raised enough to shoot in September and cover all those recovery events we went to. I was able to hire Jeff Reilly to edit and get Brendan Berry to do an original score. As the momentum built, we were able to license Eminem's song and Rob Thomas's song. It adds up. We spent over $50,000 just acquiring the rights to the archival news footage we used in the film.

B. **That's a big chunk of money and the history section is a big chunk of the film. Why did you commit so much to telling that part of the story?**

G. I didn't set out to have history as a large part of the story. Initially, I just wanted to explore the current movement that was unfolding. However, after sitting down with the people doing advocacy today, it was clear their lives had been altered and impacted by people and events earlier in the recovery movement.

Many people don't know the full history of the recovery movement. I sure didn't. And if more people in recovery did, we probably would have a better understanding of anonymity and less stigma around addiction and recovery.

I used to attend the same twelve-step group in Connecticut that Marty Mann called her "home group." I learned a little bit about her, but no one ever taught me about the precedent-breaking things Marty Mann did by going public with her recovery in the 1940s, and influencing public policy at the highest levels. I'm probably alive today because of her work and the work of Harold Hughes, who figures prominently in the film. I found my recovery, initially, through addiction treatment and healthcare resources that wouldn't exist without the advocates of the past who built those resources. They spoke out and helped bring addiction into healthcare and built those institutions of care. They were all people who were in recovery first, and then became advocates second. There's still a lot of tension around treatment, twelve-step culture, recovery, anonymity, and advocacy, but with more understanding, the pieces are coming together. The history section of the film clarifies the reality of the early advocacy efforts and surprises a lot of people.

B. Addiction and recovery are such huge and complex topics. How did you arrive at the structure and story you wanted to tell in the film?

G. The arc of the film is loosely inspired by the Faces & Voices of Recovery message training. They understood early on the media's need to tell stories, and the training clarified for me how important it was to use the media to dramatize the recovery story, in the same way the media has sensationalized the addiction story. The training takes people on a journey: The why, the how, and the what we should be doing as a community to effect change, and I hope the film captures a piece of that.

That's also where I began to really understand the necessity for putting this story in a medium that my friends could understand. There are all kinds of academic writings about the movement out there, but I had many friends in recovery who weren't in college and didn't have access to that knowledge. I believe most of our world's solutions are sitting on the shelves of academia. And the brilliant people who have come up with these ideas just haven't figured out how to best communicate and market those solutions to the world. So it was figuring out a way to mainstream this message. I see my role as a translator—to make information that a lot of brilliant people have already formulated and transfer it to people in way that everyone can understand and take action on. That's the idea of the film, that's the idea of the book—to take a complex subject and make it understandable to everyone.

B. The irony of your title. As you know, Craig and I didn't get it at first, but it is perfect. The film opens up an important conversation on the convoluted subject of anonymity, secrecy, shame, and stigma. Understanding the relationship between these things is a central, but challenging part of your film, isn't it?

G. I don't know how you talk about addiction without talking about shame. It is really fascinating to me the push back I've gotten about that element of the film. People get upset that we talk about shame; I don't know what bubble people are living in.

Remaining hidden and not talking about our recovery status publicly feeds into shame. Obviously, we take a hard line on what anonymity means and what it doesn't mean. And, ironically, AA's own World Service Office supports our position: You can disclose your recovery status publicly however you choose, just don't reveal your personal group membership status at the level of press, radio, and films.

B. Over the long course of making this film, I watched you conduct scores of interviews with amazing people. At some point in almost every one of them, I would catch a look in your eye that told me you were personally having a moment of enlightenment. Besides trying to capture wisdom for your audience, was making this film also a journey of discovery for you?

G. The process of making this film and the experience of my recovery has been all about remaining teachable. Having the opportunity to make this film taught me so much. It is the beauty of being a documentary filmmaker; you get to ask questions to incredible people and hopefully, along the way, learn a bit of what they have learned.

One slogan I love goes, "Smart people learn from their mistakes; wise people learn from others." At seventeen years old, getting sober, people would say, "That must be really hard for you." I don't know, from what I've seen and heard, it's pretty hard getting sober when you're fifty after you've been drinking for twenty-five years. So, for me, I can learn from that experience. At seventeen, I got a ticket to freedom. It's simple; there are a million things I can do in life. I just can't drink or do drugs. Accepting that identity opened the door to self-awareness and becoming teachable. I still learn every day. The journey keeps unfolding.

B. So, all along the way, while you were interviewing others, you were examining yourself. Personally, what did you learn on this journey?

G. One of the biggest challenges I have in my recovery is just trying to be in the moment, enjoying the journey, not looking at or setting destinations. I mean, you have to look toward the future for some things, like writing a grant to try and get the film funded, but you have to stay in the process. Like, when we were out on the road, I couldn't wait to get through filming, and get to editing. Then, it's like "Oh, I can't wait to finish editing so we can go into distribution," and then we have to do the international version, and on and on. It's such a challenge to just enjoy the moment. I see that every day with my son, just trying to be there in that moment with him as he grows up. I'm so blessed and grateful that my recovery has given me that freedom and self-awareness to work at being present in the moment—look to the future, yes, but certainly appreciate the importance of the now. Meeting all those people in successful recovery during our journey reinforced that for me.

B. What do you want your viewers to take away from the film?

G. To get permission, not just for people in recovery or family members, but to get permission in our communities to talk about addiction and include recovery as an integral part of that conversation. That is the huge missing component. It is a complex public health issue.

I'm not going to simplify addiction. It certainly is not a simple issue. Recovery has probably been the one piece of the conversation about prevention, treatment, and drug policy, in general, where there has been a vacuum of silence. Bill White talks about how we can fill whole libraries with what we know about the pathology of addiction, but we can barely fill one shelf with what we know about the recovery experience.

We have just as many people in recovery as we do addicted, but we don't really know how they got to recovery. Research is scarce, and we don't really know how to facilitate long-term recovery in the most effective way for people. Recovery is a reality, and it's a miracle when you see somebody, after watching the film, get up and say for the first time publicly that they are in long-term recovery. And then, you see the light go on in somebody else the second they realize that recovery is possible for them.

B. **You introduced me to Bill White and his influential book,** *Let's Go Make Some History*. **Are you making history with this film?**

G. Time will tell. It's bringing a conversation to a media platform that's never happened before. Even the *Hollywood Reporter* said in its review, "If anonymity is a successful strategy for many, its reign as the default mode of recovery already seems to be over." And AA's General Service Organization published a bulletin addressing the issues raised in the film. So it is getting attention.

But the film is about people who have already made history. I'm just the one who put these history makers in a package that tells this revolutionary story to a whole new audience. It's like making a film about Martin Luther King. The filmmaker can get credit for the film, but the history maker is Reverend King. The people in my film were blazing trails way before Greg Williams ever joined the club.

The recovery movement has been big for a long time; I just hope I can help invigorate the conversation and throw a little gas on the flames of the advocacy part of it. I get excited when I hear that Idaho is opening new recovery community centers as a result of people seeing the film. I don't know anyone in Idaho. I didn't know the film even made it to Idaho. But the fact is, the film and its message somehow got to the policymakers, and they're opening new recovery community centers this year. That's pretty cool.

B. It is. Thanks, Greg.

My brother Craig and I have been making films, mostly of the documentary and informational kind, for a long time. We've been to many places in this world and met fascinating people. We love our work because it requires us to learn about a subject and become acquainted with people at deep levels, usually for intense, brief periods of time. Once a production is over, it is on to the next, and another wondrous experience is there for our exploration, rewarding to be sure, but often transitory.

For us, there has never been anything quite like working on *The Anonymous People*. And we have Greg Williams to thank for the opportunity. It was his passion, knowledge, and focus that propelled us along the journey of miles and months through recovery in America. My interview with him touches on many of the issues we explored along the way, in a journey that was like the course of a river winding its way through a diverse landscape, picking bits of local matter at every bend and carrying them for deposit in a great ocean of knowledge. This production was different from all others we experienced—physically, emotionally, and intellectually. Like recovery itself, it was transformative.

Usually, the stories Craig and I have done are fairly localized, consisting of one microcosmic society of people and a singular experience: the acculturation of an Eskimo village; the need for medical care in Tanzania; a war in Lebanon; a samba school in Rio. You go to one place, find a few people who represent the subject, focus your story, and tell it as simply and powerfully as you can. You try to find the universal truth in the particular and communicate something that has meaning for all. And you hope that what you have done will change people in some small way.

Greg piloted us through a much wider territory of places, people, and experiences to collect what was needed to tell the story of *The Anonymous People*. Physically, it was grueling to cover that much ground; intellectually, it was an expansive challenge to accumulate so much knowledge. Emotionally, it was as varied as the powerful flow of a river through turbulent rapids that then falls into refreshing pools of serenity. As we emerged at the end of the journey, we were transformed by revelations that grew our understanding, renewed our ideals, and instilled a belief in the possibility of change, both individual and global—change for the greater good.

GETTING GEEK-Y

I have to pause just a moment to explain something technical. This may only interest all you filmmakers out there, but I feel compelled to clarify. It's another language issue. I often use the term "filming" to describe what it is we did in "shooting" this documentary. To be accurate, we weren't filming. And although we were using video cameras, technically, we weren't videotaping, either. There was no film, nor was any videotape involved in the production. Actually, what we were doing, and what most people do now, is "capture" images and digitally encode them in a silicon cage of electrons arranged in binary units of 1s and 0s. Even Hollywood is gravitating more and more toward digital production, as all those 1s and 0s can now be arranged to replicate the rich look of film. Since the dawn of moving pictures, when we slathered light-sensitive nitrate emulsion on a base strip of celluloid, sprocketed behind a lens in a light-tight box and pointed it at someone, we have called it "filming." Whatever chemical or electronic soul-capturing miracle it is that takes place inside that box, when you aim the thing and let light in through an intricate array of stacked, convex, highly-polished, glass lenses to focus it on a reactive medium, it is a process that resembles shooting. (Some say something is killed when you steal the image of a subject.) And because this all started with film, it is called filming, a unique word to come up with when you think about it. You are transforming some real thing, person, and moment into a piece of artificial reality—a random schmear of molecules, or collection of electrons, suddenly organized by light energy into a still slice of time. Rembrandt, the Master of Light, did the same thing, of course. More particularly, so did Seurat and Monet, who painted with pixel-like dabs of color on a piece of cloth to create an image. As the contemporary artist James Rosenquist said to us once when we were filming him in his studio (yes, we were shooting him with actual film): "You take these colored minerals, grind them into particles, and mix them into a medium of some sort, then push them around on a surface in some way and call it art." These great artists manipulate molecules of color to create images in much the same way filming does, it just takes them longer.

Thus, fine artists paint. Cinematographic artists film. What do videographers do? Video? Early in the '60s when video technology allowed recording of television signals on magnetic videotape, it was called videotaping. But now, what we are mostly doing with a video camera is "capturing" information on solid state cards or optical discs. What are we doing—carding? Or discing? Whatever. What we are doing is making movies, which in Muybridge and Edison times were first called "moving pictures." Later, Hollywood called them "pictures," and popularly, they became known as "movies." The point is, often, the first name we give a thing in any new technology persists through its evolution. The old name seems quaint when applied to the latest innovation, but it helps to make the new more comfortable and acceptable. Take printing—3D printers are all the rage now. An astounding, but inevitable technology whose process and end product bear little resemblance to hand printing letters on parchment with a quill pen dipped in ink. It's cool to think that the fully-formed replacement knob for your electric range that you just fabricated on your new desktop 3D printing device was "printed." Just as typesetting is printing, or ink-jet printing is printing, it helps me grasp the process.

So forgive me if I say we "filmed" this documentary. We pointed our camera and made a *movie*, just as Edison did on his Kinetoscope camera, supplied with Eastman Kodak film. In that tradition, if you please, we filmed. Just happens we used an advanced digital video camera.

More importantly, there was the artist who actually looked through the lens of this new-fangled imaging device and made the pictures beautiful.

CRAIG MIKHITARIAN
Director of Photography

"One of the strengths of the film is actually seeing so **many** different people, all different types, telling their stories, and with such purpose."

Craig is my best man, and not just at my wedding. As my business partner, he is my best man, too, as he is in life. People are always amazed that we two brothers have worked together for so long. When he moved to New York City after graduating college to join me in a feature film dream, that was only phase two of a long-standing partnership making films, which began in phase one when we were just kids making music videos of Beatles' songs or recreating Apollo space shots in miniature—all on Super 8mm film. We just never grew up.

After a freelance stint with the broadcast networks and public broadcasting, where Craig was nominated for an Emmy and we produced documentaries for an Emmy Award-winning show, we began phase three. We started our own company, ACM Productions, and continued to produce and direct documentaries, a couple of TV shows, commercials, and business films. One doc we shot, *Children of Darkness*, received an Academy Award nomination. In 1995, we moved our business out of New York and into the idyllic hills of Connecticut, where we have been ever since, pursuing our dreams and raising our families. There, we met Greg.

And lest I be accused of brotherly bias, this is what Greg said to me about Craig, behind his back:

"Craig has been with me from the very beginning on this journey through the topic area of addiction and recovery. He shot my pilot for the reality TV series I wanted to do called, *Halfway Home*, and he shot the dramatic stories on addiction risk you directed for me that we made for Western Connecticut State University. He shot all the videos we produced through the nonprofit, Connecticut Turning to Youth and Families. It's just been a growing, great relationship.

"He taught me a lot, too. I don't see myself as much a creative filmmaker, or even director, as I am a storyteller. Craig's creative eye has always been a great complement to my storytelling. He has tremendous broadcast experience and he does things at a top level. Working with him is like being on a basketball team where the point guard always knows where the small forward is and how the play is going to develop. We show up on set for an interview and we hardly have to say anything. While I'm prepping the talent or the subject for the interview, Craig composes the shot, lights it, and by the time we're ready to go, nine times out of ten, it is exactly what I had envisioned. Recovery is not an easy subject and we've had to find our way with this. Compared to other vérité subjects, it is difficult to shoot. When you're shooting groups, specifically, you never know who is going to talk next. It is a real challenge for one cameraman to shoot spontaneous dialogue within a circle of speakers and get the coverage needed to be able to edit into a powerful scene. But with his experience and familiarity with the subject, he knew what to expect and he was there with the shot the moment it was needed. Very difficult to do.

"Then there is his technical prowess. He probably knows more about the technology than any DP [Director of Photography] I've met. He not only shot the film, but also from the very beginning, thought through the whole technical approach to the production, how to shoot the film, what to shoot the film on, the lighting package, and the plan going into editing. The cachet and skill set he brought to preproduction was really helpful to me in building the foundation for the whole production, technically and aesthetically."

I second that emotion. Thanks, Greg. Here's a conversation I had with Craig after we wrapped production on *The Anonymous People* and had a chance to enjoy several screenings of the finished film. You might enjoy looking through Craig's viewfinder to see what he saw in the making of the film. You might also see why I am proud and thankful he is my brother. And my best man.

BUD. First, let's set the record straight. You're not in recovery yourself, right?

CRAIG. Other than still recovering from my last round of golf, no. I'm fortunate never to have had a problem with alcohol or other drugs.

B. You worked with Greg Williams before I did. How did you come to know him?

C. As they say in this crazy business, it's who you know, right? In this case, I got to know Greg through my son, Mark, who is a friend of his. When

Greg was doing cinema studies at Quinnipiac University, Mark said to him, "You ought to meet my dad, he's a filmmaker." There you go. So, when Greg thought of trying to do a reality TV series based on recovery stories, I shot some interviews and profiles for him.

B. **And tell everyone how we got involved in this amazing project called** *The Anonymous People*.

C. Well, those early stories that Greg pitched, unsuccessfully to MTV, were mostly about young people in recovery, and really set the stage for developing the larger idea for *The Anonymous People* movie. It proved to him and showed me that there were some compelling stories there. And then, of course, you directed and I shot a series of dramatized vignettes for Greg about the risks that college students face with alcohol and other drugs, which Western Connecticut State University used in student orientation and prevention programs. So gradually, he was bringing us into his world of service and advocacy for addiction recovery and we were learning something.

Later, as part of his master's thesis at NYU, he wanted to create this broader video on the subject, but he couldn't get grant money to support it, so he took out a loan and invested his own money. And he asked us to help him make the film.

B. **I remember the early discussions about it, and I was a little hesitant. What was interesting to you about the project?**

C. Greg certainly had a lot of passion for it. That's the first requisite. And having done some of those smaller videos with him, I was starting to learn more about the recovery movement. I saw there were a lot of interesting stories there.

When he talked about *The Anonymous People* specifically, I wasn't quite sure either about how it would work as a film, in terms of appealing to a general audience. But when he said he definitely was going to do it and had that commitment, and said he had some funding to get started, I thought it was great. I wanted to help him.

B. Like you, I didn't have any knowledge about the huge size of the recovery community and the scope of the movement, so when I first heard about *The Anonymous People* **idea, I thought the film would be pretty small. But Greg had big dreams. He wanted to change the conversation and save lives. That's a compelling reason, but I worried that he could reach the audience.**

C. I admit that I was a little skeptical in the beginning. But the thing he had built in for him was an audience of twenty-three and a half million people. You could look at it as a niche film for a specific audience, but it's a big audience. If it didn't succeed as a general audience film on the scale of say, *An Inconvenient Truth* or *Waiting for Superman*, it still had a huge potential to be seen by a lot of people. Truth is most people are not generally interested in documentaries unless they are interested in the subject of the documentary to begin with. We thought maybe it would reach the large recovery community first and then "go viral," so to speak.

B. Do you remember what we thought of his title, *The Anonymous People***?**

C. Initially, I thought it was a little confusing. First of all, I didn't understand the whole anonymity thing and I never realized it was such a big issue; I didn't understand its significance. I understood the stigma idea because I certainly understand why people often don't want to talk about such things, and how that was detrimental to affected people on social and political levels. But, not knowing anything about AA, for example, I didn't understand how anonymity played a part in all that. Now that I understand, it's a good title.

B. Yes. It's perfect. Especially if you know enough about the subject to catch the irony. What were some of the early discussions with

Greg about how we would make the film, that is, the production approach?

C. We knew it was going to be a low-budget effort. We knew from the start that the crew would have to be small, quick, and mobile. We wouldn't be flying; we'd be driving from place to place around the country. We'd be borrowing Greg's parents' Honda Pilot, not a big production van by any means. There wouldn't be much room for three people, equipment, and luggage. That dictated certain technology choices.

We all agreed that technically, it should be as high end as possible, with the idea that it was going to get into theaters. We knew it couldn't be film because of cost, but we wanted that high quality. And we also knew with a small budget, a small crew, and a small car, we couldn't handle the big digital rigs they use in Hollywood these days. I mean, it was just going to be you, me, and Greg doing everything.

Ultimately, content was king. We had to move fast and make sure we captured what was important. After a lot of testing, we settled on the new Sony CineAlta camera that was easy to work with and gave us a great look.

B. By the way, we shot about 120 hours of high definition video. That's an enormous volume of files. How did you store, manage, and organize all that information?

C. During shooting, we double-recorded everything, using the card in the camera and an external Samurai solid-state drive. Every day after we shot, Greg would back up the files from the external drive, which we could then reuse the next day for new filming. And I did the same thing with the XDCAM cards from the camera; I'd back them up on a portable drive we carried, so now we had two copies of everything we shot. Back at the editing suite in Connecticut, our assistant editor, Christian Power, created another back-up and transcoded the files so they could be edited on the Avid. I think we figured we shot about twelve terrabytes worth of video, and Greg now owns a boatload of drives.

B. As for the film itself, it turned into quite a journey for us—not just geographically and over the expanse of time, but in much deeper ways. Over the long haul of the production period, what do you remember most? What did you learn?

C. We met amazing, amazing people. I was just so impressed with the people we interviewed and how smart and articulate they were. When you think back to the terrible state they were in during their active addiction, it is easy to overlook that there was always such a brilliant person inside. But, I'll tell you, all the people in recovery who we met have a generosity of spirit and a willingness to help others that is just remarkable. These people are working in their communities, helping others who are struggling right now. I can't imagine doing that every day. To me that seems like such an exhausting job or service, and to deal with that day after day after day with people who have not yet recovered requires such an energy and a willingness to help, I can't even imagine. Plus, you're dealing with your own problem. I mean, I think they recognize that part of their recovery is based on other people helping them, so they have a willingness to give back. That idea of paying forward all the time is pretty cool, for anybody.

B. Care to mention anyone specifically who impressed you?

C. I better say John Shinholser or I'll be in a lot of trouble. I can almost hear that Marine yelling in my ear, "Give me twenty!" He was great for the film because he has a good intuitive sense for what works and doesn't work for filmmaking, and so he took us into a lot of visually interesting situations. And, personally, he is genuine, so that makes him very appealing on camera. Others? I don't know. Everybody. I'm pretty impressed with Greg, actually.

B. Well, what *do* you think of Greg?

C. He's very smart. He's able to talk with anyone, in any situation. He seems very comfortable doing that. If he wanted to get into politics, he could probably be quite successful—and I mean that in a positive way. Just to have the perseverance to see this whole project through is impressive enough. People have no idea what it takes to get a film like this up on the screen, any film for that matter. But this one, in particular, with its broad scope and long production period, is just a great, great accomplishment.

B. **It is. For a first-time filmmaker, what do you think of his methods and his direction? After all, we're not too old to learn new tricks from the new generation.**

C. It worked out pretty well, I'd say. There were days I had my doubts, you know, about what we were doing. You and I probably would have been more concerned about the details and logistics of planning production before we got into certain situations, wanting to know exactly what is going to happen, what we're going to be filming and how. But Greg had a great trust in his vision and just kept moving forward. Granted, he knew a lot about the subject going in; I mean, in a sense, he's been prepping for years. He was more willing to just jump in and "do it on the fly," as he puts it. And he made it work.

B. **Any situation comes to mind?**

C. Well, we were at that huge rally in Detroit in September and at the end of a long day somebody came up to us and said we ought to go over to this church where there was a faith-based recovery service happening that evening. Not knowing anything about what to expect, we just sped over there, jumped into a very difficult production situation, and just started shooting. It was an incredibly moving service. The sequence never made it into the final film, but I'm happy to say it's included in the DVD's bonus features section.

B. **What do you think of the final product? Does it tell the story as you thought it would?**

C. I'm glad we didn't have the primary responsibility of editing it. Because, as we were shooting it, I couldn't wrap my head around how all these many, many pieces of information and situations, and all that volume of footage could be whittled down into a manageable, cogent story. When I saw the first cut, it was amazing. It was like watching the footage for the first time because the way Jeff and Greg put it together, it took on new meaning and context. I was amazed how well the many faces and voices we met in our journey are captured in the final film. I think one of the strengths of the film is actually seeing so many different people, all different types, telling their stories, and with such singular purpose. After all, many faces, one voice, that's the concept right there, isn't it.

B. You bet. Thanks, bro.

All of us on the production team were deeply touched by the privilege of working on this film. There isn't a person in the credit list, whether in recovery or not, who wasn't invested in and uplifted by the experience. Speaking for the artists and craftspeople who brought their specialized skills to this project, I can tell you they poured their heart and soul into the film, as well as considerable talent. Greg assembled an extraordinary production and post-production team, from director of photography Craig Mikhitarian, to editor Jeff Reilly, to assistant editor, Christian Power, to composer Brendan Berry, to re-recording engineer Mike Ryan, and several others whose names you must notice in the credits. There were not a lot of technical people who worked on this film, considering the scope and beauty of it; budget constraints limited the luxury of throwing a host of specialists at it. That meant everyone gave a little more than might ordinarily be required. The beauty of it is that we can all take extra pride in the results, which in turn, intensifies our personal responses to the film's messages.

Briefly here, please meet our editor, Jeff Reilly, who is representative of Greg's dedicated team of filmmakers. Along with Craig's earlier remarks, Jeff's behind-the-scenes comments will give you an appreciation of what it took to make the film, and what we all took away from it.

JEFF REILLY

Editor

"We had so much material, it was hard to pull out the good stuff. That was the challenge."

In any discussion I've had with Jeff Reilly, he listens first, thinks, and then speaks. And his first words are always positive, suggesting that whatever we are talking about is headed in the right direction. What a fine quality to have as a film editor. I didn't spend the hours and months locked in the edit suite with him that Greg did, but I'm certain that Jeff's positive attitude throughout the long editing process contributed to Greg's stamina and confidence in making all the difficult decisions required to create the story that became *The Anonymous People*. Jeff is a creative person, which means he is a deep thinker and a sure-handed doer. But he is also a collaborator of the first rank, making him the ideal teammate in the ego-bound enterprise of filmmaking, which simultaneously relies on intense personal creativity and submission to the group dynamic. Oh yes, and the man's got "cred."

Jeff is an Emmy Award-winning editor, who won an Emmy for Outstanding Editing on the ESPN documentary, *Ali's 65* and was twice nominated for Emmys for other documentary work. He has edited many high profile programs for HBO, ESPN, NBC, CBS, Sony Pictures, Nike, Dick Clark Productions, Brainstormin' Productions, NBC Sports, Women's Entertainment, the Travel Channel, Boomer Esiason Foundation, A&E, and Biography Channel. In addition to editing, he has brought writing, directing, and producing skills to various commercials, Public Service Announcements, short films, a fishing show for the Travel Channel, and a pilot for the History Channel.

Because his involvement in *The Anonymous People* was so deep, extending beyond editing, to include writing and even producing portions of it, I wanted to hear his inside perspective on the making of this speculative and unusual film. We sat down to talk as soon as he was able to come up for air after months of concentrated effort in the editing room.

BUD. How did Greg bring *The Anonymous People* to you?

JEFF. I knew him from our days working at TeleverseMedia, and he just called me up and the timing was right. I was eager and excited to do it because I like heavy topics and this was a huge story. I felt good about taking it on because Greg had a lot of momentum behind him; he had important people involved in the story, such as William Cope Moyers and Tara Conner, and he had people in the television and film world interested who wanted to see ongoing cuts.

B. As an editor, what did you think about the amount of material Greg had amassed? And how long did it take you to find the story inside all of that?

J. There was a lot of footage to work with and that's always good. There were about 120 hours of original material you guys shot, and with the archival footage, we probably had 200 hours of video to edit. But, we had a first cut done in just three months; I think it was a manageable one hour and forty-seven minutes. Then, we just kept trimming until we had it down to about ninety minutes. So not counting the different versions, like the international version, we probably had a good fine cut in about five months time. I was pretty happy with that.

B. What was your biggest challenge editing the film?

J. The biggest challenge is always just keeping it good and tight. It really wasn't different than any other editing project—keeping the best stuff, losing the not-so-best stuff. In terms of structure, it came together when we saw the second half of the film was the answer to the first half. The first half was dark; it was about all the emphasis in the media and in people's minds about addiction and the stigma. The second half was about coming out of the darkness and into the light. I struggled with that the most. We had so much material; it was hard to pull out the good stuff. That was the challenge. Everything was so good it was hard not to get redundant, to streamline it and keep it moving.

B. What was it like working with Greg Williams on this, his first feature?

J. Greg is an excellent director and storyteller. One of his strengths is that he knows where he wants to go, where he wants to be, and he's very loose about getting there. He's not behind you holding your shirt and turning you this way and that way. You're sitting in this smallish room with somebody for weeks on end, so if you don't get along, it could be pretty rough. We got along well together; and he knows his stuff.

B. Was there anything in the film or story that particularly touched you?

J. Yes. A lot of stuff. Early on, I cut the Bridgeport CCAR meeting—an open all-recovery meeting we were allowed to film at the Recovery Community Center—into a little story and that got me. Karen Zaworski who talked early in the film about what it was like to lose a child to addiction, that got me. It always gets me, every time. Even in the screenings it continues to get me choked up. In an intellectual way and in an entertaining way, John Shinholser, definitely, was big for me, as he is for everybody. I mean, not only is he entertaining, he's smart. Those are some of the ones that stick out for me.

B. There's been a lot of comment and controversy over the history section of the film. Why did you spend so much time on that?

J. The biggest surprise for me, and it really gripped me, *was* the history part. When we were talking about it early on, I didn't envision it becoming as big as it was. It came together very nicely in the thread and build of the story. It was one of those things that when it was done, I said, "Wow, I don't know how that happened, but it came together nicely." It's an important and interesting context for the story. In the first cut, it was even longer.

B. We're privileged in our business to be exposed to so many different and wonderful stories and to meet some amazing people. We are constantly learning new things. Was there anything in your experience making this film that transformed you in any way?

J. Yes. Definitely. The stigma thing, for example. Bill White talks about how insidious it is. You don't really realize the little things you can say that sort of add to it. I think the language of recovery is something I've taken with me. I always felt like I was a pretty empathetic guy beforehand, but this has really heightened that. Like you said, one of the fringe benefits in our business is to hear these amazing stories from amazing people, which helps with empathy and connecting with people.

Here is a person, a professional who, though not jaded, has seen it all. The variety of stories, sensitive and spectacular, that Jeff has been intimately exposed to in his filmmaking career would seem to be enough to qualify him as an especially empathetic member of the human family. But, working on this film ratcheted up the empathy factor several notches. We (Jeff, Craig, and me) have not experienced addiction to alcohol or other drugs, yet we learned something vital from the faces and voices of recovery we met and studied, led by our young teacher, Greg Williams. In telling the story of those who tell their stories, we intensified our understanding of the importance of connections—those we make within ourselves and those we make between each other and the world around us.

Chapter Two

ANONYMITY TO ADVOCACY

It has been said that the only thing we learn from history is that we do not learn from history. The new recovery advocacy movement is out to change that.

First the good news . . .

Recovery from addiction to alcohol or other drugs is real. Recovery works. Recovery can be permanent.

Now the bad news . . .

Most people do not know this; especially those who need to know it most— the twenty-two million Americans who are currently suffering in addiction. They need the knowledge and hope this good news brings. Ironically, for the twenty-three million Americans who are already in long-term recovery, individually they may know this, but collectively they lack the understanding of how successful and widespread recovery is and can be. For the rest of us, who are not afflicted with the disease, well, most of us are just oblivious.

Then there's the sad news . . .

This entrenched societal ignorance is costing us lives. Three hundred fifty people will die today from addiction-related causes. That's nearly 130,000 deaths a year. And, how many more lives does this public health crisis wreck collaterally?

Add to that our neglect of the problem that is costing obscene amounts of money. Conservative estimates put it at 350 billion dollars a year. That's your money. Taxes. Healthcare costs. Criminal justice costs. Lost productivity. The car that was just stolen from your driveway.

There is another cost to this. Our character. This might be the highest price we are paying. If we see ourselves as essentially good and optimistic people, then beware the contagion of ignorance, prejudice, and apathy that mark our attention to addiction issues.

And all of this is unnecessary.

Newsflash, folks: People with addiction can be healed and they can stay well. Recovery works. In fact, we can all recover from this public health scourge.

Those twenty-three million Americans in long-term, successful recovery—anonymous people to most of us—can prove it. Once they were addicted, now they are well. And their very existence in wellness can supply the most potent medicine of all for this disease: hope. If only we knew their stories and the knowledge they hold.

I began our journey stupid. Greg was smart enough to know there were important questions. What happens when people in recovery come out of the shadows, reveal themselves, and use the power of their stories for the greater good? Is anonymity and secrecy synonymous? How have certain understandings of the tradition of anonymity in twelve-step programs actually perpetuated stigma and created obstacles to personal and societal healing from addiction? How has media done harm? Can people recover? Can society recover? What can we all learn from recovery? Do people in recovery have the secret to changing the world? I didn't even know enough to ask these questions, let alone understand their significance. I was about to learn.

Greg's conversation with Donna Aligata was one of the last things we recorded in our production period, but it is at the top of this chronicle of our journey, because Donna's influence on Greg was seminal and carried him forward in life with great momentum. Her teachings are at the heart of what changed Greg and what motivated him, ultimately, to make *The Anonymous People*. Just as Donna's perspectives and wisdom propelled Greg along his paths of discovery and growth, they also helped to launch this story of our filmmaking journey into the new recovery advocacy movement.

DONNA ALIGATA

"It's about a journey. It's about changing your whole life. The other side of recovery is not dark. It's very happy and it's joyous. And free!"

Donna Aligata is a nurse by profession and character. The Latin origin of the word, "nurse," meaning "person who nourishes," is a fit description for this wife, mother, pie-baker, gardener, and, oh yes, one of the most resourceful caregivers serving youth and families the recovery movement has. Forget that as we arrived at her home in a wooded Connecticut neighborhood where she lives with her husband Ken, the fragrance of homemade minestrone and baked bread, along with their insistence that we stay for lunch, warmed us immediately; or that their home, inside and out, is lush with plants, flowers, and herbs, all signaling that the love and care of growing good things is a natural occupation in this house. All that aside, the real evidence of Donna's nurturing is in her recovery work, saving young people from addiction and uplifting their lives. Ask Greg Williams. Although well into his own recovery and already active in helping others privately, it was Donna Aligata, more than anyone, who initially planted the seed of public advocacy in Greg and gave him the nourishing support and guidance that eventually flowered into what Greg is today—one of the tall trees in the garden of the new recovery advocacy movement.

For over three decades, Donna has worked as a mental health and addiction nurse, and a national trainer, facilitator, and consultant in the behavioral health field. For the Department of Defense, she provided clinical supervision and training for the military, including suicide prevention training for active duty Naval Officers. For the Substance Abuse and Mental Health Services Administration (SAMHSA), a branch of the US Department of Health and Human Services, she contributed to the design and standards for fourteen of that organization's National Policy Academies. Currently, she is a senior staff member at Policy Research Associates (PRA), a New York business that provides technical assistance, research, and training for public and private agencies working to create positive social change for disadvantaged people. At PRA, Donna is the project director for SAMHSA's Technical Assistance Center where she and her team work to strengthen state behavioral health systems that support the prevention and recovery needs of military service members, veterans, and their families. Outside of all that, in 2008, she founded Connecticut Turning to Youth and Families, a 501(c)(3) organization with the mission to help youth and families facing drug and alcohol problems connect with prevention, treatment, and recovery services through a statewide network of peer-to-peer supports.

Both Donna and husband Ken are in long-term, sustained recovery, and active with a program of family recovery continually since 1989. They have lots of stories to tell. As we sat around their table on a chilly autumn day warming ourselves with hearty food and heartfelt stories of recovery, it was apparent Donna and Greg have a deep bond. It was obvious to me that we might never have had the opportunity to make *The Anonymous People* were it not for the fortuitous meeting of these two just a few years ago. It was a privilege to break bread with them and listen as they reminisced and ruminated about the intersections of their recovery life.

GREG. Do you remember when we first met?

DONNA. Of course. We were having an event for families and youth, and we had tables and tables full of families with recovery experience. And you got up there and showed your video of a number of youths telling their stories, and when I looked around, I don't think there was a dry eye in the room. There were a number of mothers who were really moved, and they felt encouraged because it was pictures of other youths like their kids who were doing well and who had once been using substances. And it was the first time any of them had ever seen hope and a story about how kids can turn their lives around. After watching that they were drawn to talk with you and kids were all talking with each other. It just set the room on fire. So we got together, and I remember saying to you, "We need to do more of this. We need to go to more communities, and do you have more films? And can we film parents talking to other parents? Can parents talk about the journey they've been on?" And there you have it.

G. **So there's that power in story. I had, obviously, my own recovery story, but I was, at that time, sort of a detached voice in most of those stories and nervous about talking about my recovery publicly. Do you remember some of the concerns I would share with you about that?**

D. Yes, I remember we talked a lot about the difference between being a youth and being someone older like me sharing our stories. But in general, you were looking at your future and what would it mean if you shared your story while you were trying to get into college. Stigma was the big issue. It was discrimination. Would you be looked at the same way, would you be trusted the same way?

G. **I find it fascinating looking back at it now because I was pretty active as a young person in recovery, working with other young people, but doing it all underground. When I met you, you said, "Well, these stories have power to the wider society. These stories have power to communities, and we don't just need to do it in secret or in anonymous groups; we can bring this out into the open." Why did you see that as being important?**

D. Well, when someone looks at someone for the first time, that person will draw conclusions by the way one is dressed or what one looks like. Many people would look at you and say, "Greg, I'd love to have you as my son. You're a great kid." But when you tell your story about what happened—how you smashed your car, how your parents were looking for you, and how all those things happened—then people look at you and your life now, and they want to know how *did* that happen. How did you get there?

I'm a nurse. If I came out in the early days and said that I've struggled with alcohol and other drug use, do you think I would have been trusted with the keys to the pharmacy? I was trusted with the keys at DCF [Department of Children and Families, CT]. I worked with adolescents and would open the pharmacy door. If the other nurses there knew I came from a family riddled with addiction and alcoholism, would they look at me different? So for years I kept that quiet. Today I come out. I come out every place I go. I can't wait to get in front of people who are providers and say, "I'm a person in long-term recovery, and I've struggled with this. I'd love to talk about it." I talk about what it's about because then it makes it okay. They look at me, size me up, and say, "She doesn't look like someone I would stereotype as a person like that." Many people know me from my work and so they think, *Oh, she's highly responsible. She couldn't have been that.* And so, it's important for people to start to see that you can turn your life around, and this is how I did it.

For families, there's so much stigma. We have a lot of moms who call up and talk about the difficulties of having a child with addiction. Because their child is an addict, they stopped going to the grocery store, or they would find people avoiding them, not wanting to talk to them, and labeling them as bad mothers or fathers because their kid is using drugs. There's an immediate jump to something is wrong in that home, that someone did something wrong. We make judgment on people. And it's important that we are able to say that this is not about judging anyone. This happens to good families; this happens to everyone. It's part of life. It's a disease just like other diseases.

What's powerful is when someone who looks like you or me, or anyone out there, all different kinds of people, tell their story. What it was like before and what it's like now. The most important part is what do you do every day for your program of recovery. What is recovery like? On TV, you see all the sensational shows and they talk about the addiction side. They show the devastation. They show people at rock bottom. But what we are really showing in the videos that you do is what it looks like to be in recovery. It's a whole story about hope.

G. I had told my personal story before, obviously, in twelve-step groups and in recovery arenas, but I had never really done anything outside of that. Then you asked my father and me to come testify before Connecticut State Legislators. Talk about going public! Tell us about that event.

D. Connecticut Turning to Youth and Families had a legislative breakfast where we tried to get youth and parents to step up and talk about the experiences they had with addiction, with alcohol and other drug use, how it devastated their families, and mostly to talk about the system and how they didn't know where to go for help. We get a lot of calls from parents who don't know who to call. We prepped all the youth and families about how to tell their story, and I had the role of helping them to do that. We invited the press and a number of key legislative people were there from both sides. I remember there was an interview process going on, and some of the stories were pretty moving. Then you told your story, and it caused some reporters to come to you. Later, I read the article, which stated some things about your story and it included, "Greg W, who would prefer not to use his last name."

I remember talking with you afterward about the pros and cons of that statement because, as I recall, it gave the impression that you were afraid to give your last name. If you were afraid to give your last name, then maybe it would say to someone there's a reason to hide that.

G. I was afraid. There was a part of me that was ashamed and in fear that if somebody Googled me, then that's what would show up. But I

think another part was my misunderstanding about anonymity and what it meant and what it didn't mean. So there were two reasons to hide it, I guess.

D. I remember wanting to be very, very careful not to influence youth of any age, especially younger youth, to feel like they had to come out about their recovery publicly until they really had thought those things through. Especially since some of them were afraid about the reflections on their family or their future in school or of being labeled.

For years I didn't come out because I was worried about being compromised professionally. There are many jobs I went for where, if people knew about my recovery, they would say, "Don't discuss it, because it's better not to say that. It's not about you; it's about the patients, so don't share." People didn't realize how important it is to have someone who has been where you've been, who has lived the experience, who can tell their story, and that there are ways to heal and rebuild your life. To be able to speak about that publicly, well, that's really important. It gives a new kind of respect and hope to the whole journey of rebuilding your life.

G. What would happen when young people were motivated to stand up and talk about their recovery? How were they perceived by their communities?

D. I can picture being in one town where we literally sent text messages through cheerleaders to the whole high school and had this film festival in the evening. It was well attended. It was packed with youth and families. And a wholesome, athletic young woman and her dad got up there. She was the Campbell Soup girl, just as healthy and wonderful as anyone could dream. Well, when other kids like her got up and talked about their life, what they were doing and accomplishing in school, and other activities in the community, it was like, "Whoa, these are kids who are leaders. These are kids who have learned lessons, who are really mature, who have made some choices in their lives."

We saw kids from all different classes, cultural groups, races, ethnicities. They all got up and told their stories, and their parents told their stories. And you realize the potential of harnessing wellness and health in young people, and how important it is to intervene young, because then kids have twenty, thirty, forty years of having a recovery-oriented and healthy life. They're going to live longer. They're not going to cost our system as much. They're not going to be in our criminal justice system. They're going to be in our colleges. Regardless of the kind of home, it's possible for recovery to happen.

G. **We have all these studies, all this research and evidence that alcohol and other drugs are in every school, but yet nobody wants to address it.**

D. Denial. There's a lot of denial. First of all, there's violence in schools, there are drugs in schools, and there are teen pregnancies in schools, and these things are all wrapped together. They don't want their school to be known as a school with a drug problem. They want to keep it quiet. It is amazing though, in Bridgeport, when the leadership group took off at Central High, and all those kids started getting clean and sober, the principal, Mr. Ortiz, came forward and said violence had gone down. They started to see less school truancy, less delinquency. We saw the change. The data showed it. And rather than invest in that, there was a lot of finger pointing: "Is it the Board of Ed who should pay for this?" "Should it be some place outside?" It became a turf issue, and the best thing got squelched. But it *was* working. There's no question recovery belongs in schools. It's that simple. It's where kids spend their whole day. That's where the biggest drug trade is going on.

G. **That community denial: "This doesn't happen in our neighborhood," or "This doesn't happen in our school," or "If we start talking about the issue, we're going to get labeled." What changes that community-level denial?**

D. The best people who can help are other people who come from the same neighborhood, who've gotten into recovery and can tell their story to show others how it happened, how they got there. The kids will change it. And the parents will change it. Parents helping other parents; parents who've been there. But the kids are going to do it, despite the parents, despite the teachers. The kids who are in recovery are going to keep meeting; they're going to meet. Far better, of course, if we gave them a platform to meet at school. If we gave them an environment that was conducive to supporting recovery at school, instead of barriers and obstacles like we have now, then that would be great.

Why is it that someone can have Lyme disease and go down to see the nurse for an hour, but someone can have addiction and can't go to a recovery support group? It's ridiculous. Being a person in recovery, I've spent thirty-four years working in this field, and in the beginning it was really hard. It was all secret. Now, school's going to become a place where, just like any other condition, you go down to the nurse for your medication for your diabetes, you go down to see your recovery support group. That's what you do for your health at school. It belongs. It's part of health. So I think the world is going to change.

G. **It is amazing to me how my whole life changed after I took that leap of faith with you and said at twenty-two, "I'm Greg Williams, and I had an alcohol and other drug problem, but I'm better now, and I'm going to help other people find recovery, too." I mean, I'm making this movie, right? And it's just the power of the story, the power of sharing the lived experience that did it.**

D. It's a freeing kind of thing. When you feel like you have something to hide, there's shame. When you feel you have to be ashamed of who you are and what happened and the choices you've made and mistakes that have happened, then that secret stuff is really not healthy. We can start to be who we are and acknowledge that we're not perfect, that we've made mistakes, and share those lessons we've learned. And this idea that people have to hit bottom is gone now. We don't have to hit bottom. There's none of that. You can actually turn your life around at any point. And so with a lot of youth, we're seeing that happening.

I can remember watching the journey you went on, and it started, I think, when you were filming other kids' stories. At first, you were just the filmmaker showing your films. Next, you became the mentor to the kids at Central High who sought you out because you had longer time in recovery. They also liked what you were doing with film, and with school, and with your life. They wanted to know how you were doing that. You started to become an example without trying to be; they were just drawn to you. It was fun to watch because you started experimenting a little bit, and I just liked seeing it happen and seeing it unfold. So you grew, and your voice grew and your voice got louder. There's a need for leadership around this. I see a group of youth coming forward, leading more and more, coming out and making it okay and safe, and really being tolerant.

When you see wrong being done to people because they have a history of using alcohol or other drugs, when you see discrimination up close, it makes you realize that you have to speak up if you can.

I find in my own recovery, every chance I get, I have to tell people about my family recovery story. I grew up in an alcoholic family, grandparents died of alcoholism, grew up with physical abuse, ran away, was a hippie; I did it all. And here I am. I have to be in their face saying, "Yeah, I am this person. I've had this history, and yes, this disease is a family disease and it's in my family." Then people see that it's possible to have all that I have, and all the happiness I have, and that my life just keeps getting better and better.

If someone doesn't want to share about his or her history, that's okay, too. But the idea of feeling better about yourself kind of comes with the territory. The more you're comfortable with the fact that this is part of your journey, then that's a good thing.

G. You make a key point—that addiction doesn't just impact individuals. What do you tell people and teach them about how far-reaching the effects of addiction are and how we are dealing with it in our communities?

D. What we know is that addiction is a chronic brain disease and it's a family disease. Sometimes a spouse will get worried about a husband or a wife who's drinking too much or using too much. It affects the whole relationship. It's a disease that happens as part of the family system. And it affects the whole community. If I'm a mom and I'm worried about my kids, I have a lot of stress, a lot of anxiety. I might become hypervigilant about my child's behavior. A kind of obsession kicks in. We see a lot of parents who feel like they need coaching in healthy parenting. So, it's a disease that affects not one person, but the whole community.

And yet, we aren't treating it like that in our systems. We have systems that treat *parts* of people. We typically don't take the whole health of a person, physically, and combine it with the issues of addiction. You have your mental health budget, separate from your substance abuse funds. Our treatment system doesn't do a lot of family work. It doesn't look at the whole system, doesn't bring the parents and the kid in. We do an assessment on the youth, and we keep him or her apart from the parents; we have a few family meetings. When this youth goes back home, if there's no supports there for him or her to live differently, then that youth is going to go back with the same old people, places, and things. The changes have to happen at home. The changes need to happen in the neighborhood. So this is really about changing the way we do things in terms of prevention, treatment, and recovery in the community.

What typically happens is a lot of finger pointing: "This isn't my budget. This is your budget. How old is this youth? Oh! She's sixteen? He's eighteen?" It's very confusing for parents to get help. Which agency is going to be responsible or accountable for the kids' safety? We run into a lot of problems with parents who don't know who to call. They get pushed around from place to place. What's worse is that some of our systems say, "Oh, we treat youth," and they really aren't specialists in youth. They really don't understand family dynamics. They drop the age down and say, "Youth are the same. Whether they're eleven to thirteen, or sixteen, they're the same as eighteen-year-olds." You can get a fifteen-year-old who works the streets, who's a mom, who has been out of school for some time, or you can get a fifteen-year-old who's very, very young. It's really a very different thing. You have to look at the youth in the family, and tailor things to them as individuals. So right now, we don't have a system. Right now, we have isolated buckets and silos.

G. **You were one of the early proponents of this emerging idea that the recovery community could be organized. What were some of your first experiences trying to get the existing recovery community organized for a purpose? You were involved in that first Recovery Walk, right?**

D. I was really lucky to be part of the initial movement with Connecticut Community for Addiction Recovery [CCAR] and working with Bob Savage and Phil Valentine in the early days. There were huge concerns about money, and I remember we wrote a conference grant that actually did not get awarded, so we started moving toward a couple of ideas, and that first walk was one of those ideas. I remember being in charge of the tents, the T-shirts, the walk permits, and of course, getting the Porta-Johns. One of the funniest stories was on the morning of the walk, getting to the Porta-Johns and seeing how dirty they were. I remember being in that Porta-John with Bob Savage, and we were cleaning them together. It turned out they were the wrong Porta-Johns. They were the City of Hartford's Porta-Johns and ours hadn't been delivered yet. So that created quite a bit of laughter.

There were a lot of homeless people hanging around Bushnell Park. They ended up putting on T-shirts and walking with us. I remember one gentleman pointing out a particular park bench he used to sit on saying that's where he got high and shot-up for years. Now he is real proud to be walking. So, this was the walk. The first thought was to put a face on recovery—to walk around the Capitol and to help everyone see that we were not ashamed. It was wonderful walking around that park, and going down the street, and people passing by beeping their horns, and yelling out to us, "I'm in recovery, too!" It was amazing to see. We didn't think we were going to get that many people. But they just started pouring into the park. And the sun was shining, and the dome looked golden, and it was like one of the most incredibly moving times.

We actually had a dunk tank one of those first years; I'll never forget it. Dr. Tom Kirk, the Commissioner, and Bob Savage were such good sports. They allowed people to dunk them for donations. I mean, it was hilarious. There was another walk where we cooked 2,000 hot dogs. Standing there cooking hot dogs in the sun, you know? It was well-attended, and families came out, face painting, bounce houses. It was a festive time. It was a real celebration of recovery. It still is like that. It's a time for the community to come together.

G. **Did you know at that first walk of this new era that you were part of something historic? Because now we have this kind of thing happening all over the country, modeled after Recovery Walks!**

D. We didn't know where it was going, but as soon as it started to unfold, it was real. CCAR made these lawn signs in the beginning. Every year we put the lawn signs up in front of our yard. I'll never forget people coming by and literally driving up the driveway, wanting to know what the recovery event was, and saying, "I'm in recovery, too."

We started to meet people. That's one of the ways I started to get known for working with kids—parents coming to my house, then calling someone, saying, "Hey, there's a lady who works with kids, and really knows how to get your kid into treatment." And it just took off here in my own community. Part of it was my twelve-step meetings and things that I'd done in the community. But it was just amazing!

We even went to the dump once to get rid of some stuff. We had the old signs, and one of the guys at our town dump came to us and said, "Hey, I'm in recovery, too!" It started to catch on that people were really connecting over recovery and not being ashamed. And that created a thing: "Well, what if it became okay for us all to come out more?" It wouldn't be such a silent process. People would see that it does work, and there are a lot of people who've been where you've been. And that's the way to change the world. That's the only way to change the world. Where it becomes part of what everybody's accustomed to. This is what's in our community. And yes, it doesn't have to be that way. You have choices, and there's help available and there are a lot of people who know how to get there.

G. **So, again, we see the power in going public about recovery, being in a movement that grows and touches people. It not only raises awareness, but identifies needs and gets things accomplished. What are your observations since this new movement has broken out?**

D. A lot of people in recovery don't even know they have a voice. And it's very exciting when they realize they have a voice and if they talk about their experience, it can help others. It requires some time, some organization, and some training. The recovery community cares. They just need some help with leadership and training, learning how to do it well and how to create enough infrastructure. Give the community what it needs to give back. We've seen it grow. We've seen it take off over the years.

It's amazing to see what the recovery community centers are doing across our nation right now. Recovery belongs in every neighborhood, in every community. The problem we see sometimes is this tension: Is recovery being bundled with treatment in a way where it's just another part of the same old thing, and the same old system? I mean, there's a difference when there's a partnership formed by people who are recovery leaders and who understand how to mine recovery services in their own community. We're talking about sober and safe housing. We're talking about employment, recovery-supported employment where people can get jobs and can keep the jobs. It's really about us offering them that support and help.

Families. When a youth first comes home from treatment, moms are lost. "What do we do? Do we let them go out on Friday night? Do we do this? Do we do that?" A lot of guidance and support and coaching is needed so that parents can share with other parents what works at home. And there's a lot of support that can help kids stay out of even needing any treatment. Prevention services already exist in all our communities. It's time to marry the prevention networks along with recovery. It's a very compatible marriage. Prevention, treatment, and recovery belong together.

G. **Is youth recovery, prevention? I mean, if young people are in recovery programs, aren't we also fostering prevention?**

D. Youth recovery support services can be prevention. They can be at both ends. Yes, you're trying to prevent relapse. But there is a difference between addiction and youth who have actually gone down that road where they've actually had the compulsion. We need to be able to intervene at every level.

Addiction is not linear. It's not a straight line. We always think of the typical stereotype, someone with a brown bag and drinking from the morning till night. That's not how it happens. People can give up using alcohol and other drugs for a year or two and still have the disease. What a lot of us don't understand is that recovery is about changing a whole lot more than just maintaining abstinence. It's about changing a lot of the inside stuff—our behaviors, the way we interact with anxiety, and the way we deal with relationships. But the point about prevention is learning how to take care of our health—not smoking, healthy eating, proper exercise— as well as, "Am I doing a program of recovery that's keeping me clean and sober?" It all belongs together. Again, when we keep putting our funding hat on and saying, "This money is just for prevention, and this money is just for recovery or treatment," then that keeps us from handling the whole person. It's really about pulling all that together. So prevention does belong as part of a partnership with treatment and recovery. It's got to come together.

The other part, of course, is mental health. A lot of kids have anxiety, depression, issues with suicide, and feelings of self-destruction that come with all of this. Every path of recovery has to be welcomed. Medication-assisted recovery. Faith-based recovery. There are many paths to support recovery. And if we think that only one way is *the* way, then that's when we get into trouble.

G. **Addiction and all its adverse effects are pervasive in our society. And yet, as we have learned from more and more people as they tell their stories, in recovery there is hope. What is your vision for what it could look like ten or twenty years from now for a young person or a family who's having an alcohol or other drug problem?**

D. First, all of those problems would be screened by a primary care doctor. We have wonderful evidence-based practice tools, like *Screening, Brief Intervention, and Referral to Treatment* [SBIRT] that can help interventions happen a lot sooner with people who might be using—it doesn't matter what—alcohol, pain meds, substances to self-medicate. The vision would be that this is treated like every other disease, that it would be safe, that we wouldn't judge people, that there would be enough experts out there that you could get help and have it paid for, just like any other treatment or health issue.

I would like to see an end to some of the shows on TV. Frankly, I feel they glamorize and stereotype what people look like who are addicted. I really don't think they show the positive side of recovery because everything good happens when you're in recovery. Maybe that's not the kind of thing that's going to sell the media or TV. But I'm going to tell you that it's not doing us any good, seeing just that side of things, you know, the interventions and all. People calling constantly asking, "Can you come and do an intervention with our family?" They think that's what it's all about. But it's about something much deeper than that.

It's about a journey. It's not about just staying sober for a few months or a few weeks. It's about changing your whole life. And that's why you need people in recovery embedded in the community who know how to have fun and live a healthy life and are normal. You know, they really are. There is the other side of recovery that is not dark. It's very happy and it's joyous. And free!

Knowledge is a powerful force, as long as it flows freely. In the case of addiction and recovery, obstacles to our understanding of the facts about the disease have impeded our ability to find its remedy in recovery. Throughout history we have been led to the threshold of finally dealing with addiction openly and effectively, only to be thwarted by some societal, self-imposed sidetrack that deters our progress. At the heart of our collective inability to solve this public health crisis are the unreasonable, but understandable, factors of guilt and shame. The prime example of this is the ridiculous, though well-intentioned "War on Drugs" begun some four decades ago. About the only thing that misguided policy did was create a profitable prison industry—at the cost of labeling people "addicts" and ostracizing anyone so afflicted. Talk about laying on the guilt and promoting public shame through policy. They might have just as well pilloried everyone with a substance use disorder in the public square.

We conflate morality and addiction and the result is a society with entrenched shame over addiction. Unfortunately, this obscures many of the noble and reasoned efforts made over the years by passionate advocates for recovery and continues to do so. It is less a question of learning from history than it is of knowing there even is a history from which we can learn.

Most people are simply ashamed to talk about addiction. That goes for the addicted, as well as the affected, and even the unmindful. It is surely what led to the formation of anonymous groups, hidden places where suffering people can feel safe and have the courage to seek and share recovery. But anonymity has been both a blessing and a curse to people seeking recovery from addiction. On one hand, it is a sacred tenet of the eponymous fellowship that alcoholics founded, and of the over 250 other support groups that have adopted it; anonymity is a haven for millions whose lives have been saved because of that principle.

Anonymity has also been misunderstood and misapplied. Much to the amazement of many who hide in the safe, invisible cloak of anonymity, it was never meant to preclude public advocacy for recovery. After Bill Wilson and Dr. Bob Smith established the first twelve-step recovery program in 1935, known as Alcoholics Anonymous (AA), they still advocated outside the program for the millions of others who were fellow sufferers, and encouraged people like Marty Mann, to go forth and do likewise. Somehow, though, through the persistent prosecution of shame (it's a moral choice), the disease could not shed its stigma. Even the values and virtues of anonymity, helpful to so many, were tainted by stigma, conferring an unfair and erroneous connotation on "anonymous," forcing many to withdraw into secrecy for protection. The anonymous twelve-step program was a safe place to secure one's secret and such organizations became the inadvertent imprimaturs of anonymity outside the program. The advocacy movement stumbled against ignorance, prejudice, shame, and a mistaken belief that it was against tradition to publicly disclose one's personal recovery status.

While the path from anonymity to advocacy has had its ups and downs, it kept moving forward. Fortunately, we have plenty of witnesses to that progressive yet halting history who can set the record straight. Their knowledge is so essential to our understanding and fundamental to the validity of the new recovery advocacy movement that we begin this book with several of the key people who enthusiastically gave their learned perspectives to Greg's film.

Addiction may be the last of our hidden diseases, and recovery, the world's best-kept secret. The forthcoming people in this book are some of the ones who are brave enough to talk about it and carry the torch that both leads the movement forward and sheds light on the truth of the past.

WILLIAM L. WHITE

"...the recovery story has yet to be told."

Greg dedicates *The Anonymous People* to two individuals: his mentor, Donna Aligata, the person he credits most with helping him cast off his cloak of anonymity for the sword of advocacy; and the other, William L. White, writer, advocate, and historian. To the recovery movement, Bill White is like everyone's favorite apple tree; the fruits of his life's work nourish, sustain, and gladden his followers year after year with unending productivity. One day, Greg sat under the apple tree, an apple fell and the rest is history.

Since 1969, when he began community outreach activities for addiction sufferers in Illinois, Bill has been a pioneer in the work of addiction study and a major force in the recovery movement. He is Emeritus Senior Research Consultant at Chestnut Health Systems in Illinois, where he also founded the Lighthouse Institute, an addiction treatment research center. He has authored or co-authored, in particular with his mentor, Dr. Ernest Kurtz, more than 450 publications in the major peer-reviewed addiction journals and trade journals. He has written eighteen books, including the award-winning *Slaying the Dragon: The History of Addiction Treatment and Recovery in America* and *Let's Go Make Some History: Chronicles of the New Addiction and Recovery Advocacy Movement*. He is the past chair of Recovery Communities United and has served as a volunteer consultant to Faces & Voices of Recovery. He was featured in the Bill Moyers television special about addiction, *Close to Home* and in Showtime's documentary, *Smoking, Drinking, and Drugging in the 20th Century*. The recipient of many awards, he has been honored by the National Association of Addiction Treatment Providers, the American Society of Addiction Medicine, and the Native American Wellbriety Movement.

When you meet Bill White, you feel immersed in wisdom. Some people have that gift; when they speak, it is you who are made to feel wise. Bill is one of those. He overflows not just with facts, but also with connections and perspectives that turn a light bulb on in your brain. Enthusiastic? Ask him a question and he can barely contain himself; brilliant eyes widen behind his rimless glasses and he eagerly obliges your inquiry with a generous sharing from his storehouse of knowledge. He is a distinguished looking man, with a bit of anachronism combed into wavy white hair worn long, but neat. His sculpted gray goatee is reminiscent of an earlier age, and if it weren't for his smooth, ageless complexion, one could almost believe that he actually lived the history he describes. In fact, it is disconcerting at first to hear him speak about the past; he has a unique style of speech in which he often puts things historical in the past predictive future, as if he were back in time observing events as a contemporary and telling you what is "going" to happen next. You will see this unusual grammatical construct in the transcript of his interview below. It is quirky, but kind of fun, because once you become used to his speech, you get swept along on his timeline and feel the tug and flow of living history. His demeanor is serious in an academic sort of way, but if you listen carefully to his stories, he laces them with dry humor, which he obviously enjoys. There is a telltale twinkle in his eyes as he pauses long enough for you to appreciate the many ironies and oddities in recovery's past.

We all had been looking forward to having our private moment with this much-in-demand mentor, to have a chance to interview him and to hear straight from the horse's mouth what the new recovery advocacy movement is all about. We sat down with him during his visit to the Ostiguy Recovery High School in Boston, a day before he was to deliver a lecture at Harvard marking Ernest Kurtz and Bill's receipt of the Norman E. Zinberg Lectureship Award. We found a quiet conference room at the school and set up a comfortably attractive scene for filming the interview. We expected to be there a while because of Bill's proclivity to speak thoroughly on the subject. He didn't disappoint. While the following conversation with Greg is edited, I also took the liberty of augmenting it slightly with a few points of interest and elaboration taken from his address on "Experiencing Recovery," which we recorded at Harvard the next day.

For all this and much more, you could write a book about this erudite gentleman. For now, Greg's in-depth interview will have to do. It is a foundation for all that follows.

GREG. You're a self-described obsessive when it comes to the history of addiction and recovery. You have amassed an amazing trove of primary research materials and written extensively on the subject. Where did it all start in this country?

BILL. If we look at organized recovery in the United States, it actually begins in Native American communities dating back to the 1730s with a series of Delaware prophets who, behind their own recovery from alcoholism, organized abstinence-based movements of cultural and religious revitalization within their tribes. Thus, we have the rise of the Handsome Lake movement in the late 1700s, which called for a rejection of not only alcohol, but of all things European, and a return to Native traditions. Following was a series of Native prophet movements to deal with rising alcohol problems, such as those led by the Shawnee prophet and the Kickapoo prophet. By the late 1800s, these movements continued through the Native American Church and the Indian Shaker Church, and, into the twentieth century through the Indianization of AA in the 1950s, "The Red Road," and the contemporary Wellbriety Movement. So there's a continual history of recovery mobilization within Native communities dating back to the mid-1700s.

G. And for the "new Americans," what are some of the earliest recovery support organizations?

B. In the Euro-American communities, we get the first rise of recovery mutual aid groups in the 1830s. I actually have the first collection of recovery case studies in the United States in a pamphlet from 1833 by Sigourney and Smith that contains some of the earliest "reform" case studies. The largest organization of the time was the Washingtonians, which grew from six members of a Baltimore drinkers club in April of 1840 to more than 400,000 members within forty-eight months, and then almost disintegrated overnight. The alcoholics in that movement went underground and began to organize recovery-focused, fraternal temperance societies for what they called "hard cases." The term "alcoholism" hadn't been coined yet in 1840. They functioned very well as sobriety-based frameworks, but often became quite closed and elitist. Some of these groups, for example, wanted only "drunkards of good repute" to be part of their societies. By the 1870s we get a new movement called the Ribbon Reform Clubs, and then we get such groups as the Dashaways in San Francisco and the Drunkard's Club in New York City. Around that time we also begin to see the first recovery mutual aid groups organized inside treatment programs in the United States.

G. What were the treatment programs like back then?

B. We actually have a very elaborate network of addiction treatment in the nineteenth century. We have the early inebriate homes that are going to begin in this city [Boston] in 1857, with the opening of the Home for the Fallen. That home is going to open and close fairly quickly, but reopen under the banner of the Boston Washingtonian Home. The Washingtonian Homes in Boston and Chicago will be two of the premier inebriate homes in the United States, with both of those continuing well into the modern era. We're also going to have the more medically directed inebriate asylums beginning with the opening of the New York State Inebriate Asylum in 1864. The inebriate asylums used very physical methods of prolonged, often legally mandated, institutional treatment. We're also going to have private-for-profit addiction cure institutes competing with one another for who can cure addiction the fastest with the least amount of hypodermic injections and vomiting [e.g., the early use of belladonna and emetics in the Keeley Institutes]. These included the chains of Keeley Institutes, Neal Institutes, Gatlin Institutes, and Oppenheimer Institutes. And don't forget the boxed and bottled home cures loaded with alcohol, opium, morphine, cocaine, chloral hydrate, and other potential intoxicants. They're being offered by the same patent medicine industry that addicted large numbers of American citizens with drug-laced patent medicines. It was common in those days to see very aggressive advertising by the pharmaceutical industry offering home cures that promised a new miracle ingredient that would provide a painless and permanent cure. Nearly all of the morphine addiction cures contained morphine at higher numbers of grains than most people were then addicted to. So, in the name of treating addiction, people actually developed even more intractable addictions. My point with this is that the theme of harm in the name of help has a very, very long tradition in the history of addiction treatment.

G. What about recovery? Were there any attempts to advocate for recovery in these treatment programs or beyond them?

B. The first recovery mutual aid groups organized inside treatment programs in the United States began with the Ollapod Club in 1864. It organized inside the New York State Inebriate Asylum and grew to a number of such associations, the largest being the Keeley Leagues, which grew to more than 30,000 members scattered across the United States. In 1895, they were going to march on the capitol of the State of Pennsylvania, lobbying for a Keeley Law that would provide state funds to pay for indigents who could not personally afford it, to receive the Keeley Cure. So we get the first inklings of people moving beyond their personal recovery toward advocacy during that period. There were other early groups, including the Godwin Association, and one can find reference to other community-based recovery support groups in the early twentieth century, such as the United Order of Ex-Boozers, the Harlem Club of Former Alcoholic Degenerates, and the Jacoby Club.

But by the end of the nineteenth century and into the first two decades of the twentieth century, both the recovery support groups and this network of treatment programs almost completely collapse. In spite of excessive claims of cure, how long do you think it took before everyone in the culture knew someone for whom treatment in that era had not worked? The collapse of early treatment came from this culture literally losing faith in the prospects of long-term recovery. We entered a very shameful period of regression within the field. Alcoholics and addicts were transferred to rural penal colonies and the work farms that were often appendages to county jails. They were transferred to the back wards of what were already aging state psychiatric asylums. With addiction seen as simply a symptom of underlying psychopathology, over the coming decades, treatment of addiction in asylums in this country indiscriminately applied whatever methods were in vogue in psychiatry. And that would include periods of mandatory sterilization of alcoholics and addicts, particularly female addicts and alcoholics. It would include indiscriminate application of electro- and chemo-convulsive therapies. It would include psychosurgery, particularly prefrontal lobotomies, as a treatment for addiction. It would include drug insults of every variety and extremely prolonged periods of sequestration. We also saw the emergence of foul wards and foul cells in the large urban hospitals to deal with the issue of the chronic public inebriate, including Boston City Hospital. And importantly, the very concept that addiction was a treatable medical disorder was destroyed.

What we said as a culture was: Let's let the existing alcoholics and addicts die off, and the sooner the better. And we're going to prevent the creation of a new generation of addicts by legally prohibiting the sale of alcohol and aggressively controlling the distribution of opium, morphine, cocaine, chloral hydrate, and the newly arriving barbiturates.

G. **So then this was a challenging time for addiction recovery, if it wasn't even perceived as viable. What was the impetus for the emergence of Alcoholics Anonymous?**

B. We get this virtual vacuum of need. The early members of Alcoholics Anonymous develop their alcoholism during the late years of prohibition, and then we get the increasing rise of alcohol problems following the repeal of prohibition that further magnified this need for a recovery resource.

The message that pervades this history is when resources for recovery decline or disintegrate, recovering people and their families will find a way to rise up out of the ashes of that disintegration to rebirth new systems of care. That's precisely what happened in the rebirth of recovery mutual aid through AA in 1935.

Most people in the United States think recovery as an organized framework begins in 1935 with AA. What's intriguing is the large number of recovery support groups that preceded AA. What was distinctive about AA was a number of things. One, AA was the first fellowship that focused not on a decision to stop drinking, but a decision of how not to start drinking. So it really shifted from a focus on recovery initiation to "How do you live a life in long-term recovery?"

The second thing was the notion of transcendence. Some of the earlier groups focused on sobriety as a point-in-time decision. For example, the Washingtonians, as an expression of their manhood, would march forward and sign a pledge that they would never drink distilled or beverage alcohol again. Now, in contrast with that, AA really framed its understanding of recovery as a kind of transcendence of self, an acknowledgment that all resources within the self had, in fact, failed to produce sobriety. So this notion of failed self-help that we get in AA's first step and the transcendence that can be found in the second and third step within AA are unique in the history of recovery support, particularly outside of early religious frameworks of recovery.

Another thing that made AA unique was that through the Twelve Traditions, AA found a way to address many of the problems that had led to the collapse of its predecessors—issues related to ego, to money, to publicity, and to relationships with other organizations. AA found through its traditions a way to recognize and rein in those forces that had destroyed so many of its predecessors.

G. So it was called Alcoholics Anonymous from the start, but how did the traditions develop? That came afterward, right?

B. Yes. AA is founded in the summer of 1935. If we think of the traditions that govern the organizational life of AA today, they really didn't exist between 1935 and the early 1940s. There were incredible growing pains going on within AA and there were no traditions yet to guide local AA groups. That collective wisdom began to emerge as people wrote Bill Wilson in New York City to say, "We're having this problem. What do we do with that?" And rather than Bill say, "This is what you need to do," he would say, "It has been our general experience across the country that . . ." So, again, he was offering this sort of collective wisdom and experience coming out of the growing numbers of AA groups.

But there was tremendous turmoil during this time. There was a group in Richmond, West Virginia, for example, that met, I believe it was on Wednesday nights, and drank beer at their meetings. There were personal attacks on the AA cofounders. Bill Wilson is offered a full-time job to bring AA within the framework of Charles Towns' Hospital. The threats of professionalism and commercialization of AA are rising in the late thirties and early 1940s. The AA group in San Francisco was writing nasty letters to New York saying that if it didn't communicate better, they were going to organize an alternative fellowship called Dipsomaniacs Incognito, and on and on and on.

In spite of these challenges, there is considerable growth of AA in the early 1940s, mirroring similar successes and problems the Washingtonians experienced in the 1840s. As Bill Wilson continued to offer guidance in his letters to local groups, Earl T, an AA member in Chicago, encouraged Bill to codify this collective wisdom that was emerging across the groups into what eventually became the Twelve Traditions of AA. You can't talk about AA members breaking anonymity per se during this early period because the anonymity tradition has yet to be codified.

G. And even though it was named Alcoholics Anonymous, that didn't mean some of AA's members weren't involved in advocating publicly for recovery. Isn't that true?

B. The question of advocacy in the context of AA came up very early in AA's history and it came up primarily through the person of Marty

Mann. Marty Mann was one of the first women to achieve long-term recovery within the framework of AA, and she began to have a vision. She was actually working on a project in which she had encountered the figure of Dorothea Dix, the famed mental health reformer of the nineteenth century. And Marty began to think, *I wonder if I could do for alcoholism what Dorothea Dix did by de-stigmatizing mental illness and creating more humane resources for the treatment of mental illness?*

And out of that vision in 1944, she founded the National Committee for Education on Alcoholism [NCEA] that's later going to evolve into the National Council of Alcoholism and further evolve into today's National Council on Alcoholism and Drug Dependence. This is the kinetic moment in the rise of what's been called "the modern alcoholism movement." That includes the rise of Alcoholics Anonymous in 1935, the emergence of the Yale School of Alcohol Studies and the creation of outpatient alcoholism clinics at Yale, and the work of the Research Council on Problems of Alcohol. These multiple organizations collectively create a recovery support and advocacy movement with Marty Mann as its most visible leader. She's going to travel across the country organizing these local community affiliates of NCEA, which are composed mostly of individuals in recovery and other concerned parties such as local physicians and judges. But Marty's primary tool of organizing is going to be her own personal story.

There's going to be early tension and dialogue around this issue of anonymity. And to complicate matters, Marty Mann is going to ask the two AA cofounders to put their name on the letterhead of NCEA as part of a fundraising letter that's going to go out to large numbers of people. That letter, with Bill W and Dr. Bob's names on the letterhead, began to heighten the tension around this issue of what is AA's relationship with other organizations? And, of course, it would create the context for later traditions that would clarify AA's autonomy and distinctiveness and separation from other organizations.

Nevertheless, it is important to note that it was AA members who were the early advocates for this new movement. In fact, large numbers of AA members are going to be part of this alcoholism movement all across the country. And, in essence, what they're going to try to do is fundamentally rewire how this country perceived alcoholism and the attitudes toward its treatment. They did that through Marty Mann's core NCEA propositions. The first one was that alcoholism was a disease. It followed, therefore, that the alcoholic is a sick person, that the alcoholic is in need of help, and that the alcoholic can be helped. And finally, alcoholism was posited as a major American public health problem worthy of public health resources. That sets the framework to then argue for public dollars to support detoxification, post-detoxification treatment centers, longer-term rehabilitation facilities in the country, and local alcoholism councils that would provide public education and information and referrals. These local alcoholism councils across the country are going to be filled with local men and women—many AA members—and their families. But they're going to be there as individuals and not as members of Alcoholics Anonymous.

G. **When did these councils really start to take root in communities?**

B. In the mid-1940s, this advocacy movement is really going to take off and by the '50s and '60s, the foundation for what will become the modern era of addiction treatment and recovery support has been laid. As this era began, the AA General Service Office will issue very specific guidelines for AA members who are working in the alcoholism field, whether it be in alcoholism treatment or public education.

G. **By all accounts then, the modern alcoholism movement evolved as a result of people's lived experience and advocacy?**

B. No question about that. As a historian, I could build a very strong case that we would not have had the national legislation in the early 1970s that created the federal, state, and local partnerships to fund, build, staff, operate, and evaluate alcoholism treatment programs without this earlier advocacy movement. Those subsequent events would not have existed without the advocates who began in the 1940s, and who spent the 1940s, 1950s, and 1960s, virtually much of their adult lives, advocating for the systems of care and systems of education in local communities across the United States. People like Marty Mann were critical to the legislation that's going to get passed in the early 1970s that lay the foundation for modern addiction treatment. And people like Bill Wilson, the cofounder of AA, and other early AA members will testify before members of Congress on behalf of that legislation.

G. Some pretty high profile people came out to testify publicly. What was the climate like and who testified?

B. What began to happen was that through this mass advocacy movement of the '40s, '50s, and '60s, a growing consensus began to shift alcoholism from a moral framework of understanding to a medical framework: the idea that alcoholism was a legitimate and treatable medical disorder. As these ideas came along, we began to get the first people to come forward who really put a face and voice on recovery—very famous people of the time, like Lillian Roth [author] and Mercedes McCambridge [actor]. Marty Mann, who crisscrossed this country hundreds of times telling her story and the stories of other people in recovery, really set the stage for a dramatic moment in the history of advocacy in the country. It was a project called Operation Understanding in 1976, sponsored by the National Council on Alcoholism, in which fifty-two prominent Americans, extremely well known in business, science, entertainment, and sports publicly announced their status as being in long-term recovery from alcoholism. It was a breakthrough moment when people like Dick Van Dyke, Gary Moore, the astronaut Buzz Aldrin, and other people who this country dearly loved stepped out of the shadows and announced themselves as people in recovery from alcoholism.

G. Was this widely covered on television and in the news?

B. Yes. Operation Understanding was a televised event with heavy media saturation because of the celebrity of the individuals involved. They simply were there to stand up and say, we're individuals who suffered from the disease of alcoholism, we recovered from that disorder, and we're here to say this is a medical disorder that is treatable and that long-term recovery is possible. It was an incredible moment for people in recovery and an enormous turning point in the history of not only advocacy, but also in the history of attitudes toward alcoholism. It was an amazing moment in the history of addiction recovery.

G. Wow, I never heard about this before. I have to see if I can find news footage of that event.

B. It was a breakthrough moment. And I can speak personally about this. I entered work in the alcoholism field in the late 1960s, at a time of the most despicable conditions under which alcoholics were treated in the United Sates. I entered at a time when alcoholics were hanging themselves in drunk tanks, in city jails, and in county jails. I saw the worst of alcoholics in the back wards of aging state psychiatric hospitals, horribly depraved and hopeless places in those years. I entered the field at a time when many alcoholics could not get admitted to a local hospital even for the treatment of trauma because hospitals had morality clauses that precluded the admission of alcoholics. Now, think of that context. If somebody had told me in my earliest days entering the field that I would see prominent people from all walks of life on national television and later, I would see the wife of a president of the United States on television talking about her recovery, or I would see more than 100,000 people in recovery and their families and friends marching publicly in the streets in my lifetime, I would've thought these things absolutely impossible. And yet I have witnessed this history, and a critical piece of that was the 1976 event called Operation Understanding.

G. The president's wife you were referring to was Betty Ford?

B. Yes. A lot of people talk about the moment that Mrs. Betty Ford announced her dependence on alcohol and other drugs and her decision to seek treatment. It, too, was an incredible moment in the history of this disorder and the history of recovery in the United States. But there wouldn't have been a Betty Ford announcement if there hadn't have been an Operation Understanding in 1976.

G. Just a little more about Betty Ford … how powerful was her announcement for people in recovery and for America?

B. The Betty Ford story is an interesting one because it's important to put it in context to really understand its power.

Following Operation Understanding in 1976 and by the time we turn into the 1980s, we're going to see a real reversal of some of the positive changes that had begun to unfold in the United States. In fact, you could even build a case that the early 1980s were in some ways a heyday of recovery in the United States, but at a very superficial level. It had become sort of the "in thing" in some circles to be in recovery during that time period, but very quickly this was smothered by two things: one was the cocaine epidemic, and the other, the rise of HIV and the AIDS epidemic of the 1980s.

We got all these incredible images that got linked to addiction—issues of race, issues of social class, fear of violence, fear of insanity. They all got wrapped up in the cocaine story in very bizarre ways at a time when cocaine addiction in the early 1980s was overwhelmingly white. Yet, the images that came across TV were inner city images of young black men dealing crack cocaine on street corners or African American infants trembling in perinatal intensive care units, and the moral panic behind that created, not only a set of draconian laws in response to that epidemic, but it began to force large numbers of recovering people out of the public light and back into the shadows for their own self-protection. Combine that with the HIV and AIDS epidemic and we re-stigmatized, we de-medicalized, and we re-criminalized alcohol and other drug problems. So in that context, to have the wife of a president of the United States coming forward within this era was an enormous act of personal and family courage. Mrs. Ford's announcement in 1978 and her continued public statements in the following years tempered some of what was unfolding in the larger culture in the 1980s.

It was an incredibly kinetic moment because of another thing, too. As I entered the alcoholism and addiction field in the late '60s, early '70s, this was a man's world, in the sense that the staff were men, the vast majority of clients served by that system were men, and the policymakers were men. But we had large numbers of alcohol and drug dependent women hidden within this culture. Mrs. Betty Ford was one of them. For her to speak publicly about her treatment and recovery and to have her family surrounding her within that recovery process was an incredible turning point in our history. And, in some ways, it may have been a critical seed of what will later be called the new recovery advocacy movement in the United States.

G. Going back to the legislation, what were some of the laws that influenced our thinking and behavior about addiction?

B. In the 1980s, there were a series of laws that began to rapidly escalate penalties for possession and sale of illicit drugs, in particular, specific laws focusing on crack cocaine, as opposed to powdered cocaine with differential sentencing guidelines. That meant that individuals who were in possession of or selling crack cocaine were subject to inordinately severe penalties. That led to a virtual explosion of the prison population in the United States. This was the period in the '80s when we literally decided we were going to try to incarcerate our way out of the addiction problem and its related problems. We couldn't build prisons fast enough and we filled prison after prison with young men of color as a result of the differential sentencing guidelines of that era.

G. You have written a lot about how drug laws historically have been used to sort of "ghetto-ize" people.

B. Yes, race and social class are inextricably linked to US drug policy. We've had serial wars on drugs beginning from the 1870s in San Francisco targeting opium use among Chinese immigrants. We go forward and we have the early anti-narcotics legislation of the early twentieth century, particularly the Harrison Act of 1914 that's going to target young immigrant men who are experimenting with heroin as it's emerging in the illicit drug culture of the United States. We're going to have another drug war in the 1930s aimed at marijuana and its association with Mexican-Americans that will produce the Marijuana Tax Act of 1937. In the 1950s, we're going to have the Boggs Act that dramatically increases penalties for possession and sale, introducing the first potential life sentence under our narcotic laws in the United States. This will be the product of the moral panic surrounding the rise of juvenile narcotics addiction in the 1950s. In the 1960s and early '70s we get the rising poly-drug abuse that is going to generate a whole other set of laws that criminalize new patterns of alcohol and other drug use. And then with the '80s we probably had the most intense period of drug criminalization within American history.

G. **At the same time these drug wars were going on, what was happening to deal with the treatment of addiction . . . and recovery, for that matter?**

B. Interesting developments. Starting in the late 1970s, we began to see a real escalation in the professionalization of addiction treatment in the United States. Large numbers of recovering people who had come in to work as counselors in programs began to be progressively pushed out and replaced. There was a growing demand for educational credentials and formal training in addiction counseling, and with that, the composition of the work force began to change. We had the insurance industry begin to pay for private treatment for alcoholism and drug dependence, which set the stage for the further professionalization, industrialization, and commercialization of addiction treatment. We're going to go from less than 500 alcohol and drug programs in the United States in the mid-1960s to today's multi-billion dollar treatment industry with more than

15,000 individual treatment programs scattered across the United States.

Let me tell you what this meant in terms of advocacy. The advocates of the 1940s, '50s, and '60s, who lobbied for addiction treatment as a system of care, viewed this very large world of recovery and saw that it needed a professional adjunct. They implicitly knew that some individuals were sicker than others and needed more intensive help than what could be provided in the rooms of AA or NA. So they lobbied and created this portal of entry called "professionally directed addiction treatment." Then, treatment began to explode across the country, not only in size and sophistication, but also in terms of its preoccupation with profit and regulatory compliance. What happened was, somewhere along the line, professionally directed addiction treatment became disconnected from the larger and more enduring process of recovery. And so, what the advocacy movement, in part, was about and saying was that it's time we reconnected addiction treatment to the process of long-term personal and family recovery.

G. There was at least one person in Congress, US Senator Harold Hughes, who was an important advocate for recovery. What role did Harold Hughes play in the early days of this advocacy movement you're referring to?

B. Senator Harold Hughes played an incredibly important role in terms of the fulfillment of the advocacy work of the '40s, '50s, and '60s. The federal legislation that came into being in the early 1970s contributed to the continued resilience of addiction treatment institutions for all of the subsequent years; meaning that it put in place a unique partnership between the federal government and state government and local communities. With all the ups and downs of treatment, that partnership has remained intact for all of these years. And that partnership owes a great deal of gratitude, not only to the advocates who led up to this landmark legislation, but to Harold Hughes for leading the efforts to pass this legislation. Later, Hughes is going to observe this explosive growth of treatment and be concerned about its growing profit orientation. Large amounts of federal and state dollars began to flow into these communities and to the local alcoholism councils, who were part of the players creating these early treatment programs. Many of the advocates became board members and staff members of these new organizations and they almost felt like the advocacy battle around public information and public policy had been won. They turned their backs to create these treatment organizations, and the second they turn their backs we begin to see an erosion in public awareness and public consciousness. The very army that had done all this public education had disengaged to run these treatment systems. Hughes then began to talk about an "alcohol and drug abuse industrial complex" that greatly worried him. He felt like it was becoming disconnected from his early vision. Recognizing that, Harold Hughes creates an organization called SOAR [Society of Americans for Recovery], which was his attempt to relaunch or revitalize recovery advocacy in the United States and invite recovering people back onto the stage of influencing public policy and participating in professional and public education. SOAR was one of the predecessors of what will later be, in the late 1990s, the rise of a new recovery advocacy movement.

G. Take us into the mid '90s. SOAR collapses. Harold Hughes dies. Then what? How did the conversation around recovery begin to reignite again?

B. I remember being interviewed in 1997 by Bill Moyers, and we talked about the cycles of history. And I remember him saying, "Given this cyclical pattern you've talked about, what would you predict?" And I said, "Well, if history's true to form, as we're beginning to lose the recovery focus within the country and within the treatment system in particular, then we could probably predict a rise of a new recovery advocacy movement."

Because, again, the history is that when recovery resources erode or collapse as we transfer people from systems of compassion and care to systems of control and punishment as we did in the 1980s and 1990s, recovering people are going to rise up to forge new sources of recovery support. When that reaches critical mass, you have an emerging social movement. I remember thinking after that 1997 interview, *I wonder how soon that could happen?* And of course, I had no idea how quickly.

There are a couple things that really contributed. I began to see in 1997 and 1998 the rise of these little grassroots recovery organizations again—sort of a mirror of the old alcoholism and drug councils of the 1960s and 1970s. But these were birthed by recovering people talking about organizing recovery supports for people in their communities. And in 1998, the Center for Substance Abuse Treatment [CSAT] began a program called the Recovery Community Support Program. Everybody knows it by RCSP. And what that began to do was provide seed money to some of these fledgling organizations to do recovery advocacy, and then, within a couple of years, shift from recovery advocacy to the development of nonprofessional, nonclinical recovery support services. This was followed by a White House-initiated program called Access to Recovery, which also provided seed money to nontraditional service providers to develop these recovery support services, to sort of build themselves as an organization that could be self-sustaining without federal dollars.

G. **After twelve years, Paul Wellstone and Pete Domenici's Mental Health Parity and Addiction Equity Act [MHPAEA] was finally passed in 2008. What was it like watching that mental health parity debate? In particular, how big was it that congressmen, such as Patrick Kennedy and Jim Ramstad, through their own personal recovery stories, were able to push that legislation forward?**

B. You know, we have a wonderfully rich and long history of legislators in recovery, or who have been affected by addiction issues in their own families, going back into the temperance movement of the early 1800s. We have now come full circle with modern congressmen and women, members of both the House and Senate, coming forward publicly with their own recovery experiences. This new generation of individuals have become not only recovery advocates, but legislative advocates, and they have helped push for pro-recovery policies. If we have twenty-five to forty million people in recovery in the United States, then that is a significant political constituency. There's virtually no context in this country in which we do not have recovery people present. So, as we begin to mobilize people in recovery, imagine the impact those publicly elected individuals can have, as they bring recovery advocacy to life within the institutional settings in which they operate, including the Congress of the United States.

G. Even though parity took a long time, a lot of other things were happening outside the halls of Congress, too.

B. Yes. By the time we get to 2000, we're going to see a very rapid growth of these local community organizations in a rebirth of recovery advocacy in the United States. So that, in 2000, we began to talk "we." "We" meaning a number of us in the recovery advocacy community began to talk about "How do we connect the dots between all of these grassroots organizations that are beginning to emerge?" And we said, "Maybe it's time for a recovery summit."

And that was the early vision of the Recovery Summit in St. Paul, Minnesota, in October of 2001. The framework for organizing the Summit came through the Alliance Project of the Johnson Institute, in particular, and with some support from key people from Hazelden and other places. We found some foundation money to bring together a planning group, and then in October, representatives from thirty-two states came together in what we had no idea would be an incredibly historic meeting to launch what has come to be called the new recovery advocacy movement in the United States.

And it was new in the sense that the ideas of this new movement were very different than the ideas of the earlier movements. We were not there to talk about alcoholism as a disease or addiction as a disease. We had little to say about the nature of the disorder. We were not there to talk about the fact that treatment works or other such slogans. We were really there to talk about a kinetic message that said this: Recovery is a reality in the lives of millions of individuals and families across the country. We were there to say there are multiple pathways of long-term recovery, and all are cause for celebration. In a world where treatment had gotten increasingly coercive, we were there to say, "Recovery is voluntary." That there is such a thing as coerced treatment, but there's no such thing as coerced recovery. We were there to say that recovery gives back to individuals, in families, in communities, what addiction has taken. So there was a set of new kinetic ideas that were very different than the ideas that had preceded them. The other thing that was different is that the vast majority of the people who were there in the room were individuals in recovery from all over the country, but they were from multiple pathways of recovery. These weren't all people in twelve-step recovery. We had people in faith-based frameworks of recovery; we had people in secular recovery; and we had people in medication-assisted recovery. We had people from incredibly diverse cultural frameworks of recovery that all came together in St. Paul to rebirth this recovery advocacy movement.

But the key issue still remained: How do we create some connecting tissue around all of us as these small fledgling organizations? So we created an organization called Faces & Voices of Recovery. And in retrospect, Faces & Voices and its progeny, for example, the Association of Recovery Community Organizations, Young People in Recovery, have become that connecting tissue for all of the grassroots recovery community organizations that have since sprung up in the United States. We tended to see some of these as separate movements, but in fact they're really part of this larger movement. We've got recovery homes as a movement in the United States. And we've got a recovery school movement. We have recovery ministries, recovery industries, and recovery cafes, and on and on. But if you begin to connect the dots, what we're seeing is a whole set of new recovery support institutions that are not addiction treatment, nor are they recovery mutual aid organizations like AA, SMART Recovery, or Celebrate Recovery. Where treatment and mutual aid have historically focused on intrapersonal issues around escaping addiction and initiating and sustaining recovery, the new organizations focused on creating a world in which people can recover. And they have begun to construct that world—the recovery supportive, physical, psychological, and cultural landscapes—in communities across the country.

G. **In other words, the community is the ecology of the issue, or as you have said, the soil out of which drug and alcohol problems grow and are solved.**

B. Yes.

G. **And this brings us back to understanding that the development of professional addiction treatment has grown more and more disconnected from the ongoing recovery process, which is nested in communities. Is it fair to say that this separation has stunted the growth of successful long-term recovery rates?**

B. Yes. When we talk about the need to create a world that people can recover within, it's really about creating the soil where recovery can flourish. This comes out of the participation of Native American communities in this movement. They've been our teachers. Don Coyhis, from White Bison, stands up and says, "The individual, the family, the tribe, and the community are one. To harm one is to harm all. To heal one is to heal all." What he says is, historically, we saw addiction as a sick and dying tree and we would dig up this tree and move it all the way over here to another area, maybe even to another community, and replant it in healthy soil, and give it water and fertilizer and sun and nurture it and love it back to health. And when it came alive again and became vibrant, we would dig it up and bring it back and replant it into the same hole, and then be shocked when the tree began to get sick again. Don's message in all of this is that it's time we began to not just treat individual trees, but to begin to treat the soil as well. But there's another point to that too, and that is not only families have been insulted and deeply wounded by addiction, but so have communities. People have begun to say, "Maybe we have communities that themselves need a larger healing and recovery process." So through the guidance of people like Don Coyhis, we've begun to introduce this concept of community recovery. There's a whole larger healing process, and addressing issues related to drug addiction in local communities can really be an opportunity for whole communities to begin to revitalize and heal themselves.

G. **Are there organizations that stand out as models or leaders in community healing or community recovery?**

B. When I think of community recovery there are two or three places that I think of. The earliest of these is the wonderful story of Alkali Lake, which is a Native American community in British Columbia that suffered horrific problems related to alcoholism and all the problems that spill out of alcoholism intergenerationally. Other communities once referred to Alkali Lake as Alcohol Lake because of the devastation by alcohol in that community. But, that community began a recovery process beginning with a single individual. And it began to spiral out and create a community healing process that has continued to this day and represents probably one of the most dramatic examples of an entire community turning itself around through the individual recovery of key members of that community.

The work that Don Coyhis and others have done through White Bison, in many Native American communities in the United States and Canada, are wonderful examples of this community healing.

The city of Philadelphia has begun to transform their whole treatment system into what they're calling a recovery-oriented system of care. They have supported the development of all of these new recovery support resources. They bring neighborhoods together, town meetings. They've got recovery murals beginning to dot the Philadelphia landscape. They're bringing large numbers of people in recovery into public forums to tell their recovery stories.

So, as much as addiction is visible, and in some ways too visible, it's the recovery story that hasn't been told. Part of the recovery of a community is bringing the recovery stories of members of that community alive. And cities like Philadelphia are doing an amazing job of not hiding their addiction story, confronting that story very, very honestly and very directly, but saying there's another side to this story. The antidote to the addiction story is the recovery story, and it is emerging in the lives of hundreds of thousands of our family members in this community.

G. **What can we learn from the sensational coverage of celebrity addiction that just seems to be rampant in today's media? Do you put that in context to anything historical, or is this something new?**

B. If we look at how the media's handled modern celebrities around issues of addiction and recovery, we find an interesting pattern. One, we find a period of massive coverage when celebrities are self-destructing around problems of addiction. So the issue of addiction is incredibly visible within the culture. And we have people heading to rehab one more time following their latest crash and burn experience, also very visible. But then, the irony is, the second that people achieve stability they virtually disappear from the airwaves. We don't see them. Whether we're talking Darryl Strawberry or Robert Downey, Jr., when the crash and burn is at the highest, the media is in a frenzy of coverage related to that. But, as soon as those individuals move into stable recovery, how does the media coverage of their recovery stability compare?

My point is that we're just telling the addiction story. We're not even telling the treatment story. All we're really telling is the treatment crisis that basically gets people heading to rehab. And beyond that, we don't know. Or we're filming, in very grotesque ways, the illusion of what's happening with people in treatment, with the idea that somehow the second you turn on a camera it doesn't alter that experience, which obviously it does.

We don't need more celebrities to step forward and talk about the fact that they're destroying their lives. We don't need more celebrities to crash and burn and say, "I'm going back to Betty Ford Center this week," or wherever they're going. What we need are celebrities who can step forward and say, "My name is . . . and I'm a person in long-term addiction recovery, and what that means to me is . . . ," and then tell us that story. So the recovery story has yet to be told. And what the advocacy movement is doing is challenging a vanguard of people in all walks of life, including people who are in a very visible position, whose story would be very powerful in changing attitudes and beliefs in this country, to tell their recovery story and *not* to just retell their addiction story.

G. **Since 2001, after the Summit, can you point to any great transform-ative successes of this collective movement or even poignant mo-ments that this new recovery advocacy movement has had for you?**

B. Yes. There are policy achievements where specific barriers that confronted people who were moving from addiction to recovery have been removed. Things like, when people who had initiated their recovery and who had never gone to college because of their addiction, or had their college careers interrupted, and then, at the point they wanted to return to school, they found obstacles to getting scholarships. Some of them began to look around and say, "I want to find an environment where I can go to college that's in a recovery-conducive environment." Well, let's be honest. Most colleges and universities in the United States have been aptly described as "abstinence-hostile" environments. And what this movement did was to empower people in recovery to organize recovery support systems in whatever environment they were in. So we began to see a movement to create recovery high schools in this country, including the recovery high school in Boston [Ostiguy] that we're filming in at this moment. We began to see a movement to create recovery support services in colleges and universities around the country.

I'll give you an example of points of awakening for me. I remember visiting a recovery community organization on the campus of a large university and I asked them to describe the program. They talked about academic mentoring and recovery support groups and recovery coaching. They talked about a recovery coffeehouse or drop-in center in the middle of the campus. And they invited me to go to a twelve-step meeting on this major university campus, and I walked in and there were more than 200 people, students, there at this meeting. And I was really shocked. I turned to the people who were guiding me into this meeting and I said, "Who are all these people?" I knew there were not more than thirty or thirty-five students in the formal recovery program on campus. And what they told me was that because of the presence of the recovering students there, one to two students a week from the larger community entered recovery on campus, which really began to reinforce for me this notion that recovery is contagious. Key people in recovery who have this contagious quality to their recovery begin to "infect" and affect, these institutions that they're a part of. So a bunch of people in recovery get together and they rent a house together, they split the rent and the message is "Don't drink and drug. Pay the rent. And work on your recovery." And there's not a dime of public funding or private funding that's supporting this. When people in recovery come together to support their own recovery, amazing things happen.

I think the other thing for me personally, and I want to put it in a little historical perspective, is the very large recovery celebration events that have emerged in the United States. Within certain fellowships there have been very large meetings of people in recovery. For example, with Alcoholics Anonymous, their annual meetings have filled athletic stadiums with recovering people. But, the idea that there would be recovering people marching on public streets as far as the eyes could see was beyond my comprehension as a person in recovery. I've been blessed to be part of these very large events. In the last couple of years, I've had the privilege of being in Philadelphia in September and watching recovering people and their families and friends march down Market Street, for as far as I could see. And that's something that I never thought I would see in my lifetime.

G. Do you think people are changing their attitudes about their own recovery status?

B. We have different styles of change: The sudden hot-flash of Bill Wilson in 1934 in Charlestown's hospital. Right? And then we have the other cofounder with his slow process of spiritual awakening. Sort of setting forth the two prototypes of recovery within the fellowship of Alcoholics Anonymous: transformational and incremental. If we look at people's identities in recovery, we find some differences. If we ask people the question: Did you once have the disease of addiction but now you're in recovery from that disorder? We'll get a certain percentage of people who will say yes. If we ask the question: Did you once have a significant problem with alcohol or drugs that you no longer have today? What do you think happens to the self-reported numbers? In the second group the numbers jump. And if we actually look at which of those individuals meet DSM-IV criteria for a substance use disorder, there are a lot of people who do not self-identify as a person in recovery and have not incorporated that into their identity. On the other side, we have people with extremely positive pro-recovery identities. These are people if you bump into them at the grocery store as strangers, they tell you their recovery story in the aisle. They are not only in recovery, they're ready to let the world know they're in recovery.

It's also important to note there's another category here; and that's people who are in recovery but are deeply ashamed of that status because of the incredible social stigma that continues related to that. And I'm going to be very blunt. There are a number of those individuals who may hide behind vague rhetoric about anonymity as a spiritual tradition. But the bottom line is they're ashamed. Given their level of functioning, given their status within the culture, it would be extremely difficult for them to acknowledge their addiction and recovery history. I'm not talking about acknowledging affiliation with a twelve-step program. I'm talking about acknowledging themselves as a person in recovery.

G. How pervasive is shame among some people in recovery and their recovery status?

B. I want to tell you how pervasive. I'm probably one of the most out people in this country. And I can run around with my big Recovery March T-shirt. Right? And I get home from a march and my dear wife Rita says, "Can you run to the store for me?" And I say, "Sure." And without thinking I've pulled my recovery T-shirt off and thrown on a sloppy old plain T-shirt. And I'm about to walk out the door and all of a sudden it hits me: What the ____ did I just do? And all of a sudden I realize this stigma is insidious. It just keeps creeping back in. I'm okay as a person in recovery when I'm surrounded by 15,000 people in recovery, but I'm a bit embarrassed to walk down the aisles of my local grocery store with a Recovery Celebration T-shirt on. That's how insidious some of this stuff gets to be.

G. It's not one size fits all, is it?

B. Obviously there are changes over time as people get into recovery. We have individuals who initiate and sustain recovery without relationships with other people in recovery—what I have called an acultural style of recovery in which people do not identity and relate to the culture of recovery in the United States. We have people who have a bicultural style; meaning they can operate within distinct communities of recovery, and master the language and the etiquette and all the nuances of those fellowships, but they can also function quite comfortably with what people in the recovery community call earth people or civilians or normies. And of course, we have some people who are so deeply enmeshed in the culture of recovery that they almost have no contact with the mainstream culture. Culturally enmeshed styles are not unusual for people in early recovery. It's part of a safety net and a sanctuary, if you will. Now we also obviously have changes in these styles over time. My point with this is that we're beginning to see tremendous heterogeneity, incredible diversity, around styles and frameworks of long-term recovery across these secular, spiritual, and religious frameworks.

G. **And now, all the celebrations like you saw in Philadelphia, which have evolved into public recovery events all over the country, they are really helping erase some of the stigma, don't you think?**

B. Yes, definitely.

G. **If you look through the history books were there ever such public demonstrations in support of recovery as we're seeing today?**

B. We don't have a lot of precedence for that. And we don't have anything even remotely close to the kind of numbers we're seeing now across the country. If you look at the Washingtonians, for example, very rapidly large numbers of people became Washingtonian members who did not have addiction histories. You could have individuals' participation in Washingtonian or temperance marches, but they were hidden. They didn't have to wear "A"s on their chest to designate their alcoholism or addiction histories. They could pass as simply being part of this larger temperance advocacy movement in the United States. But in terms of what precedence did we have of people clearly identified as people in recovery publicly marching together and telling their stories from public forums? It's really interesting the speed at which this occurred since the Summit in 2001. Some of the early marches, we were lucky to get fifty or seventy-five or 100 people to come out for this day in the park. There was a lot of controversy within recovery communities about whether we should be doing that publicly and was it a breach of anonymity and on and on and on. But suddenly, there was a turning point. People began to figure out these are not people marching as AA members or NA members or Women for Sobriety members. These are people marching as people in recovery. And we began to get key leaders from within local recovery communities to step forward and be part of these marches. Again, not marching in terms of their identities as individual fellowship members, but marching as people in recovery. Suddenly, the numbers shot up to 200 or 300 and then 600 and then 800. And then, we began to see local recovery celebration events and marches measure in the thousands. We get to places like Philadelphia, where two years ago I think it was more than 20,000 people, and last year more than 25,000 people.

G. Okay, so the big question: advocacy versus anonymity. Because there's a lot of "Can I do this? Am I allowed to do this? Do I not do this?" How has the movement explained and communicated to people that they're not breaking their anonymity by simply disclosing their recovery status publicly?

B. I think the first thing is that they've had to educate members in twelve-step groups related to their own traditions. The tradition doesn't bar one to permanent secrecy or prohibit one from disclosing one's recovery status. It's very explicit in terms of disclosure of one's affiliation with the fellowship of Alcoholics Anonymous at the level of press. So one can stand up—as some people did in 1976, who were members in twelve-step fellowships—and simply stand as people in recovery without identifying themselves with those fellowships, completely within the compliance of the traditions of those fellowships. It's taken some time to sort out "What can't I do and what can I do?" within the framework of the values and guidelines that have governed people's individual fellowships. And those discussions are different, for example, in LifeRing Secular Recovery and Celebrate Recovery than they are in AA and NA. But all of them have that discussion.

G. Do you feel there continues to be a disconnect between the intention of the tradition of anonymity and the interpretation of it today?

B. There's a disconnect to the extent that some people still see anonymity equated to secrecy. I'll give you an example. You could have AA members who've been so anonymous/secret that they came together and created a closed group that functioned very well, and that group grew old together, supporting each other in recovery. The individuals died, and the group died because the recovery circle was a wall around them with limited contact with the outside world. In other words, they "passed" in the larger community. Not passed in terms of pretending they weren't AA members, but pretending that they had no addiction recovery history. There's this idea that certain fellowships are promoted by attraction, rather than promotion. But how is one attracted to those fellowships if there's no knowledge that anyone is in recovery, in terms of how they live their lives? So this segregation between the issue of anonymity at the level of press, and the issue of anonymity as a spiritual principle is sort of an antidote to self-centeredness and people's attraction to cameras, like insects to light and fire. Those are serious concerns that continually need to be addressed. But, anonymity is not secrecy, and anonymity does not prohibit the kind of advocacy that large numbers of people in these fellowships have done almost since their beginning.

G. You have often written and spoken of "recovery capital." What does that term mean?

B. The term "recovery capital" was coined by the researchers Granfield and Cloud. It's a wonderful concept because we had all these labels to capture the pathology of addiction, but we didn't have any words to talk about the resources that exist inside people or inside their families or inside communities that could help people initiate and sustain recovery. What Granfield and Cloud said was that there's another side to this story of addiction. There can be people with very severe or complex addiction problems, but they may also bring a lot of recovery capital and that recovery capital can dramatically increase their odds of long-term recovery. We've got a couple of ways to intervene with people. The traditional way is let's figure out how we can lower or eliminate the problem's severity through multiple episodes of treatment. On the other hand, somebody could say, what if we increase the recovery capital?

Let me make this real concrete. We're sitting in a recovery high school right now. Let's talk about the adolescents treated in the United States multiple times who did wonderful in adolescent treatment; pull them out of their environment, bring them into an adolescent residential inpatient unit, and they thrive inside that unit. They seem to have wonderful insights; they express great motivation for their continued recovery. We discharge them, and within forty-eight to seventy-two hours they've relapsed once again in their natural communities. So the question Granfield and Cloud raised was why don't you move into the life of their communities and build a world where they can recover? Increase their recovery capital, not only their internal assets, but let's build recovery capital within their family and within their schools. Rather than continue to recycle this adolescent through multiple episodes of treatment, maybe we need to leave our offices and institutions, go into that community and build a recovery high school, or create recovery support groups within the local high school, or create student assistance programs in that school, or help organize young people's AA or NA meetings inside the life of that community. The concept of recovery capital has been an incredible boon for us to rethink how we intervene to support long-term recovery.

G. How do you define recovery?

B. The question of how to define recovery is among the most controversial issues within the field. In 2007, the Betty Ford Institute pulled together a consensus conference that published their findings in the *Journal of Substance Abuse Treatment* and, in essence, defined recovery as three essential components. First, sobriety. Now some people are refining that and broadening it to the concept of remission, meaning people either have continuous abstinence from alcohol and other drugs, or they no longer meet diagnostic criteria for the disorder. Second, is the improvement in what we call "global health," that is, emotional health, physical health, cognitive health, relational health, and occupational health. And finally, is this third dimension referred to as citizenship, the idea that addiction is so isolating that many individuals have deeply wounded their communities through their behavior. Citizenship is a repair of that relationship between person and community. So, sobriety or remission, global health, and citizenship seem to be the emerging components of recovery definition in the United States.

And, by the way, in terms of another interesting question we've begun to address: How many people meet a recovery definition in the United States? We just finished some studies and, in general, those studies would suggest that we have somewhere between twenty-five and forty million individuals in this country who are in remission from significant alcohol and other drug problems [criteria one], but we don't have studies of the prevalence of people who meet all three recovery definition criteria. Such studies have simply not been done.

G. **Let's talk about your book, *Let's Go Make Some History*, which you wrote for the Johnson Institute. What do you mean by the title?**

B. I began writing articles on the new recovery advocacy movement even before the St. Paul Summit, and there was a point where the Johnson Institute and Faces & Voices of Recovery approached me to pull those papers into a book. And I said, yes, we could do that if we use any proceeds from the book to support the movement.

The reference to the title is an interesting one. There was a story from the civil rights movement that was passed down to me through the generations of civil rights activists, with whom I associated, and it was the story of the day in a town where there was an injunction against a march, and the civil rights marchers were prepared to march in violation of that legal order. They had begun marching from the churches, approached the peak of a hill and, as they looked over, what they saw ahead of them was a virtual sea of baton-slapping police officers, and dogs, and fire hoses, and you could sort of see the panic on everybody's faces. They began to envision what potentially was going to unfold here and, of course, the TV cameras were lined up on both sides of the route of this march. As people had to address their own fear about was to unfold, the story that was passed down to me was that one of the oldest men among those marchers said simply, "Let's go make some history." At that moment, the marchers began to move forward and marched into history, as what then unfolded was captured on national television cameras.

So at the 2001 Summit, as we thought about where do we go with this movement, I ended my remarks with the phrase, "Let's go make some history," not knowing at that point in time that there really would be a movement that would emerge out of this meeting.

G. **And what is the essence of that call to action; in the context of the addiction recovery advocacy movement, what does that phrase, "Let's go make some history," mean?**

B. The call to action we are making is not for everyone in recovery to go public with their recovery status. Stigma related to alcohol and other drug problems is still very real in this country, and people can experience significant consequences by disclosing parts of their addiction and even their recovery status. So what we're looking for is not for all individuals in recovery to somehow become public advocates. What we are looking for is a vanguard of people in recovery who are temperamentally suited for that role and whose personal and family circumstances allow them to take on part of that public role, to simply step forward with others to put a face and voice on recovery. And part of the reason we think that's so important is that we know there are a lot of issues around stigma that I can't educate you out of. I can give you all the facts; I can read all the books to you; I can show you documentaries; and nothing's going to change that embedded prejudice until you personally encounter someone in recovery who means something to you and hear his or her story. When we ask people how their attitudes have changed related to addiction and the prospects of recovery, the most powerful ingredient in their change is that they know someone in recovery, within their own family or their own social or occupational network.

Part of what we're trying to say is that most everyone in America knows someone in recovery; the problem historically is they didn't *know* they were in recovery. That means everyone continues to maintain incredible stereotypes about who are the people who develop alcohol and other drug problems in this country, who are the people who recover, and who do not recover. As soon as we begin to get this vanguard to step forward, then we begin to collectively break down the stereotype. In the same way Ryan White forever altered the face of AIDS in the United States. When we have the Betty Fords of the world stepping forward to put a face and voice on recovery, those stereotypes simply can't be sustained any longer. As the stereotypes begin to disintegrate, by the power of people's stories, then what we can do is come behind that with our advocacy and begin to dismantle the discriminatory structures that really have created obstacles for people seeking and maintaining recovery over time, and build resources that are going to dramatically widen the doorway of entry into long-term recovery for people.

G. On a personal level, what brought you into recovery advocacy and why do you do it so fervently?

B. In some ways, I've come full circle in my own life. I was a young kid in recovery, had lots of piss and vinegar, tons of energy, and didn't know what to do with it. So it was part of that "let's get into recovery and save the world" kind of thing. I was studying psychology at the time, behind my own recovery, and in the years that I was working in communities— this is the late 1960s, early '70s—they had almost no local treatment resources to speak of at all. I sort of took it on as part of my charge to try to help organize those services, participating on local councils. In some ways, I started as an advocate, worked as a street worker, went on to work as an addiction counselor in a program that I help found in 1973, and went on to become clinical director. Then I migrated into all kinds of roles related to research and policy over many years.

And an interesting thing happened. If you had met me in the early 1970s and bumped into me in a grocery store, I might very well have told you my recovery story. This was the period of the super ex-addict, dope fiend, folk hero kind of caricature we had, particularly those of us affiliated with therapeutic communities at that time. And then, as we began to get pushed toward professionalization, I became almost embarrassed by my recovery story and felt it was baggage I needed to shed if I was going to do anything of importance in this field. Because you would get discounted as a person in recovery, which meant people could put you in a little box and didn't have to listen to you. I spent the middle years of my career building professional credentials and doing professional writing and doing professional research, and I made less and less reference to my recovery status until I got into the late 1990s.

And then, I'll have to admit there was an epiphany experience that I had. I was going to speak at a professional conference in Dallas, Texas. By this time I had started volunteering evenings, during my travels, to speak at these little grassroots recovery advocacy organizations that were popping up. And I visited Searcy W, one of the old-timers in the recovery community in Dallas, Texas, to interview him about the early history of treatment in the Southwest. And I'll never forget. We took a break in the interview and Searcy said, "Now, Bill, what's this research stuff you do?" And I explained to him that I worked in a research institute and studied treatment by doing treatment outcome studies. And I was very excited because we had just got a five-year project funded and that we were going to follow people for five years. Now I'm talking to someone with fifty-four years of sobriety at this point in time. And Searcy just looked at me and smiled and said, "Five years. Very impressive." And then it suddenly dawned on me—the context and to whom I was speaking. And so, I kind of regrouped myself as best I could, and we finished the interview. But it was an epiphany.

When I was flying home on the plane that night, here's what I realized. Because here's the question Searcy asked me after that. He said, "What does your research tell you about people like me?" What do you think I had to say to him? "We don't even know you exist!" We don't know anything about people in long-term recovery. We can fill libraries with what we know about the pathology of addiction, and we're learning a lot about treatment. But we know almost nothing about recovery, particularly the lived experience of recovery.

On the plane home from Dallas that night I had this powerful experience. It was this awakening I had spent almost my whole life learning about addiction and I'd learned a lot about treatment. I'd mastered a fair amount of that knowledge. But, separate from my own experience, from the standpoint of science, I knew very little about the long-term processes of recovery. I asked myself, with millions of people in long-term recovery out there, why don't we begin to study the recovery experience? So I made this promise to myself that for whatever time I had left in my career, I was going to devote it to the study of the solution. And I said, how can I ask other people to disclose their recovery experience when for years I've been hiding my own recovery status? To be perfectly honest, I was professionally ashamed of it and I'd internalized some of the very stigma I criticized. From that trip on I came back to the research institute at which I worked saying, "We have got to study long-term recovery." I began to be more vocal about my own recovery. So again, it felt like I'd almost come full circle to going from where I was in the early 1970s to where I ended up in the early years of this new century.

G. And now, how do you see your role in this movement?

B. My role has changed a lot. I started out as the Johnny Appleseed of the movement, running around trying to speak everywhere I could to jumpstart this movement. Then I began to back up and I said, "Okay, now that things are going, I want to be the historian." I began to really try to capture as much of the history of the movement as I could. And to be honest, I've continued in both those roles. But now, I've really moved toward the question of what's the implication of this movement toward professionally directed addiction treatment in the United States, to create an intellectual legacy for this movement, and to write about this movement in peer-reviewed journals that historically have had little interest in recovery.

G. What is the implication for addiction treatment in the face of this movement?

B. The implications of recovery advocacy for addiction treatment are very profound. It is no wonder that the treatment industry or even addiction treatment professionals may be, at times, somewhat threatened by this movement. Because, in some ways, this movement is calling for a fundamental redesign of addiction treatment, as we know it in the United States. Part of that design is that addiction treatment, as it began to get professionalized and commercialized and came under increasing regulatory control, through the '70s and '80s, basically modeled itself on the acute-care hospital. In other words, the episode of this thing we call treatment began to get shorter and shorter and shorter—screening and assessing people, admitting them and assessing them, and then treating them ever briefer, discharging them, and terminating the service relationship. It's not unlike, as I'm traveling today in a different city, if I severely injured myself and went into an emergency room here in Boston, my treatment would be very much like the model of addiction treatment in the United States. They would screen. They would admit. They would assess. They would treat. They would discharge and get me out of here and get me back to my home in Florida and never see me again. Except with addiction treatment, as we treat very severe and complex problems, what we're doing now is recycling people again and again and again through these emergency room episodes. In effect, we've become the revolving door that we were designed to eliminate, the revolving door of local emergency rooms and hospitals—and the revolving door of local jails. What the recovery advocacy movement is saying is that treatment's not enough. You have to reconnect treatment to long-term recovery. So, we're calling for a fundamental redesign of addiction treatment to move from this acute-care model of intervention to a model of sustained recovery support and active recovery management.

By comparison, if we look at people like myself who have been treated for cancer in this country, they are screened and diagnosed, actively treated and are now in full remission. For most individuals treated for cancer in this country, we know that the stability point of that remission is not reached until five years. So what do we do with people with cancer? We aggressively monitor people following their treatments. We're constantly in their lives educating and screening and doing checkups and celebrating when people reach that five-year window.

In contrast, what we do in addiction treatment is, we hold graduation ceremonies, give somebody a token or chip, hug them and tell them to go have a great life and, as they head out the door, say, oh and by the way, make meetings and get a sponsor. If we really believe that addiction is a chronic disorder comparable to other primary health care chronic disorders, then why aren't we treating it that way? Recovery today means recovery for a lifetime. If we really believed that, we would be doing assertive post-treatment follow-up on people for a minimum of five years. Even for our most stabilized and highest functioning, at a minimum, we would be doing annual recovery checkups for five years. Instead, we have nothing that even closely resembles that. So the challenge for the recovery advocacy movement is to promote a fundamental redesign of how addiction treatment is delivered, how it is funded, the policies that guide it, and its clinical philosophies and practices.

G. **So what you are doing now seems the perfect culmination to all you have done throughout your career and in your life experience.**

B. Working in this whole field all this time has just been unbelievably rewarding. I can't imagine a fuller life than what I've had. I've been incredibly blessed with the people who I've had an opportunity to work with. I've been able to work on an issue I'm deeply passionate about. I've gotten to watch people virtually rise from the dead—people the world had given up on—and observe this incredible process of rebirth. And, not only people who simply come back and are no longer destroying themselves, but who have then gone on to rebuild who they are and do incredible feats of service in their communities. To be part of that . . . is as good as it gets for me.

If you've just read this entire interview with the remarkable Bill White, you now understand why Greg Williams made *The Anonymous People*. Not only why, but how. Armed with Bill's teachings, Greg was able to give his film the authority, the perspective, and the insight such a work of importance needs and can claim. I loved it when Bill White called himself "the Johnny Appleseed of the movement." He does get around. And everywhere he goes, there's fertile ground for his knowledge to be sown, take hold, and grow. Bill has started virtual orchards of recovery in locales throughout the world. His fruits have fed others and multiplied. Occasionally, he has passed the old seed sack to certain new Johnny Appleseeds to carry on the cultivation of a movement.

Greg Williams is one.

For more juicy fruit, you would be well recommended to read Bill's collected papers, especially those found in his book, *Let's Go Make Some History*. Likewise, his compelling book, *Slaying the Dragon*, is—or should be—required reading. And if you want to be armed with the best of practical resources in your own or anyone else's recovery, check out the website, williamwhitepapers.com, for his smart and useful "Recovery Toolkit," and for many other treasures there, historical and contemporary.

Chapter Three

DARK TO LIGHT

Bill White brings a scholarly perspective to the history of addiction and recovery. And more than just a historian, he was also a participant, along with some of the pioneers of the new recovery advocacy movement, heeding his own exhortation to "go make some history." We were privileged to interview and include some of these history makers, policy makers, and scholars in the film. They offer first-hand knowledge of how the current movement evolved from Bill Wilson to Marty Mann to Harold Hughes, and so on, into the vibrant force it is becoming. Greg spends a good chunk of time in his film bringing that history to light through these faces and voices of the movement's participants. Greg believes (having learned this from Bill White) that understanding the history of addiction treatment, recovery, the tradition of anonymity, and the advocacy movements helps to inform, validate, and strengthen contemporary action.

On the following pages you will meet extraordinary people who have spent their lives on the front lines of social and political change, making history. Their conversations with Greg complement the evidence shared by Bill White in his interview and affirm that whatever the part, no matter how small, anyone can participate in moving a cause forward and can help build momentum and strength toward change. Their stories take us out of the darkness of ignorance and despair, and into the light of knowledge and hope.

JOHNNY ALLEM

"We have to continue to tell our fellow citizens who are in recovery that they have a duty and a right to claim their citizenship."

Johnny Allem's modesty tends to obscure his stature among the pioneers. This soft-spoken son of a Tennessee country preacher carries his humble roots into the stories he tells. With his unpretentious and genial manner, it is easy to miss the historic import of his life experience. Then, you read his resume and realize this gentle man is one of the titans behind the emergence of the new recovery advocacy movement. In the early 1990s, he took a leadership role in SOAR (Society of Americans for Recovery) and, alongside its founder Senator Harold Hughes, worked the classic grassroots model of advocacy traveling all across the country attempting to change attitudes and policies that would lift the dark clouds of stigma and injustice that had descended onto addiction during the previous two decades. His work with SOAR led directly to his association with the Johnson Institute and the Alliance Project, which helped launch the 2001 St. Paul Summit and the subsequent creation of Faces & Voices of Recovery.

He is past President and CEO of the Johnson Institute, a founding board member of Faces & Voices of Recovery, and currently is the founder and President of Aquila Recovery, a Washington, DC, based clinical resource for people with substance use disorders. Johnny Allem's advocacy work in politics, policy, and peer-to-peer support spans three decades. His path put him in the vanguard of the movement that represents the millions of "anonymous people" in need of leadership. No wonder Greg was grateful to have this interview with one of his heroes.

We were running late the day we met Johnny in the DC offices of Aquila Recovery, which was then on Connecticut Avenue NW, one of the main thoroughfares between the Capitol and Bethesda. We had spent nearly the whole day in the center of the city filming at Faces & Voices of Recovery, and now we were trying to beat traffic out of town. We worried where we would park along the avenue close enough to Johnny's building to unload all our gear, bring it in, and set up quickly so we wouldn't keep Johnny waiting. At least, Craig and I were worried. As usual, Greg showed no concern about parking. And, typical of Greg's luck, a metered parking space good for two hours opened up right in front of the building. Perfect. There is more to that story, however. But first, let Johnny Allem tell his.

GREG. Can you explain a little about how you found recovery?

JOHNNY. The history of my family shows that there was a lot of disease over many generations, and I'm fortunate enough to be one of the first ones we know of in my family to reach recovery.

The first time I drank, I drank to get drunk. I was twenty-two, and I continued to do that for twenty-two more years. I was a person who had no defense against the first drink, so I worked hard every morning because I knew I might not have an afternoon. I moved to Washington in 1969. I did a lot of political consulting, message development, and writing for politicians. I was a pretty average drunk. I called myself an alcoholic, and I would go to the bar and say, "Nurse, give me some medicine." That was as much as I thought about it.

I did not know about twelve-step programs or things like that. I didn't know there was any hope for people like me. A doctor advised a friend of my wife's, who was in trouble, to find a twelve-step program and we went with her. I met lots of people who I was surprised about and I kept coming back. The power of attraction. I had no intention of stopping drinking. After all, I needed this chemical balance to be who I was; but I kept seeing people in recovery and eventually I got the message. I had a long crash landing from a weekend drunk and realized I needed to sit with these people who had a better message than I did. That was 1982 and that has been my story ever since. I'm still sitting with those people; and I'm still paying attention to my own recovery.

G. The business and social circles you were running with in Washington are pretty notorious for their love of alcohol. Obviously you fit right in while you were drinking, so did you encounter any negative responses from your friends or associates when you stopped?

J. In this town there's more discrimination against recovery than addiction. I remember right before I got well, I was a long-term member of the National Press Club and everybody loved me. But the day after I wasn't drinking, people would kind of walk around me. They didn't want to deal with me. It was common knowledge, once it was known that you were in recovery, you would not be able to be promoted. The discrimination was pretty heavy.

G. Why do you suppose people have that attitude about what is essentially a health problem?

J. One of the reasons is that people see untreated addiction when it's end-stage. People who are begging on the street or who show up in a criminal justice context are very visible and not too pretty. That's the face of our disease to a large section of the public. We have cab drivers; we have politicians; we have barbers; we have people in all walks of life living in long-term recovery, but that's not a highly visible circumstance. Even with the work that Faces & Voices of Recovery has done and with the number of us who have worked in the field diligently for a long time, it is hard to overcome the image that's put out on *Access Hollywood* every night!

G. So you are in recovery and despite facing the stigma society puts on your health condition and being subjected to discrimination because of it, you are not silent. In fact, much to the contrary, you set off on the path of public advocacy. Why?

J. Because the policies around our disease were different than any other disease I knew. I'm a politician at heart, and I know how policy gets developed at the county council level and at the city level. I've studied those kinds of things and I know how healthcare interacts with public opinion. As I looked at my own disease and saw it being treated so off-the-charts differently than any other disease, I became more and more upset.

I grew up knowing the symptoms for measles and diabetes and other illnesses, but was taught that drinking was a sin. So I had a moral problem. When I got sober I learned differently. I learned that I had an illness. That resonated with me—I had an illness that needed to be treated like an illness, and I needed to develop a lifestyle that would support recovery. I didn't understand why everybody couldn't get that. It wasn't that complicated, but you couldn't talk about it and it wasn't common knowledge. Why don't we know these things? And why are people in recovery hiding in the closet?

These are things fundamental to human happiness. It made no damn sense to me at all. I felt like this needed a movement, like the civil rights movement. I felt that the same tools of advocacy and awareness that I became familiar with growing up during the civil rights movement were appropriate to ever being helpful to this disease. That kind of drew me into the advocacy and policy side of things.

G. **Did you get active with the policy issues of addiction and recovery right from the beginning or was there something that transpired in your recovery to get you there?**

J. It was fairly soon. I was in recovery for five years and the mayor, who I knew here in DC, appointed me to the Mayor's Advisory Committee on Alcoholism. I didn't know there was such a thing. I didn't know there were policies. I was clueless. I learned a little bit about the science and politics of it. I was kind of stunned; the politics didn't make a lot of sense to me. We were operating a separate, parallel health system, not connected with doctors and other diseases. People were expected to pretty much lose their lives or get in custody of the police department before they ever got treatment. Those things bothered me.

In the early '90s, I came to know Senator Harold Hughes from Iowa, who I had worked for when he took a short run for the presidency back in the '70s. He was the author of the Hughes Act, which was the first step by the federal government to recognize addiction as a disease. I got to know him and help him with his organization called the Society of Americans for Recovery [SOAR].

G. **What was it like being public about your recovery and an advocate before many people were doing that? How did you navigate the issue of anonymity?**

J. I was never very private. I wasn't secret about my drinking and, when I stopped drinking, that wasn't a secret either. I didn't really think about anonymity too much. I was taught the spiritual principle of anonymity, which I respect greatly. I've always considered the anonymity tradition to be mostly about safety for newcomers. I never thought I was supposed to stick my head in the ground and never admit to anybody that I have a disease. My interpretation caused a lot of people some consternation. I had to ignore a lot of that nonsense; and it is nonsense. It's not the teachings of the founders of twelve-step programs, let alone anybody else in the long, long history of recovery that precedes the development of AA. We're just like any other people with any other disease, but we put up with this discrimination largely because of our own shame, not because it makes any sense.

G. **Let's go back a little bit and talk about your early work with SOAR. Give us a little context about the environment out of which SOAR "rose," if you will, and how that fit into your career and the arc of advocacy that followed.**

J. Well, my wake-up call to get involved on the national level was the Society of Americans for Recovery and getting to know Senator Harold Hughes. I had known him previously as a client and as a candidate, but not as a human being. Here's a guy who's a former truck driver, very charismatic, whose recovery was well known all over Iowa, but is able to win friends and influence people because he was up front and positive and had a very populist orientation. When Senator Hughes was governor of Iowa, Brinkley Smithers, one of the founders of the National Council on Alcoholism, visited him and said, "Why don't you run for Senate? We need people like you in the Senate."

Iowans liked him, and they sent him to represent them in the Senate. And, as a result of his advocacy, the Senate allowed him to have a committee on alcoholism. They couldn't formally do it. They let him do it informally. I'd never heard of this before or since; it was an actual Senate committee, but private funds funded their hearings. Senator Hughes conducted a wide-ranging hearing on alcoholism—in the Armed Services, in the community, all phases of alcoholism—and as a result of that, proposed the Hughes Act. It really spawned a lot of thinking at the government level as to what treatment was and jump-started a lot of activity in the treatment field. It was a marvelous bill. It created the National Institute of Alcoholism and Alcohol Abuse. It was a milestone in our country, as far as our disease is concerned.

And then in the 1980s, the Hughes Act began to be chipped away. And though insurance companies, for a while, paid generous benefits for people to get treatment, they were suddenly beginning to cut them off. Later on, after the Clintons' health bill went down in the 1990s, they decided to recoup some losses and cut addiction treatment altogether. And with the birth of the War on Drugs, where all America's problems were the War on Drugs, we were going to stamp it out. Forty years later, we're still stamping it out.

So, Senator Hughes, being a politician and a policymaker, recognized what was going on. He said, "You can't have good policy without good advocacy." If politicians and policymakers don't see people in front of them who care, then they're not going to care. They look out there and they see people with other diseases; they don't see us.

It was a very dark period in our history, and for people, particularly in recovery, there was lot of fear. But Senator Hughes said, "If we do not speak up on behalf of our brethren and our illness, it'll just get worse." We need to play the game the way all people do who want fellow citizens to respond to their needs and their conditions. So he formed the Society of Americans for Recovery. He pounded a lot of pavement, tried to raise money. There was none. And in '93 he asked me if I would help him, and I did. We ran some conferences across the country trying to mobilize people in recovery, but it was tough going—very tough going. But we paved the way, I think, for things that were to happen.

And then, we ran out of money. There was no more interest and no more money. Finally, we had to shut the doors in 1995. But there's no question in my mind that Senator Hughes put me on a path of awareness and passion for educating, starting with my fellow people in recovery. Because if we couldn't answer the call to be American citizens, and to claim our citizenship and do the things that other citizens do about their needs and their wants and their hopes and their aspirations, then we couldn't be asking other Americans to pay attention. Senator Hughes inspired me to stay at this, and one way or another, I've been at it since 1985. He's my hero, and I miss him very much.

G. There was still a lot of advocacy work going on throughout the late '90s. What were some of the forces that kept going and actually led to that critical summit in St. Paul in 2001?

J. Slowly, through research and documentation—William White played such a heavy role in that—and through the work of the Johnson Institute and other organizations, and with the help of a few forward-thinking treatment organizations, there was a lot of talk and discussion and mobilizing the recovery field.

There was an organization started here in Washington by the Johnson Institute, called the National Forum. And they brought all people together to discuss the field. There were government officials and treatment officials, and there were public policy people. I was working at St. Elizabeth's at the time, but I was asked to be on that committee. We met twice a year and that gradually moved forward and, with some funding, we started the Alliance Project. That was under the leadership of Paul Samuels, who is still around at the Legal Action Center. One thing led to another, and William Cope Moyers became president of the Johnson Institute in Minneapolis. He shepherded and provided the funding for the planning of a national summit and that occurred, as you know, in October of 2001, just after 9/11. There were some 235 delegates from all over the country, who had been carefully solicited to represent their part of the country and the variety of our recovery community. We worked for three days to establish a national movement. And that's really where the modern recovery movement took off.

We poured over all the questions out there and then we set a path that was a universal and broad-minded look at the field. There was a lot of stuff put on the floor about anonymity: "Do we include everybody? If somebody's on methadone, are they in recovery?" We discussed the need to reach the entire public of America with what recovery was about. We heard data that we had commissioned by pollsters that showed the public thought being in recovery thirty days was a long time. The American public didn't understand that there were millions of people in America who had many years of recovery. That's not a known fact. We had people presenting ideas of what to do at the state level and what policies to propose that would begin to turn this ship around. There was not a lot of structure there, just camaraderie and thinking and the willingness to say, "Well, we need to take this to the local level." There was no formal organization. People were afraid of organizations. It was called the Alliance Project because nobody wanted to call it the Alliance Movement. There was a good deal of skepticism like that.

G. And since those 235 people met and the new addiction recovery advocacy movement, as William White describes it, was born, what are some of the successes you have seen?

J. One of them I call the *theology*. That's the work William White has done in documenting the conversations that were held. He documented what happened in St. Paul, and he documented the work that could be done by the recovery community. So, we had some literature that we could cite and go to. We also continued national polling, so there's good tracking now every three or four years of how the mood is changing.

There was a lot of interest in getting people involved locally, because if it doesn't happen locally, it doesn't happen at all. I'd like to think my work with the Johnson Institute was helpful in community organizing. We created a program called Recovery Ambassadors, which we took all across the country and trained over 3,000 people in local leadership. Many of the Faces & Voices chapters around the country began with the Recovery Ambassadors workshops. Basically, we put thirty people in a room and they did role-playing on how to teach other people to overcome obstacles like anonymity and shame, and how to raise money. We taught them basic precinct-type politics to organize themselves into a force in their local city council.

One of the very visible things and one of the earlier victories we had is in insurance laws. Some of those laws, passed in the '40s, were very discriminating by our standards today. One of them said that if you were in an emergency room and you had alcohol in your blood, the insurance company didn't have to pay for your treatment there. That was an early target of our policy efforts and, here in DC, several of us testified to get that clause removed. All across the country, under leadership of Faces & Voices, legislators have stopped that kind of discrimination.

There's a current movement going across the country called Ban the Box. It has to do with people who have a police record, usually as a result of their disease. Many employers in our country have a question on applications, "Have you ever been convicted of a felony or have you been arrested?" That's used as a screening device to throw your resume away, and so we've been advocating to have that box eliminated. If you're offered a job, it is appropriate for employers to know everything they can know about you. They can get your police record, whatever, but to use it as a screening device on the front end, that's blatant discrimination. It has nothing to do with how good a pipe fitter you are, or a craftsman, or being in any kind of trade. So the Ban the Box movement is something that's come out of our advocacy, and we have many allies on that.

Those are two examples that are tangible at the local level. They're bringing people together and showing them that if we claim our citizenship and tell our stories, we get support in the general public and we can get policies changed.

G. One of the great policy victories in recent times was the passage of the Mental Health Parity and Addiction Equity Act in 2008. What was it like seeing that bill finally put into law?

J. It was fantastic in every way possible. But there are two major stories there that I think are important. First, is the act itself, and how it was nursed through with the help of so many people both inside and outside Congress and the coming together of allies, across the field, who helped us. It was a wonderful, wonderful victory to demonstrate, once again, that if you have a passion in a nation like the United States of America, and you're willing to do the work of organizing around that passion and bring citizens together around a cause, you can be successful. I think it was a great demonstration of democracy at work. And there are many, many heroes to that. Jim Ramstad [US Representative, R–MN] and Patrick Kennedy [US Representative, D–MA] led us through so much, as did Carol McDaid who mobilized so much support.

The other part I think is so important is that we influenced the thinking in Congress that the American public would not tolerate this kind of discrimination anymore. This was a basic right, number one. And number two, it saved lots of money to do it. It set the stage, then, for healthcare reform. We went into healthcare reform assuming we had to fight this battle all over again, but the technicians, the staff up there, said, "No, no, we fought that battle. You won it. You can go into this next battle [i.e., The

Affordable Care Act] as a peer," meaning, now we're walking arm in arm with cystic fibrosis, with multiple sclerosis, with all these other health issues, and we're now in the same class. We may have differences, and we have to each fight for our own causes, but we're in the game now. So, it's not just winning the actual vote on parity itself, it's that it gave us a place at the larger health community table, and that's huge.

That will play out for years, and we have to maintain that place at the table. We have to continue to tell our fellow citizens who are in recovery that they have a duty and a right to claim their citizenship. We still have to have our community understand public education and do these practices for the next generation. But, parity was huge, and it was a thing I'll never forget as long as I live.

G. You have been public about your recovery for so long and advocating for the rights and welfare of addiction sufferers and people in recovery for decades. You obviously see the importance of that and have no problem doing it. But what about the person in long-term recovery who is reluctant to share his or her story publicly? What would you say to that person who might still feel the stigma and fears associated with public disclosure?

J. Well, I would say two things. I would say to somebody who's in recovery that you need to take care of yourself, number one. There's no question about that. Where there are threats that are real, you need to be respectful of that. And certainly, we all want to make sure that a safe place exists for the newcomer and that nothing can compromise that. But beyond that, after you have done the work to build your own defenses, to build your own care for your health, you have an obligation and a duty to do two things: not let somebody keep you from being a full citizen on the one hand; and on the other hand, do something to give back, so the person after you can have those same rights. It's another step toward recovery.

I've always said the thing that has driven me most in my advocacy is the picture of my three grandchildren. I know where the disease comes from. I know about my family, and I'm one of the first ones to have a successful story to tell. And now, in my generation, we have a number of people who are going to family illness meetings. I want my grandchildren, when they graduate from high school, to have the same knowledge of the symptoms of addiction that they have about measles or diabetes or any other illness. With an illness definition of this disease, if they or their friends ever have a difficulty with this disease, then they will know they don't have to just live and die with it, that there are answers for them. They will know they're not weird or different kind of people; that one out of ten people have something in their genes that allows them to have this illness and that there are steps that can be taken. That's what drives me, to know that that's the kind of world my grandchildren will grow up in.

G. What is your vision for the recovery movement itself? What role do you see advocacy playing in ten or fifteen years?

J. We have a lot of work to do. It includes demonstration. That's part of it. It includes knowledge dissemination, putting the science out there. Because the science is very clear. The new science tells us that there's a huge quantity of people who are at risk that we've been ignoring. We're still working on the margins here. We are not working in the mainstream of healthcare like we need to be. We need to be demonstrating for all behavioral health, not just addiction, but all behavioral health.

The knowledge we have to dispense is tremendous. We're just getting started. You don't change public opinion overnight. Look at the smoking thing. I was amazed when we finally turned a corner on that. Well, it didn't happen overnight. It happened after years and years and years of advocacy, published science, and people standing up with great courage and being examples of change. We need to do the same thing.

Does that make any sense?

G. Perfectly.

Practically speaking, the issue of anonymity applies to two non-conflicting situations: keeping your personal addiction private or not; and protecting the privacy of others in your anonymous support group and not disclosing your specific membership affiliation at the level of press, radio, and films. The latter is sacred and inviolable; as to your personal story, well, that is your own, or the world's, as you see fit. When Johnny Allem put his story out into the world, he says it was met with "some consternation." But his interpretation of anonymity certainly had the founder's imprimatur. And, by the way, AA officially sanctions public disclosure as we were reminded in a recent letter sent out from the General Service Office Public Information Desk of AA, in response to members' inquiries and concerns over the release of *The Anonymous People*. It says, in part:

> "On page 11 of our pamphlet, 'Understanding Anonymity' the following suggestion can be found:
>
> > 'AA members may disclose their identity and speak as recovered alcoholics, giving radio, TV, and Internet interviews, without violating the Traditions—so long as their AA membership is not revealed.'"

This is not an issue to be taken lightly. The question of anonymity is central to the subject of Greg's film, and it is obviously not without its controversy. The matter is one of dual responsibility. The safety one feels in an anonymous group support meeting should never be compromised; such an environment provides immeasurable healing and strength for its members, especially for newcomers.

On the other hand, outside the group, personal anonymity is not so inviolate. One's decision to go public about addiction or recovery rests entirely on the individual's comfort level in doing so, taking into account all sorts of factors, internal and external, that involve health, family, job, friends, and peer support. The heart will know if and when. Then, whether disclosing or advocating, simply do not mention the name of your anonymous group affiliation, if any.

We met many people in our journey who were open about their addiction and recovery. Greg was meticulous in preserving their anonymity with respect to any of their anonymous support group affiliations. Generally, members would express their affiliation by saying simply, "I'm in a peer-based recovery support group." And, as we know, there are many of those, some anonymous, some not. It is interesting to note that the common characteristic of all those who openly disclosed the secrets of their recovery was how empowered they felt. It was as if a great burden had been lifted, and now life and spirit were lighter.

We left our interview with Johnny Allem thinking of all the historical connections he made for us, how plugged into history he is, and how he is still lighting the way. In fact, it is Johnny Allem who found the rare VHS tapes of Harold Hughes speaking that Greg used in the film, helping to illuminate the truth of history and correcting our misconceptions.

Remember that parking space out front? Well, there was a traffic ticket on the windshield and our car was marked for towing. Apparently, we had failed to read the signs correctly, which, on closer inspection, told us that avenue parking was prohibited during rush hours, metered or not. It was the *fourth* parking ticket we had received thus far on our trip. Proving, I suppose, if you go blindly forth in this world, you don't always learn from history.

STACIA MURPHY

"We have to find and open the hearts. And I think those hearts want to be opened."

Some people are destined to be leaders. Stacia Murphy is one. Despite seeing herself simply as a teacher, helping people, one-on-one, to navigate the work-a-day paths to recovery from addiction, she was thrust into a larger leadership role in the advocacy movement. She led the Alcoholism Council of New York from 1990 to 1999 as the organization's executive director. After that, she served nearly seven years as the president of the National Council on Alcoholism and Drug Dependence (NCADD). At first, she resisted taking on these high-profile positions, but ultimately surrendered to her destiny. "I began to get a sense that it was always what I was supposed to be doing," she says, adding that she felt "guided." Once she was called to the national stage, her message never really changed, only broadened. Her mission, large and small, for the better part of four decades, has been to fight the stigma of addiction through education, prevention, counseling, and advocacy services.

For her interview, Stacia welcomed us to the Alcoholism Council offices in New York, where she was the interim executive director. As we sat down, we were immediately struck by her warm and gentle manner. It's that humility again, that people in recovery seem to possess. Here was a national leader with a long career at the head of the march and, frankly, I expected a louder voice. But, her communications skill lay not in grand oratory, but in the quiet, intimate persuasiveness of a spiritual teacher whose inner strength carries such a charismatic force it can motivate either a single individual or a national movement.

This proved to be an emotional interview for all of us. As the conversation progressed, the power of Stacia's words grew in direct proportion to the increasing softness of her voice. Her quiet speech commanded our attention and deepened our feelings. I think it will become obvious where our waterworks were turned on. This is one of several interviews we did that might be enhanced by reading portions out loud, as if they were your words. In a sense, they are. And, I daresay, Stacia Murphy intends them to be yours.

GREG. How did you first get started doing addiction and recovery work?

STACIA. My involvement in the field of addiction was quite accidental. In 1978, I was working with men and women in prisons who had problems associated with alcohol and other drugs. I wasn't interested in the work after a period of time because of the stigma, the attitude of folks. We used to walk into the prisons, and they'd say, "Here come the drunks," and I said forget this. My own personal recovery is extraordinarily important to me, and I don't need to have that muddied by people who don't have the information they need. And so, I went away. But, I was called back quite purposefully.

We would go into the prisons and do groups, and one day I said, "You know, you can't tell a person in jail, 'Don't drink. Go to meetings.' That's not who they are, and that's not what they believe." So, we started an aftercare program, a reentry for them to just come home or come by the center; a place to land and feel safe. I've never met a person in prison who didn't say, "I'm never going back." And I always say, "And how do you plan to do that? If you don't have a plan, you will go back." You can get a job; but if you don't stay sober, you won't keep the job. You can get your family back; but if you don't stay sober, you won't keep your family. So we focused on their addiction and giving them time to experience recovery, sobriety on the street, and to get on with their lives. That was the beginning.

G. And you were involved for the next three decades or so, on a national level taking part in and observing some of the changes in the fields of addiction and recovery that occurred over that time. Overall, from your perspective on the history of the recovery movement, which development do you think was the most important?

S. You put me on the spot there. Certainly, the founding of Alcoholics Anonymous; there's nothing more phenomenal than that. At the seventieth anniversary in Toronto, they had a flag ceremony. Ninety countries. And the person who had the flag from Saudi Arabia was a woman. These are people in recovery. So, to me, it is the founding of Alcoholics Anonymous and everything that has happened since that time to change how we look at alcoholism and addiction in this country and to create hope in people's lives. Alcoholics Anonymous, and then the National Council, obviously, because I'm a part of the National Council. I think it's an important part of history because it really galvanized people around the country—scientists, researchers, communities, families, individuals. It gave voice to the hopeless, to individuals in despair.

G. **You were president of NCADD for a significant period during the '90s. What can you tell us about that organization and your experience serving as president?**

S. The National Council on Alcoholism and Drug Dependence is an advocacy program, founded by Marty Mann. It is reported, though old-timers will dispute this, that she was the first woman to achieve long-term sobriety in Alcoholics Anonymous. And Marty got sober after a horrendous time with alcohol, not understanding it was a disease. She began traveling around the country with Dr. Bob and Bill W, the cofounders of Alcoholics Anonymous, helping people to get sober and learn about alcoholism as a disease.

She experienced stigma, no programs, and no services for alcoholics and their families. And she said, "This is terrible. We need to do something about it." And Bill and Dr. Bob said, "We can't, but you can." And from there, she founded the National Committee for Education on Alcoholism in 1944. It is the oldest advocacy organization in this country dealing with the problems of alcohol. It changed its name in the late '90s to include other drugs and became the National Council on Alcoholism and Drug Dependence. Marty was a very smart woman, and she quickly engaged the medical community in this movement by going around the country, talking to doctors and getting them to think about this being a disease, not a willful act of individuals who were totally out of control. And it caught hold. She was a public relations genius, I thought.

When I was a part of NCADD it was really a prevention program, offering information, referrals, training counselors, working with unions, working with corporations, and getting people into treatment programs. With the right kind of information, you can change the hearts and minds of people. We also did advocacy work in Washington, on the Hill, to initiate legislation. The local affiliates followed suit in their local community. It was not only doing work on a national level, but also trying to be a model for political advocacy at the local level for affiliates. They've been doing that political advocacy for years.

G. **How were all those public activities of NCADD funded in the beginning? And how did they navigate the close relationship with Alcoholics Anonymous?**

S. Well, Alcoholics Anonymous is a separate entity. But early in the establishment of the organization, Bill W was on the board. And when Marty started, they had no money. There was a gentleman named Brinkley Smithers, who had been in about fifty detox treatment centers. They began talking to Brink and told him, "We need a rich philanthropist," and he said, "You found one." And for many years, the Smithers Foundation was the only foundation that gave to projects dealing with alcoholism in this country. That has been their mission to this day; it's a foundation that's almost sixty years old. During the 1970s and '80s other foundations followed suit.

G. **As funding came and the public advocacy campaign started, how did Marty Mann reconcile public disclosure of her recovery status with anonymity and the traditions of AA?**

S. What Marty understood was "No, I can't stand up and tell you where I go for my help. I cannot mention where I get my support and my help. But I can say I'm an alcoholic, and I'm in recovery and not break the tradition of anonymity." I can tell you all day long I'm in recovery. How I got there is not important. I don't have to name names, but I can talk about my own personal recovery.

And I think it's important because if I can't tell you about my struggle or my journey, then I can't expect you to feel comfortable about your recovery or your journey. I continue to promote the stigma and the shame if I can't say that I'm an alcoholic and I'm in recovery.

G. What else happened that had a big impact on how we view or treat alcoholism?

S. The Hughes Act of 1974. Harold Hughes was a person in recovery. He was a member of Congress, and he worked with "Brink" [Brinkley Smithers] and a lot of other people behind the scenes to create legislation. The Hughes Act began to "put money into the field." The National Institute on Alcoholism and Alcohol Abuse was formed. It's the oldest government organization devoted to research about alcoholism. And the National Institute of Drug Abuse, which deals with illicit drugs. Those are the two research organizations funded by the government that continue to do research about addiction, and some incredibly groundbreaking work has been done.

Then in 1976, Marty, again, the woman, the thinker she was, gathered together luminaries, celebrities from all walks of life, from all fields, sports, entertainment, in Washington for what was called Operation Understanding. There were all of these folks who were not homeless, who didn't live under bridges, talking about their recovery. It was a groundbreaking moment, and it got a lot of attention. I think it helped reduce the stigma dramatically.

Then came a lot of attention in the '70s and '80s to treatment programs everywhere—detox centers, rehab centers, psychiatrists, psychologists. I call it a greed industry because that's what it spawned, a greed industry. You have people going into detox centers twenty times and going into rehabs and never getting well and so there was a real belief that people just never got well. You never got sober. We were immersed in the pathology of addiction, so there was no sense of hope. That's what was being promoted.

G. What perpetuated that attitude of emphasis on treatment and the lack of attention given to recovery?

S. I think there are a lot of culprits. I think the media was a big culprit because it always showed the bad stories—the wrecks and the gunfights and the debris and all of the chaos. And I think it was a lack of understanding. I really believe that people's inability to understand and accept this as a disease, a complex medical problem, influenced how they reported the news. It influenced stories. It influenced attitudes. And so, if you're a stigmatized group, you're going to retreat from that and say, "Yeah, okay. I'll just do what I do every day, and I don't have to be a part of a national scene." I believe that's part of it.

G. **At a personal level and as a person in recovery, what was it like going out during those times, working as an advocate?**

S. Well, understand as an advocate, going around the country and just listening to people, talking about my own recovery, it was extraordinary how you can create hope where there is very little. People would come up to me and say, "You know, I've been hiding for ten years, and you just told me I don't have to do that anymore." You recognize that in order for our movement to grow, we have to release ourselves of that shame.

G. **Easier said than done. What has it taken for people to step out with their recovery stories and do so without the shame?**

S. It was folks tired of being blamed, and being ashamed, and wanting very much to be seen in a positive light. And angry, because advocacy is about anger. And knowing that by their voices being heard around the world, you help give voice to others. It was interesting because when Whitney Houston died, Wendy Williams, who has a TV show, said on that day, "I want to tell you something. Fifteen years ago I was where she [Whitney] was, and nobody ever knew that. To this day, I will no longer hide because my saying this will help someone else." And that's what the movement does. That's what Marty did. Marty helped women, because there were not a lot of women in Alcoholics Anonymous. She helped women understand that they had a disease, and they could do something about it. But also in doing something about it, they could help other women do something about it. Bill and

Bob understood that this idea of two alcoholics talking to each other was simply what helped people stay sober, and it continues today, over and over and over—a conversation in a coffee shop, a conversation in a drug store, a conversation on a bus, a phone call here, a phone call from a mother. And you talk with them, and they get something that makes them feel better and gives them hope. And that's what recovery's about. Hope.

G. But there's still the stigma, the perception that this is about bad people.

S. We underestimate the power of stigma. People who have diabetes don't shoot you, they don't beat you up. They don't throw their children out of the window, they don't stick up stores. So it's the behavioral aspect of this—good people do bad things. When we pick up that drug, whether it's legal or illegal, something happens that causes us to behave in ways that are unnatural to who we are as human beings. And for those people who are affected by those seemingly unforgivable deeds, they're still locked in the pain of that. And until individuals, who have been affected by those who are afflicted with alcoholism, can release their own pain, then we continue to stay stuck. When I'm talking to people, talking to students, or talking to family members, I say that it is the inability to embrace this as a disease. It's not just my brother, it's lots of brothers. It's not just my sister, it's not just my mother, it's mothers all over the world. It's fathers. It's children. It's the notion that this is not just about me, but it's about hundreds and hundreds and hundreds of thousands of people.

G. For many people who can drink without a problem, I think it is hard for them to accept the fact that others just can't stop.

S. I believe this very strongly, and I don't think it's complicated: I think that some people get diabetes, and some people don't. Some people get depressed, and some people don't. Some people become alcoholics, and others don't. Most people can drink. A lot of people can't. It's what alcohol does to people when they drink it, or take other drugs. It's pain, and it's a journey. There's the addict on one hand, and then all of those folks on this side. They're on the same journey. They don't get it. The same journey of pain and suffering, of powerlessness, of lack of understanding, of all those occurrences that make them feel shame. When the afflicted person on this side starts to get well, everybody over here leaves, they abandon that person. For whatever those reasons are. Pain, lack of understanding, anger, sort of that emotional whirlwind we alcoholics drag people through.

G. **Recovery is a long process. And those of us who are fortunate enough to have a continuing support structure thrive when we have the understanding of others. How can more people begin to get that ongoing support?**

S. I talk about addiction as very powerful, and I talk about recovery being equally powerful, transformative. Both are processes. Addiction is progressive. Recovery is progressive. What people want you to do is stop drinking and just be. Everything then just goes away. But it doesn't. We're left with memories; we're left with lack of forgiveness; we're left with all those things that were done to us on both sides.

It's an individual journey. But it's a journey over time. I learned that when I came into recovery. I was told, "You will be better over time. Not overnight. This is not a microwave problem. It's not a crash course." So much damage has been done emotionally, spiritually, and mentally, to the mind, the body, and the soul, and the spirit. And you have to find out what that is. There's work you've got to do. There's forgiveness, there's redemption, there's honesty, there's accountability, there's responsibilities. All those things that "good citizens" are supposed to do. And that's a process. A child isn't born today and is an adult tomorrow. A child grows. It's a developmental process. We don't appreciate that because you're dealing with adults. And I sometimes think people just refuse to get it.

I'm pretty blunt about things because I think it's a time to be blunt. You have to look at yourself in this. Get over this. Some people cannot drink alcohol or use other drugs without it causing havoc in their lives. It happens. The science tells us some of it's genetic, it's a brain problem, it's a lot of theories. But, look at those individuals in your own life and how different they are, and if you can't come to a place of forgiveness and acceptance, then you have to look in your own soul because there's something wrong.

G. Did you experience any of this personally?

S. It was not my intention to become an alcoholic. When I was a little girl playing in the sandbox, being an alcoholic was not a goal. I wanted to be a doctor. I wanted to be a lawyer. I wanted to be a writer. But "alcoholic" wasn't on the list.

I spent from eighteen to thirty-three drinking. As I continued to come out of that and grow and change, that's a process. It's emotional, it's ups and downs, it's uneven. But what I do, consistently, is stay sober.

It took my family ten years to even discuss my alcoholism. But I had a moment, years later when I was celebrating my twentieth anniversary. I was at a family reunion and my brother came over and he said, "We want to celebrate this." And in that room were a lot of my cousins and my nieces and nephews who didn't know that about me because they were young and I had been sober quite a while. But, they got something that let them know that there was a life lived one way and a life now lived another way, and the one they were experiencing was the one lived without alcohol in it. And they understood the passion, the power, the pain.

G. Did you ever feel challenged or uncomfortable about sharing your sobriety publicly?

S. I'll give you an example of that. We had a walk years ago, early '90s, in Riverside Park. We were trying to create a recovery walk. It didn't work. But, we had T-shirts, and I had my T-shirt on, and I was walking to my car, fifteen blocks, and I said, "If I keep this T-shirt on, they'll know I'm an alcoholic." And for just that moment that thought occurred to me. I didn't take the shirt off because I realized that I had internalized the stigma of my disease, and at that moment, I decided consciously, "I'm not gonna take this T-shirt off." That has to happen for each of us because it is so demonized. It is reported so badly.

I listened to a medical doctor say, right after Whitney Houston died, that once an addict, always an addict. That is an irresponsible sound bite. A responsible medical practitioner would have said, "There's no cure for this disease, so once you get it, it either goes into remission or you continue to stay addicted to alcohol or whatever your drugs are. It's certainly related to the brain and its pleasure centers, and you sort of get hooked. Sometimes it's very hard for people to get unhooked from that which they become so accustomed to doing. And for some people it takes years and years and years."

When I first got sober, I met a man who took twenty years to make his first anniversary. But you can't condemn that. It's a process. It's a tough disease. It's tough. It's very complex, and we don't talk about its complexities. We don't talk about the struggle. We don't talk about the challenges people face trying to stay sober just on a daily basis. Do I still get cravings? Absolutely. But I have enough tools in my portfolio to say, "I don't have to do this. I can do this, or I can do that."

So it's not one size fits all. It's where you are, and what seems right for you to do in order to overcome. I had most of the symptoms of an alcoholic when I was nineteen years old. I didn't know anything about it. I just liked to have a good time. I'm seeing younger and younger people in recovery, and I am applauding that. But I see the struggle because they think their lives are over. But what they don't realize is they're on this incredible journey that is transformative. They will know a freedom that passes all understanding. They will know a life that they never imagined happening, if they just simply stay away from that drink or that other drug, one day at a time. It's just as simple as that; but, it's also very, very hard because society doesn't normalize recovery. We just need to normalize it. People become alcoholics. People become addicted to other drugs. People become addicts; they get better. It's normal. It's what happens. If there were more support, if there were more of a supportive community, I believe we would diminish relapses significantly. I believe that.

G. **It all comes back to the education and advocacy that you and so many others have been doing for decades, doesn't it? Do you think a mobilized recovery movement can reach everyone in society, not just people in recovery, but also people in active addiction, as well as everyone else who is affected by addiction, and help everyone understand this a bit better?**

S. The recovery movement gives that audience, gives those individuals and those families, another perspective, another view. There are so many people in this country who just stay sober every single day, and they go about their lives. They get up, they go to work, they pay their taxes, they go to PTA meetings, they go to church on Sunday, because they're good citizens, but they're faceless and voiceless. The more they become faces and voices, the more the numbers will increase. It becomes a modeling. It becomes a reflection of the possibility of people transforming their lives. Harvey Milk was an advocate—Sean Penn did a brilliant job in the movie—and said, "You gotta give 'em hope." Our current president talked about hope. It's this notion of hope, because when people are in the darkest parts of themselves, when they feel there is hope, that's when they can pull something out of themselves that allows them to live again, when they have been so much in the dark. Recovery provides a light that shines in an extraordinary way.

G. **How do we get there? How do we make those faces and voices visible and heard so the modeling can take place?**

S. You have a walk of a million people in recovery. Or you have a concert, a million people there. Two million or three million in recovery who are proud, whose children see people who are sober. Talking, rallies, conversations, education, bringing together a group of media folks and saying, "Folks, y'all gotta change these stories and talk about what happens to people when they overcome this, what happens when they face this challenge." We need to be in churches. We need to bring those folks to the pulpits and to the community centers and to the schools. It's the stories of transformation that get other people to know their lives are not over. And I think more and more of us need to be out there, telling those stories. I was there one day, and now I'm here today, and look at that difference. I'm a good citizen. I do good things, but I couldn't do those good things when I was under the influence of alcohol and other drugs. And now I can.

G. You have seen the new addiction recovery movement grow. Do you think we're moving in the right direction?

S. Absolutely. I do. And I actually made that statement the other day to one of my staff, who's getting her master's in public health. She works here and sees the work we do and is involved in it, and she is aware of the challenges. I said, "Mark my words. Within the next eighteen months to three years, you will see a major shift in how we deal with alcohol and other drug problems in this country." We laid the groundwork, the voices are out there, we have the science, and we have the data. I think it's our time. I absolutely believe it.

Recovery is a moving experience. It's a moveable feast of pleasure and purpose and growth and learning. Each day is a new day of possibility. It's excitement. It's joy. It's tears. It's passion. And to share that . . . you get someone to see the light because addiction is dark. You get people to see the hope, the possibility. You do it with humility. You do it with grace. You do it with love.

We have to find and open the hearts. And I think those hearts want to be opened.

Greg's appreciation of the past grew the more he spoke with knowledgeable and experienced advocates, such as Aligata, White, Allem, and Murphy, and so many others we can't include here. He began to see the significance of understanding the historical arc of the recovery movement, how it began, who and what kept it going, why it stalled, and more recently how it reignited. One key person in the movement kept coming up—Senator Harold Hughes, who took public advocacy to a new level.

Historian William White recommended a book to Greg, *With a Lot of Help from Our Friends: The Politics of Alcoholism* written by Nancy Olson, who served on Hughes's staff until he retired in 1975. It's the inside story of Hughes's advocacy at the highest levels of government on behalf of the common suffering citizen. It was at the Senate hearing on "The Impact of Alcoholism" before the Special Subcommittee on Alcoholism and Narcotics in 1969, chaired by Hughes, that AA cofounder Bill Wilson testified. Recognizing the import of his own testimony, Wilson said, ". . . this is an extremely moving and significant occasion. It may well mark the advent of a new era in this old business of alcoholism." The next year, President Nixon signed the Comprehensive Alcohol Abuse and Alcoholism Prevention, Treatment, and Rehabilitation Act of 1970 (the Hughes Act). This first-of-a-kind legislation authorized a comprehensive Federal program to address prevention and treatment of alcohol abuse and alcoholism. And of course, in 1976, Hughes attended Operation Understanding, a dramatic event that put a public spotlight on scores of celebrities and their recovery.

As Greg delved into the history of the movement, he saw its relevance to validating and refreshing the ideas of the new recovery advocacy movement. He was looking for ways to introduce Harold Hughes into the film and shed some light on those early, groundbreaking years. Were Hughes or Olson still alive, you can bet Greg would have been on the phone trying to secure an interview with one or the other. That's why Johnny Allem's help in acquiring the archival videos of Hughes was so important in bringing alive Hughes's contribution to the history of recovery.

All those seminal events—the hearings, the convening of celebrities, the legislation—received much press at the time, but they soon faded into history, as stigma-inducing policies of the next two decades, notably the "The Drug War," obscured the positive advances in public perception that Hughes and others had won. The emerging recovery advocacy movement stalled. More recently though, the pendulum has swung back as recovery has begun to find its voice again, and the ranks of advocates have swelled to revitalize the movement. We met a few of the warriors who have been out in front carrying the torch.

PAT TAYLOR

"One vision is to have a million-person event here in Washington, DC, bringing forward the reality of recovery."

I remember the anger of the 1960s. When people speak of causes, social action, and protests, I think of that time when we had heroes in the streets rallying, marching, doing sit-ins, and raising hell to raise awareness.

When I first met Pat Taylor in her office in Washington, DC, where she was Executive Director of Faces & Voices of Recovery for over twelve years, I had an immediate '60s flashback to my own time of civil rights marches and war protests: I saw her dedication, belief, passion, and maybe even a flicker of vestigial anger burning in her eyes. Her voice, mellowed with humor was, nonetheless, strong with conviction and determination. We came to learn that Pat's entire work life has been spent advocating for something—campaigning around issues local to national and working to change public policy for the good of people and communities. She has raised her fist, carried banners, chanted in the streets, and argued for causes in the halls of Congress. She is an experienced and steely activist with a kind and optimistic heart. Easily, she could have been a rousing captain in any of our demonstrations of another era, exhorting us flower children to passionate participation. On this day, what I saw in the eyes of this professional was something very personal. It was the same deep commitment I had once seen in fellow protesters marching for peace or equality, for whom social change was more than mandatory; it was existential. The recovery movement is that profound; it is also about death and life—needless death that makes you angry, and redemptive life that is joyous.

What is it going to take, I thought, to right the wrongs addicted people suffer? Death? Thousands die of preventable breast cancer and of HIV/AIDS. We rally. Do 75,000 people dead each year from alcohol use mean anything? How about 38,000 dead from other drug overdoses? What about those additional thousands and thousands of deaths by crime or car accident that are directly related to alcohol and other drugs? How many deaths will it take? It's dawning on me: Recovery is more than a process. It is a cause for life.

What Pat Taylor said in her conversation with Greg that day got me angry again.

GREG. Why does Faces & Voices of Recovery exist?

PAT. Well, for too long, people in recovery and their family members haven't been represented where decisions are made that affect their lives and the lives of people in their community. So, we're advocating here in Washington, DC, and in state capitals all across the country to end discrimination and make it possible for people to get the help they need to recover and also to be treated with dignity and respect. Unfortunately, in our country, we pass laws that discriminate against people who have taken the time to get well, so that they can continue and get their lives back on track. Part of our work is redressing these discriminatory laws, so people can live their lives to the fullest, just like people with other health conditions. Addiction is a health condition just like any other, and it's high time we treated it that way.

G. Faces & Voices of Recovery has done quite a bit of public opinion research on the issues of addiction and recovery. What have you learned that is significant and how do you apply that to your work?

P. It's outrageous that our country, our government, spends millions of dollars each year to investigate and research the "problem" of addiction. I mean, we know how many sixth graders in Washington, DC, have smoked a joint. But we don't know how many eleventh graders are in recovery. Our government isn't researching how people get well.

One of the things we found was that no one knew how many people are in recovery in our country. There are over twenty million Americans in long-term recovery from addiction to alcohol and other drugs, and they're benefitting their families, themselves, and their communities because of their recovery. Part of what we're doing at Faces & Voices of Recovery is working to let people know that these twenty million Americans are well. They're next door neighbors. They're teachers. They're bankers. They're all across our country, these twenty million Americans who are in long-term recovery. Unfortunately, there are over twenty-two million Americans who still need help to get well and recover from addiction to alcohol and other drugs. So what we're all about is supporting people who are in recovery, but also making it possible for many, many others to get the help they need to recover.

G. Which is what the 2001 Summit in St. Paul was all about, where Faces & Voices of Recovery really began, right?

P. No one knew whether or not people in recovery would be willing to come together and organize, just like people with other health conditions have. We have a breast cancer movement in our country, people with HIV/AIDS and many other health conditions have come together and organized and have been public and demanded their rights to get the care they needed. We did this first-ever public opinion survey of the recovery community to see if people would be interested in being part of a new national movement. We were delighted to find out that they were. That was really the genesis of what has become a new national organization: Faces & Voices of Recovery. We're building on a rich history of people coming together around this health issue. And as we look to the future, we have many, many opportunities ahead to really build a civil rights movement for people who need help, as well as people who are in recovery.

G. **Why is it important to mobilize people who are in recovery and have them tell their stories?**

P. People with addiction have the right to recover. They also have the right to information about how people can and do get well. One of the founding principles of Faces & Voices of Recovery is that there are many pathways to recovery, just like with other health conditions. We make a special point of letting people who are in recovery talk about what worked for them, offering hope to those who are still struggling, but also letting the public and policymakers know that there are many pathways to recovery. If you go to the doctor or a healthcare provider, you have the right to know what's available, what the options are. For example, if you were diagnosed with cancer, your doctor would tell you about five or six different treatments to find the ones that would work to help you get well. The same with people who have addiction. People can and do get well, and if you try one way and it doesn't work for you, the exciting and good news is that are other ways to try. You can and will recover.

G. **What's it been like mobilizing a national advocacy movement around this issue, with public perception and all the challenges?**

P. Yes, this is a very exciting time in terms of the recovery advocacy movement all across our country. There are over 200 recovery community organizations. They're formed by people who are concerned about these issues, who are speaking out, who are mobilizing, who are educating elected officials and others about the reality of recovery. I can't tell you how much fun it really is doing this work. People in recovery and their families are totally committed to making it possible for others to get the help they need and to end these discriminatory barriers that are being faced when people do make the commitment to stop using alcohol and other drugs. So just like some of the other civil rights movements, we have our struggles, but we also have our opportunities.

G. One of the struggles you face, of course, is stigma. In the film we're making, I want to explore the way mass media depicts addiction and how that affects public perception of the issue. What's your take on the media and their role in hindering or helping us find recovery solutions?

P. This is a big topic for me. I am very concerned about the way people are portrayed in the media and also the way programming uses people with alcohol and other drug problems to draw viewers. When A&E's *Intervention* first went on the air, we did a letter writing campaign to A&E saying, "Hey what's happening to these people after they're on the show, number one, and how are people being portrayed in this particular program? And think about it." One thing that came about because of that campaign we did was, A&E is investing in something called The Recovery Project. They now have programming where they talk about recovery, where we can now see people no longer using. It's just not this fascination with people in their active addiction. A&E is sponsoring our town hall meetings around the country, and things like that. That's something. It's not the end, but I mean, that's a response to an outcry.

When *Celebrity Rehab* with Dr. Drew was first launched, similarly, we did a national campaign talking about what it means to have people in their active addiction in that kind of programming. In many ways, that programming has been a real setback for our movement because it's prurient interest. What are people's lives like when they're addicts? Oh, it's drama. You know, people like it. It's good TV, and there's no drama in recovery. Well, I counter that. I think there's a lot of drama in recovery, and I would love to see reality TV shows about how people find and sustain their recovery for the long haul. We called on producers, network executives, and others to think about a reality show about people getting well. There is a lot of drama in recovery, and it's time that that's what we see on TV.

G. And then, there is this pervasive, obsessive coverage in the news media of celebrities who are acting out in their addiction.

P. An era of celebrity fascination is how I describe it. Celebrities who relapse, who go into rehab, recycle in and out of rehab, I mean, those were the kind of storylines always. We're living through it right now. It can't end soon enough because it is really hard to counter when images fill our screens of what people are like when they're addicts and not what people are like in their recovery. That's a challenge in terms of changing public attitudes. That's why it's so important that what's going on in communities across the country be what we profile, be what we talk about, and get those stories out into media in a different kind of a way. Hopefully, we will live to see the day when there isn't such a fascination with celebrity addiction.

But I do think there is a growing awareness on the part of reporters in the media to have real people who have experienced recovery to be part of their stories. Five or ten years ago when they were doing a story, there weren't people who would be willing to be part of those stories. And so that message of a lived experience of recovery is now much more present than it was in the past.

G. How can we move that message to become more "present" now?

P. Building the capacity of recovery community organizations so that they can inform the media of what their activities are so the media is covering those activities, as well as the problem. When groups have advocacy days where hundreds of advocates walk the halls of state legislatures, there are media representatives covering those events. That's why events like Recovery Month are so important. That's why the growing sophistication of recovery community organizations is so important. We are behind this solution and we want to have the media be covering that solution. Recovery community organizations are an important part of making that happen.

G. And the individual people in recovery.

P. Absolutely. And their family members. You know, I think it's really important, as we talk about our growing national and international recovery advocacy movement, that we understand that family members are as affected by recovery as they are by addiction and that they are critical parts of local recovery community organizations. Often, when they speak to elected officials, they may be more likely to listen to a mom or a dad, you know. So we need to make sure they are at the table, as well.

We also have our own kind of celebrities in the recovery community. People like Congressman Jim Ramstad, Congressman Patrick Kennedy, and other elected officials who are not only open about their recovery, but are also leaders in setting public policy and creating better public understanding about the policies we need to support people in recovery. There is a growing cadre of people in recovery who are state legislators now and in other kinds of policymaking positions. And that really makes a tremendous difference for us. Using their profile is really critical.

G. Your very name, Faces & Voices in Recovery, suggests exposing identities and stories to public light. How do you reconcile what for many seems to be a conflict between advocacy and the anonymity tradition?

P. Many of the twenty million Americans who are in long-term recovery we don't see every day. Part of the reason may be that they believe if they are using a particular twelve-step program in their recovery it means they cannot speak out and advocate. Nothing could be further from the truth. I mean, one of the things we've done here at Faces &

Voices of Recovery is to develop messaging so that people in recovery, and family members, can speak out about the reality of recovery in a way that does not violate other traditions of a twelve-step program. It is okay to speak out and advocate on behalf of your rights and benefits. We encourage people to take a look at our brochure, *Advocacy with Anonymity*. Use it to move forward so that people can know and understand the reality of recovery, offer hope to others who are still struggling, but also to influence public policymakers. It's like with other health conditions or with the women's movement or with other civil rights movement. We need to come together and speak out and advocate. Everyone has a right to do so.

G. I think one of the cool things you have done is to unite the diverse recovery community. With so many pathways to recovery, it must be hard to focus the big issue and make it relevant to everyone. It is powerful when you can do it.

P. It is. We want to make things personal so that people understand our personal journeys. But then, we want to come together and unite and speak with one voice. That's why this recovery messaging we've developed is so important. It allows individuals to share their personal experience, but also broaden it to be more inclusive and be part of our unified community. Speaking with one voice is how we talk about it. It's telling you a story with a purpose, letting people know that recovery is a reality. It's speaking out to end the injustice that people still struggling with addiction face: Be it restoration of voting rights for people with drug histories; be it access to care that people aren't getting; or doing something to stop drug overdoses. I mean, there are incredible economic and social problems facing our country that are due to people still struggling with alcohol and other drug problems. So coming out of the basements into our nation's capital and state capitals, going to a PTA meeting, talking about recovery, talking about the fact that people can and do recover is critically important.

G. William White writes about the "new advocacy movement," pointing to different kinds of recovery movements in the past and suggesting we're on the cutting edge of something new. Where do you think we've been, where are we now, and where do you think we're going?

P. There's a long history of people in recovery coming together and speaking out. We're building on that history of advocacy and have been doing that over the last ten years. But we're really just at the tip of the iceberg in terms of our potential and our capacity to mobilize and organize a recovery community—people in recovery, family members, friends, and allies—all across the country.

I think we're on the cusp of some dramatic changes, partly because of a growing understanding and the advocacy over the last ten years about the reality of recovery: Our victory, in terms of the federal ban on financial aid to students with drug convictions; our victory in Wellstone/Domenici; our Mental Health Parity and Addiction Equity Act; ending insurance discrimination; the fact that Congress did not even question whether or not addiction should be part of the Affordable Care Act; the fact that we are fighting back against drug testing; the fact that recovery community organizations all across the country are at the table when states are thinking about essential health benefits; that recovery community organizations are at the table where decisions are being made about the types of services that will be funded by public funders. None of that would have happened ten years ago. I think we made tremendous progress. But we have a long, long way to go in terms of making it possible for those twenty-two million Americans who are still struggling to get the healthcare they need. And then we do not discriminate against them once they stop using alcohol and other drugs.

G. If you had a vision for the new addiction recovery advocacy movement, what would that be?

P. One vision is to have a million-person event here in Washington, DC, at some point in the not too distant future, bringing forward the reality of recovery. And I think that demonstration of recovery needs to come with an agenda for what we would like to see happen to make it possible for more people to get help and to support people in long-term recovery.

My vision is hundreds and hundreds of recovery community centers all across the country; public policy that supports and doesn't discriminate against people getting help; that we see portrayals of people in active recovery and their families as part of our everyday lives; and that we just assume that people can and do get well; people who go to the doctor's office with an alcohol or other drug problem at age sixteen or seventeen are identified as having that problem and get the help they need to recover, early, so that they lead full and rich and healthy lives. We're making it possible for that to happen.

G. Great. Thank you.

At least forty-five million American lives are at stake here. This is more than a health issue. It's a cause for social justice and civil rights for those struggling with addiction. That's why recovery needs a movement.

Pat Taylor is one optimistic woman. While she is completely realistic, she does have great hope for the future and success of the new recovery advocacy movement. Nevertheless, it made me angry to realize how entrenched stigma and discrimination are in our society—both an irrational and a systemic bias against people with addiction and even against those already succeeding in recovery. Discriminatory policies and warped media portrayals exacerbate the problem; and more to the point, actually cause the false perceptions that inform negative opinion. The harsh truth is, that too many of us are mindless, media-manipulated idiots without the gumption to get off the couch and take some positive social action. And people die. Needlessly. It's an old, old story.

I want to be there when the recovery movement holds that million-person march on Washington. It'll be like the '60s all over again. We'll change things.

TOM HILL

"...it's not going to change unless people come out and start demonstrating what recovery looks like."

Tom Hill is a cool guy. He's a former artist (actually, still is) from New York, who changed careers when recovery changed his life. It has been over twenty years since he simultaneously found long-term recovery and the power in community support and social activism. That's when he got a degree in social work and began a professional career that led to community organizing and leadership positions in two areas: addiction and recovery issues; and Lesbian, Gay, Bisexual, Transgender and Transsexual, Queer (LGBTQ) causes, including HIV/AIDS. His perspective and experience as a gay man and person in recovery inspires and informs his work and is expressed well in an article he wrote for *The Good Men Project Magazine* entitled, "Come Out, Come Out Wherever You Are." In it, he points out that people in recovery can learn from the LGBTQ community; being visible, honest, and starting the conversation can erode the stigma that otherwise prevents people from living openly and improving their lives. Tom is a founding board member of Faces & Voices of Recovery and was its director of programs at the time of our filming.

From Greg's conversation with Pat Taylor in the surprisingly small suite of offices at Faces & Voices of Recovery, we moved a mere ten feet into Tom's office to talk with him. Just outside his window, an adjoining office building crowded close by, obscuring any sunlight. The symbolism of the building's looming stone wall was not lost on us as Tom recounted his own coming out.

GREG. As an advocate for both the LGBTQ community and recovery, what parallels do you see between the causes? And what have you observed about the growth of the new recovery advocacy movement in the time that you have been involved?

TOM. One is stigma—when a group of people are looked down upon by society and despised, ostracized, marginalized. When you look at other social justice movements—civil rights, or LGBTQ, or the movement around breast cancer—there are always lurches ahead and there are always setbacks. Look at the LGBTQ movement that happened since Stonewall in 1969, some forty years ago. Has public opinion changed? Absolutely. Has it changed to the degree that everybody would like? No. But, there is a public debate about gay issues in a way that didn't surface forty years ago, and people's lives have definitely improved.

A huge thing I learned was the power in the early part of that movement of coming out. A lot was written about the need for people to come out, to step out of the shadows and openly declare themselves as a gay, lesbian, bisexual, or transgender person. When I came to recovery advocacy that seemed to be the stumbling block—to get people to feel powerful about talking about their recovery. It's coming out as a person in recovery. It is a very powerful and liberating thing.

Beyond that I've also seen a huge change in the demographics of our movement. I've seen people of color in much larger numbers. I've seen women and gay people. I've seen young people. Things are very, very different than they were twelve years ago in terms of what we look like. I think that our movement reflects greater society much more now than it did originally. Building a movement that has that kind of inclusion and also includes all pathways to recovery are really dynamic things that have changed and need to change more. I think we still have a tremendous amount to go. But when I disclose my recovery status, people no longer take a step back like they did in 1998. Awareness has changed, and I think consciousness has been raised a little bit. I think that public opinion is going to be hard to change, and I think it's not going to change unless people come out and start demonstrating what recovery looks like. That's always the first step.

G. Do you remember the first time you went public with your recovery?

T. Coming out for me was embedded between coming out as a gay man and coming out as a person in recovery. I came out early in my recovery, and I was out a little bit before, to colleagues and family. For me to hide my recovery, I couldn't understand why I would ever want to do that. This big impetus was changing my life. I was coming out as being gay, why would I ever want to be secretive about the very thing that was making me happy and making me transformed? Also, everybody in the community had seen me as a public nuisance, so why would I ever want to not show that I had the capability to change? It just seemed natural that if they saw me on the addictive end, then they should see me on the recovery end.

G. You bring that personal, cojoined experience coming out as a gay person and a person in recovery to your work. What transpired to make that happen all at the same time?

T. I got sober in the early '90s in New York City, and part of my coming out process was joining an LGBTQ community of recovery. And what was also happening at that time in New York City was the AIDS epidemic. There was a lot of community activism, and part of my service was not only through recovery venues but also through the LGBTQ community. That led me to sort of rethink my career and rethink what my purpose was, and I went back to school and I got a social work degree in community organizing, and got things going in a direction that just seemed very real and right and purposeful for me.

G. What was your pathway to recovery? How did you end up getting help and finding recovery?

T. Well, it's funny because I was a freelance artist, so I didn't have insurance. I didn't even know treatment existed. All I knew was various mutual aid groups that were pretty much abundant in New York City. I really liked the sort of community aspect of it and I connected with sources of help and support pretty easily. I was in therapy before I got into recovery and that was really sort of a portal for me—that and the combination of mutual aid groups.

G. **And you saw some kind of value and appeal in those mutual aid groups that interested you enough to pursue a profession in community organizing?**

T. When I was at Hunter College, one of my internships was in the public policy department at the LGBTQ Community Center. I actually created that internship because I wanted to work there and I wanted to do that kind of work. Then, my first job out of school I directed a senior center for LGBTQ people. I was engaged in sort of a national network of things regarding how people aged in queer communities. I was doing a lot of creative programming. And I was at a conference where Barbara Warren from the LGBTQ Community Center offered me a job to start up this recovery advocacy project called RCSP, Recovery Community Support Program. This was in 1998, and I took that job and that was the beginning of being a part of groups across the country that got grants to do mobilization and community organizing. None of us really knew what we were doing. It was tremendously confusing and enormously fun.

G. **So you were sort of learning on the fly. What were you discovering in your community work? Any surprises?**

T. With that RCSP grant in 1998–1999, one of the assumptions was that we were going to find people in recovery, organize them, and mobilize them so they could go out and talk about how great treatment was and advocate for treatment dollars. But when we started working in communities, folks wanted to talk about recovery, what kinds of things were conducive to recovery, what things in the community supported recovery, which nobody was really talking about then. It was a very, very different conversation than before. I really cite the recovery community as being a major impetus in that shift of talking about going from treatment to talking about a much larger paradigm of recovery. I said we were all confused because this had never been done before. It was exciting to exchange that information with other people. I met people like Phil Valentine and Bob Savage. I met people like William White, Beverly Haberle, Joe Powell, you know, leaders in this community now. We all were coming together as a group and trying to figure this out in our own communities. It was an amazingly fertile and productive time. I still look back on it and get goosebumps thinking about it.

G. Was there a particular inspiring moment you recall?

T. In 1999, we brought community people down to DC for the first big RCSP grant team meeting. I brought a black lesbian, a woman of transgender experience, and a Puerto Rican gay man, and we showed up like, "Well, the queers are here!" And we started talking about what recovery looked like to us in a set of cultural contexts. And one of the folks who really resonated with us was Don Coyhis from White Bison because he was talking about the same thing in a very different way— what recovery looked like in a Native American experience. He was in the process of doing amazing things, translating recovery experience, like twelve-step stuff, into a Native language or a Native cultural context. It was a great sort of cross-pollination that was happening. We talked about what people bring to the recovery community in terms of their own personal stories, and also their cultural experience that nurtures and welcomes recovery. I think that's been an important piece of our movement and those kinds of things are still really pertinent today as we move forward.

G. How did you find that it was even possible to organize the recovery community? I mean, besides cultural differences, it would seem the traditions of anonymity would be a barrier to trying to organize people.

T. I think one of the powerful lessons we've learned in organizing the recovery movement is helping people, especially people within the Twelve Traditions, to understand the difference between safeguarding their anonymity and being able to talk about their recovery in an open honest way. They can separate those issues in such a way that they don't break any of the Twelve Traditions, and at the same time, they can also teach people and talk openly about their recovery status.

When you work with any oppressed group, it's always good to have people understand their history, such as learning about people like Marty Mann and learning about Bill Wilson testifying before the Harold Hughes hearings in Congress. Learning about things that happened beforehand that all pointed the way toward a recovery advocacy movement, and that you didn't have to jeopardize your anonymity in a program to be able to speak out for pro-recovery policies and against discriminatory policies and programs.

G. You mentioned recovery support services and seeing how they've evolved. How do they work to complement existing mutual aid groups?

T. There was a major shift in 2002 in the RCSP. It moved from support program to services program. There was a policy shift and programming shift that went to peer services. I had had a lot of experience with senior centers, so I sort of knew about the idea of "peer-ness." About that time, people started talking about many pathways to recovery, and we were looking at all these other kinds of ways that people recover other than in twelve-step programs. Peer services really took hold in terms of this idea of what people needed that they weren't getting. They needed emotional support but they also needed housing, they needed employment opportunities, they needed ways to help them get their GED and go back to school, all in a recovery setting. Not in a generic setting, but in a very recovery, nurturing kind of setting. And so we looked at how people could start to make programs around those things. It was also how recovery community centers came about. There were a couple of grantees who started recovery community centers, and we had a meeting in El Paso in 2004 and brought all the grantees together and did two-and-half days on talking about what recovery community centers could look like. After that, everyone went home and started up recovery community centers. Now, in 2012, we see this whole network of recovery community centers across the country and a lot of that thinking came out of RCSP grantees in those early days.

G. So what's special about a recovery community center?

T. First of all, it was radical to be able to hang a shingle on Main Street that said, "Recovery Community Center." People went in the front door with a great deal of ownership and pride that they were citizens of the town and they belonged to the recovery community center. It made recovery visible and, if I can say, proud on Main Street. I think that was a great contribution. The other thing is a recovery community center is a great hub for community organizing. It's a community organizing engine because people can go, assemble, talk about ideas, and do advocacy and mobilization work in a way that's very physical. So, it provides a plant, a factory for recovery programs to happen, for recovery ideas to happen, for recovery engagement to happen among the recovery citizens in town. And they've been very popular and really effective. And I think we're going to see a lot more of them.

G. How do you deal with local resistance to recovery community centers or to recovery residences—the "Not in My BackYard" [NIMBY] objection?

T. NIMBY issues come up with recovery community centers. Folks were aghast that the addicts were taking over downtown. Putting a shingle out that says we're a recovery community center sends a powerful message that we're an integral part of that downtown or that community, that we do community service, and that we give back. Regarding recovery residences, they're usually based on ignorance of people who think people are actively using. They don't like that a lot of cars are being parked around and things like that, so it's important for recovery residences to fight those things in the courts, and to prove themselves as good neighbors.

I think it's a matter of changing public opinion and changing community views on what recovery is. The thing about people in recovery is that we're thoughtful about those things, we make good neighbors, we make good employees, we're earnest, in many ways, about how we go about living our life now.

G. What is the Recovery Bill of Rights?

T. One of the great contributions of Faces & Voices of Recovery, and one that I'm especially proud of, is the Recovery Bill of Rights. That came out of the idea that everybody in this society deserves the right to recovery and deserves that right in many, many layers. Whether I'm accessing services, whether I'm being affected by public policy, I have earned my right as a person to be here, to be a part of, to participate, and to engage in society in ways that I choose, which is to be open about my recovery and to make that a part of my participation.

G. That's a great ideal to work for. Is that your vision for what the recovery movement could achieve?

T. My vision for this movement would be that we'd be out of work. You know, that somebody who has a problem with using substances or has addiction is treated the same way as anybody else with a health condition. We don't stigmatize people for eating cake if they have diabetes.

Once again, there's a war on people using drugs. There are a lot of state bills out now that are requiring people who are accessing public assistance to be drug tested, and I don't see that happening with other people who are accessing any other kind of federal funding. It's a war on poor people; it's a war on people of color; it's a war on people that has nothing to do with the manner in which they receive public assistance. I think it's important for our community to come out and stand up for the marginalized. Everybody has a right to get the things they're entitled to in this country, whether it's public assistance or college education or the right not to be criminalized for certain activities, the right to reenter from prison in a way that is conducive to someone's recovery and the betterment of their life, instead of recycling them back in that system. I think those are pertinent issues that are not going away. And we have a responsibility to stand up and speak out.

Both Pat Taylor and Tom Hill bring that inspiring activist spirit to the new recovery advocacy movement. The passion was evident in Greg's conversations with these two dedicated individuals and left us all a little roused up, even a little angry. In a good way.

JIM RAMSTAD

"There's no room for politics when you're talking about a disease."

Do good things happen to people in recovery from addiction? Ask former US Congressman Jim Ramstad from Minnesota. He got sober in 1981, and for the next ten years served in the Minnesota State Senate. Then, in 1991, he was elected to the United States House of Representatives, where he served for the next eighteen years, representing Minnesota's Third Congressional District. For more than twenty-eight years of his thirty-three years in recovery, Mr. Ramstad was, in his words, "blessed" to be given the public trust of elected office. Fittingly, he gave back. For over a decade he worked in the House, under both Republican and Democratic majorities, to end discriminatory practices against people suffering from mental health and addiction problems. In 2008, all that work paid off with the passage of the Paul Wellstone and Pete Domenici *Mental Health Parity and Addiction Equity Act*, a bill he had co-sponsored in the House with Massachusetts Representative Patrick Kennedy. Mr. Ramstad rightly regards this law as one of the most important legacies of his work in public life.

Since retiring from Congress in 2009, he hasn't stopped his advocacy and education around the issues of addiction and recovery. Currently, Mr. Ramstad is a resident fellow at the Harvard Institute of Politics, where he leads a study of the "Policy and Politics of Addiction." Clearly, he doesn't confine his advocacy to the halls of higher learning or Congress. He is continually available, offering his knowledge and support to any and all, as he did for us. Greg contacted him and, without hesitation, he invited us to his office in Minneapolis for an interview.

His office, on the second floor of a modest building in his old district on the outer edge of the city, can barely contain all the memorabilia of his distinguished career as a legislator. Occupying all available shelf and wall space are signed baseballs, awards, and photos with celebrities and dignitaries of every political stripe, suggesting a public life that considered all points of view. Jim Ramstad is a tall man, and as he folded himself into the chair behind his desk amid the forest of lights and grip stands that we had crowded around him, he focused on each of us with a cheerful welcome. He had the comfortable manner of a skilled and engaging politician, in the best sense of the word, the kind who understands that every human being matters, and every vote counts.

GREG. How did it come about that you disclosed your addiction and recovery so publicly, first to your constituents in Minnesota, and then more broadly to the nation when you went to Congress?

JIM. I woke up in a jail cell in Sioux Falls, South Dakota, on July 31, 1981, under arrest for disorderly conduct, failure to vacate the premises, and resisting arrest. It was my first term in the State Senate and I was mortified; I was humiliated; I was embarrassed beyond words. I wanted to be dead. But instead of being the end of my life and the end of my career, it was merely the beginning.

I remember talking to my parents from that jail cell, and my mother told me to just tell the truth, the whole truth, and nothing but the truth. For the first time in my life, I was able to tell the truth about my drinking. I was a binge drinker, and I was an alcoholic. I didn't want to be an alcoholic. I had two uncles who both died from this disease of alcoholism; one was a contractor, highly successful; the other one was a doctor, highly successful. Both proved that alcoholism is an equal opportunity disease, as my counselor informed me the first day in treatment. And so, wherever I've gone for the last thirty years, I found it very natural to speak openly about my recovery. And that's only because of the grace of God, the access I had to treatment, and the love and support of recovering people wherever I go. I thought I owed it to the people of my district, the people I represented, to tell them what happened and to tell them the truth about my drinking, and I did from day one of my recovery.

G. **Did you ever consider keeping your addiction secret or try to remain anonymous in your recovery?**

J. I never had anonymity; the newspaper and television people took care of that. Even though it was humiliating and embarrassing to wake up in jail and to be under arrest, it was also freeing to be able to talk about who I really was—to let the truth ring out and to let the truth prevail. And I did. It was like a great burden had been lifted.

G. **What has your personal recovery been like since breaking that denial and speaking your truth?**

J. I learned the efficacy of treatment first-hand, and I went through aftercare, and I'm still recovering. I remember asking the counselor one of the first days in treatment, "Will I ever be a recovered alcoholic?" And he said, "Not until they put you in that pine box under the ground. If you stay sober, keep going to meetings, don't have another drink, you'll be a recovering alcoholic for the rest of your days on this earth." But, I wanted to be fixed. What do you mean I can't be recovered? One day at a time is all he could guarantee. It's all any of us can guarantee, if we go to meetings and work the program. Now, I'm just grateful that I'm a recovering alcoholic and able to share with others the joy of recovery and the blessings that have come my way and the way of other recovering people.

G. In your profession as an elected representative of the people, you are by definition, and unavoidably, a highly public figure. Have you seen or felt any negative consequences in your life as the result of talking about your recovery?

J. I've seen and felt a lot of love and a lot of support from other recovering people. I rarely gave a talk, during the eighteen years I served in Congress, where afterward people didn't come up to talk to me about somebody in their family with an alcohol or other drug problem, about their own addiction, or inviting me to a meeting to speak at their group. It's just a real blessing to be part of the recovery movement. I still see, as a former congressman, the blessings of recovery every single day.

G. Not many people have had the experience of giving testimony as a United States Congressman and announcing that you're a person in recovery. What is that like?

J. I think being a recovering alcoholic is not just a policy issue with me, nor is it with other recovering alcoholics—it's a matter of life or death. We know this is a fatal disease. That's why we feel so passionate about the need for equality in treatment and for removing the insurance barriers that are discriminatory. And so, as a recovering person talking about it on the floor of the Congress, I think there's a little bit more attention paid to somebody who has experienced the ravages of chemical addiction and has also experienced the joy of recovery, the promise of a sober lifestyle.

G. Prior to the parity initiative Congress passed in 2008, were you involved in any earlier policy and legislation around this issue?

J. The first major legislation related to addiction and recovery I worked on in Congress was authorization of the drug courts. I strongly believe in the efficacy of drug courts. They're the biggest civil justice reform in our lifetime and they prove that treatment works. First time, nonviolent offenders who go through drug court have a recidivism rate of less than 30 percent, compared to 76 percent of people in the general prison population.

In 1996, Senator Paul Wellstone—my dear friend who died tragically in a plane crash in 2002 and who was so committed to helping, as he said, the "little feller" not the "Rockefeller"—got me interested in the parity legislation. It would remove the discriminatory barriers against people with addiction who are in health plans; in other words, treat diseases of the brain, such as addiction, the same as the diseases of the body. If addiction is categorically a disease, then you can't justify discrimination in insurance coverage.

G. The parity bill was really a bipartisan issue and a bipartisan collaboration. That's not the usual practice in Congress these days is it? How did it work that both sides of the aisle got behind this bill?

J. Unfortunately, it has become unique to work in a bipartisan, pragmatic, and common sense way down there. There's so much polarization and so much acrimony, hostility, and lack of comity. There is a lot of comedy, too! There's not the collaboration that existed when I first went to the United States Congress, and it's really too bad. Everything has a political connotation, and that I think is harmful to the country, and certainly harmful to good legislation being passed. That's one thing I admired so much about Senator Kennedy; he reached out to the other side. Whether he was chairman of the committee or ranking member, he'd reach out to the Republicans.

For example, he reached out to John Boehner to work on the education legislation and reached out to me to pick up the mantra when Paul Wellstone died. He came to see me with Patrick [Kennedy], who was then a fellow member of the House, and said he wanted to pick up the mantra of Paul Wellstone in the Senate and see this parity bill become reality. And until his dying day, he was on the phone calling Harry Reid, the Senate Majority Leader, saying, "Harry, when are you going to bring up the parity bill," because the House had already passed it. And Senator Reid was delaying it for tactical reasons. Senator Reid amended the $700 billion bank bailout bill to the parity bill and passed them as a package. But we didn't care how it got passed. Finally, after twelve years, it deserved to be passed, and we were grateful it was.

G. What does it take to get our policymakers and legislators on board with these issues so more people can be helped?

J. Well, that's a really good question. When I first started working on the parity bill, I had colleagues and friends in Washington on both sides of the aisle who would come up to me and say, "Jim, I really admire your own personal recovery, but if I get on this bill, I'll never get reelected because the people back home don't believe chemical addiction is a disease. They think it's a moral weakness or moral failing." And I'd say, "Well, where have they been since 1956 when the American Medical Association, the experts, the nation's top doctors who did the research, categorized it as a chronic disease and a fatal one, if not treated?" There's no question, we're still fighting that stigma today. There are some people who have actually told me they'd rather have cancer than alcoholism. They'd rather have diabetes than drug addiction. Well, I tell them, for many cancers, there's no cure. There's no cure for alcoholism or drug addiction, either, but you can recover, one day at a time. There's no question that stigma is still a huge barrier to recovery and to more dollars for research, more dollars for treatment, more dollars for drug courts, and for other measures to help people.

G. Do you think progress in addiction treatment or addiction recovery policy is held back in any way because it is a political issue?

J. There's no room for politics when you're talking about a disease. This has never been a Republican or Democrat issue in my twenty-eight years of legislating. We have always had good bipartisan support, not unanimous support, sometimes, but it seems like we've always been able to get majority for the major legislation that we need both in the Minnesota legislature and in Congress. It's because enough people have been educated and realize that addiction is a disease and that it is treatable, that treatment does work and people can get into recovery, and that in the end, the taxpayers save money. It doesn't cost money. When was the last time that Newt Gingrich and Ted Kennedy agreed on anything? Well, they agreed on drug courts, the efficacy of treatment. I can name people like Bill Bennett who has never been accused of being a liberal, who strongly supports treatment and drug courts. And I can go on and on mentioning some good, strong conservatives who support treatment and who understand recovery. Many of those people have siblings or spouses or children who have been impacted by alcohol and/or other drugs. There's nothing like seeing this disease up close and personal.

G. It's funny the issue doesn't gain more traction than it does because it makes a lot of dollars and cents, too, doesn't it?

J. For every dollar we spend on treatment in this country, we save over twelve and a half dollars. For every dollar we spend on drug courts, instead of sending people to the criminal justice system, we save over fifteen dollars. So, there's no question that treatment is cost effective. If you can get people on the road to recovery, you're going to save a lot of bucks for the taxpayer.

G. Looking ahead, do you have a vision for what the recovery movement can be in this country, or what recovering people can do to advance policy to help people overcome addiction?

J. At major league baseball parks around the nation, I want to see whole stadiums full of faces and voices of recovery. I want to see the people lined up in the state legislatures across America and in the Congress of the United States to get into those hearing rooms to support recovery issues. I want to see more people go public with their own addiction. I'm not talking about violating any traditions of any organization; I'm talking about telling their own stories and sharing with others so that others can have hope and have the opportunity to enjoy the blessings of recovery.

G. Do you think filling baseball stadiums and filling up the halls of Congress and state legislatures can change the misperceptions and stigma of addiction?

J. Absolutely. I've seen it. I think people like Patrick Kennedy, who was called by the *New York Times*, the face of recovery in the Congress, have made a big, big difference. Various athletes, various high profile people who have the courage and the faith to tell their stories of recovery have made a difference. There's no question about it. I see that locally. I see that on a statewide basis here in Minnesota. And, I've seen that across the nation.

G. Great. Thank you so much.

J. Thank you.

G. I mean, thank you for putting your influential face and voice out there.

J. Oh, thank you. You're a good interviewer. You don't even work from notes.

PHIL VALENTINE

"A man does not light his lamp and put it under a bushel."

Phil Valentine doesn't look the least bit tired, though he should. Being married, the father of five, and coach of a travel soccer team require no small amount of attention, but he is also the Executive Director of Connecticut Community for Addiction Recovery (CCAR), which in itself is a twenty-four/seven job. Phil takes it all in stride and makes it look easy. With his warm smile and calm demeanor, you feel this internationally renowned leader of the recovery community has it all under control. He exudes an inner peace born of a strong spirituality. He says a higher power is the fundamental force that guides, empowers, and through his recovery, blesses him.

Obviously, it works for him. He found recovery in 1987 and found CCAR in 1999 when it was just getting started and focusing on advocacy. In 2000, he was instrumental in initiating the surprisingly successful "Recovery Walks!" event in Hartford, Connecticut, believed to be the first public march of the new recovery advocacy movement supporting recovery from alcohol and other drug addiction. When CCAR began developing peer-led services for people in recovery, Phil designed and facilitated several innovative programs that gained recognition near and far. With the opening of the first Recovery Community Center in 2004, in Willimantic, Connecticut, and subsequent ones in Hartford and Bridgeport, CCAR programs and services exploded, as the recovery community responded in hungry need for more. First, there were the boldly public centers themselves with the visible signage out front that identified the centers and welcomed people. This explicitness was revolutionary. Inside, creative solutions arose and resources grew to meet growing need: Employment Services; Recovery Housing Project; Recovery Coach Academy; Telephone Recovery Support; All-Recovery Groups; and many others. All were innovations that transformed CCAR from a purely advocacy organization into a vital, peer-led services organization. Its success in providing recovery support services and promoting the reality of recovery has become the engine that drives and validates the organization's advocacy.

We met Phil at CCAR's Hartford Recovery Community Center, which occupies all three floors of a handsome old Victorian house in a respectable neighborhood not far from the downtown business district. Its white-cream exterior, trimmed with the slate-blue and cranberry colors typical of New England, presents a homey welcome, and except for the sign out front telling you this is a recovery center, you might assume a wonderful family lives there. Truth is, a wonderful family works there.

This was my first encounter with any such group of recovering community people. I'm not exactly sure what I expected, but I did assume I was in for a serious, rather glum experience. I mean, weren't people in recovery sort of, I don't know, sick, or in crisis, or at best, struggling to make it? I wasn't particularly looking forward to meeting depressed people. I was prepared to be quiet and respectful and reassuring when I met "these people." I certainly was not prepared for what we encountered the instant we set foot inside the Center and began meeting staff, volunteers, and clients: We were greeted with warmth, good cheer, optimism, and positive purpose. These qualities beamed from everyone's face and could be heard in everyone's voice. It was a place infectious with friendliness. I realized my preconceptions were misconceptions. Rather than wading into a heavy, gloomy atmosphere, those rooms were light and airy and full of busy people. The air, I sensed, was filled with hope.

Then we met Phil Valentine's smile.

GREG. How did it happen that as a person in recovery you began working in this field?

PHIL. I was sitting around at home in 1998 and I was a stay-at-home dad. At that time, Joshua was about four and Sammy was about two, and frankly things weren't real smooth with the marriage. I was at home and Sandy was working and we wanted the roles to be reversed. So, I started to look for a job and I came across Bob Savage, who was looking to hire someone as an associate director for CCAR. He told me what the recovery movement was all about, which in those early stages was focused on putting a face on recovery. At first, with about twelve years of recovery, I had some difficulty with the idea that I could be open and public about it. I had grown up in a twelve-step program where it was really hammered into you about anonymity, and that you are anonymous at the level of press, radio, and film. I had to wrestle with that. Then, I was reading in the New Testament in Matthew about "a city on a hill can not be hidden. A man does not light his lamp and put it under a bushel." No, he puts it on a stand for everyone to see. That rang true for me because I believed God worked a miracle in my life. He lit the light of recovery in me, so who was I to hide it under a bushel or in a church basement, if you know what I mean. So I was hired at CCAR and things just unfolded.

G. Do you remember the first time you said in a public venue that you're Phil Valentine, a person in long-term recovery?

P. I do. I was saying in twelve-step meetings that I'm an alcoholic or an addict. The difference with this movement is that you say you are a "person in recovery." I remember SAMHSA came to Hartford to do something about national planning, and they asked me to be on this panel in the legislative office building. There were all these people with initials after their names—doctors, attorneys, researchers—and they asked me to say something. I said, "My name is Phil Valentine and, but for the grace of God, I have not had a drink or a drug since December 28, 1987. I am a person in long-term recovery." And, when I said that, it just got quiet and everyone was looking up, looking at me and I was like, "Uh-oh." It's the whole idea that when you declare you are a person in recovery, people take notice. People listen.

G. Were your initial fears about public disclosure ever realized?

P. Not at all. The more I tell my story, the more comfortable I am with it, and I've never received any backlash here in the United States. We have a lot of freedom to tell our story and people are accepting and welcoming and, in some ways, even honor it. Not that I tell my story to be honored, but people understand the struggle, the story of the underdog, and that when you're down and out, we have a country where we can really turn our lives around and make something of them.

There are a lot of gray areas, but for me, it's been clear that my program of recovery is not just for the rooms. My program of recovery transcends everything I do, everyday. However, when I go to a twelve-step recovery meeting, people don't know what I do for a living. I like to sit, absorb, contribute, so in that sense, twelve-step meetings are a refuge for me. I don't bring CCAR or the recovery advocacy movement into twelve-step rooms. I don't think that's appropriate. I don't think that's what it's about. My work is my work. I'm very lucky that my work is my purpose and my purpose is my work, so I'm one of the few blessed people who have a good understanding of what my call is. I think that's what God wants me to do, and I'm able to do that everyday.

G. Tell me about the beginnings of CCAR. What was the mission?

P. When we started CCAR, the first thing we wanted to do was to put a face on recovery. We did that in everything we planned. We were speaking, offering ourselves as living proof that recovery is real. Those are the words of Bill White. He believed that a vanguard of people in recovery is needed to lead this movement, and I felt called to that vanguard wherever that may lead. Twelve years ago there was so much about addiction—this is your brain on drugs, the classic fried egg on the frying pan. We wanted to promote recovery. If the public saw people recovered, they'd be more likely to support all those programs that help people get into recovery. Our whole foundation was laid on the idea of putting a face on recovery and that's still very much a part of our roots today. You'll see people here who are always willing to tell their story of recovery because they know they are helping other people; they are offering hope. And there's no greater purpose in life than to offer hope to other individuals. Recovery has a lot of promise, and people believe in promise.

G. **You then transitioned from what you might call the public relations side of recovery advocacy to providing actual services. How did that come about?**

P. You can only speak at so many places, sit in so many meetings, or be on councils or boards and bring that recovery perspective. I came to believe that people are wired a couple different ways: People who were willing to put their face on recovery; and people who wanted to work behind the scenes, just helping people maintain and sustain their recovery. So out of that notion, we started to design services that would help people stay in recovery. It blossomed when we opened our first Recovery Community Center in Willimantic in 2004. It was kind of like *Field of Dreams*, you know, "build it and they will come." When you look at our foot tracks today in our three centers, you will find that they average 15,000 visits a year. People are coming.

G. **I have heard you define that thing you built as a "bridge" between treatment and recovery. It seems so obvious now, but how did that notion of connecting treatment with recovery, and vice versa, first develop?**

P. Early on, probably 1999, I had to present at a CSAT [Center for Substance Abuse Treatment] conference, and they wanted to know what we were doing in this whole advocacy world and how the recovery community was interacting with treatment. Bill White was in the audience, and I didn't know who Bill was. I was very nervous, very nervous with all the suits, and everything. We got into a discussion about recovery support services being one of the bridges between the two worlds. I said something along the lines that recovery support services are best provided by people in recovery who have that lived experience. And some researcher type asked me if I had any evidence to prove that and without batting an eye I just said, "No. Not a shred." And Bill White started to crack up because he thought, *Wow that was a good answer.* One of the most refreshing things about people in recovery is that they tell the truth. It's an honest program.

I found out there was this vast treatment system I knew very little about and I saw how CCAR was the natural bridge for this. We had people from both sides working with each other, and so we wanted to bring the recovery perspective into treatment, and we wanted the treatment world to bring their knowledge and expertise into the recovery community. We could all form like one circle together because we're all in this together; we're all about getting people well.

What we tried to work toward all these years is building evidence. I think at CCAR, we have a lot of evidence that shows recovery support services are viable, they're less expensive than treatment services, and they really help people sustain a healthy lifestyle. When you do that people don't end up back in those expensive treatment services. In recovery, we move out of crisis; we move into a useful way of living.

G. Did you find that to provide the support services needed for recovery you had to remove the barriers to recovery that people struggle with?

P. You know, I don't even look at removing barriers; I look at finding solutions. It's really this idea that if you are a stream, or in biblical terms "living water," and there's a barrier, you flow around it. You start to get clean and sober and into recovery. And what do you need to maintain? You need social support, other people doing what you're doing, and you need a safe place to live, and you need employment of some kind. So, we help people do all of that. I think if you get people healthy and productive, everyone benefits. It's not rocket science, but it's very powerful.

G. One of the ideas of bringing people in recovery together was the Recovery Walks! event. What is it like now to see how that activity has

grown over the years from the seeds that CCAR planted with their first walk?

P. Right, and it's called Recovery Walks with an "s"! Back in 2000, we wanted to put a face on recovery, and if we could bring fifty people together to walk in our capitol city of Hartford, we thought that would be great. Nobody had ever done anything like that—an annual walk for recovery from alcohol and other drug addiction. That first year, more than 700 people showed up, so we had hit upon something. Now, we do that every year and have thousands of people in recovery walking on Bushnell Park and offering themselves as living proof that they are in recovery or they support recovery. And it's grown from there to walks all over the country. Who would have thought? When you put all these events going on in the same day, it's just extraordinary. There are tens of thousands of people participating, so what it really says is that this is a movement. We think it's a wonderful concept; I call it a large-scale intervention of hope.

G. You frequently talk about being a cancer survivor and how the health system saved your life. Can you draw any comparisons with the way you were received by the health system and its support systems versus the way people struggling with addiction are received by our systems?

P. When I was first diagnosed with Stage 4 cancer, I was immediately referred to specialists who treated me with kindness, concern, and incredible expertise. They laid out my options and gave me some choice in the matter. If I had presented with a heroin addiction, I don't think that would have happened. I don't think I would have been referred to two or three doctors specializing in heroin addiction. I don't think I would have been treated with a lot of expertise. That's a huge difference. And I think the factor is the stigma. It's the discrimination.

It's understandable. They see a lot of people who are addicted, a lot of people who are high or drunk, and who cause a lot of damage. That's a frightening kind of dynamic to deal with, especially for a healthcare professional. Their first reaction is "Why? How did you get yourself to this point? Why are you like this?" Instead of compassion, we're treated with scorn.

G. How do you define recovery?

P. People all over the world are struggling with what the definition of recovery is. I think it's God's way of smiling upon us and saying, "You can't define me; you can't really define recovery, either." We came across a definition of recovery that's not really a definition, but it helps us. It's more of a philosophy. You are in recovery if you say you are. When people walk into our center, you're in recovery, if you say you are. And that really hinges on the concept behind twelve-step programs. AA says all that's required for membership is a "desire to stop drinking." It doesn't say you have to be stopped, doesn't say anything else. All you need is a desire. Greg, how could I ever say you have a desire? That's up to you. And however you want to work on it, we're going to encourage that. We might have strong suggestions for you; if you decided that alcohol was your primary problem and went on the marijuana maintenance program, we might ask you, how's that working for you and make some suggestions. But really, that's kind of up to you. Everyone has to find their own pathway to recovery.

G. Thanks, Phil.

It is hard to pinpoint when the new recovery advocacy movement actually began. As we learned from the remembrances of some of the early advocates, the efforts to organize the recovery community have been constant nationally, yet sporadic locally, over many decades. National leaders inspired; local leaders perspired. Eventually, together, they built a movement. Just like politics, ultimately all recovery is local, and that is where many of the tangible milestones of the recovery movement surfaced.

In Colorado Springs, one significant outcropping was White Bison, founded by Don Coyhis, of the Mohican Nation. White Bison was an early grassroots organization formed to bring addiction prevention, sobriety, recovery, and wellness to Native American communities throughout the country. The Wellbriety Movement it generated is a model for bridging individual sobriety to a larger commitment of community healing and has contributed widely to the knowledge and teachings of recovery at all levels. If Greg had one regret in the making *The Anonymous People*, it was not having the resources, the time, nor the opportunity to interview more leaders among the many pathways to recovery. High on his wish list was Don Coyhis, whose natural philosophy of healing centers on the interconnectedness of individual, family, and community, offers essential insights for the larger recovery movement. The White Bison vision is referenced in the film, but Greg would have loved to give it a more prominent place in the story. White Bison is well worth further exploration by anyone seeking alternative pathways to recovery.

Budget issues, production logistics, and time all weighed against pursuing many such inspiring stories around the country. Thus, we were fortunate that our home state of Connecticut has strong roots in the development of addiction treatment and recovery and we have ready access to the history, the individuals, and the organizations that have influenced the growth of the recovery movement. Marty Mann rehabbed and found recovery support in Connecticut. In fact, Mann's twelve-step home group is still active and, by coincidence, Greg attended it for a time. The vital lineage of CCAR, now an international model for recovery community organizations, is represented in the film by its founder Bob Savage, its standard bearer Phil Valentine, and through to its field people like Michael Askew. These and many more local and personal connections surely helped Greg make his film and enrich it.

Shortly after we filmed the CCAR story, a truly miraculous event occurred. On June 16, 2012, a male white bison was born on a dairy farm in Goshen, Connecticut. Such a birth is thought to be as rare as one in ten million. The event received worldwide coverage in the press, and a month later several tribes from Native American nations sent representatives to perform a naming ceremony. The white bison calf was named Yellow Medicine Dancing Boy. A rather healing name, isn't it. We saw great meaning in this event; we have come to believe that the appearance of this spiritually significant white bison in Connecticut is a sign of connection between all recovering peoples. It is a unity symbol that brings together the vision of Don Coyhis's White Bison group, CCAR's mission, and the efforts of individuals and organizations everywhere in the recovery movement. Connecticut's white bison can be seen as a revelation and a reminder that recovery is real.

With the perspective of history and our first-hand looks at recovery in action today, we were gaining an appreciation of the miracles and power of recovery. We heard about the architects of advocacy who, over time, built the movement that continues to help make recovery real for millions today. We witnessed for ourselves what happens when people take a bold step into the light and undergo a transformative experience that leaves the darkness of addiction behind. That recovery works is cause for celebration and pride. But it is not easy to take that first step into the purifying light of truth and openly share success—not when the weight and fear of shame hold you back. Then we met some extraordinary people who told us how they did it.

Chapter Four

SHAME TO PRIDE

Many of the heroes of the recovery movement spent their active addiction days in unimaginable darkness, and yet somehow found their way into the light. What were the factors that led them out of the dark? What has been the media's role in perpetuating the stigma of addiction and recovery, and what should the media's role be? How have some of the victims of media sensationalism dealt with the issue? Why are successful recovery stories ultimately more important than the lurid addiction stories we are most used to seeing? What is the stigma issue all about? Why are people in recovery so ashamed of "coming out"? What's holding the recovery movement back? And what happens when people do go public with their recovery stories?

These were just some of the questions that continued to crowd my thoughts as we rolled across the country gathering story after story. Every individual we met had a little bit different take on the experience of addiction and recovery, and it was hard to find an overall answer to these questions that would deepen my understanding of the issues and help me become sincerely sympathetic with the advocacy movement—and as enthusiastic as Greg.

One insight was helpful. If you take anonymity out of the equation, everything seems less complicated. We were privileged to meet several people for whom anonymity was hardly even a question. To one degree or another, they were celebrities, or at the least, public figures. Anonymity? As they tell it, that was never an option. Living in the spotlight flushes out any semblance of secrecy for these good people. When they accepted their individual public disclosures, their lives changed. It is instructive to hear their stories and what it means when "*everybody* knows."

TARA CONNER

"While I was in rehab they were running news stories that I was in a bar standing on a table drunk, swirling my crown around my finger. And I'm like, 'That's impossible because I'm in treatment.'"

You think you know Tara Conner's story. But you don't. It is likely that all you know about this former Miss USA is what you have seen on television or in the tabloids. But I can tell you this: the Tara Conner media creation is *not* the same as the beautiful and real young woman we had the privilege of meeting. When you hear her complete story, when you get to know her even a little bit, you come to appreciate one of the main ideas Greg was trying to get across in his film: Popular media sensationalizes the addiction story, in lurid exploitation of suffering people's deepest health crises, and fails to tell the inspiring stories of recovery that as John Shinholser says, are even more sensational—stories that if widely told would uplift us all.

But the headlines scream at us about downfallen celebrities, almost as if the press were trying to sell us *schadenfreude*, by gleefully stroking the shame finger at human beings in distress. Shame on the media for foisting this trash upon us. Shame on us for buying into this crap. It is disgusting. The problem is even when we recognize the media is sensationalizing a story and not telling the whole truth, we consume it. Like sugar. We eat it up even when we know it is not good for us because it is tempting, goes down easy, and is everywhere. But it is poison, and it affects us in insidious ways. A constant diet of sugar builds up to contribute to obesity and diabetes, to feed cancer, or to cause any number of physical ailments. Media trash about addiction is the same. We absorb daily doses of it, and it poisons our perceptions until it grows into a serious case of stigma—an unnatural condition of prejudice and discrimination toward people who genuinely suffer from a disease and who need empathy and help, not scorn or derision or shame.

Unfortunately, Tara Conner has been through this media mill. The story you know is the one ground out by the national press: The beauty queen diva, druggie, and disgrace, absolved in a teary public spectacle of a press conference led by Donald Trump, only to be calumniated further because of the drama of that event.

Given all that she had been through, we didn't quite know what to expect when we met her for our interview. Would she be understandably defensive, hidden, or equivocal as she faced yet another media inquisition? We had nothing to worry about. When Tara walked into the conference room provided to us by the Caron Treatment Centers on that chilly, rainy spring day in New York City, she brought her own sunbeams. They seemed to follow her about the room, like a key light illuminating the shine in her hair and the sparkle in her eyes. Upon seeing her, Craig whispered to me, "I don't think we have very much lighting to do here." She already had the sweet light of truth and serenity.

Tara was poised and confident, betraying only the tiniest tinge of wariness—or was it weariness—as Greg began their conversation with the obligatory questions about "her fall from grace." This was something Greg was clearly uncomfortable doing because that part was not the focus of the film. Yet it was important to understand the shame and stigma Tara faced in her very public ordeal, so that we might better understand how misperceptions about addiction and ignorance of recovery are perpetuated in our culture. Her behind-the-scenes story about being in the spotlight during her darkest days sheds light on how the media actually keeps us all in the dark about these important issues. Awkward as it may have felt rehashing the subject, Tara recognized its relevance, and God bless her, she immediately took charge and put us all at ease, disarming us with her openness and light, good humor.

GREG. Would you mind telling me a little bit about your personal journey to recovery?

TARA. My journey to recovery basically started in 2006 while I was Miss USA. A lot of people didn't know that I had been using since I was fourteen years old. And I tested positive for cocaine during my reign, and it kind of became this huge media mess. All of a sudden, the world was pointing a finger at me and it made me actually look at myself. I had the opportunity to go to a care and treatment facility while I was still Miss USA, and I started my journey there.

G. What was it like to experience the Miss USA competition under the influence and then have this all come out after you won?

T. Well, the pageant usually lasts for about three weeks before the finals. I was basically sequestered in Baltimore, Maryland, and it was just me and the drugs I had on me. And there were some other girls who also had some different pills and stuff on them. The night I won I took a Xanax probably five hours before the competition, and I took a little bit of a nap. I woke up and during the competition I basically wasn't feeling any pain and I was just going with it. When I won, it was such a shock; but, at the same time, I wasn't present for the moment. And, if I said I had a regret, I would say that it was not being able to experience it to the utmost, the fullest, because I just wasn't there. I was just going through the motions.

When you win Miss USA, you move to New York for the year. All of a sudden, I'm whisked away to New York City and I don't know what a cross street is. I had never had Starbucks before. Donald Trump is my boss. It was crazy. My disease had progressed to doing cocaine; that was my go-to drug there because I wasn't able to access the other drugs I was doing while I was in Kentucky. I was all alone and it was the first time that I was sitting by myself. All I had to do was manipulate these people. I didn't realize I was trying to protect my disease. I didn't know I had a disease. I didn't have the capacity to be honest with anyone. I was going through depression, and life was getting really hard for me. I was just trying to check out. But I wasn't really aware that I was trying to check out. I used so that I didn't have to be in that moment because I just didn't have the tools to be a Miss USA. I think, finally, it got the best of me. I got tired and run down and it just caught up. Then, one day, I got drug-tested and I was like, "Oh, here we go."

G. **You failed this drug test and the media is coming down on you left and right. That must have been a difficult moment for you. There you were, all that you had hidden up to that point in your life was suddenly exposed. And not just to a few, but to the world. What was that like for you?**

T. The day before I took the drug test I actually had this weird moment. Some people call it a psychosis, but I call it the "Big Guy" or "God." I always had this sketchy relationship with God. I felt very unlovable, like, "He's not into me; I'm damaged." But I had this moment where I was told, "There's a thunderstorm coming through and you're going to be drug tested tomorrow, but if you flush away everything you have and don't touch it again, I promise I'll carry you through this." That night was December 10, 2006.

And then the next day, December 11, they didn't tell me I was getting tested when I went in, but I just had this feeling that it was going to happen. And, I actually did get drug tested and I knew I was going to fail. For me, that was proof so I flushed what I had and I didn't use again after that.

I had never been honest with anyone about what I did, even my closest friends at the time. But I was like, "I'll be damned if my boss knows that I'm using before my mom knows," because she's the closest person to me. So I called my mom, and it was the first time I was honest with her, and I said, "Mom, I'm getting drug tested, and I'm about 99 percent sure

I'm going to fail." She asked me what I was going to fail for and I was like, "Well, a lot!" She rightfully could've said, "How dare you? I've tried to protect you for so long," but instead she came at me with love and told me, "Well, whatever happens, I love you and I'm going to be here for you, and if you need help with anything, just let me know." She gave me love. And it made me feel okay with being honest about what was going on.

The next morning when I was driving into the city, I turn on the radio and, "Miss USA fails a drug test for cocaine. Will she lose her title? Blah, blah, blah, blah, blah." And by that night it was on *SportsCenter*, of all things. I was on every media outlet. I'd never been followed by the paparazzi before, and now people were stalking my apartment building. It was insane, like, "Everyone is watching me right now." I was mortified because the thing that bothered me the most was that they started pointing a finger at where I grew up and at my family. They started going into my small town of 2,300 people, knocking on my grandmother's door and offering her poinsettias. It was Christmastime and she said, "Aren't these people sweet? They're giving me poinsettias." And I said, "Granny, don't talk to these people. They're jerks." They were taking pictures of the home I grew up in, which looked a little beat at the time because they were doing construction on it. They made me and my family sound so redneck and just pitiful. I think my family being dragged into it was probably the hardest thing for me because this was my battle, not theirs. I'd already done enough to embarrass them.

I was friends with a lot of the people who were running stories against me and they would call me and say, "Tara, I've got to write a story. Is there anything you don't want me to say?" I do appreciate some people trying to protect me when they did, but at the same time others were nasty. They were so mean to me. They were saying I was promiscuous because I had dated a couple of people who had a name. I didn't throw up in bars and I didn't make a mockery of myself, but they started making me sound like I did. While I was in rehab, they were running news stories about how I was in a bar drunk and standing on a table, swirling my crown around my finger. And I'm like, "That's impossible because I'm in treatment!" They were dragging all these innocent people into it and airing their dirty skeletons. It was so unfair. It was mortifying.

G. **Obviously the press conference with Donald Trump couldn't have been more public. What was that like?**

T. Before the actual press conference I went to hide out in Columbus, Ohio, where my mom lives. I had to lay low because there were so many people in the city trying to find me, and it wasn't safe for me to be there. Donald Trump called me a couple of times and said, "You're going out and you're kissing girls, and you're on cocaine. What am I supposed to do with this? I'm so disappointed." He's reaming me, and I couldn't really say anything other than "I'm so sorry. I'm so sorry. I don't even know what to say." And then my boss calls me five minutes later, "We're going to have a press conference in New York. We need you to fly in."

It was on my twenty-first birthday. I flew back to New York that night and I didn't know what was going to happen. For some reason, I just had this odd sense of peace, probably because I had been honest for the first time in twenty years. I knew that if I didn't keep the title that I would end up being okay. And I knew that at the end of the day the people who really cared about me were behind me, and they were going to support me in whatever happened. I thoroughly expected to lose the title because they told me to pack my bags. The day before the press conference I didn't sleep at all. That morning we got into the car and the president of the organization had my resignation papers in her hand. They were so ready to get rid of me. And I don't blame them because I was such a little hellion; I was so hard to deal with.

We go to Trump Tower, and I take the elevator up to Trump's office and he sits me down and says, "What am I supposed to do with this?" And I think I had just a little bit of manipulation left in my tool belt and I said, "Well, sir. I think it would say far more about the organization and far more about your character if you gave me the opportunity to turn this around." And he says, "You're right." And it could've been his idea all along. He may have known from the beginning that he was going to let me stay. My boss at the time was basically trying to convince him asking, "Sir. Are you really sure? She's crazy." But I had a feeling I was going to keep it. I thought, *This is bizarre.*

He didn't say anything to me before I went down to meet the press. It was just a sea of people. I remember walking in and covering my face and I felt like I was on trial where I was getting ready to be bludgeoned to death with stones or something. It was crazy. I felt like a witch at the Salem witch trials who they were going to hang up. So, we go down and he says in his infamous way, "Terra," (it's Tara, which he pronounces correctly now), "Terra is a good girl. Terra will be given a second chance." And it was fascinating to me because even as he was telling everyone, "Obviously, she has a drinking issue and she needs to go to rehab," I stood up and I said, "Well, I don't think I need to go to rehab. I think that's pushing the envelope a little bit," still trying to save face. I didn't even know that I said that, until I looked back at it four years later. I was like, "Did I really say that? Holy crap." Obviously, I'm crying because I'm mortified.

G. **There's this fascination with people's downfalls in our culture, and with your story, the emphasis was on the crisis, the sensational. Was there anyone in the media who treated your story as a health issue or even sympathetically?**

T. If there is a media outlet out there that treated it as a health issue, I didn't see it. No one had compassion. They weren't saying, "Oh, my gosh. This poor girl. Something's going on with her. My heart goes out to her." I wish I had heard that, but I didn't. I don't want to say that no one said it because I don't know. The only ones who I saw and heard were saying, "She's a disgrace." And they still call me that. "Disgraced Miss USA." Five years later. Five sober years later. If you Google my name and read the headlines, I almost committed suicide. I was suicidal. I used coke. I was a cutter. I was raped. I was this. I was that. There were no headlines of

"Tara Conner Celebrates Five Years of Sobriety Today." You know what I mean? Rarely do I see that. It is getting a little bit better now. But at that time, it was all about "Secret Late Night Outings" and "Hooking Up with Miss Teen USA." And blah, blah, blah. It was just crazy. They made me out to be such a little crazy nugget.

G. People forget how young you really were when all this happened. You probably had the most memorable twenty-first birthday of anybody I've ever heard. But, seriously, despite all your worldly experience, you really entered recovery at a young age. I'm fascinated with young people in recovery—how would you describe it for you? What's it like in your early twenties to be in recovery?

T. Actually, I was really proud of myself for not drinking on my twenty-first birthday because I wasn't in treatment yet. I was in Columbus and I could've done whatever I wanted to and I didn't. I think I was done. I did enough damage in the six years that I used. I wasn't freaking out; I was kind of peaceful. My mom was so afraid that I was going to kill myself because I was so much at peace. She kept asking, "Are you okay?" I would reply, "Yeah, I'm fine." I had reached a point where all of my skeletons were out of the closet. "Take me as I am. Take me or leave me. This is it. I can only go up from here." I didn't have to try to prove myself anymore. There was such a freedom that came with that realization.

I see a lot of young people come in and get sober, and it is tough because they say, "But I'm so young. What about when I get married? I'm not going to be able to toast on my wedding." Only an alcoholic thinks that way, by the way. Or they're like, "Maybe I'm just young and stupid." To which I reply, "Are you? Are you really young and stupid? Do you think it's normal to pop thirty pills a day?" Probably not. "You've been arrested how many times? And you're what, twelve?"

I love being sober young. People meet me and often they say, "There's no way you're twenty-six years old." I can sit down with anyone and have a decent conversation about life because I have so many life skills that take so many people so long to learn. I have recovery so early, it makes me appreciate success even more. It makes me appreciate failure. It makes me appreciate hard times, good times. I wouldn't trade it for the world. For me, trading my peace of mind for a drink, for one fun night, it's not worth it. It's just not worth it. I don't ever want to go back to the way I felt when I was using.

G. Part of this film is going to compare how other health issues in the US are treated—in the media, in terms of stigma, insurance, etc. Do you see a difference in the way famous people are treated in the media when they go public with a different condition or struggle?

T. It depends on what type of celebrity you are. It really depends on which media outlet thinks you're good and which one doesn't.

I do feel that people who publicly come out with stage 4 cancer or some type of illness, generally are treated with compassion. For people struggling with addiction, it's getting a little bit better. Not much. I hate to make that comparison, but at the end of the day, addiction is deadly, too. It's so similar and people don't know that. If I pick up again, I don't know that I'll make it back to recovery. I don't know that I would survive. Because my disease is still progressing even though I'm not using, and the amount that it would take for me to get high will kill my body. It is absolutely deadly. I'm going to have this for the rest of my life and I'm going to have to work on this for the rest of my life. I'm not saying, "Please feel for me," but at the same time, don't judge me. Do you know this is an epidemic? Do you know this is happening in your own home? Do you know you could be me and not even know it? It's sad.

G. As you've progressed in your recovery, you've taken on this role of becoming a public advocate for recovery. Considering your celebrity status, that's pretty unique. There are not many people like you doing it. Why did you commit to putting yourself out there so

publicly as a person in recovery? Especially with the tenacious media we talked about.

T. I feel like I didn't have a choice, right from the beginning. Not many people go to treatment and then have to do a media tour about their treatment stay—a day after! I had a therapist from Caron who told me, "I didn't think you were going to make it." She said, "Not because I thought that you were unfixable, but you were basically sent out to the vultures and you had to put yourself out there. Not many people could've handled that." I found that it held me accountable for my first six months. Because when you think everyone's watching, it is helpful. For some people, it may have been too much, but for me it kept me in my place.

G. **You did a show for A&E with a big personal profile and interview with you. Tell us about that experience. How they treated your story, and how you felt about the whole show they produced.**

T. It was called "Fame and Recovery." And they shot my story for two full days and they had so much footage. And then when I watched it, I was so disgusted. I seemed like this pitiful little mess. I think for the last shot they have me putting my hands over my face and crying my eyes out. I couldn't believe it. They didn't show anything about my recovery.

The media doesn't care what it's like now, and I hate that. They don't care about the advocacy work you're doing. They don't care if you're helping save lives. You're going out and you're trying to help people and tell your story and to be vulnerable and real, and then, all they focused on was "I did thirty pills a day." I was taken aback by that. I kept watching the show, waiting for them to say something positive. Just say something positive. And it was just so pitiful, "Oh, poor little addict."

After I did *Oprah*, I was like, "I'm never talking about my story again. I hate this. I feel miserable. I feel belittled." I felt like a walking stigma because they only focused on the stigma part. They didn't focus on the good part. So I said, "I don't want to give these interviews anymore unless it's for good, unless it benefits someone, or it's in a safe setting because I'm constantly giving myself to all of these people who are just tearing it apart after I do it."

Hey, we go on to be awesome people. We do cool stuff. We live. We live bigger than most people who are living it up. And you don't see that. It's just all the boo-hoo. Speak to me about my recovery. Let me tell you what that looks like. I don't want to talk about the bad stuff over and over and over again because you never get to see the blessings that come from being clean and sober for five years. Or the relationships you build. Or the level of maturity you gain. There is so much good that comes with recovery. I'm rejoicing in life right now.

G. That's great. So when you do tell your recovery story, how do people receive it?

T. When I have young girls walk up to me after I've spoken to their community or their school or their parents, they'll tell me, "Wow. I related to that so much it was scary." If I affect one person in a room every time I speak and it helps to change their life in some way, or if they identify with something that I say, or if they relate and they don't feel alone, then that's the biggest reward you can get.

So if my story—the good, bad, the ugly—affects someone to the level of seeking more awareness about this disease or just taking it home and opening up a better line of communication for them and their family, bring it on. I'll do that all day long.

G. It's not simple or easy for people to speak publicly about recovery. How did you overcome those impediments to public discourse? How did you navigate those issues of anonymity and stigma?

T. Well, my anonymity was broken immediately. So I never had the opportunity to have anonymity. And, for me, that's okay. I really do feel like we all have a path, and now I realize that if that's my purpose, while I'm here, to air my dirty laundry in the hope that it helps someone's life, then I'll take it.

As far as stigma, I've already been through the hard stuff—sharing my story openly and not reserving what I say at the risk of making me look like a fool. Sometimes I can get pretty graphic, and it gets a good reaction. But the more I talk about what once shamed me, the smaller it gets.

G. You're connected to a lot of other famous people in recovery. Is there a culture growing over the last few years, as you've been in recovery, of people with status in society talking publicly about their recovery? Do you see that?

T. I do. I'm not going to name names, but I do see more and more famous people coming out and talking about their story. And some of these people you would've never known they were an addict. I see them around in my little recovery groups and I'm like, "Oh, wow. I didn't know they were sober. That's great." And I see some of them appearing on news channels and speaking or you'll see a piece on them. I do hope people get to see more and more of these celebrities coming forward and understand their story and see what recovery looks like. You can be an A-lister, you can be a famous rapper, you can be a Miss USA, you can be a politician, or you can be a journalist. We're everywhere. I would love for that stigma to be broken a little more so that people know it's not just the old man under the bridge. It's not just the female in Hollywood who goes out every night and is completely wrecked. There are people in society who are very successful, and they still suffer every single day. They suffer.

G. How powerful would it be if the next Tara Conner doesn't have that image of the homeless guy with the brown bag? In other words, here's a normal person or a successful person, who is simply

perceived as having a health problem just like anyone else. How powerful would that be?

T. I couldn't identify, even one week into rehab that I was an addict because I didn't relate to what I thought addiction looked like. I looked different. I was successful. I didn't lose everything. I didn't lose anything. I gained. I won Miss USA. I'm walking red carpets. I have a driver. I have a stylist. I have everything that a little country girl from Kentucky could ever want in her entire life. It's on a silver platter; and I'm empty. Empty. Nothing's going on in there.

If I would've known what addiction looked like, I think I would've figured it out sooner. I think I may have known. I wish that a Tara Conner had come to my school and spoken to me, instead of showing me a sizzling egg on a frying pan and saying, "This is your brain. This is your brain on drugs." And I'm like, "Oh, that's cool." You know what I mean? That's not scary, really. I needed to hear my story. I wish I had heard my story. I would have related so much, you know?

G. Yes.

So many facets to Tara Conner and her story. But, one telling remark she made says a lot: "I just never, never knew there were people like me out there."

What if she *had* known? What if there had been visible and available people she could have turned to when she was fourteen, who could have told her she was not alone? What if there had been young peers of hers in recovery, who were public, and happy and active, in whom she could have found identification, support, and hope? What if her high school had had a recovery program? What if more people in recovery had been out there telling their stories?

Tara Conner's path may have been entirely different. That is why Tara is doing what she is doing today. She is totally out there. She is telling her story, the whole story, not some hyped up, salacious version of it. Now, she's an ambassador for recovery, mostly to young people, letting them know they are not alone. Showing people, who just don't know, that there are so many others like them, and like her, who have this disease and what it looks like. And she travels the country, on her own, speaking, meeting people, and offering real hope for recovery.

Here she is . . . Miss USA, Tara Conner. She is still in the spotlight, but now on a much bigger stage. Imagine if all the other twenty-three million individuals in long-term recovery in this country joined her under that spotlight. What a beauty pageant that would be.

LAURIE DHUE

"People in our society still think of addicts as home-less people living under bridges, who are wearing trench coats and clutching a paper bag full of whiskey, and that's just not who we are."

Laurie Dhue belongs on TV. She knows how to tell a story and present it with authority and grace. That is, no doubt, why this veteran broadcast journalist is the only person to have anchored and hosted news shows on three major cable networks. Laurie began her broadcasting career at CNN, becoming one of the youngest full-time anchors in the network's history. She then moved to MSNBC, hosted several shows and was a news anchor on NBC's *Weekend Today Show*. She followed that with eight years at Fox News Channel, where she hosted *The Fox Report Weekend Edition* and appeared weekly on *The O'Reilly Factor* and *Geraldo at Large*. She recently joined TheBlaze TV News to anchor their prime time news updates and will host *For the Record*, TheBlaze's original documentary series.

Laurie found recovery in 2007 and has become a committed and active advocate for recovery. She travels all over the country, speaking, moderating discussions, and emceeing recovery events. We can attest to that. During Recovery Month we attended several rallies and events and Laurie always seemed to be there, tirelessly working the crowds or offering support to some individual.

Somehow, among all these commitments, Laurie found time to sit down with us at Joe Schrank's Core Company in Williamsburg, Brooklyn, and tell her personal story. What a pro; she walked in "ready for prime time" and gave us more polished sound bites than we could ever possibly use. A few of her gems are in the film, but here's the rest. When Laurie speaks it all comes together. It was like turning on the TV, sitting back, listening, and learning.

GREG. **Millions of people saw you on television while you were suffering with your addiction, but they had no idea at the time what you were going through. Describe what life and work was like for you before recovery.**

LAURIE. For many of the years when I was anchoring my own shows on national television, I was in the deepest depths of my alcoholism, and yet, somehow I managed to go to work day in and day out. A lot of people ask me how I did it. Well, I'm a very determined person. I could go to work several mornings a week with the skull-crushing, stomach-turning hangover and somehow manage to get into the TV studio, read the teleprompter, interview people, and sound somewhat intelligent. Life is exhausting enough as a sober person, and I look back on that old behavior and truly do not know how I did it year after year after year. I drank for almost 6,000 days; I added it up. A lot of those days, unfortunately, were spent hungover at work. And, I didn't just have some desk job; I was an anchor on the national news, and so I had to look my best, I had to sound my best, and frankly, I was operating on about 50 percent capacity. In fact, there were days where I would lie in the fetal position on the floor of my office at Fox News Channel and think that I would rather be dead right now. When you're saying that to yourself, you know something's wrong. It's time to get help. Unfortunately, I literally thought I could not live without alcohol. I drank for a lot of reasons. I drank because it took me away from my pain. I drank to make myself more interesting to other people. I drank to make you more interesting to me. I drank to have fun, to escape, all the normal reasons people drink. That was me; I am just a garden variety drunk. I'd like to think of myself as special, but I'm really not. I'm just one of tens of millions of Americans who have this disease.

G. What was your experience like hiding your addiction from others?

L. We alcoholics are crafty. We hide things. We're good at keeping people out. And while I certainly didn't hide my drinking publicly, I hid the shame and the fear and the pain that my drinking caused. I mean, I was "good-time Laurie." You invite Laurie Dhue to a party, she's going to be the ring leader. She's going to be on the bar. She's going to be doing shots, and you're going to have a good time if she's at the party. But you know who wasn't feeling good the day after the party? Laurie Dhue. Sometimes it would take me two or three days to recover from a drinking binge. I'll say this about drinking: Drinking made me a lot of promises. It told me a lot of lies. A drinking world is not a happy world. It's not particularly glamorous. It's not even that fun. If you've been to one party, you've been to them all. I don't care if I never go to another party as long as I live. It's incredibly isolating, and on the outside, it seems like you are being very social. You're out and about, you're drinking, you're having fellowship with your friends, but really, for me, I was becoming more and more isolated. It's a common thing among alcoholics, we have tons of people around us, but we're really alone. It goes to the point where you enjoy a couple of drinks a week, socially, to suddenly, you're going out every weekend and you're getting drunk, to I'm going to have a quick pop before I go out, to I need to have three vodkas before I go to dinner, and I'm going to have at least a bottle or two of wine and I'm going to have after-dinner drinks, then I'm going to go to an after-drinks club, and if I get home at 3:00 or 4:00 in the morning, it's no big deal. I'll get four or five hours of sleep, and then I'll go back to work. So, it goes from being a fun thing to being something you are dependent on.

I definitely became dependent on it. I know that for a fact because when I quit drinking and detoxed, those first two weeks were living hell. I couldn't sleep, I couldn't eat, I had night sweats, and I could barely function at work. It was the hardest period of my life, but I knew if I made it through the first thirty days, I could do anything. And now, I think about all those things that I accomplished when I was a TV anchor, and all those things pale in comparison to getting sober.

G. Then, all of a sudden, everybody knew. How did it happen that your addiction and recovery story became public?

L. It was not my intention to go public exactly how or when I did, but that decision was made for me. I was giving what I thought was a private speech at a private dinner in Washington, and I was talking off the record about my journey through alcoholism and sobriety and the role of faith in my recovery program. Unbeknownst to me, there was a reporter in the audience. Without consulting me first, she broke the story that Laurie Dhue, Fox News anchor, is a recovering alcoholic. Early the next morning I was at President Obama's prayer breakfast and I was so happy to be there. I'm walking in and my blackberry goes crazy. It's all kinds of texts from my friends: "OMG. You're all over the Internet." "Oh my gosh, Laurie, your story is out. What are you going to do?" "Does your agent know? Does your family know?" Et cetera, et cetera. I thought, *It's over; I'll never work again. I'll be a complete pariah. What TV station is going to want to hire me?* But, my agent said, "You know what, Laurie? I think this could be a very good thing for you." I realized that he was right.

G. Why?

L. Because having my recovery status disclosed that night turned out to be one of the best things that ever happened to me. Once the word got out that I was a recovering alcoholic, it took my recovery to a different level. Rather than feeling any shame about it or any embarrassment, I felt good about it. I felt like it was a real opportunity to share my experience, strength, and hope with people who may be watching or listening to me and thinking, *Oh, my gosh, I'm just like her.*

It has given me the opportunity to speak freely and openly and publicly about this disease that affects between twenty and thirty million in this country, a disease that affects every single American family, a disease that is an epidemic in this country. So I actually have that reporter to thank for being where I am today.

G. What happened in the immediate aftermath of that story breaking?

L. A couple of days after the story broke on the Internet, the *Today Show* reached out to me on Facebook and asked if I would like to come in and tell my story. I said I would come on the *Today Show* on the condition that this is a message of hope I'm delivering. I'm not going to tell you how many drinks I had in one night. I'm not going to give you any salacious stories. I'm not going to gossip, but I am going to talk about how alcoholism doesn't discriminate. It doesn't care who you are, how much money you have, where you're from, what the color of your skin is, or what your religion is—it doesn't care. It's a deadly disease that can affect anybody, but there's hope. And while it's not curable, it is treatable, and I'm here to say that a program of recovery can work, but you're the one who has to make the decision. You're the one who has to put the hard work into it.

G. What was the *Today Show* experience like? Did they honor your conditions?

L. The *Today Show* producers agreed that would be my message. The whole staff was respectful. I went on with Meredith Viera, who was incredibly respectful and let me tell my story and talk about what my recovery had been like, and sharing the message of hope, and that you don't have to suffer alone. I said, "If you think you have a problem, or you want to talk to somebody who understands, anybody who wants to, can reach out to me on Facebook." Within an hour, my Facebook was flooded with messages. I had several hundred, and they kept coming to a point where I actually had to start a second Facebook page. I got so many messages of hope and encouragement. I got messages from people who said, "Thank you so much. I'm an addict too, but I've been afraid to talk about it"; or "Thank you, my mother's an alcoholic and I haven't been sure what to do, but you're giving me the hope to talk to her"; or "Thank you for sharing your story." And that was the whole point about going public, and that's why I continue to try to be an advocate for recovery.

G. **After the initial reports came out and you did the *Today Show* interview, what kinds of reactions did you get in the media? Were you welcomed with more opportunities to tell what you wanted to tell or did you face any negative reactions to your disclosure?**

L. The *Today Show* interview changed everything and opened a lot of doors for me, and I'm really grateful. It led to several other interviews with major media outlets, and rather than being a woman with a problem, I became a woman who had a solution she was willing to share. Reaction toward my going public has been extraordinarily positive. I've gotten very few negative emails or negative messages on Facebook. I've gotten a lot of encouragement from people who were and are in the TV industry. I hear a lot of "Thank you for being so brave."

My email inbox was flooded with various recovery organizations asking if I can help, would I like to be part of this discussion, or would I like to moderate this panel, or speak at a conference. I never would have had these opportunities had I not gone public with my addiction and my recovery.

But it's not about me publicizing myself; it's about me being one of tens of thousands of advocates for recovery out there. If I can help one person or ten people or a hundred people, just like you're helping them by doing this documentary, then great, I would have done my job as a recovering person because it's all about helping other people.

G. What do think are the biggest misperceptions people have about addiction?

L. People impacted by addiction are everywhere. We are your pizza delivery guy, your doctor, your mother, your minister, your uncle's wife, the President of the United States, your senator, and your next door neighbor. You, me, we're everywhere, and we all share one thing in common: this disease. One of the biggest misconceptions in our society is that people don't think of alcoholism as a disease. I think the stigma that still very much exists in our society comes from the fact that people really don't get addiction at its core. It's a dirty little secret; it's a dirty little word. I think so many people in our society still think of addicts as homeless people living under bridges, who are wearing trench coats and clutching a paper bag full of whiskey, and that's just not who we are.

G. From your lens as a journalist, where do you see addiction ranking alongside other health issues that have social movements attached to them?

L. I believe that addiction is the single biggest healthcare issue in this country. It's an epidemic; it's a crisis that we are not effectively dealing with, and that's because of a lack of education, a lack of information that's out there about addiction. If you think back, you can make a lot of parallels to the AIDS crisis and breast cancer. Think about this: Remember back in the early '80s and the movement to raise money for AIDS or for breast cancer? Nobody wanted to get near anybody who had AIDS. Nobody wanted to touch a person who had AIDS. Oh, it's a gay man's disease. They deserve it because they had anal sex with another man and that's dirty and that's wrong, so they deserve to be sick. Then, people like Princess Diana came forward and went to AIDS hospices and put her arms around people who had AIDS and said, "You're not going to go through this alone. We're going to raise money and we're going to learn more about this disease." Then came amfAR with Elizabeth Taylor and several AIDS scientists. Then, Magic Johnson came forward as a straight man and said, "I have HIV." And we know what has happened in the last thirty years—billions of dollars have been raised and millions of people have been saved.

It was the same thing with breast cancer. Nobody talked about it until Betty Ford, God rest her soul, came forward to not only talk about breast cancer, but also that she suffered from addiction. We owe so much to Betty Ford. There was a time when people didn't talk about breast cancer, and now you can't go anywhere without seeing a pink ribbon somewhere, or a Susan G. Komen breast cancer sign. October is breast cancer awareness month, but who knows that September is National Recovery month? Most people don't know that. It's all about cancer and AIDS and heart disease. That's not to take anything away from these movements, but if we could get to a point in this country where we're talking as openly about addiction as we do about AIDS and breast cancer and colon cancer and diabetes and heart disease, we will be so much better off.

Addiction costs this country hundreds of billions of dollars each year, when you talk about people who miss work because they're hungover, or they're incarcerated, or lost productivity, or hospitalization, or diabetes, heart disease, liver failure, and all the complications that come from drinking and drug use and other manifestations of addiction. If we could just begin to chip away at the stigma, to educate more people and get more information out there, and raise more money for prevention, then we would be a much healthier country than we are now.

G. What role or responsibility do the media play in our perception and understanding of addiction?

L. Media has a very interesting role here. A sexy story sells. So a story about Charlie Sheen going ape and being surrounded by his goddesses and saying he's drinking tiger blood, well, that's a story about addiction that sells. It's sexy. It's tragic. A lot of people made a lot of money off Charlie Sheen because of that. I think the media likes to focus on people who are known as train wrecks, rather than telling the stories of people who are making it through recovery and who are thriving, productive members of society. I think there's a real opportunity here for the media that's being missed. Cover addiction in the balanced way you would cover any other public healthcare crisis, like AIDS, like breast cancer, like diabetes.

I can't blame the media a 100 percent for bad coverage of addiction. Maybe some of it is that celebrities are reticent to talk about their recovery. You and I know plenty of famous people who are in recovery. We obviously can't talk about them because we want to protect their privacy. I wish that some of them would come forward and tell their stories because I think they would have the opportunity of helping thousands of people.

G. How about reality television? Shows like *Celebrity Rehab* and *Intervention* have all been popular, but are they delivering the right messages about addiction and recovery?

L. I'm a big fan of Dr. Drew and what he has done in terms of raising awareness of addiction. His show has been incredibly effective. I'm not the biggest fan of *Celebrity Rehab*. I think some of their issues are hyped up and I think, just like any other reality TV show, it doesn't necessarily show the truth of what's going on in recovery. It's kind of salacious. A lot of people talk about the show *Intervention* on A&E; love it or hate it, it's been very influential. In fact, while I was drinking one night alone in my apartment, I saw two back-to-back episodes of *Intervention,* and it got me thinking, *My God, I don't want an intervention to happen to me. I need help!* About two weeks after I saw those episodes of *Intervention,* I decided to get sober. So I'm actually grateful for that show.

G. Wow. You never know what's going to trigger the start of a journey.

L. To me, it was incredibly powerful. I remember crying in my bedroom, having a glass of wine on my bed stand table, knowing that I had to do something. I saw the show and I thought, *My God, is this what my life is going to come to?* I'm going to show up at a friend's apartment and there will be everyone in my life sitting on a couch saying, "Laurie, are you ready to go to rehab?" And, you know what's funny? I almost planned what my intervention would look like. If I had been intervened upon I would have gone to rehab; I was that ready to get sober, I was so hungry for it. I just couldn't say the words out loud, "I am an alcoholic, and I need help." But, once I did that, once I admitted that I had a problem and asked for help, that's when this wonderful journey began. I'm so lucky to be sober. I can say without a doubt that I would be dead today if I didn't get sober five years ago.

G. Obviously you have no regrets now about your public disclosure, which was unique, because of your visible position in the media. But, for the average person in recovery, what are your thoughts about secrecy and anonymity?

L. There is so much discussion about breaking anonymity and whether or not it's a good thing, and whether or not it actually helps the cause. Clearly it's an individual decision. Nobody forces anybody to go public about his or her recovery, but I feel that too often, people in recovery confuse anonymity with secrecy. Secrecy just foments the stigma that exists in our culture about this disease. I believe if more people came forward and said this is what I've been through and this is what recovery looks like, it would help untold thousands of people. I think by sharing their stories, people create an environment of knowledge and of understanding that's free from shame or embarrassment—one that makes it possible for more people to feel free to get help.

There are endless stories of recovery, and we need to tell them and share positive messages of recovery because in these stories are education and hope and strength and love. I know this: All the good things that are happening in my life are because of recovery.

G. Great. Thank you, Laurie.

CHRIS HERREN

"Most people don't pass the mirror test. I can pass the test today because of recovery. The only reason."

Chris Herren is a superstar. He's a devoted husband, a loving father of three children, and one of the All-Stars out on the frontlines of recovery advocacy, bringing his message of inspiration and hope to young people all across the country. If there were a "Recovery Hall of Fame," he would be inducted in the first round.

He used to be quite a star on the basketball court, too. In high school, the six-foot-two-inch guard was Massachusetts Player of the Year three years in a row; then, at Fresno State College under legendary coach, Jerry Tarkanian, he was selected to the All Western Athletic Conference First Team for two years running. From college he was drafted into the NBA, where he played for the Denver Nuggets and the Boston Celtics.

While he was celebrated on the hard court, it was hard-core drugs that brought him down. As former New York Knicks guard and now broadcaster, Walt Frazier might say, Herren took some "ill-advised shots"—starting with cocaine, then Oxycontin, and then heroin. His addiction cost him. He not only lost his game, more importantly, he nearly lost his family and, literally, his life. One time, he was found in his wrecked car with a needle in his arm and pronounced dead at the scene.

You can learn more about his story in his memoir, *Basketball Junkie*, written with Bill Reynolds, or in the Emmy-nominated ESPN Films documentary, *Unguarded*, directed by Jonathan Hock. Or you can go hear him speak. Go. He speaks frequently to students and families in high schools and on college campuses and he is also much in demand as a speaker to many professional sports teams. When you hear him, fair warning, be prepared not to breathe for several minutes at a time, as this all-American athlete recounts in gripping detail the ugly depths to which he descended under the push of every imaginable addictive substance. Yes, that part is a sensational story. So if, as advocates urge, it is time to start telling and celebrating the recovery story more, why does Herren talk so much about this dark side of his life?

For one, he controls the story. His no-holds-barred accounts are honest, and they preempt any misinformation by the media. It is his story, and he uses the facts of his life, once held secret, to illuminate for young people, in particular, the dark path that is the all too common consequence of trying their first Solo cup or blunt. They can see the reality when he reveals it; they even seem to experience it, vicariously. He gets them hooked on his addiction story; then, comes the kicker—his sensational recovery. By contrast, the place where Herren was a few short years ago compared to where he is today is simply stunning to kids and their parents. We saw that in action.

When we caught up with him, he was in Connecticut speaking to students and parents in a packed high school auditorium in a well-to-do community of high-achievers and social advantage. Yet their idyllic town was experiencing the same drug epidemic that was ravaging young people in communities across the country and across all strands of society. On this night, people were gathered looking for answers. Herren gave a deeply emotional presentation and, as we listened transfixed by the horror of his addiction story, one couldn't help wonder how it was possible that this now healthy all-American was even alive today. And that's what makes the recovery part of his story so powerful. Standing tall and strong, Herren is the absolute manifestation of the reality and possibilities of recovery. Tears of empathy and recognition fell freely in this audience during his addiction chronicle, and turned to tears of joy and hope as he shared his recovery story. By making the consequences of addiction real and recovery even more real, he reaches about half a million young people a year in this way.

Greg pulled Herren aside after the presentation and asked if he would give us a few moments for the film. It was late at night, and he had been traveling all day from an earlier presentation at another high school in another state, but he did not hesitate to say yes. He was clearly tired, but he was the kind of tired you get after playing four quarters of a basketball game to a tie and now you were facing overtime, relishing the moment, taking the court with a second wind, and wanting the ball in your hands so you could make the winning shot. For Chris Herren, it was a good kind of tired. The way a winner feels.

GREG. What made you decide to do the film, *Unguarded*, and be so public about your life in addiction and recovery?

CHRIS. The decision-making process didn't come from me, it came from friends of mine, the Mullin family. Liz Mullin thought it would be a good idea to share that story. Jonathan Hock is critically acclaimed and had just got done doing the Marcus Dupree story for ESPN and it all worked out. I had already released the book; my secrets were out, and I wasn't scared to tell my story in front of a camera. The book was much deeper and revealing than what I talked about on film.

G. We heard your story tonight about how fellow NBA star Chris Mullin and his wife, Liz, offered you treatment. Obviously, he's public about his recovery. What did his support mean to you?

C. He's public about his recovery, and his wife, Liz, she lived it. Chris Mullin is someone who had reached out, but really it was more so his wife. I had known Chris because I had lived with them for a couple of weeks getting ready for the NBA draft in 1999. And when I was in the hospital, Liz was really the one who contacted me and said, "I'm gonna get you into a place. Would you be willing to go?" His involvement had nothing to do with basketball and everything to do with just one family, who understands the struggle, helping another. So, it was that gift they gave me on that day that has changed my life.

G. There's one line from your brother in *Unguarded* that really struck me. He talks about what people used to call you, and what they call you today. How did society perceive you when you were addicted, and how does society perceive you today as a person in recovery?

C. It's not about how society perceives me; it's about how I perceive myself. It's how I look at myself in the mirror. People still call me "junkie." Not as many, but there's still those people out there. But it doesn't matter. It's what I call myself. As long as I'm good with myself, I couldn't care less what everybody else says. It's too good now to worry about the past or the future. I'm good right here, you know. At one time, I had 14,000 people yelling, "junkie," in a basketball arena. Today that stuff has no bearing on me. If you look at my Twitter feed, you'll see that people call me a junkie every day. A kid sent a message tonight saying, "Hey, show up. I've got two bags of dope for you." I've lived with that since I was twelve years old, so I don't pay attention to it anymore.

G. How do you feel about the way addiction and recovery is being treated as a health issue in America?

C. I think we should be ashamed of how we deal with this health issue. I think every cause, like breast cancer, like the Heart Association, like diabetes, like autism is worthy of social and financial backing, but why not addiction and recovery? Why are we so afraid to say, "I want to help. I'm gonna extend my hand like I do for autism, like I do for diabetes, like I do for heart disease. I'm gonna do it for addiction." That's how I look at it.

G. You are asked to speak all over the country. With so much secrecy around addiction and recovery, what has your experience been like telling your story and where did you find the strength or confidence to do it?

C. It's freedom, you know. It's letting go. I was told early on in recovery that people can't hurt you with what you tell them. So expose yourself; let it go because nobody can come back to you with it. I was coached and mentored very early on in recovery by some pretty powerful people with a solid foundation in recovery. Those men educated me on how to live my life in my early stages of recovery, and I believe that's been a key, critical part of my recovery that allows me to stay sober today.

G. A lot of people stood up tonight after you spoke and they disclosed their recovery status. A lot of those people probably had never done that before. Have you ever gotten any negative reaction to disclosing your recovery?

C. *Unguarded* was viewed by millions, and I have received one email about breaking the tradition of anonymity. I respect people's views and how they perceive the traditions. But if the media can write about me being found overdosed in a Dunkin' Donuts with heroin in my vehicle, why can't I talk about recovering from that? That's how I look at it.

G. How does the media generally treat you in terms of your story?

C. When I do a radio show or a TV show, the introduction is former NBA basketball player who threw away his basketball career due to drugs and alcohol. I don't know why they don't throw my kids in there, too. Like, I look at them and say, "How come you didn't mention my kids. I almost threw them away?" Who cares about basketball? Basketball should be last on that list. I was to the point of walking away from my children, my life, ending it. Basketball is just a game, man. You know? So sometimes I think that gets lost. I didn't throw away a basketball career. I mean, I broke my kids' hearts for many years and my family's heart, and that's what I believe should be talked about in the introduction. That's how powerful the illness is.

G. Explain a little bit about your drive to speak to young people. How are you trying to reach them?

C. Getting out in front of the young kids is what it's all about for me. This week, I was with the Minnesota Vikings; I was on the campus of Notre Dame, Purdue; I did the New England Patriots, the Chicago Bears, Green Bay Packers, Boston Celtics, Oklahoma City, West Point, Annapolis; I've done them all. Where I want to be is with the kids. I believe that's where I can have the most impact. I can tell with my eyes. I tell people, "Watch from behind me when I talk to high school kids and you'll see how many people are affected by it." When you watch from my view, and you see hundreds of little kids reacting, then you realize what an issue it is. Last year, I spoke in front of close to 500,000 kids. It's a lot of work. It's a lot of moving around—this morning in Long Island, tonight here, tomorrow two high schools. That's what it's all about for me because I want kids to walk away and say, "You know what? He's kind of cool. It's kind of cool to be sober." Like, recovery's cool, you know? It's not a sign of weakness. It's not a sign of regret and shame. It's not a scarlet letter. It's not any of that. It's cool. Like, you overcame. That's how I look at it, and hopefully kids will get that same reaction to it.

G. You talk about the four high school girls wearing purple T-shirts who were in your audience once and how they bravely disclosed their choice to live sober to the entire school. Tell us what that inspired you to do. And now, you have Project Purple. What is that?

C. We created the THP Project Purple Initiative, which is all about the kids. It's about educating, raising awareness, inspiring, and getting kids to really look deep down within themselves to find out *why* they need to change who they are. And when I ask that question in front of 2,000 high school kids, you'll see 50 percent of them drop their heads. Their eyes go right down because they're thinking, *Why?* And they know why, but they need to talk about why. And I think that's half the problem; I think none of these kids talk about why. I would kill to go back to that age and talk about why, instead of living with all those little secrets that eventually grew to be monstrous.

G. You're inspiring others to stand up and give this illness a voice. What's your dream? Ten years from now, twenty years from now, how does society look at this illness?

C. Well, the dream is that it's not the most underfunded health issue in this country. The dream is that we're worth more than five-day detoxes. The dream is that it's okay to fall. Get back up; there's a bed for you, you know. When diabetics go off their sugar and they show up to the emergency room, they get treated with great empathy. They level them off, they put them in a room, they feed them, they give them the correct food. An addict walks in after a relapse, and he's thrown back on the road. Hopefully, someday, addicts won't be looked upon as throwaways. Because you step over me, you step over little Chris, you step over Sam, you step over Drew, you step over my wife. You step over that one addict, you're stepping over a whole family, and there's heavy fallout and repercussions for that.

G. **Since your recovery, what do you look at that is significant in your life? What tells you that recovery is working for you?**

C. My chips [recovery anniversary medallions]. I give them to little Chris and Samantha, and they get it, they know it. They know when it's coming, they look forward to it, and they keep them on their dresser. They're the little trophies we share together. I'm a sober dad. You know what I mean? There's nothing better than that.

When I tell that story about shaving in the mirror, you know that was pretty deep. I was a late bloomer and I started shaving at seventeen or eighteen years old, and I did it in the shower. At thirty-two years old, nine months sober, I did it in front of the mirror for the first time in my life. That was a pretty powerful moment for me. And I think if you ask most people, they don't pass the mirror test where they can really look at themselves and say, "I like it." You know what I mean? And that's important. It's important to pass that test. I can pass the test today because of recovery. The only reason.

Drug and alcohol-free since August 1, 2008, Chris Herren now puts his recovery and family above all else. His celebrity and unique ability to relate to young people combine to be a potent platform for his advocacy, which, in turn, strengthens and helps maintain his own recovery. He founded The

Herren Project, a nonprofit organization that provides educational and mentoring programs to help those touched by addiction and to offer guidance to treatment pathways. In 2012, inspired by those brave high school girls, he launched the THP Project Purple Initiative with the mission to erase the stigma of addiction and get people of all ages to stand up for prevention, treatment, and recovery. Time to get off the bench and play ball.

WILLIAM COPE MOYERS

"It's public perception that drives public policy. If we want to change public policy in the state capitals or in DC or anywhere in our communities, we have to change public perception."

It was a personal thrill for Craig and me to meet "young" William Moyers. We had worked along side his dad, Bill Moyers, albeit in separate units, early in our career as producers at WNET-13, the New York area PBS station. Among our peers, Bill Moyers was much admired and respected as a journalist and as a man with high standards of truth-telling and possessing a clear moral compass. Craig and I had always wanted to work on his shows, which were informative, provocative, and seemingly purposed to elicit some societal action for good or, at least, to stimulate fruitful contemplation. We never got the chance to contribute to Moyers's programs, but we tried to emulate his thoughtful and honest approach when producing our own documentary projects. We also knew him to be a Master of Divinity (he was a former Baptist pastor) and a family man. Plus, he and his wife, Judith, ran their own production company, *Public Affairs Television*. If not a hero, he was certainly an ideal to which we could aspire.

Imagine our shock when we learned, along with the nation, that his adult son, William, was discovered in a crack house in Atlanta near death from addiction. How could this be? He was a member of an upstanding family, imbued, we could only assume, with the good values and rational thought that must have permeated his upbringing; yet, here was the incongruous news that this privileged son was in such ignominious circumstances.

We didn't know son William was an accomplished journalist in his own right, or that he had grown up a popular, high achiever throughout high school and college—a scholar, an athlete, a musician. His professional success was high, writing for major newspapers and television, but he was not as famous as his father. That changed overnight when his harrowing story made headlines, linking him to the celebrity of his parents.

William's addiction story is hair-raising. If you ever have the opportunity to hear him speak, he tells it in mesmerizing detail, or you can read about his remarkable trip to hell and back (taken three times) in his memoir, *Broken: My Story of Addiction and Redemption*. We'll not tell it here. It is his recovery story that is even more remarkable. In no small way, he became a major force in pushing the new recovery movement forward and effecting change in national policy. He now works for the Hazelden Betty Ford Foundation as Vice President of Public Affairs and Community Relations. On smaller, more personal levels, he continues to help others navigate the process of treatment and recovery. His latest book, *Now What? An Insider's Guide to Addiction and Recovery*, provides the kind of informed guidance and support that so many addiction sufferers lack and simply don't know exist.

One sunny Sunday afternoon, we headed to the historic Basilica of St. Mary, which occupies a city block along Hennepin Avenue in downtown Minneapolis, to hear William speak before a large community gathering of people in recovery. He spoke for about thirty minutes, then received people individually for more than an hour, listening to personal stories and offering advice. Without a trace of weariness, he joined us afterward in a quiet meditation room off the main nave and sat down for a conversation with Greg, sounding as enthused and fresh as if it were his first of the day. When he spoke, his cadence, timbre, and faint remnant of a soft East Texas accent was so like his father's, we instantly took a liking to him. Then, as he told his story, with both candor and humility, we grew to admire him on his own merits.

GREG. You started talking about your recovery before many people started talking about their recovery publicly. How did you get to that point, and what was it like when you first disclosed publicly?

WILLIAM. I got sober finally in '94, and I started working at Hazelden in '96. And sometime after that, I think it was in '98, I was invited to give a presentation at the Rotary Club in downtown St. Paul. I was honored to do that. It was part of my job to promote public awareness about Hazelden and about addiction. I had this talk prepared, and it was pretty good, and I had all these startling statistics about alcoholism and drug addiction in it. So I started my talk, and was telling them all about the statistics of alcoholism and I saw people just sort of nodding off, and checking their watches, and looking at their cell phones, and people were sneaking out the back door, and I was losing them. I could see it just as clearly as I'm talking to you right now that the audience thought I was a nice guy, but they could have cared less.

I then decided if I was going to hold this audience and was going to take advantage of this unique opportunity to speak at a Rotary Club, I'd better grab them. I literally threw the speech to the side of the podium there, and said, "Well, actually let me tell you about this from my own experience." And some people started to perk up just a bit. I said, "I'm an alcoholic and an addict. I'm talking today about people like me." And people were shocked. They were shocked for two reasons. One, that wasn't what the talk was supposed to be about; and secondly, they didn't realize that I was what I was—a recovering addict and alcoholic. I guess the other piece to it, which surprised them, was that I was somewhat well-known in my community of St. Paul/Minneapolis, and they just couldn't imagine that Moyers could be one of those. So I sort of winged it. I told them my story. Not my twelve-step story, but my story of addiction, my story of recovery, and the multiple treatments I had had. And people were putting their forks in their mouths, and they would stop. And I remember there was a man or two walking at the back of the room, getting ready to leave when they heard me say, "I'm an alcoholic and an addict," and they turned, and I knew I had them. I didn't mean to do that. I mean, I meant to tell my story at that point, but I didn't know it would resonate like that.

That was the day, a long time ago, with just a couple of years clean, still young, that I realized the real power is in the personal story. And from that day on, I've always tried to weave my own story into the public policy story about addiction recovery. I say, "My name is William Moyers. I'm in long-term recovery from addiction to alcohol and other drugs. Addiction doesn't discriminate; this is what one of us looks like." It shocks people because I don't look like that. Because I don't come from "that kind of family." That's where I learned the power of telling stories.

The other thing I'll tell is that when I got to Hazelden in '96, Jerry Spicer, who was then our CEO, said, "I want you to go out and I want you to change public policy about addiction recovery."

And I said, "Great, Jerry, where's the money?"

And he said, "Well, we don't really have any money in this field."

I said, "Okay, all right. Where are the constituents?"

He said, "We don't really have any constituents."

There were no faces and voices of recovery. There was no real grassroots advocacy going on in an organized fashion. So I figured the best way to lead is by example. And, if I were going to ask other people to stand up and speak out in their communities in single voices or in unity, I needed to lead by example. Winston Churchill always said, "The scariest thing about being a leader is looking over your shoulder and seeing that nobody is following." So I didn't want to be a leader of one, I wanted to be part of a bigger experience. So, I led by example, and it worked.

G. After you started talking publicly about your recovery did you experience any changes in your life?

W. Totally. Remember, I got up there at a Rotary Club in St. Paul, first public talk I'd ever given about my own experience as an alcoholic, and that was a big shock to me, just like it was to the audience. But the biggest shock, if you will, the most significant unintended benefit—not consequence—of being public about my story was that I became a lightning rod for people who had nowhere else to turn. They were "Oh, that's where I can get help. I can go to that person." Because, you see, I'm not a famous person. I don't live in Hollywood. I don't live in New York City. I live in St. Paul, Minnesota. I've got a listed address in the White Pages or on the Internet. I'm easy to find, and I work for a reputable organization. So when I started to tell my story of addiction and recovery, people began to come to me with emails, phone calls, and letters. They've even come up to my front porch in St. Paul, unannounced, or they'd call ahead of time and say, "Hey, can I come over and see you?" And I became what I always call the lint brush of recovery in my community. I sort of roll for the community and pick up all these people who need help. Being public with my story and working for the organization I work for has allowed me to help other people. And that was not what my plan was when I started being a public advocate.

G. In those late '90s, when you started disclosing publicly, how did you navigate the anonymity issue in your own life?

W. I never grappled with the anonymity issue, and here's why: Because with some notable exceptions, I never stand up at a Rotary Club or at the Library of Congress or on C-Span or in an op-ed in the paper or at a church and speak out as a member of any twelve-step group. I speak out as a person in long-term recovery from addiction to alcohol and other drugs, somebody who works for Hazelden, and somebody who knows first-hand the power of addiction and the power of recovery. I never worried about violating the tradition that is so important to some people in recovery because I didn't speak from, nor pretend to represent, any entity like AA or Al-Anon or any other twelve-step fellowship. It's clear I violated the Eleventh Tradition when I wrote my book, *Broken*. I had to. But I felt really strong about this, Greg. If I were going to share the intimate and somewhat sordid details of my downward spiral into addiction, then I owed it to the reader, I owed it to the recovering person, or the desperate family member; I owed it to all of them, to explain how is it that I recover. It's not magic, and it's not a miracle; it's a program. And so, in the book, and in some of my other talks and presentations, I have talked about my participation in that recovery program because I feel to do anything less than that is to not give people the opportunity they need, the hope they need, to recover. I don't do it regularly, and I'm trying to always be careful. I make it clear that when I do speak about the Twelve Steps, I'm speaking as a person who is in recovery, not as an expert or as a representative. And I think it's really important that people who are in those kinds of programs recognize that they can be public. They can speak out in Washington. They can speak out in their communities. They can speak out in any public forum, as long as they do it *not* as a member of AA or any other twelve-step fellowship.

G. **Your mother and father, Bill and Judith Moyers, created a five-part series on addiction called, *Moyers on Addiction: Close to Home*, for PBS in 1998. That was probably the first of anything like this that's been done in such depth. Can you explain the idea and the decision your family went through making this?**

W. It was out of my relapse in '94 that both my parents and I recognized the gravity of this chronic illness. People can be recovering and do well, and then all of a sudden make a sharp left turn or sharp right turn, and go off the deep end again. I mean, I had been sober for three years in the early '90s, and I went back out. And I almost didn't make it back. That experience and that relapse shocked my parents. They sort of intellectually knew addiction is a chronic illness, but they expected their son, who had everything to stay sober for, to stay sober. But I didn't. So when I relapsed, it shook my whole family to the core.

From that experience, my parents decided to do a five-part series for PBS that started when I relapsed in '94, and came of age, if you will, in '98. My folks did that series to try to help explain everything there is in the continuum of this illness. They didn't want to do it about their son, and they didn't want to do it about our family. But the fact that their son and our family had been through it gave it validity, gave it some oomph, and personalized the issue so many people know. In that five-and-a-half hour series, I'm in about two-and-a-half minutes of the whole thing. I mean, I think my dad mentions early on why they're doing the series, but I don't think I'm even identified as William Cope Moyers in the beginning. They asked me, "William, are you okay doing it?" I said, "Yeah, I'm okay doing it. I'm a public advocate, and I work for Hazelden. This is what I'm supposed to be doing." But the series wasn't about me, it was about people like me. The series wasn't about the Moyers, it was about families like the Moyers, and I think that's why it resonated. It would have been sort of hokey if it had been my story.

G. Let's talk about policy for a moment. Why do we even need public policy change around addiction?

W. Addiction is the most misunderstood of all illnesses, I believe. There's been a stigma in this country since the colonial days. Dr. Benjamin Rush, who was a signer of the United States Declaration of Independence and Martha Washington's doctor, was grappling with this problem back in the 1770s. Alcoholism and drug addiction, as we now know it, had been endemic in our families, our communities, and our societies since America's been a nation, probably even before. For a long time, people didn't recover from the illness, not in mass. The point of it is that the disease has been not only marginalized but stigmatized. People do not understand the chronic nature of this disease. They don't see addiction as an illness; they see it as a behavioral problem or a spiritual problem. And it is part that. Plus, they don't understand the pervasiveness of it. They don't understand that addiction doesn't discriminate.

If somebody has cancer or heart disease or diabetes, there's no shame around that. But there's so much shame, private shame and public intolerance, as well as public policies that are against addicts and alcoholics. Public policies reflect the fact that people still, even in this day, don't really get it when it comes to the impact addiction has, not just on individuals, but in communities. The recovery advocacy work I do and the recovery advocacy work that's represented in the film you're making is really all about standing up and speaking out, and shedding light into the dark corner of an illness that knows an awful lot of shame. Advocacy work around addiction is important, particularly putting a face on it, doing what we're doing right at this moment because we have a long way to go in eliminating stigma and removing those barriers to care.

G. It's been a long struggle. Insurance discrimination is one example. Tell us about your involvement in the twelve-year battle for parity.

W. It was actually longer than that. There was a lot going on back in the mid-'90s around eliminating discrimination by insurance companies against people with mental illnesses, including addiction to alcohol and other drugs. Up until the mid-'90s, healthcare conversations generally did not include treatment for addiction or treatment for mental illness. And those of us in the addiction field and those in the mental illness field recognized that that was wrong. That was discrimination. It needed to change.

Paul Wellstone [US Senator, Minnesota (D)], who was a great champion of people with mental illness and addiction, Jim Ramstad [US Representative, Minnesota (R)], and some others in Congress and other organizations, all came together and started to really push legislation. In 1996, Congress did pass a parity bill for mental illness, but it specifically excluded addiction treatment. And the reason why it excluded it was because a lot of politicians on both sides of the aisle were wary about expanding access to care for "substance abusers." The mentally ill, they're one thing, but those alcoholics and addicts, well they're, "Ah, we're not quite ready for that yet!" But Paul Wellstone always used to pound the table, literally, in my kitchen or in Washington in his office, and say, "We're going to get this fixed!" And eventually we began to move that legislation. Faces & Voices of Recovery came around, and people began to stand up en masse. Politicians, elected officials, and the media began to say, "Oh, hmm, well, we'll listen to the argument."

The big blow came in 2002; Paul Wellstone was killed in a plane crash here in Minnesota. It was not just an incredible personal loss for me and a loss for this community of the Twin Cities in Minnesota he represented, but when Paul died, there was a big gasp from those of us in the field saying, "Oh, my goodness. We've lost our greatest champion in the Senate." We all weren't sure what was going to happen. But the field rallied, and we came together, probably more so as a result of Paul Wellstone's death and continued to push until 2008, when we finally got the insurance coverage legislation through Congress.

G. You were involved in that milestone St. Paul Summit of 2001. What role did the Summit play in influencing policy change, and even in the greater arc of the story of the new advocacy movement for recovery?

W. The work that was already happening in Washington, DC, with Paul Wellstone and Jim Ramstad and others around parity, or insurance coverage for addiction treatment, the Johnson Institute, the Legal Actions Center, NCADD, and others—they were all sort of talking in the late '90s about how to mount a recovery advocacy movement that was different than anything we've ever done. It all came together and resulted in that summit in October of 2001. We actually had two of them. We had them both here in the Twin Cities because this was sort of a hot bed of recovery community organizing, but also because it's in the middle of the country. It was easy for people to come here from California and New York, and Texas and Florida and other places. And so, we gathered here.

I was working with Paul Samuels and Stacia Murphy and others in national organizations. A group of us realized we needed to get some money and try to fund this recovery advocacy work in some sort of cohesive, coordinated fashion. I knew Jeff Blodgett personally. He'd been organizing Paul Wellstone's campaigns and I knew Jeff from the Twin Cities. Our kids went to school together. I managed to get us an appointment with the president of the Robert Wood Johnson Foundation, and Jeff and I went to Princeton, New Jersey, in the spring of 1999. We made a presentation on the importance of recovery advocacy and we highlighted the stigma around addiction and its history. They were like "Oh, wow!" and we got a half a million dollar grant. That, plus some other monies we raised, allowed us to bring together all those advocates who'd been doing their own work in locales across the country. We brought them all together, twice. Out of that came the Alliance Project, which is now Faces & Voices of Recovery. It was this really remarkable moment.

By 2002, we'd been working for a long time. Faces & Voices was up and running; but, Paul's death in a plane crash while campaigning in the fall of 2002 was probably the last catalyst we needed to not give up. That helped push us over the finish line, even though it would be another six years before that legislation with his name on it was approved by Congress and signed by President Bush in October of 2008.

G. **How did you feel when that legislation was finally signed?**

W. At the time, it was a validation for everything all of us had been doing: our own individual advocacy work; a willingness to tell our stories in small settings and venues; the effort of the field to coalesce around an organizing entity; Paul's work; Jim Ramstad's work; Hazelden's work. It was a great moment. But somewhat bittersweet, you know. Paul wasn't there. The country was kind of falling apart, the economy was in shambles, and the country was going into a recession. It's ironic that the legislation was actually part of the Bailout Bill in October of 2008. It was a really important moment; I mean, we've really succeeded in recovery advocacy. But there's still a lot of hard work to do. Healthcare reform, insurance policies, and politics of addiction are still formidable obstacles.

G. You have inside knowledge of journalism and the media. Part of what I hear from people in recovery is that the media tells only one side of the story, the face of addiction, and we don't necessarily see the other side. As a journalist, do you see any change at all in the way the media tells addiction stories?

W. The media is very powerful in this country. It's public awareness that drives public policy. If we want to change public policy in the state capitols or DC or anywhere in our communities we have to change public perception. I think things are changing ever so slowly, but steadily. I can see it. There are more stories in the media now about the other side of the issue. In the old days, the focus was always on the problem. But I got tired of the story of the problem all the time. I didn't need to go into any legislator's office in Washington or go in front of the TV camera and say, "Addiction is a disease that takes a terrible toll on your constituents." Everybody knows that. In this film endeavor that you've got going on now, we are talking more about the solution than we are about the problem. And that's really good. A lot of the media I do now is not just about addiction as a chronic disease, but the fact that people do recover and you can be in long-term recovery. You can be in remission from the illness. I've been in remission for eighteen years. And it does work.

G. Throughout the years that you have been active in advocating for recovery, what do you see as evidence, outside of parity and other legislation, that change is really happening in the hearts and minds of the public?

W. Well, it's happening. There is a movement. It's a disparate, localized movement that is stitching itself together in a way that is actually beginning to change the momentum around drug policy in this country, where we, as a nation, are beginning to embrace addiction as a healthcare issue. That's really good. When I see the rally at the capitol in St. Paul last year or when I go to Washington and see a lot of people going up to the Hill to make visits on recovery-related issues, I say, "Yeah, yeah. It is changing." And there is the younger generation, you and others, who are actually taking the lead in continuing this good work. I wasn't the first one to do it, and I won't be the last one to do it. The key is to keep pushing and not give up. To stand up and speak out and recognize that we've come a long way, but we still have a long way to go. In the meantime, whenever we do stand up and speak out, we put a face and a voice out there and become a beacon of hope for people who are hopeless and helpless.

G. Do you have a vision for what the recovery advocacy movement might become?

W. I think the vision I have is the reality of today, which is that it's happening. I don't know where it's going. Never could I have imagined that my casual use of substances would ever lead me down into the abyss. Never did I imagine that I could recover from it at one point. Never did I imagine that from my recovery would come this coincidental opportunity to work for Hazelden. Never did I imagine that these disparate groups would come together in a summit. Never did I imagine that parity would pass and become law in this country. Never did I imagine that documentaries would be shot about recovery advocacy at the grassroots level. What I see is that this isn't an issue for the closet anymore. Addiction is a disease that doesn't discriminate. It's actually an issue that has a solution. Recovery is real. And when we stand up and speak out, we put a face on the solution, and we help other people who don't know the faces or the solution. That's what the movement should be—standing up and speaking out. And it is happening.

G. Great. Thank you.

TOM CODERRE

"When you go from being a lawmaker to a lawbreaker, that's a good story for the press and they took it and ran with it."

I call him Tom "Ubiquitous" Coderre. It seemed for a time during our year and a half of production, wherever we went, Tom would be there, to help, to participate, or just to support by his presence. We filmed him conducting a training session in Boston. We recorded his activities at the Recovery Caucus at the Democratic National Convention in Charlotte. We tried to keep up with him in the Senate Chambers of the Rhode Island State House. We saw him attending a meeting at a Recovery Community Center in Pawtucket. When we weren't shooting him specifically, suddenly he would just show up, say hello, and ask if there were anything we needed. *Doesn't this guy have a life,* I wondered.

He sure does. When we met him he was Chief of Staff at the Office of the Senate President of the State of Rhode Island. That is basically your normal, straightforward twenty-four/seven job made no less easy by the fact that Tom had been a State Senator for eight years. At the same time, he was also the Chairperson of Rhode Island Communities for Addiction Recovery Efforts (RICAREs). More recently, Tom was appointed by President Obama as Senior Advisor to the Administrator at the Substance Abuse and Mental Health Services Administration and has since relocated to Washington, DC.

Tom has a life, all right. A recovery life. In case you haven't noticed, people in recovery apparently have more time than you and me. I think it is because people now in recovery once faced the prospect of totally running out of time. That's the moment when the Grim Reaper appears and says, "Sorry friend, your time is up." In 2003, Tom came close to having his clock stopped. He got busted for cocaine, but was lucky enough to stand before a judge who stood between him and Mr. Reaper long enough for Tom to get an opportunity to find recovery—and a new life. When you get the help you need for recovery, you also get a blessing. More time. More sand in the hourglass of life. And you make the most of it.

Tom makes the most of every one of his grains of sand and helps everyone around him do the same. Over ten years in successful recovery, Tom has amazing energy, all purposeful and positive. So when you need him, he finds the time, as he did for us the day we searched him out at the Rhode Island State House. Greg managed to collar him and sit him down for a conversation in his small, but elegantly appointed office just off the Senate floor. I think it was the only time we ever saw Tom sitting, and it may have been a record. When Greg gets an important interview subject seated, trapped under our lights, and wired to a microphone, he doesn't let go quickly. Here are excerpts from a candid and heartfelt hour and a half with the (just-for-the-moment) *not* ubiquitous Tom Coderre.

GREG. How did you get involved in politics in the first place?

TOM. I remember sitting around the kitchen table with my parents talking about politics. I remember my grandmother being a huge fan of John F. Kennedy. There was a portrait of him in her living room, and I remember hearing stories about how my grandmother would pack my mother and my aunt in the car when they were kids and drag them out to Cape Cod when the President was landing for one of his summer vacations. When I was about fourteen years old, a family friend came to my parents and asked my father if he was interested in running for state representative and my father said, "Nah, I can't do that. I can't. My job won't allow me to take time to go to the State House every day." But, pointing at my mom, he said, "How 'bout Elaine?" And my mom was like, "Me?" She had never thought about running for office. We talked as a family about it and she decided that she was going to run and I got involved. I was a fourteen-year-old computer nerd, running the computer for the campaign. My mother would walk door-to-door everyday and she'd come home at night and I would be in charge of punching into the computer the people she had met, and then we would print out postcards and letters to those folks asking them for their support. My mother was successful in that race; she won a Democratic primary and then she won a general election. That was back in 1984, and I guess if you were to say that I was bitten by the political bug, that's probably when it happened. It's something I had in my blood from that moment on.

G. **In 1994, at only twenty-five, you were elected to the State Senate of Rhode Island. You must have felt like you had arrived.**

T. I was the youngest senator at the time. There is a moment when you feel like you have arrived, I suppose, when you're that young and you show up at the State House and the average age of the people in the Senate Chamber was probably sixty. And here's this young whippersnapper coming in and wanting to change the world. I guess, yeah, you feel a certain sense of power.

G. **With the remarkable success you achieved early in life, there also came circumstances that led you into addiction. Would you talk about that?**

T. Sure. Rhode Island, like many other states, has a part-time citizen legislature, so to serve in the legislature you also have to have another job. Because I was involved in the community, I got a job being a nonprofit fundraiser. I worked for United Cerebral Palsy and I worked for United Way, and I was always trying to maintain my duties here at the State House. With my job and my family life, it was really tough to balance that and there was a lot more stress in my life than I normally would have had as an average twenty-five year old. So I started drinking around that time to cope with stress I was experiencing. I never thought anything of it; I was always able to function at a pretty high level and, as a result, I didn't see any of the signs that I was drinking too much. Family members would politely mention it and suggest maybe I was drinking too much, or maybe I had a problem, maybe I should stop, or maybe I should take some time off, all the things people say to you when you're starting to cross the line. When you get elected as a senator at age twenty-five, you feel powerful and invincible to begin with. So when people are telling you that you have a problem with alcohol or other drugs, there's a disconnect in your mind and you don't believe it. You don't feel as though something is going to be more powerful than you. And I think that's what happened to me. I think I easily slid into thinking I can control this; this is not going to be difficult to control, just like I control everything else in my life.

G. And so, it got worse and you eventually lost your Senate seat.

T. My disease progressed. The more I drank, the more I wanted to drink, and the worse it got. It started out being social and fun and, you know, maybe having too much to drink a couple nights a week. But then, I was having too much to drink every single night of the week. Things started sliding, my work started sliding, my responsibilities in the Senate started sliding. I kept a lot of that secret, though. When people would mention it, I wouldn't acknowledge it. The way it all ended was that the Senate was redistricting and we were downsizing; we were going from a fifty-member Senate to thirty-eight and the folks in leadership thought I couldn't handle being here anymore and eliminated my Senate seat. At first, I became indignant and I was going to move into another district where I thought I could win and run for that seat, but my addiction had progressed too far by that point and I wasn't able to do that.

G. There was a lot of press about you and your addiction. Was that after you left the Senate?

T. The easiest way to talk about it is to talk about my bottom. After I left the Senate, my disease progressed even further. Because I didn't have those responsibilities anymore, and I lost the job I had running a large nonprofit agency in Providence and couldn't handle those duties. So I started using cocaine, which really helped me escape from my problems and life on a daily basis. Alcohol wasn't even a close second. And the progression of my disease was all that much quicker. After being out of office probably only three or four months, I was arrested for possession of cocaine. I had been seen buying drugs in my community, pulled over by the police, searched, and arrested on the spot. Obviously, when you go from being a lawmaker to a lawbreaker, that's a good story for the press and they took it and ran with it. But it wasn't enough to help me stop and so I went on using probably for another four or five weeks until I was arrested again, held without bail, put in jail, and another whole round of news stories abounded about that. And that's when I ended up going to treatment and getting into recovery. That was May of 2003.

G. Were you ever aware of how your addiction was impacting your family and others around you—that it wasn't just about Tom's life anymore?

T. I knew I wasn't just impacting myself, but I was trapped so deeply within my addiction that I really didn't spend a whole lot of time thinking about it. I knew I was creating damage everywhere: the damage I was creating to my family whom I love very much, the damage I was creating to the institutions that I cared about, the Senate, the public service organizations I had belonged to and held so dearly. Even after I was arrested, I wasn't thinking clearly. It was almost like it was surreal; it was happening to me and I was kind of watching it from outside myself, almost like an out-of-body experience. It wasn't till much later in my recovery that I started to deal with some of the shame and the guilt and the harm I had caused.

G. How did recovery go for you?

T. I would like to say that I willingly got into recovery, but that wasn't the case. I had to be arrested. I came into recovery kicking and screaming. I didn't want to go back to treatment. I didn't want to live in a recovery house. I didn't want to do the things I knew were necessary to get well. But somebody told me early on in my recovery that if I walked ten miles into the woods, I would have to walk ten miles out. That was very meaningful for me because I realized that I didn't have to recover overnight. I could recover over time, and that I could take the time that was necessary. I spent five-and-a-half months in treatment. I spent another six months living as a resident in a recovery house, and I ended up getting asked to be the assistant house manager, and eventually the house manager. I was there for two-and-a-half years in a recovery house and it was during that time, from treatment to the recovery house, that I started getting some stability back in my life, to heal my mind and my body from the devastating effect of addiction. It needed time to do that.

I also took the time to deal with some of the issues that were going on in my life, like the relationships I had lost with my family and my friends, with the organizations and associations I had belonged to, and the institutions I loved. Those are the things I had to rebuild, and I had lost contact with all that through my active addiction. That was something I was able to do, little by little, through my recovery. I would schedule a meeting or I would go to an event and it was hard at first, because the guilt and the shame that I was feeling about my addiction and the articles that people had read about me in the paper, about people seeing me on the six o'clock news in handcuffs standing before a judge, and thinking everywhere I went that people were looking at me saying, "Oh, there he is, there's the guy they locked up, and that was the former Senator who was a drug addict." I mean, those tapes played over and over again in my head everywhere I went. It was hard to drag myself out of the cocoon of the recovery world of that treatment center, or the recovery house I lived in, or a twelve-step meeting, or anywhere I was where I felt safe, then venturing outside of that and actually being with real people and thinking they would accept me again, and believe in me, and love me the way they had previously. It took a long time for me to be able to figure that out and to be able to get to a point where I felt comfortable doing that. But, it really happened. It happened.

G. It happened big time. You moved to Washington, DC and started some amazing work teaching people how to talk about recovery. How did that come about?

T. Through the process of getting back out into the community, I was introduced to an organization called Rhode Island CAREs, which is Rhode Island Communities for Addiction Recovery Efforts. I started going to their meetings because I heard they had free pizza. I was still in that cocoon of safety with other recovering people, but that was the way I was able to start venturing back out into the community. Then I heard them talking about all these projects they were running and I wanted to be involved. I started hearing them talk about the fact that they run a legislative day at the State House. And I was like, "Well, I used to be at the State House. Maybe I can help with that." They were going to have a rally and people were going to tell their recovery stories. And I was scared to death of that. I said, "I don't want to be part of that, but I can come and volunteer and serve soda at the rally or something." Eventually, I became the chairman of the Legislative Day Committee and I ran the Legislative Day. And I remember coming back to the State House for the first time and standing in the rotunda with a microphone in my hand and screaming from the top of my lungs that I was a person in long-term recovery, and how long I hadn't used, and that I had once served in this building, and now we're here to take it back, and that there are a lot of policies affecting people from finding and sustaining their recovery for the long term, and that we, as people in recovery, have to tell our stories so that public policymakers will know that it's not okay to treat us the way we've been treated, and not discriminate against people in recovery.

It was through that work that I learned about Faces & Voices of Recovery in Washington. Faces & Voices of Recovery was hiring a national field director and I applied for the job. I had been in recovery just over three years, and I thought, *I'm never going to get this job because I'm just like a new kid on the block in recovery*, and there were people who had multiple years of recovery interviewing me. For some reason, they liked my energy and they liked my enthusiasm and they liked my background, and I got that job.

I started traveling around the country. We had the local recovery community associations host events and use it as an opportunity to tell their own recovery stories and to talk about and shine light on things that were going on in their communities that weren't right. And it was through that project I realized that people in recovery didn't have a lot of training about how to talk about their recovery. In fact, I didn't have a lot of training about talking about my own recovery. When I first went to Faces & Voices of Recovery, they said, "We've developed some messaging. This will help you. Let us have you sit down with our media folks and they'll train you so that when you go on the road you'll be prepared to do that."

When I took that training for the first time, it was transformative. I was physically transformed. I felt, "Oh, my God. These are the words I've been looking for to tell my recovery story the whole time. This is what I've been uncomfortable about. This is what I've been uneasy about. This is the answer I was looking for." When I stood up at the State House for that first time and held the microphone in my hands, I had an uneasiness because I didn't feel like the general public or my former colleagues really knew what I was talking about because I was using therapeutic language. I was using twelve-step language. I was using the language we use in recovery. Taking that training helped me understand that there's a better way to talk about this. And when I went around the country, I realized this is something we really need to train people to do. You don't need to be the national field director of Faces & Voices of Recovery to be eligible to take this training. If we can train recovery armies how to talk about their recovery, we'll be able to affect public policy, not just in Washington, but in all fifty states, wherever there's a recovery community organization, wherever there are people in recovery who are willing to come out and publicly speak about what they've been through and what life's like today for them as a person in recovery, instead of fading into the woodwork. We'll have accomplished something.

G. It definitely was transformative for me. As you went around the country doing the message training, what were some of the problems you found in the way recovery communities talked about recovery?

T. I would cringe regularly at the things I would hear people say publicly about their recovery. People were getting up in front of large groups of people in the general public and trying to share their story as if they were going through therapy. I noticed that when I was with other people in recovery, they got it. They understood what was going on with somebody, but when we were with the general public, they didn't get it. A story about somebody drinking all night and using cocaine, getting in their car, and then running over a fence and trash barrels and other things, well, people in a recovery group would laugh about something like that because they would identify with it at a therapeutic level. But people in the general public, they were shocked. They thought it was disgraceful. I noticed that we needed to find a way to separate what people were saying in public about their recovery and what they were saying in more therapeutic kind of twelve-step groups—that there was language that people could use inside the rooms and language they could use outside the rooms. If we were going to build a case for more support for people in recovery, for people changing their lives around, for people stopping using and finding new ways to live, we were going to have to message around that. We're going to have to show the general public that people in recovery don't get in their car and run over trash cans and fences anymore, that what they do now is get up every morning like I do and eat breakfast and go to work. That's what they do now. They have families, and they're involved with their community, and they sit on boards of directors, and they're presidents of banks, and they're Chiefs of Staff in State Senates. They even serve in the US Congress. That's who people in recovery are.

G. After your time in Washington with Faces & Voices of Recovery, you came back to Rhode Island and actually reentered politics. Did your public recovery play any role in that move?

T. I wasn't looking to leave Faces & Voices of Recovery, but a unique opportunity presented itself when a former colleague of mine was elected Senate President. I had conversations with her about coming back here to be her Chief of Staff. First of all, that was a humbling experience to have those conversations because on one side of the ledger, I had almost been run out of this building as a result of my addiction. And then, to talk about coming back in the role of Chief of Staff to the Senate President, well, that was the ultimate redemption for me, quite frankly. And to have the Senate President believe in me and believe in second chances as much as she does was further evidence to me that being a person in recovery has its benefits. Being a person in recovery, you really can get your life back. You really can redeem yourself to your colleagues, to your peers, and to your community. If I hadn't been so public about my recovery, then she would never have had any idea about what I was doing, about where I was, about how I was interacting, and about my ability to do this very job that I'm in today.

G. How confident were you that you could work in this arena again?

T. I remember I was talking with one of the most important people in my recovery network and I said, "Do you think I should go back and do this? Or do you think it's too dangerous?" And he said to me, "You know, Tom, we don't get into recovery to *not* do the things we enjoy in life. We get into recovery so we have the *ability* to do the things we enjoy in life." And what I found was that he was right! I love politics. I really enjoy the political world. I've been able to raise issues and concerns about things that would affect people in recovery, and I know I've had an impact in public policy since I've been here. I've been able to talk to individual senators or representatives. I've been able to be in meetings and be part of discussions that have gone on, where I've been able to lend my own personal experiences, like I've never been able to do in any other job. And I think that's a result of my recovery. So being able to talk publicly about your recovery can be beneficial on many different levels.

G. Awesome. Thanks for all your time. One last question, if I may. Do you have a vision for the recovery movement?

T. This is a tough question. I should have anticipated it and expected it. Let's see.

Okay. My vision for the recovery movement is that we won't have to be segregated as we are now; that stigma will be erased; that communities of recovery will continue to flourish; that we'll have places and people and support systems; that we won't have to worry about having medical care when we need it; if we have a relapse of our disease, we'll be able to get the help we need and get back on the road to recovery as quickly as possible; that the medical community, the law enforcement community, and the general public will treat us as fellow citizens, instead of as a stigmatized group of folks.

G. Great sound bite! Thank you.

Immediately after the interview, Greg went down the hall to get the family side of this story, and found Tom's mother, State Representative Elaine A. Coderre, who, at the time, was serving her twenty-ninth year in the Rhode Island House of Representatives. Her longevity and popularity in the State House contributed greatly to the support Tom and his family received from colleagues and friends during his journey to hell and back. In one respect, the Coderre's were lucky to have all the understanding, all the resources, and all the opportunities that Tom had to achieve and sustain his recovery. But, their celebrity was a double-edged sword; it brought both support and shame for Tom's illness. Mrs. Coderre told Greg about the pain and suffering they went through as a family and confirmed that, like most families, they didn't have the knowledge or tools to cope effectively with Tom's addiction, despite any advantages they may have had. For a year and a half, she said, they lived with the fear "that a policeman would come to our door and tell us he was dead."

Addiction can strike anyone. And it leaves each victim and the lives of every family member and friend in utter chaos. If chaos is the worse that happens to you when addiction strikes, you're lucky. If you find recovery, you're blessed. Just like the Coderres.

DON FERTMAN

"If I can just touch one person and send them on the right path, then the job is done."

Here's a delicious story. The fact that it involves the Subway restaurant chain merely adds to its tastiness. It's about a top executive at Subway who told his recovery story on national television and changed one man's life.

Our story begins in 1980. Young Don Fertman was playing in a rock 'n' roll band called The Crayons. He was the one with the orange hair in a group of Crayola-colored musicians who were struggling to succeed in the music business. To support their art, they created commercial jingles for a small, local chain of sandwich shops, called Subway, but it wasn't enough to keep the band together. When The Crayons started breaking up, Don was asked to join Subway to help open more shops. He uncolored his hair, put on a tie, took the job, and was good at it. Unfortunately, prior to Subway, music hadn't been his only obsession; he was also addicted to alcohol and other drugs. After two years on the job, he crashed.

Don's employer, Fred DeLuca, the founder of Subway, sent him to treatment. Not only that, DeLuca offered him his job back and a second chance. DeLuca's enlightened act transformed Don's life and, though unforeseen at the time, also helped to change the fortunes of a company and to influence untold numbers of other people. Especially one person living almost a thousand miles away in Indiana.

Some thirty years later, on the night of November 21, 2010, Harold Andrews was sitting at home watching television, his mind on other things. He had recently moved north from Texas to start a new life. In Texas, he had been arrested for drunken driving, half-heartedly went through a court-ordered treatment program, continued to drink, and lost his job. Now, it was Thanksgiving time in a new town, he was still out of work, and three weeks earlier he had again been arrested for driving while intoxicated. He was trying hard to remain sober, but there he sat distracted by a nagging desire to have just one beer, when something on TV caught his attention.

Don Fertman was on *Undercover Boss*, the CBS Emmy Award-winning reality series that follows high-level corporate executives as they secretly slip into the rank-and-file of their own companies to examine the inner workings of their businesses. As the show explained, Don was the Chief Development Officer of Subway. He had been with the company thirty-one years and under his tenure had seen it grow from 166 stores to over 41,500 stores in 104 countries and become the largest franchised quick service restaurant in the world. He was now disguised as a trainee going into Subway shops across the country, learning on the front lines what made his business tick, and what it took to become a true Subway "sandwich artist."

Then came the lightening bolt that struck Harold: Don revealed that he was in long-term recovery from addiction to alcohol and had been sober for twenty-eight years of his productive career at Subway. Further, Don had built his successful recovery in much the same way he had helped build the success of Subway—one day at a time, one store at a time, one quality sandwich at a time—in other words, steadily, step-by-step, always building capital.

Harold was moved. He sat down and wrote Don a letter. At first, he wasn't going to send it—just the act of writing it was cathartic—but, after a time and with his fiancé's encouragement, he sent it. Here, edited and condensed, is Harold's letter to Don:

Mr. Fertman,

I saw you on *Undercover Boss*. I was extremely surprised to see an alcoholic as the boss. I mean that in the best possible way.

Please understand I am not asking for anything. I am, however, sending you praise and letting you know you have made a difference in my life. Just because I am an alcoholic doesn't mean I cannot succeed. I can reach the top of the ladder. I'm still looking for the ladder, but I will find it and when I do I will strive to be the kind of person that you have become. I know I can only take one day at a time. But if you can do this and become one of the top people at a prestige company like Subway, then I can do this as well.

Please let me thank you once again for being brave enough to go on national television and let a fellow recovering alcoholic know that, with determination and hard work, anything is possible."

A year later, Greg was at home when he received a text message from a friend advising him to turn on CBS. *Undercover Boss* was re-airing Don's episode. Greg was impressed with the positive way the program handled Don's recovery story and immediately saw its potential to be part of a film he was newly hatching. Greg was thinking he might call it *The Anonymous People*.

In the weeks that followed, Greg got to know Don personally and discovered that his story was even richer than he thought. He learned that Don was the go-to guy at Subway whenever an employee needed help to navigate the addiction treatment system or find support in recovery. Within the company and throughout his community, Don was open about his recovery and loved to talk about the second chance that Subway had given him. But until he went on national television, he wasn't public in a big way, nor was he a loud advocate. He preferred to help people individually, one at a time—as they do at any Subway restaurant counter.

By the time we began production on *The Anonymous People*, we were all certain Don's story had to be in the film, so off to Subway headquarters we went for one of the earliest interviews on our year-long schedule. While Craig and I set up the scene in a Subway conference room, Greg and Don huddled, preparing the topics for discussion. Greg happened to ask what kind of feedback he had received from his appearance on *Undercover Boss*. Don said that among the many messages he received, one letter stood out. It was Harold's. He retrieved it, read it aloud, and Greg, the great storyteller he is, knew immediately that Harold had to be in his film, as well. The whole time Greg was conducting his interview with Don, he was trying to figure out how to make that happen. Here's an edited version of their discussion.

GREG. **How did it come about that your addiction and recovery story became a part of that whole episode of *Undercover Boss*?**

DON. Well, it was kind of interesting. This producer, Damon, came in prior to production and started asking some questions about my life, about my background, what I do with my time, and that kind of thing. I realized that recovery is a big part of my life; it's given me the life that I have today. So, it kind of slipped out and I mentioned that I happened to be an alcoholic in recovery.

G. **Wow, they certainly grabbed onto that. But I was impressed with the way they presented it in the program because so many of the media do not know how to handle this public health problem and don't realize the power they have to help people. Were you comfortable with the way the producers handled it?**

D. First of all, I can say some really good things about the producers of *Undercover Boss* and the production company that does the show. As we talked about my being an alcoholic in recovery, they were willing to listen to my recovery story, in terms of how it would be portrayed. They were very careful to portray things appropriately. So, I felt really good about that.

G. **Was this the first time at this level of media that you've disclosed your recovery status?**

D. This was the second time I talked about my recovery publicly. The first time, I was anonymous. I was interviewed for a publication that was related to a hospital and they were talking to people in recovery who had some measure of business success. I was "Don"—no last name, no company mentioned, nothing specific. But it was one of those things where I didn't get a whole lot of feedback because nobody knew who to give feedback to. *Undercover Boss* was the first time where I've talked about something like that on a grand scale. I've revealed my recovery here at headquarters. Actually, I've been pretty open about it. Our folks in HR know that I'm in recovery because I've made myself available to anybody who might want to discuss recovery. And there are other people in recovery here who have either come to headquarters because they know me and I've helped them to get into the company, or they've talked to me about things over the years. They know my background and I know about theirs. But for me, it's kind of an open book; I have nothing to hide. It's part of who I am and if I can help somebody, somewhere, then probably the more people who know, the better.

G. Reflecting on the show, what was your experience like when you first saw the broadcast?

D. When I watched the show itself, I had an assortment of people over to the house. I was there with my family, my in-laws, and some friends. I was very curious as to how the producers were going to portray me. They had spoken with me and we kind of reviewed the approach that I'd like to see, but there's no guarantee they were going do that. When you do a show like that, they have you sign off with no control over the editorial content. For all I knew, they could have said, "Oh, look at this guy, he's an alcoholic and what a mess." But, they treated it with respect. The story they told was one of hope: A guy who could've lost it all was given a second chance. It couldn't have gone any better than it did.

G. And what kinds of reactions did you get from others?

D. By the time the show was over, the folks I was watching it with were very enthusiastic. And the moment the credits started rolling, I started getting texts and emails and messages on Facebook. The first one I got was from Fred DeLuca who said, "Don, great job." After that came a lot of my friends in recovery saying it was a very sensitive kind of portrayal and that I respected the traditions of anonymity and it showed that somebody can indeed have a second chance at life. Everyone expressed the hope that somebody might get something out of it. And then, what started to come afterward were messages from people who did get something out of it.

G. **A few minutes ago, you showed me a letter from someone named Harold who was obviously touched by your story when he watched the show.**

D. Ah. That one letter. I got hundreds of emails and communications and Facebook postings, and all of that. I received so many great messages from people, and that particular one was the one that touched me the most.

G. **If you don't mind, there was one thing he said I'd like to hear your reaction to. He writes,** *"Please let me thank you once again for being brave enough to go on national television and let a fellow recovering alcoholic know that, with determination and hard work, anything is possible."* **When you read that, how did you feel?**

D. It really made me feel good about discussing my recovery on national television. But it was interesting that he said, "... being brave enough to go on national television ..." That's the funny thing, bravery didn't enter into it. It never crossed my mind to be afraid to talk about my recovery. I was very comfortable with it, because to me it's not something to be ashamed of, or afraid of. It's part of who I am. And because I have been an active alcoholic and in recovery now, I have more to offer someone than I would have ever had, if I were just a regular Joe, so to speak. It's such a source for strength for me, getting strength out of my past.

I think people suffering with addiction hit some kind of bottom; we get to that point where we can't do this anymore, or we're just going to go on until we die. And then, that jumping off point comes and hopefully something triggers some change. I believe that if I can touch just one person and send him or her on the right path, then the job is done. The reality is, at this company, I was given that second chance and I was able to keep going. There were a lot of second chance people in the *Undercover Boss* story, which was terrific.

G. Great story. Thank you.

By the time the interview was over, Greg had a plan. At this point, Don and Harold had never met. In fact, no one knew about this amazing and private story of how Don had inspired Harold—and vice versa. Greg asked Don for an introduction to Harold and over the next couple of weeks, Greg had discussions with Harold about meeting him during our trip through the Midwest the following month.

In February, we were about to leave Louisville, after filming Mike Barry, Karyn Hascal and others at The Healing Place, and head to Minneapolis where we had a heavy three-day shooting schedule planned. We were pressed for time and worried whether we could afford to detour east into Indiana to interview Harold. Harold came through with a solution; he would drive down from Indiana to meet us before we took off straight to Minnesota. What a guy. I was learning quickly that people in recovery will do anything possible to make something good happen.

Harold came to our hotel in Louisville and, for expediency, we set up a scene for his interview right in our room. Harold was accompanied by his fiancé, who gave him moral support and the occasional cigarette. He was nervous; who wouldn't be? Our set and lighting and cameras and microphones make our intention serious and our process understandably intimidating to the uninitiated. I'll say this, though, Greg has an easy, calming way about him; he is unpretentious and humble, something his brothers and sisters in recovery perceive immediately. Harold began to relax, confident and secure in Greg's trustworthiness. The result is story-sharing that is honest and powerful, and it was emotional for all of us.

HAROLD ANDREWS

"The longer I go being sober, the sweeter this is."

GREG. Just go back a bit, if you will, and set the scene for us. What was your life like before you stopped drinking?

HAROLD. Sure. At the time I thought life was great. I had a good job, got a nice house, a great fiancé. Everything was awesome. I get paid on Friday, go out to a bar or a nightclub and have some drinks with the guys. The problem came the next morning when I finally found my way home. I had to explain to my fiancé how I already spent half, three-quarters, if not all of my paycheck. I kept doing this more and more often and she didn't see a penny. But yet, she has to pay all the bills. I felt really embarrassed with myself, but I wasn't ready to quit drinking. I was telling her one thing while living a different life. It was rough.

G. Did using alcohol affect your job?

H. Alcohol had a lot to do with my employment. Now that I got two DWIs, it's a huge issue for me. I had applied for a position at an IT solutions company. I got the offer letter, contingent on my background. They said, "Well, you have a felony." And I said, "That's not true. They were only misdemeanors." They re-investigated and they found out that I didn't have a felony background. Unfortunately, it was too late. The position was gone, so now I have to start over, looking again. It upset me that I had to go through something like that. But, I have nobody to blame but myself. I'm the one who put me in that position. I'm the one who decided to drink and drive and I'll take the responsibility for that.

G. You told me earlier that your fiancé gave you an ultimatum and helped you to stop drinking. How did that happen and how did you find recovery?

H. I remember waking up in a jail cell, in a drunk-tank. My fiancé let me pretty much sit there for a few days, think about what I had done. She finally came to see me, and she said, "What do you want to do? "I told her, "I have to quit drinking. It's a second DWI, and this is no way I want to live my life." She stood behind me, and that meant a lot to me. I was also fortunate that I had a good attorney, the prosecutor was good to work with, and the judge was a stand-up judge. She believes in giving people a chance.

Once I got out of jail, my attorney said, "Look, if you're serious about wanting to quit drinking, you need to get some help." I started going to a few meetings around town and I found this little church that's right down the street from my house. So, I went and I felt at home. There were some older fellows like me in there and they have twenty, thirty years of sobriety, which helps me a lot.

G. You had been sober only a few weeks and then something happened that changed your life. Tell us about that.

H. I had a month or so of abstinence under my belt, I'm still pretty nervous, pretty embarrassed, and still got things going on with the court system. I happened to be watching TV one night and the show *Undercover Boss* came on. In this particular case, Mr. Don Fertman of Subway was on, and he disclosed the fact that he's an alcoholic. That really caught my attention. At the time, I was sitting watching the show, thinking a beer would be nice, and I'm still trying to resist the temptation. But in hearing him and seeing what he went through, I know how hard it is. Sometimes it's hard to say no, and not to pick up that drink. And then to see a guy who's in charge of a billion dollar company, who travels internationally, go on national television and be open and honest, to realize that there's a company that will actually help him, not just fire him because he's a drunk . . . well, that meant everything to me.

G. You obviously felt a very strong connection with Don. What did you do?

H. After the show, I grabbed a laptop and I started typing a letter to Don before I even knew how to get a hold of him. I just wanted to put down how I felt. I finished and my fiancé says, "What are you doing?" I read her the letter and she said, "Well, I'm glad you feel that way, send it. If this guy can go on national television and admit he's has an issue, and he's in recovery, then Harold, that's not unlike you. You're doing the same thing." It made me stop and think.

G. So you sent the letter and you actually heard back from him. What did his recovery story mean to you coming from a person like that?

H. I'm only a month or so into recovery and, of course, I'm feeling sorry for myself. I'm also on the verge of realizing there's more to life than drinking alcohol. When I was watching the show, I'm thinking, *Wow, this guy's got it all together. He's got a beautiful wife, beautiful home, terrific job. This guy's on top of the world.* And then, I thought, *Yeah, but he's still going to think about that drink the next day.* I never realized what "one day at a time" meant. I was thinking, *I wonder if Don goes through that every day.* I didn't really know.

So yes, Don and I exchanged a few emails over the course of the last year. He checked on me from time to time, and every time I got an email from him, I thought, *Wow, this guy who's in charge of a huge operation has the time to email somebody like me.* I don't quite know how to say this: I didn't know anyone in his position or at his level. I never talked with anybody like that who was an alcoholic. But to see somebody like him going through this, I realized that alcohol doesn't discriminate in any way. It made me pretty proud to see him on TV and then be able to talk to him.

G. That's a wonderful story. You wrote about hope in your letter, and I know you were early in recovery and there were a lot of consequences of your drinking that you were dealing with at time, but through all that, where did the hope come from? How did you finally see the possibilities of recovery as something real?

H. It's more of a feeling. I don't really know how to put it into words exactly. For me, I had to go to that higher power. I had to seek out somebody or something to help me find the direction I needed to go. When I was watching *Undercover Boss* and I saw Don, I was like, wow, that's the person I want to be. I don't know if it was just that one particular moment that hit me, but in watching his show, and hearing his story, and seeing the respect he got from his peers and his boss, well, that was awesome. And, it was such a little thing that he had to do—just quit drinking. It sounded so simple, but I felt that was the toughest thing in the world for me to do.

I realize that while it is a little thing, it will probably always be the hardest thing for me to do for the rest of my life. I know now, I can't drink at all; however, there's always an alternative. I don't want to be back in jail. I don't want to be verbally abusive to my fiancé. And looking at people like Don and others who I can look up to and sponsors I talk with, well, they give me that hope and that desire.

G. Describe, if you can, what recovery has brought to your life, the gifts it has given you.

H. It has been a rough road to travel, but I never thought life could actually look this bright again. I enjoy things more during the day because I'm not drinking. I sleep better at night. I've lost a friend or two, at least what I called a friend, because they're still into heavy drinking and I just can't put myself around that. I still have a couple of friends who do drink, but they respect me enough not to try to push that upon me. I've got a good meeting group. I've got a great higher power, and I've got a very loving fiancé who has stuck with me through thick and thin. She says,

"I'm proud of you." After everything I put her through, she can still be proud of me. It means a lot. It gives me the desire to continue. Excuse me. This is really emotional for me. All these things mean more to me than anybody could ever imagine. Having a good mentor, having people to look up to, seeing people who have gone through this and who have gone on national television and shown that they have the courage to stand up, to not only admit their mistakes, but also to try to help others, is a huge thing for me. I was fortunate enough to find that and, I'll be forever grateful.

G. Your recovery is working.

H. The longer I go being sober, the sweeter this is.

Here's the dressing on top of this delicious Subway story:

It's now April of 2013. We're at the famed Bushnell Theatre in Hartford, Connecticut to screen the first release cut of *The Anonymous People* before a crowd of 500 supporters, friends, and recovery advocates and celebrants. It's an exciting event; the press is there, and the entire filmmaking team is there, proud and anxious to have this first public screening of a work that has become so important to all of us. But there is something missing from the film.

Don and Harold's story did not make the final cut of *The Anonymous People*.

Despite all our preconceived notions, despite all our beliefs that this was one of the best stories Greg found, and despite our amazing editor Jeff Reilly's herculean efforts to find a place for it in the film, it did not fit. How to explain this? It isn't easy. Film editing and storytelling is a mysterious art. At some point in the process, a story takes on a life of its own and begins to dictate the elements that will propel it forward. The arc, the thread, the juxtapositions, the points and counterpoints—they all come into play and combine with structure and pacing to let you know when the story is stalling or going off-track. The other big tyrant is time. Whether it be artificial standards and practices or our own psychological limits, stories need to conform to certain lengths for public acceptability. Don and Harold's story took too long to tell properly.

Greg had the unenviable task of trying to explain the omission of the story to Don, after all his support and help in creating it in the first place. Give Don credit. Maybe it is the musician in him, but he had the artistic insight and understanding to appreciate Greg's storytelling dilemma and accepted it most graciously.

There was another surprise in store for everyone that night in Hartford.

The producers of *Undercover Boss* found out about the story that Greg was making of Don and Harold and decided to do a follow-up episode on Don, which would include Harold. CBS flew Harold to Connecticut and, with their cameras, followed him to the premiere of *The Anonymous People* in Hartford. Before this day, Don and Harold had never met in person.

The theater was packed. Greg took the stage and began telling everyone he had prepared a short featurette to open the show. It was one example of the powerful stories he had found while making *The Anonymous People*, but which he couldn't include in the main film. The lights went down and there was the complete Don and Harold story—Harold's letter and all. The audience watched the short film transfixed, moved, and inspired. The lights came back up and Greg again took the stage to make another introduction. Out of the darkness, two figures approached from the opposite wings. And there on the big stage, Don and Harold, brothers in recovery, met and embraced for the first time—in public.

The Don and Harold story is significant in the collection of celebrity and media stories we examined. It illustrates how powerful the other side of the addiction story—successful recovery—can be. The media money machine could take a cue: There are at least forty-six million Americans who would love to hear that kind of story. Kudos to *Undercover Boss*; they learned there was an audience for a good recovery story, so much so, they were compelled to do a follow-up program to their original broadcast, which focused on the touching story of Harold Andrews that Greg uncovered.

Therein lies the lesson we can learn on how to influence media's coverage and to encourage a more positive depiction of the human struggle for redemption and healing. In Don's case, he controlled the message. Yes, *Undercover Boss* retained final editorial control, but the only information the producers had to work with was what Don gave to them. How Don told his story and how he expressed it influenced the content and tone right from the beginning. He spoke truthfully and used positive expressions such as "person in recovery," instead of "addict." There was no shame evident; in fact, there was just enough pride in his recovery story to make it blossom into something beautiful. Behind the Subway counter in his incognito *Undercover Boss* role, he may not have been an accomplished "sandwich artist," but in front of the camera, no longer anonymous, Don Fertman became one helluva "recovery artist."

All of the celebrities and public figures we met during the making of *The Anonymous People* developed the skills and the purpose to use various media to promote recovery in the best ways. As we have seen, some were early victims of insensitive and harmful publicity. By virtue of their celebrity or position, they may have had no choice in controlling initial accounts of their addiction, but now they do control the story. And they are changing the way people look at them. Likewise, the average person in recovery, whether privately or within a larger community, can help change the common, negative image people suffering with addiction have had to endure. Shame and stigma are perpetuated by secrecy and media exploitation. Show the world what the face and voice of recovery truly looks like, and the world, along with yours, will change.

As Patrick Kennedy, William Moyers, and others have said, if we change public perception about the disease of addiction, we can change attitude and public policy overnight.

With a nod to Neil Armstrong, it need only be one small step to make that giant leap from shame to pride.

But it takes courage.

Chapter Five

FEAR TO COURAGE

The Anonymous People is a story, after all, about coming out of the shadows of shame into the full light of public disclosure for advocacy and healing. It takes courage for addicted or recovering individuals to do this because the insidious nature of the illness causes many to be fraught with fear. Achieving healthy socialization is a difficult maneuver for the addicted. It is a challenge acknowledged by the fourth of the Twelve Steps, which encourages participants to make "a searching and fearless moral inventory of ourselves."

Fear and anxiety would seem to be at the root of addictive behavior in the first place, and no one is more susceptible to these elemental forces than adolescents. Until about the age of twenty-five, when our prefrontal cortex, the region of the brain associated with calm reasoning and judgment, becomes more or less fully developed, we are strongly influenced by another area of the brain, the amygdala, which matures earlier. The amygdala houses our fear center; when we perceive something that is threatening or strange or unknown to us, the amygdala reacts by sending a message to our cortex looking for a way to deal with the fear or anxiety we are facing. Often, due to the simple biologic incapability of the yet undeveloped cortex, our brain cannot offer a reasonable solution. Alcohol or other drugs do, though. These artificial salves calm the alarm, and their feel-good properties go directly to our reward center, another area of the brain that develops early. It is easy to see how the cycle of problem perception, reflex, reward, and learning can be wrongly wired in our brains during such a vulnerable developmental period of our lives. Those chemical patterns, if you will, can stay with us a long time; 90 percent of addicted adults began drinking or using other drugs during adolescence. Addiction compels us to find some artificial way to deal with fear; recovery offers other solutions, which, though they may represent a more difficult leap of faith, are real.

There is much still to learn about all of this. President Obama's "brain-mapping" initiative continues to inspire new understandings of the neurological pathways that control our behavior and feelings. In the meantime, as research goes on, science and medicine also continue to argue about the causes, diagnoses, prevention, and treatment of addiction. On one polarized side of the debate are those who believe the answers lie in chemistry; the other side believes cognitive behavioral therapy is the remedy. Most of those in the field fall somewhere in the middle.

One thing is for certain: addiction is best addressed during adolescence, when we learn our lifelong lessons. In fact, we have our best chances to overcome future fears when we can be taught how to do so at an early age. There is reason to believe that young people in recovery will actually have an easier time moving into advocacy as their recovery matures. If they have learned how to deal with their anxieties early, then later it will be easier to find the courage to come out and stand up proud and loud to inspire others to recover or even prevent addiction in the first place.

We see this happening already among the youth of this country, as they are becoming a strong force in the new recovery advocacy movement. Nurturing our youth and giving them the knowledge and strength to move from fear to courage is our essential responsibility. At home, that means setting some limits on behavior—which kids *want* us to do, by the way—and providing a communicative, safe, and secure environment for them. Some of that is being accomplished in recovery programs, which are cropping up in high schools and universities across the country. Successes there create considerable hope for the future, because they are proving that young people are ready, willing, and able to be healthy, productive citizens.

Hey. It's simple biology.

ROGER OSER

"[Supporting recovery] can take you to places you never even dreamed of—positive places."

William J. Ostiguy High School is in the heart of Boston, literally and figuratively. The school is in a small, five-story brick building wedged between shops, restaurants, and quirky businesses, just yards off historic Boston Common, and within sight of the gold dome of the Massachusetts State House across the park. And, as school Principal Roger Oser proudly tells it, Ostiguy High School arose out of the hearts of Boston citizens who saw a desperate need to help young people beat addiction, solidify their recovery, and achieve academically.

Ostiguy High School, founded in 2006, is one of five such schools in Massachusetts, three of which are in the greater Boston area. Ostiguy High is a public school, not a treatment program. It combines a standard high school academic curriculum with supportive recovery life skills, administered by a staff of certified educators and specialists. It is open to any student in recovery from a substance use disorder who qualifies on at least two accounts: be motivated to remain sober and be committed to earning a diploma. Students must have thirty days of sobriety before they can attend Ostiguy High and must consent to random drug testing while enrolled.

The principal goal of a recovery high school is to create a safe environment for students in recovery. Evidence shows that when young people, just out of residential treatment for addiction, return to their old school and friends, they are more likely to succumb to the pressures and behaviors of their former life. According to SAMHSA, 75 percent suffer relapse. A recovery high school provides a peer-supported environment for living and learning away from the harmful influences of the past—at least long enough to establish a strong recovery.

We caught up with Principal Oser on a busy Friday afternoon at the school. He was between meetings and we corralled him in a cheerful classroom that was just emptying of students. He knew them all by name and they exchanged good-natured greetings as they left, teasing him about his apparent celebrity status as he stood before our camera.

GREG. Ostiguy High is part of the greater Boston Public School system. What is your relationship with the regular schools and how do students find you?

ROGER. A lot of our referrals come from different treatment programs and then, we connect directly with the public schools—with guidance counselors, school nurses—to give them information, not just recovery high school, but about counseling and treatment options. That way, young people can have conversations with licensed substance abuse counselors. That might set the stage for them to be able to come to Ostiguy High. We want young people to have access to counseling treatment, to get a foundation in recovery. And so, in addition to the sixty to seventy young people we serve a year, we're trying to have a greater impact on the entire school system, in Boston and surrounding areas, by making sure they're aware of the systems and the counseling options that exist for young people who need help for this issue.

G. What do schools need to do to be able to support recovery in a school setting?

R. We know that for young people in recovery to be successful, they need a peer-driven environment where other young people have the same issue. They need mandatory drug testing. They need a licensed substance use counselor on staff who can provide support. They need staff who understand their situation. So, I think the school district has a responsibility to create opportunities for young people to be in that type of environment. But I want to stress that recovery high school students aren't more special or better or different than other young people. We can show through research, and we can show through experiences that for this group to be successful, they need a specific set of supports. And public school systems are always trying to provide opportunities for all types of students.

G. **You've traveled around the country and talked with other recovery high schools. What are you and other recovery school leaders talking about in terms of advocating for more acceptance and growth of the recovery school model?**

R. I think a lot of it is about awareness and understanding what addiction is, and the specific supports and needs of a young person who has this issue, and that there's a growing number of young people who face this issue. Once people get into recovery, it's the old people, places, and things that bring them down, especially adolescents. If they go back to the same school, hang out with the same people, and do the same things they did before, their chances of staying sober are almost zero. When you talk with the students about their experiences, you can see the impact it has on them. One thing they will always say is "If I went back to my old school, I would not have been able to stay there. I would've relapsed. I would've been failing school again. I would've been back on the streets."

Once they make that effort to get sober, give them a place they can come to where they can continue to grow, not just academically, but socially and emotionally. That's what we're trying to do with recovery high schools. We have a model that works, and we're continuing to find ways to sustain it financially. That's the message we're trying to get out; there's a different way to do it for this population. And we're just trying to get as many people as possible to be aware of it and find people who support this type of concept.

G. **What did it take to get Ostiguy High School started?**

R. I think it's a great lesson in civics. William J. Ostiguy, a private citizen and Boston city fireman; State Senator Steven Tolman, a politician; and Greg Hughes, who oversaw the Governor's Council on Substance Abuse, plus, Action for Boston Community Development, a community-based organization [in collaboration with the Gavin Foundation], and the Boston Public Schools—all came together. Senator Tolman and Willie Ostiguy visited other recovery high schools. They came back and said, "We have to be able to do this for our young people." They got the consensus behind them and were able to pass some legislation that supports recovery high schools to this day. And now, we continue to grow and build relationships in the school districts to make sure we can sustain it. When you get a group of people together, if you have the will and you can work together, you find a way to make it happen.

G. You speak with a lot of pride about Ostiguy. As well you should—nearly 80 percent of your graduates go on to college. This must be very rewarding work for you.

R. This is incredibly rewarding. Any time you work with people in a community to achieve something that makes a difference in people's lives, I mean, how can that not be rewarding? On a day-to-day basis, like, we're filming this on a Friday at two o'clock, I just stepped out of a staff meeting. I'm exhausted. I have tons of frustration. You know, this isn't happening, that's not happening. But then, you sit back and you look at the bigger picture, the staff here, the students here—we just finished our student meeting and we had some graduates there, and you see how their lives are going and how well they're doing. The students who are here, how well they're doing compared to when they were in dark places deep in their addiction—that's the beauty of recovery. And then, you find a community that will support that. It's like anything else, what you do is important, but the people you do it with is what makes it special. And so, to be part of that process is extremely rewarding. It can take you to places you never even dreamed of—positive places. It's amazing.

It was easy to catch Roger Oser's enthusiasm. The students at Ostiguy are extraordinary. You sense such a life purpose in them, a determination to succeed, a level of maturity that belies their age; yet, they are still kids and they horse around and have fun. It is a promising combination. There were many exceptional students willing and eager to share their stories with us, along with their ideas and hopes for the future. One young man started talking, with stunning maturity, about the world outside of himself:

> "There's an image of drug addiction today, but there really isn't an image of recovery. I think the public needs to know that recovery is very, very possible and it's happening all over the place. There are people coming back from drug addiction, becoming better people and living a normal life and doing good things, and changing things in the government. People can change. Today, I just try to give back what I've been given, just trying to make good things happen, trying to change the image of recovery . . . and the world."

When I hear pessimistic, old fogeys complain about the "younger generation," I say they have to know more young people like this young man and all the others we met at this recovery high school. They are typical of the many young people who have come back from addiction and who are now in successful, productive recovery.

Think about this bit of irony. Some of the best hopes for our future may come from the two million high school students who currently have a substance use disorder. Could this be true? Can addiction, one of the major forces tearing our families and society apart, also be its salvation? Yes—if we gave those two million kids a chance to recover. Why? Because successful, long-term recovery from addiction is life-changing; thus, there may be no group more well-equipped and motivated to change the world for the better than young people in recovery. We must think of it that way, encourage it, and make it happen.

Then there is this. Using addictive substances in your teen years is much more likely to begin the onset of addiction than if you start using after the age of twenty-one. Statistics and science back that up, and common sense tells us that bad habits start early. Study after study shows that early intervention saves lives and reduces costs. So, why do we continue to foster an environment that fuels bad habits, instead of one that nurtures the good? Why are two million teenagers left suffering instead of encouraged to strive for a bright future?

Joe Schrank and Kristen Johnston, who have been advocating for a Recovery High School in New York City, wonder why, too. They are frustrated with the obstacles they have encountered from people and systems that block their progress to establish the city's first such school. Knowing the power of recovery and the benefit to youth and to our society, it should be a slam-dunk. But the problem is not enough people know this story yet. Most of us don't realize the staggering fact that there are over twenty-two million Americans who are addicted to alcohol and/or other drugs. And we are woefully unaware that this enormous problem, for the most part, begins in youth. What's more, most of us simply don't know about the other twenty-three million Americans who are in real recovery, living productive lives. If we did, and if we knew the truth, all kinds of pathways would open up. That's why people in successful recovery, living the proof, need to step up and teach us, to tell us their stories and change the conversation. As it is, our ignorance gives rise to many reasons why good healing ideas, such as recovery schools, are difficult to put into practice.

Ecole Nouvelle, later named Sobriety High, one of the first recovery high schools in the US, was established in 1986 in Minnesota. But, despite its early success—it had the advantage of being in a state with a high density of addiction treatment, support services, and issue awareness—the idea was slow to catch on elsewhere. By 2014, there were only about thirty-five recovery high schools operating throughout the United States. Why is such a good idea so hard to implement?

When we were in Minneapolis, we stopped in to see Monique Bourgeois, the former Executive Director of the Association of Recovery Schools, a national nonprofit that advocates for recovery schools at both the high school and collegiate level across the nation. She has been involved with the Association of Recovery Schools since its inception in 2002, and told us that besides the general lack of awareness and understanding among the public about the efficacy of recovery schools, there are practical reasons why they are difficult to start up and sustain.

> "Part of the challenge is finding supporters who are going to work at the grassroots level to help find sustainable funding for a recovery high school or collegiate recovery community. Also, recovery schools are locally based, and must respond to the needs of their local community, and because education is controlled at the state and local levels, it is difficult to apply one type of model school to every state in the country."

Bourgeois is optimistic, though, that recovery schools will take hold and help create vital solutions for addiction and recovery for our youth. She pointed out that there is now a convergence of forces that is driving change, including new and better research about addiction, treatment, and recovery; growing awareness of mental health issues; revisions to the *Diagnostic and Statistical Manual of Mental Disorders* (DSM-5), making it easier to qualify youth for health services; and the Affordable Care Act, which is expanding mental health and substance use disorder services to more adolescents who need treatment and continuing care.

There's a progression in these forces that is notable and instructive. Policy does gradually change . . . because policy makers finally get the facts . . . because knowledge of issues grows . . . because awareness is raised . . . because more and more people tell their recovery stories.

Greg knew one person who was extraordinarily successful in teaching people how to tell those stories. We went to meet him, several times, in fact.

AARON KUCHARSKI

"We're the experts on recovery, and I think we should be empowered to go out and have that voice heard, and put a positive face on recovery."

Greg is jealous of Aaron Kucharski. He says Aaron is one of the luckiest guys in the country because his full-time job is to advocate for recovery and train others to be good advocates. Plus, he works in New Jersey, a state that can boast being at the forefront of building an active addiction issues constituency. In truth, New Jersey's success owes much to the Advocacy Leadership Program that Aaron runs for the National Council on Alcoholism and Drug Dependence (NCADD-New Jersey), which turns out knowledgeable and trained leaders who are dedicated to confronting the state's most pressing addiction treatment, prevention, and recovery issues. Since it began in 2008, the program has graduated nearly 200 advocates and enlisted over 500 leadership partners who support the advocacy efforts. Over the course of a year, participants receive trainings on a variety of subjects that include how to tell one's story of recovery, the legislative process, addiction issues, such as treating non-violent offenders, and the state budget. With these skills, participants can, among many other things: give testimony before legislative committees; address high level budgetary matters at the Department of Human Services; conduct informational forums on addiction; speak for stigma reduction; and communicate with the media. The ultimate goal is to establish advocacy leaders and leadership teams throughout New Jersey fully empowered to change systems and promote good public policy.

Aaron is one of those omnipresent soldiers—actually, he's more like a general—of the national recovery movement who seemed to be at every major event we attended. And like many people in recovery, you would never know how important he was to the movement by his quiet modesty and humble demeanor. Yet, you know he has earned his Four Stars by pulling off such accomplishments as being one of the lead organizers of the Wellness Room of the Recovery Caucus at the Democratic National Convention.

When we caught up with him, he was giving a workshop on messaging training and the media with Tom Coderre in Boston. This two-day class was similar to the one Greg had taken, which so greatly influenced his life, and the two of them had a lot to talk about; however, our camera time with Aaron was too brief because of his full schedule. Nevertheless, you can glean from the following short interview something of Aaron's clarity and knowledge on the subject of advocacy and the recovery movement. His message is simple. And profound.

GREG. Taking a cue from your own training, tell us how you would introduce yourself.

AARON. Sure. My name is Aaron Kucharski. I'm a person in long-term recovery, which to me means that I haven't had a drink or a drug since September 6, 2003.

G. What transpired in your recovery to motivate you to transition from just a person in recovery to become such a public advocate for recovery?

A. Taking this language training was a way my recovery evolved. There was this moment in my recovery when the shame of addiction turned into the pride of recovery. And I think there was always this passion in me to help other people, but it was lost for some time. I wanted to show other people a way to do it, get people to where I am. And recovery gave me back that passion to share with other people, and work to organize the community around these issues.

G. I know that taking this training years ago certainly changed my life, but it was a little strange at first. The first time you took this training, did you buy into it and put it into practice?

A. It took me a little while, actually, but when I did, I used this language training everywhere. You have to practice to get used to it; it did feel like learning a foreign language, in a sense. You're learning a different way of speaking, and you're challenging your old ideas. And I really liked that because I had to look at some of the biases that I had. I use it in advocacy efforts, when I talk to elected officials, or even when I talk to family members. I use this language training when I write in blogs and make comments on articles online on addiction. I've actually used this training when a police officer asked me, "Have you been drinking tonight?" I said, "No, I haven't. I haven't had a drink since September 6, 2003." It's pretty specific, okay? So, I work, and I use this training in all aspects of my life.

G. **As we shot your message training session today, we saw the class write down a list of words—synonyms and phrases—that describe an "addict." Some of them were pretty harsh and derogatory, like junkie, crack head, and dope fiend. What is that exercise about?**

A. That exercise shows the need for training like this, and why there needs to be an alternative to the offensive words that portray people who have had a problem with alcohol or other drugs in the past. The words that people came up with were negative and offensive. I read them and get sad; it makes you sad that this is how people in recovery are perceived. This training is all about offering an alternative to that. That way, people can identify themselves in a more positive light and talk about their recovery, rather than their past addiction.

G. **Why is it important to train people to speak out about recovery?**

A. Well, it's important because for a long time people have been silent around addiction issues; and we look at this as a growing recovery advocacy movement. And when you look at movements in the past, like civil rights, or women's rights, voters' rights, they all had leaders, they all had people speaking out on the issues. And it's a much-needed voice; we need to define what people in recovery should say to show others that there's help, that we can remove barriers, and make sure that more people get into recovery.

G. You do a lot of advocacy work in New Jersey and elsewhere. What does advocacy really achieve, and how do you go about it?

A. I think speaking about it in public really does address that negative public perception. That's the victory. It's about reducing stigma. For a number of years, we've been doing trainings to get people to be comfortable talking about it, whether it's a family member who has somebody else in recovery, or who may have lost somebody through addiction, and how to tell their story in the most effective way. We've done a lot of organizing at the State House in Trenton, through rallies or through letter-writing campaigns and letters to the editor. We have ten regional advocacy teams in New Jersey, so no matter where you live in the state there is a team you can meet up with and help set the direction for solutions to addiction.

G. You also do campaign organizing and voter registration. Obviously, you see that as an important component of public advocacy.

A. In 2008, a national campaign called Recovery Voices Count began, which was a nonpartisan civic engagement campaign that focused on educating voters about recovery, and about candidates on recovery issues, empowering people to vote in their state, and reminding them to vote on Election Day. I think that not only does the recovery community need to educate themselves on the issues, but they also need to ask candidates questions and figure out where they stand on these issues.

G. From your perspective, what do you think is important for the re-covery movement to do as it continues to grow and expand?

A. The vision I have for the recovery movement is that people understand the harm in being quiet about it or using the wrong words when describing recovery. I think it's really important to improve those words and use the language in our training. Also, it's important to find the leaders out there who are going to talk about the issues. We're the experts on recovery, and I think we should be empowered to go out and have that voice heard and put a positive face on recovery.

G. I agree. Especially the language piece. Elevating language helps to erase stigma and the fears of prejudice and discrimination. That's empowering and can create the courage to speak out.

A. Exactly.

Chapter Six

DOOM TO HOPE

It's not just the physical component of addiction that beats people down and fills them with a sense of doom; external forces of shame and stigma intensify feelings of hopelessness in people already suffering from guilt and low self-esteem. There often seems to be no escape. Even if you could overcome your addiction, you face a societal scorn that damns and dooms you to a life hardly worth living. At least that is the feeling and the fear as long as you are in the compounded darkness. All of the people in recovery we met found the courage at some point in their lives to lift themselves—or be lifted—from the doom and find blessed hope. Over and over again, we heard their unique stories and came to appreciate how many different ways there are to find hope, and how many pathways there are to find recovery. Strengthened by their successes in recovery, they eventually began to bring that hope to others by quiet example or dynamic advocacy. And they continue to do so.

The faces and voices you meet in the following pages are just a sampling of the many extraordinary individuals who gladly shared their stories with us. Each, in their own way, is devoted to helping others find a path from doom to hope. Just as each of their paths to recovery was different, their commitment to advocacy takes many forms—person-to-person, institutionally, creatively, or sometimes organizationally, galvanizing great numbers in public advocacy.

It struck me how different all these people are, how they break the stereotypes of the addicted person, and how they speak with one voice about their journeys. It only proves that no matter who you are, doom is not inevitable and hope is real.

JOHN L. SILVERMAN

"I would always encourage someone not to be frightened, to go out and talk about how they stopped, and now what recovery is like for them."

John Silverman has fought more adversaries than most people. In his NYPD days, his foes were the criminals and miscreants in the streets of the city. They were nothing compared to the demons that later rose up to give him the fight of his life. His bout with addiction was John's personal main event, a grueling fight that went round after round until he was knocked out. But in 1984, like a true champion, he climbed back into the ring, faced his toughest opponent, and made a comeback. He got sober and began his successful path to long-term recovery.

John grew up during an exciting time in the 1950s on the lower east side of Manhattan. As he puts it, "My neighborhood was a haven for boxers. I remember seeing my father hang out with light heavyweight contender, Tony Johnson. Rocky Graziano grew up there and his family lived a few doors down from me. Even LuLu Consentino, a lightweight contender, opened a bar there, LuLu's, on 13th Street. I would play pool in the back while the great and not-so-great boxers told stories at the bar. I guess you could say that my heroes have always been boxers."

Maybe that's how John became such a fighter, with the heart not to stay down, the moxie to get up and become a mover and shaker in the very city in which he humbly grew up. Recovery has given him the opportunity to succeed. He runs a thriving international private investigation firm that employs over 500 people. He is part-owner of a four-star restaurant in Manhattan. And, he owns a boxing management enterprise with some promising fighters in his stable. While recovery has enabled him to enrich his life, recovery also compels him to give back.

Besides philanthropy and mentoring, recovery has made this real-life boxing aficionado into a heavyweight champion of recovery advocacy, a cause he lives and breathes daily. He was definitely there in our corner when the film was at a critical stage and needed support. Next time you see *The Anonymous People*, read the credits; you'll see John's name as Executive Producer, which means that he was key in helping Greg go the full ten rounds and get that film made.

GREG. **It is fair to say your life changed dramatically since your recovery. Where were you at one time, and how did you get here?**

JOHN. The person who's sitting here now obviously isn't the person who came into recovery twenty-eight years ago. I was a New York City police officer, and I was a good cop. I worked hard. But the alcohol got to me and, after I left the police department, my drinking took a downward slide. I was homeless for almost nine months. I didn't have to be homeless, I mean, I had a great family. I could have gone to my mom, but I think pride is what kept me from doing that. I couldn't let anybody see me in the condition I was in. I lost my apartment and lived where anybody would have me. The end for me was a mattress in the back of an abandoned building in "Alphabet City" in New York City. I'm laying on this mattress, I'm thirty-five years old, my future's behind me, unemployable, very sick. And that's where they found me in the back of this abandoned building. The next day my friend, Louie, brought me upstate and I detoxed there for four days and I didn't know how I was going to stop. I made a phone call to my friend, Barbara, who had gone away for a month or so, and when she got back she wasn't drinking. So, I called her and I told her, "I need some help," and she told me, "I've been waiting for this phone call." That started my recovery.

G. What was your early recovery like? Did you keep it secret or were you open about it?

J. I finally was able to get a job after about nine months sober. I took a job working at this one particular restaurant, a wonderful restaurant in New York City, and I freely talked about what happened to me. I talked about my recovery and there was no shame there. For the first four or five years, I talked about it all the time. Because when I talked about it somebody else would say to me, "Hey, I think I might have a problem. Could you take me with you? Where do you go? What do you do? How did you do this?" And I made myself available for that.

G. But then later, you started being less open about your recovery status. Why was that?

J. A few years into my recovery, I decided that I wanted to make a difference in life, and I knew I could do more, so I took a risk—I took two risks. I got married that year, and then I started a business, the business that I'm in now.

I do security work and investigative work, and it's work that's very confidential and it's work that's extremely important to someone's life who's in trouble. Either their personal life or their business life is in big trouble and they'll come to a firm like ours for help. And when I started, I had to embrace the idea of anonymity because I thought, *I can't put this out there. I can't tell a guy that four years ago I was laying on a mattress in the back of an abandoned building, and now, you want me to step in and help you fix your business, your life?* So, I really couldn't say anything, and that went on for a while. People would say, "Why don't you drink?" And I'd have to make excuses. I'd say, "Oh, I'm on medication." I'd say anything because I didn't want to have to explain that I was an alcoholic. It was a terrible feeling to have to hide it from someone. It was a terrible feeling to have to lie.

G. I had the same sort of journey. Before I entered recovery I lived two separate lives—the addicted one and the front I would put on for

**my family, friends, and the police. Then, in recovery it was similar—
I was open with others in recovery, but then I kept it secret from
school, employers, and even some friends.**

J. Keeping a secret, that's right. Addiction loves secrecy; it festers and
grows in secrecy. Well, I was keeping a secret to the rest of the world,
but I wasn't keeping any secrets when I was going to the meetings that
were helping me with my recovery. I was very open about my life and
what was going on. When I got into this business, I think I had to get
comfortable with my own self-worth, my own self-esteem, how others
viewed me, before I was able to actually talk about it with a client or talk
about it with a colleague. I mean, how many people would be honest
enough to speak to a roomful of strangers and talk about what happened
to them? I found, once I was able to do that, it changed my perspective
completely. I had nothing to fear anymore, nothing to hide.

**G. But it's hard telling your secrets, whether it's about your addiction
or your recovery. Why do you think it is better to bring those secrets
to light?**

J. The problem is when people hold these secrets, they can't get help. They
can't. Where do you go for help if you don't talk about it?

G. What was the tipping point for you to become more open again?

J. I thought, what's this all about anyway? I believe we were all created
with a purpose in our lives, and that purpose for me was to help the
alcoholic who still suffers the way that I did. And I wasn't doing that; I
couldn't put myself out there. I realized when I started to share openly
about what happened to me, colleagues and clients all just fell into "Hey,
would you mind talking to my brother? My brother's got a problem with
alcohol," or "Would you mind talking to my son?" And it just went from
there, and I decided that this is my purpose; this is really what I'm put
here for. So, I had to be up front about what happened to me and how it
happened. I couldn't hide in the church basement anymore.

G. What is it like for you to carry that message of hope and see the light go on in other people, watching them find the hope that you found?

J. Well, let me kick something else around about that. When I was new in recovery, my mom would give me five dollars a day. Five bucks! I'm an ex-policeman, thirty-five years old, and my mom's giving me five dollars a day so that I can go to a recovery support meeting and get a slice of pizza and then come home. I was going to two or three meetings a day and I was stretching that five bucks, walking to meetings. There was this meeting at night that was a regular meeting, Monday through Friday, and there was a bunch of guys there who were so nice to me, and they were so kind. They would always ask me, "Hey, why don't you come on out with us? We're going to have a bite to eat." And I'd always say, "No, thanks. I'm not hungry." But meanwhile, I was very hungry. I was hungry, not only for the food, I was really hungry to hear how to stay sober. But my pride kept me from going into that restaurant because I couldn't ask somebody to pay for a meal for me. So today, when I go to a meeting and I hear a newcomer to say to me, "No. It's all right. I'm not hungry," I ask him a second time. I'll tell him my story about how I felt at that time, and almost every single time he'll come and have a burger with me and sit and talk. So I had to learn how to be honest. When I came in, I wasn't an honest person, I just wasn't. It's part of the illness, and I had to learn over a period of time how to become honest.

G. What kind of reactions do you get from clients or other business people who don't know you when you tell them about your recovery?

J. You get various reactions, but I've never gotten a negative reaction. When I tell them what happened to me they can't believe that I'm the same guy I'm talking about twenty-eight years ago, and I'll go into as much detail as they would like me to. And I'm telling you, there's almost always someone who comes up to me later on and wants to talk to me confidentially, either about themselves or somebody in their family who might need some help and what should they do. To make a recommendation for them or be available to help, that's my purpose. That's my real job. That's where I spend most of my time these days; I spend most of my time *in* recovery.

G. **And you would encourage people in recovery to just put it out there if they can, live their lives, share their stories—because . . . why?**

J. I would encourage it. An investigative technique is to tell somebody something about yourself and you'll be surprised how they'll tell you something about themselves, and it's the same thing here. I would always encourage someone not to be frightened, to go out and talk about what happened to them, what happened while they were drinking, and how they stopped, and now what recovery is like for them. Until I made that phone call to my friend, Barbara, I had no idea there was a place that I can go and find recovery. I didn't know there was some hope. I thought I was going to have to do this the way I stopped smoking—I did it on my own and it was hard. Yeah. I didn't know there was a place to go, so if we don't put it out there, if we don't talk about it, then how is anybody going to really know? Recovery is the greatest thing in the twentieth century. It's changed so many lives.

John L. Silverman is not the only fighter we found who took the punches, but eventually emerged a winner. We traveled to that well-known barrio of boxing, Louisville, Kentucky, where we met another champion in the ranks of the recovery movement—in the women's division.

MAETTA BROADUS

"At the age of twelve, I was a full blown alcoholic."

She grew up poor in the West End of Louisville, Kentucky and was a neighbor of Muhammad

Ali. She remembers seeing the young Cassius Clay playing with friends in front of the modest white house that was typical of their African-American working class neighborhood. At the time, neither of them realized they were both destined to become champions and heroes to many.

Today, Maetta Broadus is active every day in the new recovery advocacy movement. She holds an organizing chair with Addiction Recovery Advocates of Kentuckiana (ARAK), a local organization serving Metro Louisville and Southern Indiana. She is also a member of People Advocating Recovery (PAR), a statewide organization in Kentucky dedicated to removing discrimination against people in recovery and assisting those in need of recovery. Her recovery date is February 10, 2007, a date that marks the beginning of the richest period in her life.

Maetta Broadus carries a serenity that belies the chaos of her youth. Her soft eyes, full of love, embrace you the moment they meet yours. You feel good; you smile. Then, you notice her hair—a riot of multi-colored dreadlocks, a rainbow that frames a face full of sunshine—and your smile widens because now you feel even better. Joyful, in fact. Until you hear her story, it is hard to imagine the journey from what seemed inevitable doom to the life of hope that this champion of recovery took. Maetta tells a story I have never been able to get over.

GREG. What was your early life like and when did your active addiction start?

MAETTA. I'm the middle child of three, had a single-parent mom, and grew up in poverty. I had some ill behavior going on in my life—molestation and abuse from extended family members. At the age of nine years old, I took it upon myself to go to the library and read about and understand sex, so at the age of eleven, I started prostituting for money because I hated being poor. At the age of twelve, I was a full-blown alcoholic. At fourteen, I became pregnant and delivered a child at fifteen. And from then on, drugs and alcohol were a normal way of living for me. I didn't know anything other than trying to kill the pain of my childhood memories of the molestation and the abuse with alcohol and other drugs.

G. **What kind of substances were you using?**

M. After becoming that alcoholic at twelve, I gravitated towards other substances—pills, cocaine—and by the time I hit thirty-five, I had a $1,500-a-day habit of smoking crack. I would do anything I could do to get that drug.

G. **Did you think you were a bad person?**

M. I was raised up going to church every Sunday. Mom made us go to school. She taught us good moral values—don't steal, don't lie, do unto others as you would have others do unto you, the golden rule. But I became different from my sister and my brother by having addiction and I couldn't stop, even when I wanted to. I had times where I prayed with the Bible in one hand and the crack pipe in the other and tears rolling down my face, praying to God that I could stop.

G. **What did you believe about yourself when you were in active addiction before recovery became an option for you?**

M. Before recovery, I believed that I was retarded. I believed that I was mentally incapable of comprehending the word "stop." I believed that I was destined for doom. I believed that I wasn't worthy of going to school.

I felt that because of my addiction, I didn't deserve the right to vote. I believed I didn't need a good job. I believed I would never get in an airplane because I was born poor. Before recovery, I believed my hair wouldn't grow. I believed I would have to walk around with rotten teeth. I believed my name wasn't worth signing on anything, no bank accounts, no paychecks, no car titles, no houses, no lease. I believed the government was supposed to take care of me and I'm supposed to get food stamps and welfare and live off of child support.

I believed I had a right to become a drug addict. I believed I had the right to come and break into your car and steal it because I didn't have mine. I believed I had a right to break the law because I was poor. I used to tell people, "I'm born this way, what's your excuse?" I also believed I was ugly, stupid, and dumb. And that I deserved everything I got in a bad way. That's what I believed.

G. What do you feel about the stigma associated with addiction?

M. Once you're seen in society as an addict, you're an abomination. You're something that no one wants in their community. You're that thing they have to hide. The stigma is they're doing it because they want to.

I didn't become a drug addict because I wanted to. I didn't become an alcoholic because I wanted to. Sometimes we have no choice, especially those of us who are not educated and informed about our condition.

G. So how did you finally find recovery?

M. At the age of thirty-five, I knew I needed help and that I needed to stop, so I put myself in treatment. It took me twenty years—twenty years of battling, staying sober, sometimes for thirteen months, eighteen months, a year, six months. I've had nineteen sobriety dates. But now, I'm proud to say that this is the first time I've ever had five years.

G. What have you learned in your recovery?

M. Since recovery, I know I'm intelligent. But, for the first twenty years, I wanted perfection out of it. And now I see that it wasn't the perfection, it's the progress. That's why I'm crusading for advocating recovery. It's the progress . . . maybe I can make a difference in one person's life, get him or her some help. Maybe it's to get voters' rights restored. Maybe it's to get a law to remove the stipulations of sending people to prison because they had a drunk driving accident.

G. **In your work, what message do you convey to people who need recovery?**

M. That there is a better way. The message I carry to the people in my community who are on crack or heroin or alcohol is that there is a better way. That it's not mind over matter; it takes work. It takes two people to have a child; it takes a community to raise a child. No man is an island; it takes a host of people to be involved in one person's life to get him or her away from what he or she thinks, feels, and believes. There's a better way and I'm living proof. From a $1,500-a-day habit to being an ambassador for recovery. Wow. Wow.

G. **How does working with an organization like PAR help strengthen and sustain your own recovery?**

M. People Advocating Recovery offers me a place where I can get strength and be able to share my knowledge and my personal experience of what recovery is. It allows me a sense of belonging to a group of people who understand the difference between having a disease and being a bad person. And it also allows me the blessing that I can totally forgive myself for being addicted and all my ill behaviors and insane actions and insane thinking, in order to give back. It allows me the freedom to accept being a helpful entity, a helpful product of society, and that I can become a voice for the people who don't have a voice.

G. **Many in recovery believe the secret to one's own recovery is in helping someone else in recovery. You seem to be proving that.**

M. I can offer a way out for the helpless and the hopeless. It gives me a sense of accomplishment that for me to offer a sick person a way out of his or her sickness is a pretty good deal. I'm so overwhelmed, and I'm so proud of myself. Although it took me twenty years! In that twenty years I've learned so much; all those sobriety dates I had, not one of them went unnoticed by me, because through my experience I know what to do and I know what not to do.

I tear up because the battle is so hard. I owe a debt to the alcoholics and drug addicts. I owe a debt to society because for so many years I thought I was crazy and didn't know that my mind could fight against my body. It's a good feeling to be relieved of the terrible curse with which I was afflicted. Today, my life is excellent. My mom has her daughter; my sister has her genuine sister whom she can trust. My brother has a big sister, finally, and my children don't have to wonder where I am. I'm trustworthy. I'm loyal. And I'm dedicated to the cause and to the crusade of removing the stigma and the barriers associated with addiction.

G. **What has recovery been like for you in terms of opening doors to new and positive experiences?**

M. I know I make a difference. I get the opportunity to do things that I never could have imagined. If I had made an itinerary of where I thought I would be at the age of fifty-four, it would have listed this: dead by drug overdose or alcohol poisoning. I'm grateful. I know I'm one of those ones who is blessed to have never gone to prison, but the prison I was in was more hideous than steel bars and concrete walls. PAR and ARAK offer me an opportunity to continue to forgive myself and continue to realize my self-worth. And it's not just about Maetta; it's about a society of people struggling for a way out. And if I can't do anything else, I can continue to stand and be a voice for the helpless and the hopeless and the lost, and I can take a stand on what I believe in. And my belief comes from my experience.

G. **What was it like bringing your family into your recovery experience? Your children and your grandchildren, for example, how have they reacted?**

M. My son, I've always been his all-in-all, no matter what. And even through my drug addiction, he held me in high esteem. Every year at the rallies, I would ask him would he come and sing and he said, "Mama, I'd do anything for you." My grandchildren, I asked them would they participate at the recovery rally, and they did. Kids would comment and congratulate them on their achievements in school, the grades had gotten better and they say, "Yeah, because my mom found recovery." Now their life is whole. For me, that feeling right there is priceless.

When my granddaughter was born, my son and his wife told me I couldn't even hold their baby. That's when I was getting high. And now these same children are in my life every day. There are no words to express my debt that I need to pay the recovery society for this.

G. You are a powerful messenger of hope. What do you say to the world about recovery?

M. We need to have a voice. Somebody has to say something about what recovery is and what it isn't. That's why I stand as a pillar of society saying, "This is the face of recovery." Today, I'm so alive. I am effervescent and bubbling with life. So when it's time for me to take a stand and go to the meetings and participate on getting bills signed and talking to the legislature, the senators and the people in the domed building, I speak loud and I speak clear on recovery. Addiction is not a choice, and recovery is a better way out.

The courage Maetta shows in telling her gut-wrenching story of addiction, paired with her inspiring story of recovery, is just what the movement needs. On the one hand, we are devastated by her addiction story and wonder how it is possible for someone to be so open and candid about such personal, hellish experiences in life. But then she uplifts us with the contrasting story of her recovery and redemption. In that respect, the Saul/Paul story of Maetta Broadus is, I suspect, easier for her to speak about publicly than we might imagine. She recognizes that her ego is subordinate to the good her whole story does for the world-at-large. How freeing it must be to realize that one's reputation—one's name—is sanctified by such a story, and not sullied.

DAN GRIFFIN

"It's a lot easier to break the cycle if you yourself are healthy in recovery and taking care of yourself."

Dan Griffin: author, public speaker, consultant, trainer, husband, father, musician, and tennis player. Dan is the kind of lively and learned guy you like to sit down with and solve the problems of the world, or examine Jimmy Page's guitar licks, or discuss brain-mapping, or talk endlessly about David Foster Wallace's endless sentences, or . . . well, you get the picture. He's a cool guy with a lot of interests, especially addiction, recovery, and the differentiating experience we males of the species have in the twelve-step culture.

Dan Griffin's books, *A Man's Way Though the Twelve Steps* (2009); *Helping Men Recover* (2011), coauthored with women's issues expert, Dr. Stephanie Covington and addiction specialist, Rick Dauer; and *A Man's Way through Relationships* (2014), examine the unique needs of men in recovery, integrating the latest thinking on addiction and recovery, as it relates to men's psychological development, the experience of trauma, and the process of socialization, particularly what Dan refers to as "The Man Rules."

After finding recovery in 1994 and with a degree in English and sociology, Dan began a two-decade long career in the mental-health and addictions field, including research, public advocacy, case management, and counseling. In 1998, Dan was the first recipient of the Hazelden fellowship to train as an addictions counselor. He served as the state drug court coordinator for the Minnesota Drug Court Initiative from 2002–2010, and as the judicial branch's expert on addiction and recovery. In 2010, Dan started Griffin Recovery Enterprises, Inc. for consultancy and training.

He lives in Minneapolis with his wife, Nancy, and daughter, Grace, where he invited us to his home on one of those ultra-wide residential thoroughfares typical of the pioneer city that anticipated the traffic of westward expansion to the edge of the prairie and beyond. Greg and Dan sat talking in the windowed front room of their neat, cape-style house as the reflective surfaces of cars driving by outside sent flashes of sunlight into the conversation, as if punctuating Dan's insights. It was an illuminating discussion.

GREG. **I suspect your recovery story has something to do with your career path and where you are today.**

DAN. I've been in recovery since right before my twenty-second birthday in 1994. I've basically grown up in recovery; I was far from a man when I got sober. I didn't have a clue about how to live and so everything I have in my life today is a result of being in recovery and learning how to live life, as they say, "on life's terms."

G. **What happened before age twenty-two? How did you find recovery?**

D. I was fourteen when I started drinking. I was sixteen when somebody took me aside and said, "I think your father's an alcoholic and you need to be careful." I was watching my dad, and he was drinking himself to death. By the time I was seventeen, I would have been easily diagnosed with alcoholism. So, by the time of my senior year of college, I was watching my life deteriorate and my will to live was almost gone. Then, during Alcohol Awareness Week, I went to a talk for anybody who grew up in alcoholic families and as a result of that meeting, a small group of us started a group for children of alcoholics. I began taking a serious look at my drinking and other drug use and I decided I was going to quit—forever. Of course, to celebrate thirty days of sobriety, I got drunk. I mean it's logical to a lot of us. But a month later, I had my last drink after throwing a "rager" party for a friend of mine. By the grace of something much bigger than me that I call God, I haven't had a drink or any other drug since.

G. **What was it like to be in early recovery, in your twenties?**

D. I had no idea how afraid of life I was until I couldn't use anymore, to deal with people, to deal with problems, to try to escape from the world. It was hard. After graduating college I took a year off and worked at a restaurant where I saw vividly how few skills I had to live on my own. I got fired. I couldn't pay bills. I didn't know how to be in a relationship. I didn't think I could have friends who didn't drink, and I wasn't connecting with a lot of other sober people. I was just lost and scared. And then, I got into graduate school and moved to Kansas, and a month after I moved to Kansas, my dad died. That made it even tougher. But, in other ways it was like, "Okay, my dad is dead. Am I going to throw this all away?" It just gave me more resolve to stay sober and to do what I needed to do. So I completed a master's degree focused on the social construction of masculinity in the culture of Alcoholics Anonymous. I was twenty-four, and then I moved to Minnesota to train at Hazelden, and I've been here ever since.

G. **But, in Kansas, you were pretty much on your own and in a stressful environment—the pressures of a master's program and a culture of drinking in college. What was it like trying to maintain your recovery?**

D. I was living on campus and I would go to dining hall every morning and I would just hear all these people—they were all connected, having fun, and all of it seemed to be around drinking, around the parties that weekend, or the parties that night. I would sit there and eat my food and I just felt incredibly lonely. I would often say, "God, why has my life turned out like this?" I think when you're young in recovery, there's a lot of that. Why me? Why do I have to be separated from such an enormous number of people? I didn't know how to be around people who were drinking. But I had my regular support meetings, a sponsor, and had made a couple of really close connections with people in recovery. That was my lifeline.

G. Then your master's thesis evolved into your first book, *A Man's Way Through the Twelve Steps*. That's a big step going from a personal, sort of private academic study on recovery to publishing something that was going to be so public. What led you to the public advocacy side of the issue?

D. One, here I am at this university, and everybody's acting like addiction isn't real, and I'm watching all these young people drink and use drugs to death. Two, I find out from my mom that my dad was in the hospital and when she called the insurance company they said, because he'd already been medically detoxed, they would only cover a week in treatment. So he went to a treatment center in Maryland for one week and was dead three months later. That angered me, and I started on this path of speaking out. I started speaking at classes. I got involved with a group that was trying to raise awareness about safety and health issues around drinking and college life, and I got a job as a community mobilizer trying to raise awareness about addiction. That's when I first realized there was power in being open about my recovery, and there was power in telling the story and letting the silence be broken. The majority of people living with the pain of addiction—theirs or a loved one's—don't know what to do. And they weren't talking or getting help. In particular, as a man, and having lost my father at a relatively young age, and watching so many men struggle with their recovery I was very interested in men's experience. And almost nobody was writing about that. And so, publishing enabled me to bring a clear message to society that there's another side to the story about the people they're seeing all over the news, all the people who are dying, all the people who are behaving so badly. It gave me the chance to help men to begin to share our unique stories and voices to the narrative of recovery. I believe the only way we can know that side is for those of us who are in recovery to be open about it.

G. People know who you are today, and they know about your addiction and your recovery. In your everyday life, have you encountered any positive or negative reactions?

D. I think this is what it comes down to: The more comfortable I've become with it, the more comfortable it seems other people are with it. People tend to be fairly compassionate about the human condition, in general. And when they know somebody's trying to change their life and improve their life, I don't think the majority of people minimize or disparage it. So, for me, it's like I'm six foot tall, I've got dark hair, I'm a recovering alcoholic. And it doesn't have to be any more than that. I used to think it meant we were special or almost deserved special treatment. I don't think that is true. It means this is our particular story of being human and it matters as much as anyone's story. And we absolutely deserve equal treatment.

G. Some people have talked to me about not being able to own their recovery like that. To what degree do you think shame plays in all of that?

D. It's funny. I used to be one of those people who quickly said about the guys who aren't being open, that it's shame. But I've had conversations with men I really respect who choose not to do it. And it's not shame. It's not. It's an idea that their experience of recovery is so sacred to them that they don't feel the need to take it out of the context in which they live it. They are deeply committed to helping those still suffering, volunteering at treatment programs and working with men in recovery. For some, yes, I think it is shame. For some, I think they hide behind traditions, what they think are rules or expectations or guidelines they don't completely understand. But, for others, I believe that in their hearts, they say they're being most helpful right here, right now—one-on-one with other men in recovery. There has to be room for that in our narrative.

G. For people who don't understand the recovery process, what do you think is important for them to know about people in recovery? It's not just about *not* using drugs or alcohol, is it?

D. There's a saying: "It's easy to get sober. The challenge is staying sober." The things we do that cause us stress can put us in jeopardy, or vulnerability for relapse. That's why behavior change is so important, because the better behaved we are, probably the less stress we have. I have truly come to believe that the most critical factor in many people's recovery is trauma, and to help them see how trauma is affecting their lives and to give them the tools to support their healing process.

Healing is about better understanding who we are, improving our relationships, looking at the areas of our lives where we can improve, and getting support. Then, it's developing some sort of spirituality, not necessarily a god, but something that says, "This is me and here's the rest of the world, and I'm just this little part of it."

G. Looking at the larger picture, how do we go about making the changes that we need to solve our huge public health crisis? Do you think it falls squarely on people in recovery to do that?

D. If the change that needs to come is our duty, it will never happen. It's an American problem. It's a world problem. Pure and simple. To create a rational policy in this country, it's going to take everybody getting honest about our most significant social health issue and the effects it has. There's nobody in this country anymore who can say they don't know somebody who is suffering from an addiction, or somebody who's in recovery. The family members of those in recovery are some of the most powerful people, and telling their stories can help change the conversation.

[At this point, Dan's wife, Nancy, came into the room with their toddler, Grace. Greg took the opportunity to get the spousal side of the story about this family who, besides living in obvious successful recovery, also lives it in the spotlight.]

G. What kind of impact does Dan's recovery have on your family? How do you integrate someone else's recovery into your family's life?

NANCY. It's very important to have a program of recovery for the entire family. There's no way to take away your recovery and separate it from the recovery of the family.

D. And I wasn't actively addicted when we met, so you had no experience with addiction, understanding it or the process of recovery beforehand.

N. Exactly. The framework that recovery brings, the dimension it brings to your relationship, and the ability to apply it and use it in all areas of your life, including parenting, is great. It is profound.

G. Before you met Dan, what was your perception of a person with addiction?

N. I think I probably had a pretty stereotypical idea about what an alcoholic was. I don't think it ever occurred to me that a young person could get into recovery in his or her twenties. I thought of alcoholism as a chronic disease that one could potentially die from. I had worked in social services prior to meeting Dan, and my office was right next to the detox center. We toured the detox center and so that was kind of my framework for what it meant to be in addiction.

G. Was Dan the first person in addiction recovery that you met?

N. As far as I know.

G. And how did that transform your ideas of addiction?

N. For sure, that it's a family disease. Dan was already in recovery when I met him, so I think the stuff that became more front and center are the residual effects of Dan having grown up in an alcoholic family. That's the family experience he was bringing to our lives, as we started to create our own family. So yes, I had a pretty one-dimensional understanding of what an alcoholic is, but now I have this very comprehensive understanding of recovery. It's the dynamics of interpersonal relationships. It's the family system.

D. And that's a huge piece. What Nancy's talking about are the childhood traumas I experienced that I brought into our relationship that I had no awareness of. There are so many men and women walking around having grown up in violent alcoholic homes, or addicted homes, or experiencing other trauma. It comes up and it comes out when you get into an intimate relationship and when you start a family. All the pain of growing up in an abusive home can come out and the cycle of abuse can continue. That's why I'm a champion now for adding childhood trauma and other trauma to the list of necessary elements in recovery. Many people lose their recovery as a result of not doing that deeper work, what many of us refer to as emotional or second stage recovery. I didn't see it in my life for the first twelve years of my recovery!

G. So this is what recovery looks like?

D. This is it, man. This is the real gift of recovery. I fought having a child, and a lot of my fear was based on the trauma stuff. I refused to be in a situation where I might do to a child anything like I experienced. I feel so sad; my heart breaks for the children still growing up in that kind of insanity. But having Nancy, having Grace, and being able to experience a loving, safe family is one of the greatest things. The idea that this young girl is going to grow up not once questioning who she is, and having a sense that she knows her place in this life, and has a great sense of self, I can't imagine a better gift to give to somebody. To be able to truly love someone and be in a family . . . this, to me, is what makes all the hard work worth it.

G. And you're ending the cycle?

D. Well, so far so good. I really believe so. I mean she will know I'm in recovery, obviously. And she will find her own path. But the reality is it's a lot easier to break the cycle if you yourself are healthy in recovery and taking care of yourself.

BEVERLY HABERLE

"We see them journey from shame to hope and then from hope to celebration, and it's very exciting to watch."

Beverly Haberle was a bit breathless and apologetic as she arrived about two minutes late for our interview with her. She could well be excused. As Executive Director of the Council of Southeast Pennsylvania and the Project Director for Pennsylvania Recovery Organization-Achieving Community Together (PRO-ACT), she was in the midst of last minute preparations for the massive Philadelphia Recovery Walks! event, which was taking place the following morning. Tens of thousands were expected to march, with a lively program of speakers and music to follow in Penn's Landing, Philadelphia's spiffy park and events center on the city's historic waterfront. As we tweaked the lighting, she was on her cell phone answering questions and offering solutions and encouragement to staffers who were on site caring for details. She ended each call with a smile. Beverly is a normal person, who apparently does extraordinary things.

With the Council, she works throughout Southeastern Pennsylvania to promote recovery through community programs and activities, shape public policy at all levels, and reduce the stigma of addiction. PRO-ACT is a well-respected, highly visible, and vibrant grassroots organization for people and their families affected by substance use disorders. The Philadelphia walk has become its marquee activity.

Beverly began working as a volunteer with an affiliate of the National Council on Alcoholism and Drug Dependence (NCADD) where she started her journey in advocacy. She was also involved in the grant process of the Recovery Community Support Project (RCSP), which under the Bush Administration funded local recovery-oriented community start-ups. She is currently on the national board of Faces & Voices of Recovery and, at this writing, is gratefully celebrating forty-one years in long-term recovery.

GREG. You have had terrific success the last fourteen years with PRO-ACT in mobilizing a recovery community here in Pennsylvania. You've been very much involved in public recovery issues and activities for a long time. Yet, early on in your forty-one years of successful recovery, you, personally were not always so public. What changed for you?

BEVERLY. I always thought sharing your recovery was a gift and that I had the right to share it with individuals I thought could benefit from it, on a one-to-one basis, but I did nothing public. Actually, until fourteen years ago, I was very *un*-public about my recovery. But, as I have seen—the importance of things like Operation Understanding—there needs to be a voice for this illness. Certainly being part of the RCSP project made it clear why it was so important. I learned there were many more people who needed to hear that recovery on a long-term basis was possible, and that you could indeed have a life that was productive and pay taxes and raise a family and do lots of things that, you know, normal people do.

G. You are also a breast cancer survivor. Did your experience with that disease shed any light on how you look at the issues of addiction and recovery?

B. When I was diagnosed with breast cancer, I got off the floor of my oncologist and there was a big sign that said, *How Can We Help You with Your Recovery?* And I thought, wow, maybe I was in the wrong place because to me, recovery was addiction-related. But what happened in that experience is that they offered all kinds of support. And I said, "How much is this going to cost?" And they said, "Nothing. It's just all part of your treatment. We want you to have the best chance of recovery that you possibly can have."

I started having waves of people tell me about their experiences, and I learned from another illness the absolute importance of peer-to-peer work. I had been a product of peer-to-peer recovery forty-one years ago, but it wasn't called that. It was because of somebody else sharing her story that I was able to take the journey I did. Now in another arena, I had women calling me out of the blue and sharing their stories with me. It was very helpful, but it also in some ways angered me because we don't do some of those things with recovery from addiction. We don't automatically say, "We want you to have the best shot you can possibly have, so we want to give you all of these things."

G. **That's amazing—the disconnect between how you treat one health problem versus another. It would seem obvious that a robust treatment protocol would always involve good follow-up.**

B. With breast cancer, before I did any surgery, I had people helping and supporting me. We need to make sure that recovery support services are intertwined with the engagement phase, helping people transition through the entire recovery process. I think there's a misunderstanding out there that it's aftercare, and it's really not aftercare. It's helping to be connected through the whole recovery process, and being able to have somebody from early on walk through it with you. Something else that's not understood—the choices and the many pathways to recovery. When people hear that, they feel like a huge weight's been lifted off their shoulders. There's more messaging that needs to go out about that. But I'm excited about some of the possibilities with healthcare, where the recovery community and peer-based recovery support services are going to play a bigger role.

G. **Why doesn't recovery have the cause visibility that breast cancer has today?**

B. Some of it is because of anonymity. We have not had the breadth of people standing up and talking about their experience until recently, so, it's very misunderstood. When we first began to mobilize and receive grant money, people with longer-term recovery were not the people who were championing this movement. They had moved on in their lives. They were no longer experiencing stigma. It was people who were in much shorter-term recovery, who had had barrier after barrier after barrier, who were the pioneers for us—people who were dealing with stigma and had first-hand experience with it, prison experiences, having doors shut in their face, not being able to get an interview for a job because they had a record, or health issues. And what has happened in this movement over the years is as people in earlier recovery have come out more and more, some of my colleagues and friends who have been in long-term recovery are coming out and talking about their twenty, thirty, forty years of recovery. Maybe before, they would have been afraid they were breaking traditions or they didn't see it as an issue they needed to talk about.

G. What is your understanding of the tradition of anonymity and how it applies to speaking out about recovery?

B. It means I'm not going to go out and say that I am a member of a certain twelve-step organization. I also think it has become one of those things that a lot of people have hid behind, when I really think they didn't have the courage or the knowledge to be able to talk about it. I think now that's getting much better, particularly in this area where there is such a celebration and such a reframing of the recovery experience. I think we've done a lot of work to help people understand the traditions, and understanding what's said here stays here. Respecting people's confidentiality is very important.

G. It's still a lot about overcoming stigma, isn't it?

B. I can remember growing up, people whispering, "They have cancer," an illness that, in my lifetime, was incredibly stigmatized. You certainly never said "breast" publicly, you know. Now, the first year I was diagnosed, twenty-nine people signed up as my team for the breast cancer walk, when I didn't even start a team. There were 41,000 people walking. So, in some ways, it made me advocate for addiction recovery at a very different level and realize the importance of that voice from a different perspective. Whereas before it was an important thing to do on a very personal level, now I see it as a wider obligation.

G. Do you think by giving more weight to recovery support, you can make an impact on the problems of addiction?

B. If we could continue the [recovery] momentum we have now, we could make a huge change in people who are currently suffering through addiction, *and*, for the next generations. I don't think people have any idea how much addiction is hidden, and how many people are out there living in shame and desperation, and how many families are affected by this illness. As we help people access and sustain long-term recovery, we're also having a huge impact on their families, their children, and other people who see them. That hope for recovery is going to spread like wildfire. By doing walks and rallies across the country and having people publicly share their stories, we can get past just experiencing hope, and make some concrete changes in how we deal with addiction in this country.

G. The growth of your council here in Southeast Pennsylvania suggests you've had success in reaching people with that message. Tell us a little bit about how public advocacy is growing in your area.

B. We now have people in every zip code in the city of Philadelphia, mobilizing. We have people who can go to their City Council. We have people who can talk to their legislators. We have people who can tell their stories at a local level, and so our profile has grown. But more than that, it's the pride of people in recovery that has grown. People are no longer ashamed. We see them travel the journey from shame to hope, and then from hope to celebration, and it's very exciting to watch.

G. What are some of the things that have changed in Philadelphia and the counties over the last fourteen years? What are some of the successes?

B. There's so many. One of the things I'm very proud of is that so many of our folks have criminal records and they are shut out of the opportunity to be interviewed for a job. City Council enacted a law in the city of Philadelphia that you can't ask if someone has a criminal record on their job application, so people are not shut out before they get a chance to get their foot in the door. They can certainly do a background check after they get the interview, but at least they are no longer banned from getting an interview. That's very exciting for people who have had no hope.

We also have a group of lawyers who donate their time to help people get their records expunged. People come out of the hearings with tears running down their faces, so emotional about having that weight lifted from them and have some hope. Now, it's not a magic thing, but it's something that creates hope for people who have been able to access recovery, but then, still get doors shut in their face.

There are opportunities for people, who never thought their voices would mean anything, to sit on committees and to participate in decision-making at all levels. There's a transformation internally that happens, people gaining that confidence, being able to speak at City Council. We took four people yesterday to City Council to receive a proclamation and five City Council members stood up and cheered for recovery month. That's huge when probably five years ago nobody would have cared. It's progress.

G. Tomorrow there will be a lot more cheering going on, this time in the streets. I mean, people all over the country have told me about Philadelphia's walk. What can we expect to see?

B. Philadelphia's walk has grown over the years. This is our eleventh walk, and each year we've seen more people. Last year we had 15,000. We're hoping to top that this year. We have an Honor Guard of people who have at least ten years in recovery, and what's exciting to me is, each year the Honor Guard has grown. I have people who say, "I'm really working to get ten years 'cause I want to be in the Honor Guard."

There are people who carry signs saying, "Five years," "Ten years," but you'll also see people with signs that say, "30 days." It's everybody congratulating people. We now have people stepping out as whole families. Last year, we had a family who had matching T-shirts, and they must have had six dogs with them, and they were all walking in unison, celebrating recovery. You know, people try to be a little creative. Then, after the walk we have a program. A lot of the legislators come. Also this year, we have "Recovery Idol," which is kind of modeled after *American Idol*. There is something really emotional about joining with a group of people who have dignity in recovery and who are on the streets of a major city walking with pride. It truly is a celebration.

And celebrate they did. A crowd of nearly 20,000 people marched through the historic streets of Philadelphia in support of that 2012 PRO-ACT Recovery Walk, led by a 340-member Honor Guard of people in long-term recovery. As Greg navigated a golf cart, directing and excusing us through the crowds, Craig and I perched on the back to film the entire length of the two-mile procession. It was exhilarating to be in the midst of these smiling, chanting, singing celebrants of recovery as they coursed through the narrow, cobblestoned streets of the City of Brotherly (and Sisterly!) Love. Their voices echoed off the brick walls of eighteenth century buildings, and when the demonstration reached Chestnut & Fifth, it took on a new significance. The marchers' voices, declaring their newfound freedoms in recovery, rang even louder as they passed Independence Hall. I realized at that moment that this march—this community rally—was more than just about recovery; it was truly a declaration for life, liberty, and the pursuit of happiness.

Chapter Seven ■

CHANGING
THE WORLD

"Small is big," Dr. Estomih Mtui said to me as we celebrated the occasion of the tenth anniversary of the founding of the Bugando Medical School in Mwanza, Tanzania.

My brother Craig and I had just been recognized for *Touching Tanzania*, a film we had made more than ten years prior, which told the story of an impoverished region of East Africa where there was only one doctor for every 25,000 people. The film had helped kick off a campaign to raise awareness and funds to improve medical care in Tanzania by building a college and hospital that could turn out Tanzanian medical doctors and professionals capable of serving their own population. The campaign raised over $24,000,000. When Bugando Medical College first opened its doors, ten medical students enrolled; now, ten years later, there were 600 students enrolled, studying medicine, dentistry, and nursing. A center of excellence, Bugando has since become a model for medical care in other developing countries.

Our part in this project, besides being another mind-opening adventure in filmmaking, was humbling. The need, the scope, the dream, and the contributions from many others were all so huge, we felt embarrassed to be singled out for what we saw as our relatively small role.

When I sincerely protested as much to Dr. Mtui, that's when he wisely reminded me, "Small is big." With that, I remembered something else—how it had all started. This twenty-four million dollar medical miracle in a distant land began with a story. A quiet, personal story.

We had been invited to lunch with Father Peter Le Jacq, a Maryknoll medical missionary who had been doing the work of God and Hippocrates in Tanzania. He told us of the nearly inconceivable conditions under which the sick were being treated there, or more accurately, not treated. People would die in their hospital beds waiting for a doctor to come, a doctor who never came, because there were none. He related personal stories of his experiences attempting to care for the sick—needing to perform an amputation even though he was not a surgeon, or carrying a patient in his arms for miles through the bush to hospital because there was no medical care in the remote village. He touched us with these stories and the need they revealed. He and others shared a dream to improve these conditions through education and facility building. And so, we were motivated to make *Touching Tanzania* because we were touched by Father Peter, and we were inspired by the way Father Peter put his face and voice out there to tell his story.

Father Peter did that, over and over again, one-on-one, and sometimes to small groups, until literally thousands of people became involved in the project. Thousands, if not millions of people will live healthier lives. All because of a personal story.

Yes, our *Touching Tanzania* became big. But it started small.

The people you are about to meet all have big dreams, too. They are deeply involved in public and personal recovery advocacy, and even though they know millions of lives are at stake, they are not deterred from acting because of the daunting enormity of the addiction problem. They recognize that the only way to attack the problem is at the personal or local level and to build successes one at a time. Their work ripples outward and soon change happens, and is perceptible.

They think big, but begin by acting small.

It took this journey with Greg, meeting the faces and voices of recovery, to re-learn an old and obvious truth: Each of us has the power to make a difference in other people's lives. What I hadn't learned yet, and what hundreds of people in recovery taught me, was how to put that power to use for the greater good. How? Let the advocates and agitators tell you how they do it in the following interviews Greg conducted.

JOE SCHRANK

"There is nothing that impacts American life more than addiction. Nothing."

Joe Schrank is more than an advocate—he's an agitator. He does like to stir things up. But it's all to a purpose. Using truth as his weapon, applied with equal measures of candor and wit, he takes aim at anyone and anything that obstructs his number one goal: helping people recover from addiction, especially young people. He attacks hypocrisy, contradiction, and ignorance, and if that means offending someone or some institution or some sacredly held belief along the way, then so be it. His views may be controversial and he may have lost supporters here and there, but it is a small price to pay, in his mind, for provoking any dialogue that promotes recovery on a bigger scale.

We met up with him at Core Company, NYC, where he is Founder and CEO of a transitional living care program for people who are just coming out of treatment for chemical dependence. Core is housed in a huge, totally cool loft space in the now center of the universe, Williamsburg, Brooklyn. It is an upscale home, really, with private rooms, and inviting common areas, including living room, dining hall, and an enormous open kitchen. Joe and his full-time staff of on-site managers provide interventions, crisis management, and a sober living experience with sober companions. The environment is clearly designed to reflect and facilitate Joe's belief in the power of peer-to-peer recovery support and real life management.

As for Joe's interview, be forewarned. His conversation with Greg is frank and sometimes profane. I kept saying to myself, *Doesn't he know or care that he is being filmed?* He is so open and honest, and quick, he doesn't allow time to fabricate diplomacy or delicacy. He tells it like it is. Make no mistake, Joe's shoot-from-the-hip style, laced with sarcasm and the occasional exaggeration, is compelling and even charming. In fact, this is one of the most entertaining interviews we did. At times, he will make you laugh out loud. But, don't let his humor and salty language detract from the seriousness of his message or its sincerity. Because beneath all the bluster—and not very far from the surface—he cares. Deeply. One close friend of mine confided something I had not known, "Joe Schrank saved my son's life. And changed mine."

So, be prepared to be offended, but don't take offense. And be prepared to be provoked, perhaps into taking action. Everything he says is designed to get our attention, move us off our pusillanimous posteriors (Joe would use a more graphic term), and join him in simply wiping the scourge of addiction from the face of the earth.

GREG. **How did you get into this business of addiction recovery?**

JOE. I'm in recovery myself—fifteen years without a drink. Like many, I was in my twenties at the time and, like many people in their twenties, when they hit addiction treatment, they're pretty lost. I did not have a career path or much of a plan. My plan was to marry someone successful and stay home and drink and call myself a househusband. That was actually going okay, until she dumped me for my drinking problem. I started in a social work program. That was always my interest, and I was working in a hospital detox, and it just kind of grew and grew into a master's program. I've worked in many different levels of care over the last twelve years.

G. **At some point, you moved away from traditional clinical work toward your own unique brand. Could you describe that?**

J. I was a clinician at a very fancy rehab in Malibu for a while, and clinical work with addicts in that world is where I don't think I do well. You can put them in an office and talk about their feelings for forty-five minutes once a week, but I don't really know what it does. I think of clinical work as very much *in vivo,* which is a theory of social work practice—in-world treatment—like, going to the mall with agoraphobics. I think effective addiction treatment recognizes they want you in their boat on a day-to-day basis. I let them sleep on my couch. That's how I do it. I follow ethical standards of practice, but I have no boundaries.

It's interesting that the science of addiction is progressing way more rapidly than the culture of addiction. We paint it with such a broad stroke, even as treatment providers. If you are a housewife popping Valium in the carpool line, or if you are smoking crack in a hotel room, it's all the same. I don't think that's true. There's not nearly enough research. We don't know enough about it. It's crazy. I don't think anybody really understands addiction. But look toward other health issues, one of them being diabetes. You're an adolescent diabetic, for which there is a different treatment plan than being a type 2 diabetic, which is different than being a gestational diabetic. But, it is all diabetes and, in a certain sense, with addiction, it's the same thing. We do know more, now, about the health aspects of addiction than they did in the thirties. So we cannot apply standards from 1930 to the modern world. Just can't do it. It doesn't help enough people.

G. **One thing I hear from a lot of people in this arena is that everyone's got their own little niche and everyone's got their own little pathway that they believe in. People argue with each other and bicker, when we have this giant health issue, this giant epidemic to address. Everyone just wants to fight over little pots of money.**

J. And there's a lot of grandiosity. There's the whole dynamic of sponsorship, which is, "You could be me, if you just listen to me," which I think is very weird. There's the problem with practitioners and clinicians who like to present the "sample of one," which is one of the biggest problems. I was at a conference about Suboxone. You want draft policy for all of America based on the maintenance and the rates of success your one guy was having? That's what you're telling us? Everyone was just enraged. Everybody wants to be the person to have the magical solutions, and I don't really think any of us do.

G. Talk a little more about the gravity of the issue and what's at the bottom of our seeming inability to deal with it.

J. There is nothing that impacts American life more than addiction. Nothing. Nobody even knows the cost in terms of accidents and lost work. How do you put a cost on destroyed families? How can you monetize the perpetuation of it?

One of the things I learned in social work school is that it hemorrhages into every area of practice. Like, domestic violence nosedives when addiction is stable. All the other things we talk about as social work practitioners, addiction is in every single one of them, and they are all improved when that's improved. The point being is that everything is improved by reducing the rates of active using—mental health, productivity, absenteeism. And you and I both know that when you stop using you're such a better student, miraculously.

I was advocating for a recovery school in New York City once and somebody said, "How is that paid for?" I said, "Well, they gotta go to school anyway, so you tell me. I don't know, I'm not an educator. How about a twenty-five-cent tax on mixed drinks in nightclubs in New York City? How about that?" "Oh, my god, that would be like . . . really? That's gonna kill the night club business in New York!" You mean you can't tax alcohol appropriately to pay for the damage that it does? That's insane. Whoever says that alcohol has this free pass of being taxed eighteen cents a gallon since 1943?

G. So, why do you think it is so hard to break through and find solutions that will be more effective?

J. I think there's a tremendous lack of creativity and honesty about the problem. I look to the recovery community and I say to them, myself included, "Is a dollar in the bucket at a twelve-step meeting enough? Is that enough public advocacy?" We have Harvard lawyers in twelve-step meetings in New York City setting up chairs as their service. Great. How about some *pro bono* legal work for a community advocacy group or some grant writing? "We can't do that, it's 'anonymous.'" Advocacy for a health problem as extensive as substance use disorders in this country is not "anonymous." You don't *not* look at HIV stuff just because you don't have HIV. Every year, I've gone to the Michael J. Fox Parkinson's pow-wow; I don't have Parkinson's. And so why it is that people think they must be directly impacted by addiction to advocate for change or better use of funds? I don't know; I don't have that answer. I don't think we have an economy, which is probably a big part of the problem.

G. What do you mean by "economy"?

J. I always knew that there was a market of people in recovery. We're a pretty big sub-culture to not have a voice in the media, considering the people who do. I mean, yoga has a very prominent web presence, if you're a yoga person. One of the things I want to create with Starbucks is that I've wanted them to advertise on our website as a mainstream brand. Do you know how much money recovering people spend on your fucking pumpkin spice lattes? A shit ton. What if we had meetings and community events organized in our own cafes and we kept the money? What if we kept our twenty million dollars a year in lattes, then would you want to advertise? I just don't think we are organized in that way. Nobody wants a recovery dollar, unless it's for a treatment center, which is a horrible message because it's "Well you are an addict. Clearly you'll fuck up in a year or two and go back to rehab. So I guess we will just advertise treatment to you." You know, it's never mountain bikes, or travel, or jeans, or water, or anything that fit, stable people in recovery would consume.

G. Getting back to the struggle to find solutions to addiction and recovery issues, what role do you think the government plays in this? I mean, not that our government has all the answers, but . . .

J. Not that the government has all the answers, but they spend an awful lot of money shooting and incarcerating the problem, and that doesn't work. If you could threaten addicts into not using, I'm all for it, but the government approach is ineffective. You could make a border war budget—triple it, quadruple it, whatever. People will still be snorting coke in New York City. That's not going to change it, ever. People will still be smoking pot all over America. The problem is not accessibility—it is a mental health issue. And you can't treat mental health issues or health issues with Black Hawk helicopters. You just can't do it. It's like saying we have an obesity problem. I mean, "I'm sorry, we're going to have to shoot all the fat people going into Burger King." Or the diabetics. "Let's get some helicopters; we're going to defoliate sugar cane fields in Hawaii, because diabetics eat too much candy and they're costing us money with their amputated feet and their heart attacks." It doesn't make any sense. The climate, and the economy, and the rhetoric are dominated by wasteful government spending.

G. Do you think policy makers and legislators believe that people like us don't vote, so why even bother to take it on as a policy issue?

J. Well, that's part of the problem. Addicts don't vote, and I think that's up to us as stable people in the recovery community to support other people in recovery. People who have seen the transformative experience know that treatment does work and recovery does work. People do get better, and we not only need to vote, we need to organize into an economy. I always look to the gay community for guidance because if they had said, "That's anonymous; we can't talk about HIV," where would that be twenty years ago? "Oh no, no, no, we can't talk about that." They understood right away that silence was going to kill the entire community. They had to organize and they had to demand a different approach to the problem of HIV from politicians and government. It had to be done, because people were dying so quickly.

G. Do you think it's the public's lack of true knowledge about addiction that is holding back progress toward real solutions?

J. I think, in general, people are angry with addicts and they want them punished, which I understand entirely. I mean, I understand being a frustrated spouse or family member. We've heard it all before—the heartbreak and frustration of dealing with an addict. They don't have accurate information and, as long as there's that punitive thing injected into the culture, that's probably what's going to continue to be supported. There's still a deep sense of shame. There are wealthy and famous individuals and families who do not want to support this as a health issue. Nobody wants to cozy up to addiction. It is still largely viewed as character-logical. You know, "Stop doing it" sort of thing.

G. Let's turn to the question of anonymity and secrecy. How do you view these issues? Do you see any connection between them and the wider acceptance of recovery?

J. I never got the anonymity thing. There are thirty of us standing in front of a church smoking. Like, what secret is this? Who doesn't know what's going on in here? My perspective has been that I've done some incredibly embarrassing things as a drunk young man. Why would I be embarrassed that I go to twelve-step meetings? I'm not. I'm really not. In fact, I think its one of the best things about me, the fact that I don't drink. I've never totally understood the necessity for anonymity. It's always been shrouded in secrecy; anonymity and secrecy are very different. You are told—as a basic tenet of twelve-step life—that you are as sick as your secrets, but live the secretive life. I couldn't reconcile that. Look, I'm not going to out anybody; I get that other people don't want to talk about it. I don't care; it's their business. I understand the rhetoric and I understand the need for the tradition, but even the church had Vatican II. To me, what the anonymity thing means is that I'm not going to tell people you were there, but I have zero reservations about telling anybody that I am in AA.

In the modern world, I question the validity and the necessity of anonymity. I do think the anonymity thing holds the recovery movement hostage because it makes people believe you can't talk about that kind of thing. The truth is, yes, you can.

G. **You're very public about your opinions on this. Do you get push-back from people?**

J. We get those angry emails all the time: "What part don't you get about anonymous?" Whether you love anonymity, and/or you think we're crazy, I don't really care. To me, it indicates there's something about it that people hold sacred. People who have been in twelve-step fellowships for many, many years seem to be much more connected to it. Younger people in the age of instant communication are much more nonchalant about it than we are.

I just think there should be an open dialogue about it. All solutions to problems stem from the acknowledgment of the problem.

G. **There certainly are models, such as gay rights and breast cancer, for example. They had stigma and they had shame and secrecy, but they didn't have anonymity.**

J. But they didn't have anonymity. Exactly! There was a time when people were very much ashamed, when women did not reveal they had breast cancer because they could be fired or they might not get their jobs back. There was certainly a time when I was in my twenties, when my mother said, "Oh, my God, their son died of cancer." "AIDS, Mom, he died of AIDS, not cancer." And now, my mother is on Facebook asking all Catholics to pray for the end of persecution of gay people. It's just such a dramatic change in twenty years from where the gay community was to where they are now. I do hope there's a time when my mother tells me that she was at Mass and they were praying for someone who had died of alcoholism. When have you ever read an obituary that says someone died of alcoholism? You hear heart failure, cancer . . . but nobody says acute alcoholism killed this person, and it's really awful. Those are little measures of things that can be changed, but not until families come forward and say, "I'm not ashamed." My father served two terms in Vietnam. He never got it together. He could lead men into battle, literally, but could not beat alcoholism or stabilize it. And I'm not ashamed to say that. I'm not ashamed to say that every man in my family drank himself to death. I think that's something that has to be open.

G. For so long we've been taught that addiction was a moral choice and that it was just about bad people. Do you think that's changing?

J. That message is still out there. If you look at the DARE website, which is one of the great cultural icons of addictive behavior in America, the message is, don't do drugs—losers do drugs. They offer you, like, dancing alternatives, which is great, all well and good. But to me, as a child of an alcoholic, to sit and listen to some cop as he told me that my father was a loser would have been torture. As an adolescent, there were people telling me, "You're heading down a slippery slope." And I was like, "Hmmm, I don't care." The messaging of the DARE program, and of our culture, is still really rooted in "you just say no"; that's what you do. So complicated biochemical problems centered in the primitive brain, fueled by your family dynamic, and your community exposure, you just say "no" to all of that. Oh, really? God, why didn't I think of that? And so, as long as we minimize the problem with that kind of rhetoric, it's not really going to change. I do think anonymity is one of the pillars that holds the entire movement back. I almost think once we reconcile the anonymity question, it'll be the pebble to start an avalanche. Once people feel safe in coming forward or talking about their own experience or being able to reveal themselves without shame or stigma, more and more people will.

G. With the prevalence of shame and guilt still around, it is hard to reveal yourself because you just don't know what the responses will be.

J. It is very hard to predict people's reactions. I'm so steeped in this world I forget there are people who are not comfortable or educated or don't have experience with the reactions when people in recovery reveal.

I don't think people want to be around the sober guy. I mean, when other fathers say, "Well, we're gonna watch the Giants game," they don't really want me to come, you know. They don't because that's their day to drink beer and I'm just going to sit there. They feel judged; they feel like I'm on some evangelical mission to make them sober. Really, I'm not that nice of a person. I don't care if they drink or they don't. It doesn't make any difference to me. So I don't know that people get it, and I've gotten to a point where I don't dance around the issue.

The truth is it isolates you. You're not a part of. It's not easy to be sober. It's not easy to function in parent groups or barbeques. It's still not an accepted lifestyle, unless you're with other people who have chosen it. That whole idea of where do you fit and how do people react to you, in terms of being supportive, is very much in its infancy. It's not normalized.

G. Is it because we haven't experienced recovery widely enough in our society to make it normal?

J. The politically correct thing in the world is to applaud somebody for not drinking. I don't think it operates on many different levels of support. There aren't characters on television who are in recovery as a normal thing, in a subtle way demonstrating how you live your life as a person in recovery. It's always the brick to the head, or the crash and burn, or the freak show, those sorts of things. I don't know that the integration of people in recovery has even remotely started into mainstream America. We are still shrouded in mystery and underground misunderstanding.

G. Even in the face of the stigma of addiction, no one can argue that recovery isn't a positive step. Why is it still so difficult to find the kind of support that will kick our movement into a higher gear?

J. For years, we've been trying to get New York City to have a recovery high school, a high school that would support kids who had been to treatment already. Well, they don't see the need. "Where would they come from?" Really? Where would they come from? You're kidding, right? There are designated high schools in this city for automotive repair, for desktop publishing, for history, and we have a gay lesbian transgender high school here, which is great. I'm all for it. But the idea that our kids are less important than kids interested in automotive repair or desktop publishing, and there is not a designated high school for people in recovery, I don't get it.

G. A robust recovery movement would create change and chances for millions to lead normal lives, wouldn't it? What would happen, for instance, if there were a recovery vote?

J. We would see a lot of the changes people have seen throughout history. I hope someday history teachers and civic teachers say, "Can you believe there was a time in America that we incarcerated people for a health issue?" I mean, we should be ashamed of the drug war and the incarceration, as we are of Manzanar and of locking people up for being a specific ethnicity. Those are the kinds of changes I would hope for if there was a galvanized recovery movement. I think we would see dramatic changes in social policy and approach to the problem and also an understanding.

But the problem does stem from anonymity, it really does. As long as we are supposed to live shrouded in secrecy and mystery, then how can we organize?

LAURA ELLIOT-ENGEL

"You just don't know where the ripples are going to go."

Laura Elliot-Engel found recovery in 1975 and ever since has been helping others do the same. Her commitment to individuals and to the entire recovery community is widely known, especially in New York State where she travels extensively working in prevention, education, and counseling in both outpatient and inpatient settings. A Licensed Mental Health Counselor and a Certified Addiction Counselor, Laura's first work in the field was with women, case finding, and counseling in two rural counties. In 1991, she moved into management and became active in public policy. She was Executive Director of the Livingston Council, Executive Director of the Cattaraugus Council on Addiction Recovery Services, and a member of the Finger Lakes Region Consortium of Alcohol and Substance Abuse Services. She is currently a board member for the Council on Addictions of New York State (CANYS), an organization of prevention, education, intervention, and treatment agencies throughout New York State, and is also the President of Friends of Recovery-New York (FOR-NY). FOR-NY is an organization comprised of New York State residents, whose mission it is to demonstrate the power, proof, and value of recovery from addiction to everyone. Its members mobilize to speak as one voice to advance public policies and practices that promote and support recovery.

I have had the privilege of appearing on discussion panels with Laura, following local screenings of Greg's film. There isn't a more committed, passionate, and knowledgeable face and voice of recovery out there, and she'll go almost anywhere to deliver the message. She knows the advocacy landscape well and is always willing to share the secrets of winning hearts and minds.

We spoke to Laura in the Albany office of FOR-NY at the end of a long day of celebrating September Recovery Month, which FOR-NY had helped organize in the capital city. After an impressive march involving participants from all over the state, the celebration culminated in music, speeches, and a ceremony in Riverside Park, a picturesque venue along the Hudson River, which is within sight of historic downtown Albany and the seat of state government.

GREG. The Recovery Rally was quite an event today. You had a great turn-out and I would describe the mood as being celebratory. It was certainly loud and fun. What are your reflections on the day? Did you achieve your purpose?

LAURA. This is our fifth year doing the statewide New York Celebrates Recovery. And while there's been some pushback about having it out of New York City, by having it in the capital, it's much more accessible to people coming from all over the state. The opportunity for people to gather on the Hudson River, at the foot of the Capitol in Albany, New York, which is just a glorious, beautiful place, is an incredible thrill. So it's about, yes, showcasing. It's about celebrating. We weren't necessarily driving policy today, although there was a bit of that. As people are leaving an event like this, you start hearing, "I can't wait until next year." Or people will put their hand out and say, "I was sober, I was clean at that event, and I'm going to hang in there a little longer because that gave me a perspective about what it can be like, and what it is like." That's why we do it.

G. Today wasn't the only day we've seen you in action. Earlier this year, we filmed you and a large contingent of advocates and supporters marching up to the Capitol here in Albany and going into the building. What were you pushing for and what were you trying to do?

L. Our Advocacy Day. Each year, FOR-NY hosts a statewide policy advocacy day early in the session for the New York State Legislature. We worked well over three months honing a shared message with other advocacy groups in the state. Our primary thrust for policy and our message was to reinvest in the community—put it back into a recovery-oriented system of care. This was important because of the Medicaid redesign process that's occurring in New York State, with the use of dollars changing with the Affordable Care Act. Four of us met with a person, one step removed from Governor Cuomo. Others met with every single legislator in the Senate and Assembly, and it was all the same message. Now, *how* the message was delivered was clearly individualized. Like, "This is the change in my life, and this is what you can do to help impact change for others." I mean, it's pretty simple, isn't it? If you keep it that simple and straightforward, the listener begins to go, "Oh! I get it." And then we followed up with emails and we followed up with calls. We followed up with visits to the local district offices, trying to reinforce that message.

G. **You identify and advocate for specific policies, but what are some of the larger problems we face that concern you?**

L. First off, if you look at the current system, we do not have adequate resources. There are not enough resources available for people who are asking for assistance—simple as not having enough treatment beds or slots or whatever kind of bureaucratic jargon you want to use. You have few pathways for people to find an entry to even the possibility of something called recovery. We have to create a depth of opportunity that enhances the potential for people to get well. Physicians should have a recovery coach as a part of their stable of referral possibilities, so when they screen people, they can say, "Do you want to make some kind of change? You might want to talk to this person who can walk with you and figure it out."

The other thing that is wrong is the stigma and the discrimination. People still don't understand this is a chronic disease, an inheritable disease. Those of us who know that have a clear responsibility to educate.

And there's the response from communities, where denial is a part of addiction: It's not here, it's the next block, it's the poor neighborhood, it's across the railroad tracks, it's down the road. There is a lack of community acknowledgment and response that calls people to join together in a commitment to community wellness.

G. **Your advocacy work takes you all over the state, all over the country. What motivated you to get on that train and become an advocate and to work the system for change?**

L. What brought me into this work was my own personal journey. I am an example of recovery that is successful, that works, and I want you to know about me. I want you to know about people like me. My recovery gave me the opportunity to get a degree in social work, and then a master of divinity. This is my ministry, if you will, and the education was about giving me knowledge and a skill set to strengthen what was maybe an inherent gift. I wanted to teach people how to advocate for themselves and on behalf of this anonymous community, this hidden community, and to know the wonderful work that Faces & Voices of Recovery does around how to talk to the media. And no, you don't have to tell the war stories, you don't have to talk about how horrible it was, just to understand there is a place you come to and move forward.

G. **How do you get other people fired up and to feel empowered to effect change? What is the message that rallies people?**

L. The message that rallies people has to come from a very person-centered place. You have achieved great things because you're in recovery. And if you choose, you can help other people achieve that as well. That's message one. Message two—and this is probably the one where you see people uplifted and almost spiritually infused, and you see the light go on—is when somebody says, "I've never advocated for myself or anybody else about anything before," and then that person claims his or her right to be on the face of the earth, in this space and time. It is incredible. What a gift!

JOHN SHINHOLSER

"So I say we make history. That's what I say."

"Well, good mornin', ladies!" said John Shinholser, as he welcomed us to breakfast in his sunroom at 7:00 A.M.

It was the way he drawled, "Well," that implied we had missed early reveille and had a lot to prove before we passed muster with him. Obviously, this US Marine Corps veteran had already been up a couple hours—his breakfast dishes were cleared, his paper read, and the dog was back asleep after a walk. We were about to get our marching orders for a day of recovery discovery.

We had arrived in Richmond the day before, tired after an unseasonably warm three days in Washington, DC seeking out recovery advocates for interviews. One was with John's wife, Carol McDaid, the lobbyist. (More about her later.) She had invited us to stay at their house when were in Richmond, or rather, she insisted we do so, employing that genteel, no-other-option way of southern hospitality, telling us to expect John would be home when we got there and to bring our appetites. They live in a rural suburb of Richmond, past subdivisions of old homesteads, horse farms, and straight miles of pine-tree-lined country roads singing with cicadas. It was early evening and raining when we pulled into the driveway of their modernized farmhouse. There was John, under the shelter of two huge patio umbrellas, barely visible in the hovering smoke of barbecue, putting the finishing touches on slow-cooked ribs he had been preparing for us.

So this was John Shinholser, a man we were soon to find out was a multitasker with many irons in the fire. With a hard-boiled exterior, John comes on strong; yet, with a sly smile and a penetrating, sympathetic look in his eye, you can tell there is good humor and a warm heart inside this drill sergeant. Among his talents, he is a BBQ king, an artist (he's won national awards for his faux-finishing painting skills), a storyteller, and, chiefly, the President of the McShin

Foundation, cofounded with Carol. Since its inception in 2004, the McShin Foundation has pioneered the use of peer-to-peer recovery support services, successfully employing persons in recovery to educate and mentor individuals new to recovery. Serving the greater Richmond area, his nonprofit organization runs a 4,200 square foot recovery center and several recovery residences.

All the time we were in Richmond, we could never pin John down for a formal interview to talk about all this. Like a platoon leader, he led, we followed, and he showed us first-hand what McShin does.

We certainly earned our stripes trying to keep up with John and record his activities, as he led us on a ceaseless march through Richmond and beyond. We visited two of the most modern and progressive county jails in Virginia, Henrico County Jail East and Jail West, where John is active in recovery programs and services that play an important role in inmate rehab, reducing recidivism, and saving public money. We filmed John and also Laurie Dhue, who was visiting, speaking to various inmate groups. We were privileged to do interviews with inmates and staff, and had a chance to sit down with Henrico County Sheriff Michael Wade, a proponent of prison reform. We also visited the hard-core Richmond City Jail to film an inmate recovery graduation ceremony John conducted. We spent a lot of time at the McShin Foundation offices and recovery center filming an advocacy-training group, a board meeting, and several interviews. In between, John made sure we were well-fed, always on the look out for a roadside purveyor of Virginia's quintessential, vinegary pulled pork or biscuits or, God help us, timing it so that we got to a Krispy Kreme just as a fresh batch came out of the oven. John knows about these things.

So magnetic was this southern hospitality of his and Carol's that we were drawn back six months later in September of 2012 to shoot the McShin Foundation's Eighth Annual Recovery Fest and Third Annual State Championship BBQ Cook-Off. And what a McShin-dig that was! Over 3,000 people attended the hoedown, which featured plenty of reminders that recovery does benefit individuals, families, and society as a whole. Counselors were available, as were political action volunteers who helped people register to vote and to sign petitions to restore voting rights for rehabilitated ex-felons. This is a feel-good community festival that does much to publicize the positives of recovery, a spirited event that perfectly symbolizes what John does on a daily basis, making his loud, proud voice of advocacy heard far outside the tent.

John is a smart, plain-speaking guy, and he grabs your attention with equal amounts of volume and veracity. His southern accent, countrified to beguiling effect, is spiced with an occasional profanity, yet he is more funny than profane—earthier than Will Rogers, but similarly wise and disarming. You had better be ready for the biting truths that come out of his mesmerizing rants.

The scene: We were in a spacious activity hall on the first floor of the Hatcher Memorial Baptist Church, where, in the basement, the offices and meeting rooms of the McShin Foundation are housed. John was conducting a group of over thirty people in recovery, several of whom had spent time in jail, some recently. John had also invited his friend, Levar Stoney, who is now the Secretary of the Commonwealth of Virginia. At the time, Levar was Deputy Campaign Manager for Governor Terry McAuliffe and was helping to build a policy platform on the issue of addiction and recovery. We were grateful to film the discussion, having received the open and gracious permission of all the recovery people in the room, although some in the group wished to remain anonymous, which we respected. John led an energetic discussion, and he was intent on making sure Levar got the messages. Here are some excerpts from the freewheeling discussion.

ON WHY IT'S SO CHALLENGING TO ACCESS SERVICES TODAY

LEVAR. My question, John, if all the peer-to-peer recovery support services you talk about are so effective, why aren't more available?

JOHN. One reason goes something like this. In the 1980s, we had 3500 quality rehabs around America. And then, HMOs came along. And HMOs' main purpose was to whack reimbursement for medical services from big corporate America thus saving money. The first industry they cut out reimbursement for was the treatment center industry. They did that because a) the recovery people had no advocacy organization, and b) it was a shame-based disease that they knew nobody was going to rise up and say anything about because most of the recovery people were members of anonymous programs. So they whacked out reimbursement for insurance—overnight moved people to services that could not adequately serve them. They've done a good job carving us out, and we haven't been able to get back up there. Now, with the new healthcare bill, we're in there strong. This will be academic if all of the states provide services. We will be on a level playing field with everybody. That's why we've got to advocate.

We, as recovery people, have to rise up and start advocating for our rightful place in society. Most of America's best soldiers for recovery are addicts and alcoholics who got clean in twelve-step programs and who are anonymous. They confuse advocacy of an illness with representing a twelve-step program. See, I'm advocating, but I'm not representing anyone's twelve-step program.

ON HOW THE SYSTEM HAS FAILED THE RECOVERY COMMUNITY

J. When I got clean in 1982, anybody in America who wanted rehab could be inside of a quality treatment center within one hour whether they had money or not. And the people who were delivering the information in those treatment centers were recovering people. So at nighttime, they were taking you out to the town twelve-step meeting, so you were linked into the recovery community. I knew where all of the safe people, places, and things were by the time I got out of the rehab. I had been in the Marine Corps, so it's pretty difficult to get that connection to all that many civilian people in a short period of time. Today's system is designed to keep our people from the resources. Our bureaucratic system has inadvertently created probably the worst delivery system they could. It's a design, a barrier that we've got to break down. That's important to understand. If you access services today, they don't let you co-mingle with the recovering community. They keep you apart. When you go to jail and the prisons, most of them keep you apart and isolated from what you're going to need when you get out.

While the disease is leaving the body, getting clean and sober is the time to be putting in a recovery message. If the message is delivered by recovery people who are linked to the community, then newcomers get linked to the community during that process. So when they get out of rehab and they get out of jail, they don't miss a beat.

ON BRINGING RECOVERY SERVICES TO PRISONS

J. Our jails and prisons are full of addicts and alcoholics. They're all pooled up in one spot. I've never been to a jail or prison yet where I couldn't walk into it and say, "Okay, who wants to talk about addiction and recovery?" and then have most of the population say, "Yeah, that's exactly what I'd like to talk about while I'm here." So when you have that captive audience in the jail and the prison, it is the best time to deliver recovery information.

ON THE DISPARITY OF TREATMENT OFFERINGS IN OUR JUDICIAL SYSTEM

J. Drug courts only take non-violent offenders. Well, we take anybody in recovery. I would have a violent offender in jail or prison get a drug court to get him the services too, so when he is released, he knows where to go and what to do. It's ridiculous to treat people different like that. Most everybody who goes to jail or prison gets out. Why only try to help the ones who have the best records? Everybody who has been in recovery for a long time knows you cannot tell who makes it and who doesn't make it.

ON PROVIDING RE-ENTRY SERVICES FOR PRISONERS IN RECOVERY

J. It may be 80 to 90 percent of people in prison are there related to alcohol or other drugs. If you're going to go to jail for four years for drugs, then why can't your last year be a re-entry type? Let's spend your last year in a halfway house or a recovery community organization so by the time you get out of the system, you've got your driver's license back. You're paying all of your fines. You have your birth certificate. You take care of all of these things. Instead, they're turning people out cold. You come out of jail or prison, your time's up, here's a $13.00 check, and a cab ride to your city of choice. Here's your PO's [parole officer] number you need to report to within so many hours. That doesn't give that person a whole lot of hope, I don't think.

ON THE "PRISON INDUSTRIAL COMPLEX"

J. The largest surge in the criminal justice system that took place in the history of the world happened in the last twenty years. They did it on the backs of the taxpayers and the crack addicts. We've built up this huge criminal justice industry centered around addiction. All of these agencies were developed—we're talking jobs, industries, and agencies. Can you imagine us going to the Department of Corrections, the Commissioner and saying, "I've got an idea on how to cut back on half of your prisons." They're going to do a back flip. "No, you're not. We are not cutting back on my watch." Well, don't you realize that we not only can reduce recidivism, but we can take a serious bite out of addiction in Virginia by utilizing our recovery community resources? We could actually save a lot of that money and spend it on education. Let's spend it on children who need help and the foster care families and whatnot. There are a lot of other industries we can build up with that money we're going to save. Bureaucrats are in denial. The best scientific evidence is conclusive that if you can engage a person in treatment *and* recovery, you'll get, by far, your best outcome.

[Then, there was this exchange with the group . . .]

WOMAN IN GROUP. I had a thought about the CSB's [Community Service Boards]. They're getting all of the money. And it just seems to me like it's wasted. I mean, it took me three months just to get my foot in the door to see somebody, to then get scheduled a month later to come back. If I could stay clean for four months, I wouldn't need their help! I called here and I told Honesty [Honesty Liller, McShin's Chief Executive Officer] I need a bed tonight or I'm going back to jail tomorrow, or I'm going to die. I was in that night, five hours later. I had a place, ready to go. And I've been helped greatly ever since. It just seems, like you said, you're getting more effective recovery in a way shorter amount of time. And so, why spend the money over there, when you've got something working better over here?

JOHN. You just said the most powerful thing. You nailed it. When is the best time to help an addict?

GROUP RESPONSE. Immediately. At the moment.

JOHN. Now! When they ask for help. You're an addict, dealing with a drinking problem for ten years and all of a sudden you call on a Sunday morning and say brother, sister, mother, father, I have a problem. I need help. That is the window of opportunity, which is really short. That window closes. When does that window close?

WOMAN IN GROUP. Real quick.

JOHN. Real quick. An hour? Fifteen minutes. Five minutes, whatever. You go to a community service provider and they say, come back in twenty-five days! Have you lost your mind? Do you know how many circular saws we're going to steal from Home Depot by that day? But, when you get busted for stealing from Home Depot they give you services *immediately*. You get arrested right away. You get $50,000 a year worth of services! And all of that could have been avoided if the Community Service Board would have said, come, we've got you covered right now. That is the barrier I'm speaking of in the criminal justice system. I have been explaining it to every policymaker for the last thirty years. It falls on deaf ears. They say, "Are you nuts? We can't do away with our sheriff's department, our police department. We need these people. That's 'public safety.' We have to *build* public safety. We can't *decrease* public safety."

So let me get this straight. We know your number one customer in the criminal justice system is an addict. And we know half of those addicts are going to ask for help, but we won't give that half help because that'll cut into half of the prison industry's pocketbook and their business. That population should be served when they come into a recovery community center asking for help. Don't you policymakers know that you could still have jails and prisons? We just need about half of what we've got. I'm saying, for 10 percent of what we're spending in the substance abuse sector, if we spend it in the recovery support service provider sector, we could eliminate 50 percent of the criminal justice needs. But we would have to be prepared to reduce recidivism and cut back on the criminal justice needs. And I don't think our policymakers are ready for that because that's how they get elected. They get elected on public safety issues, not on recovery issues.

In this circle alone, how many of you all have family or loved ones who vote? Raise your hands. Everybody. Families get burned out driving their loved ones around to their job because they can't get a driver's license, because they're behind on court costs or a fine, or child support, or whatever. They get burned out watching their loved ones being held back by a bad system. You think they wouldn't vote for a politician who is going to change that and turn that around? You bet your butt they will.

This is the advocate piece I'm talking about. But the people in Virginia don't know that. We are the largest group of unheard people in the state. AARP, we know about them don't we? The Susan Komen cancer people, we know about them, right? We know about every issue out there. But people don't know how important the issue of recovery is. And how vital it is for us to advocate for intelligent policies. The sad part about it is that we've got probably more advocates in voters than any other block out there.

Let's do the math. Seven hundred thousand Virginians meet the clinical criteria for needing substance abuse treatment by definition of the Joint Legislative Account and Review. That's 10 percent of our population. We currently have 120,000 people in our criminal justice system and over 70,000 are in a jail or a prison. These are big numbers. We've got 400,000 to 500,000 felons. They all have loved ones and family members and friends. And this rotates every five years; we get a fresh, full crop come through. So we should probably have what it takes to elect 100 recovering delegates, and forty recovering state senators! We've just got to organize and get it done, gang. We're shooting ourselves in the foot by doing nothing.

SHARON. How many politicians have family members, like their children or their spouses, who have had substance abuse problems or even themselves? If their family members need help, they can get help because of who they are or the money they make. Why? Because they are a certain person, an individual in our government system versus somebody who works at Wal-Mart. Why is that person more important? The Golden Rule—treat others as you want to be treated . . .

JOHN. I support a state delegate who is a friend of mine. And when I go to his fundraisers or his parties or whatnot, he's got a family member in recovery that's right there. So they understand it. But, they are afraid; everybody is afraid of taking the first step. And we're afraid to be part of the recovery movement. It's a stigma. It paralyzes even family members.

NANCY. I've known John for most of my life. And McShin is trying to break down the stigma of addiction. And what he's trying to say is unless we unite as a group and show them we're productive people, they're going to keep shutting doors and being scared off. We have to show them that we are intelligent, and we can recover. Once we recover we can be that much more of an addition to a society.

SHARON. But that's society for you; if you watch a show and you see somebody who has a mental illness, right away, you see somebody on the street. They label that person. Oh, this person is high on crack and they just killed . . .

JOHN. They sensationalize the illness. Sensationalism sells TV commercials. I mean, that's why Greg's documentary needs to be made because we want to sensationalize *recovery*, because recovery is very sensational. Not only that the disease is contagious, but recovery is contagious, too. And advocacy is contagious, as well.

SHARON. But everyone is in here to get help. Why look down on people who are getting help?

JOHN. Because addiction has a bad boy component to it. We have one of the only diseases you can get that tells you, you don't have it and some of our main symptoms are cheating, lying, stealing. So it takes a lot to overcome that. There is some legitimacy for some concern. When you come to McShin, we know right away who the bad boys and girls are. And you know what, we'll tell them that they are not ready for us. You need to go to jail or prison. Or you have another mental illness. You're above our pay grade. But we want you to get the help and help guide you in that process.

You have wonderful thoughts, you know. Any others?

TANNER. I feel like the public, when they think of the word "addict," all they think about is addicts in active addiction. They think about us cheating, stealing . . . like what John said. What they don't see is what goes on behind these doors, the recovering aspect of being an addict. When I came in, I had cheated, I committed crimes. But when you come into the rooms here, you're talking to addicts who have been through what you have been through and who genuinely care about you. There's no judgment. It gives me a sense of comfort, and a sense that I can open up and express my feelings and grow as a person. When you come into recovery, you work on yourself the whole time. It's really interesting the way people think about addicts. We have a disease. It's not like we're bad people. We did bad things to support our habit.

NEIL. You asked us what we thought about voting for a politician who wants to help us people with the disease of addiction. But honestly, maybe I missed something, but I've never seen any politician on the campaign trail bring that up.

JOHN. You rarely see that, do you? Anybody ever seen that?

GROUP RESPONSE. No.

JOHN. I've seen Levar's boss talk about it and want to help. What did he say?

LEVAR. Why are folks locked away for years on end when they can be contributors to society? When folks—and John said 700,000 people out there—get to be contributing members of society who will pay taxes because they buy goods instead of stealing. It should be about addition and not subtraction; you put someone in jail, that's subtraction. You take them away from society, putting people away, that's costing us money. Adding them back to society gets them integrated back into everyday life so they can contribute to society, to government. It seems logical.

JOHN. We're borderline making history here! I've been around a long time and this is the first time I've seen a Chief of Staff from a guy running for higher office sitting in a think tank group like this. And not only participate from the bottom of his heart, but actually grasp, develop, and understand not only the issues, but also the process. I mean, you guys have no idea what you're being part of right now. You need to know there's a whole lot of people who have been trying to get rid of us. They don't understand us or recognize us or they can't justify it. And it's up to us to make sure we make that difference. I mean this is historical!

MARK. Yeah, I've been in jail. I've seen a lot of people going in there; I tell them to go into the recovery program. Now, tell no lie, I'm ninety. I have seen people come in who are very sick—my brothers and sisters—but they come back, and then they are well, you know what I mean? We're communicating. That's amazing. That's how much love we have for this group. We meet strangers, you know, drug users, alcoholics, whatever, we're all the same, but we talk—communication, man. You see them coming in here, dragging, but then you see them with that smile on their face and that makes me feel so good. I'm here every day. We can give it all we can. It's going to work.

NEIL. I have to agree with you, especially these groups, it's like we've all become one big family. We all look after each other, ask how you're doing, if you're stressed out about something and maybe thinking about using, or thinking about taking a drink, we talk you out of it. We all look out for each other. Exactly like you said. It's great. It really truly is.

BARBARA. I think it's absolutely amazing that I can even be a part of this today. I struggle with peer-to-peer because I'm a loner, isolator. The peer-to-peer contact, they tell me like it is. I can't get away. I have to face myself, who I am, without drugs, yes, that's part of it. I'm very grateful. I can't tell you how amazing it is to have this. And, as I go along, I'm hoping I can get registered to vote in one state, stay there long enough to cast a ballot for someone who, if they tell the truth, will make a difference and will genuinely care about people in recovery. And we do recover.

STUART. You know, John, when I think of politicians, you're talking dollars and cents. What does it cost to house an inmate per year? If you take the money it costs to house an inmate per year and take them in this recovery group on their last year, look how much money you're going to be saving the taxpayer. Now, when I think of politicians and their programs, I think all about money, and I think that's the final picture most politicians look at.

JOHN. There's a bill in the House right now, they want to drug test people getting TANF payment [Temporary Assistance for Needy Family]. Now, there are scientific documents, outcome studies out the wazoo that show, financially, that is about the dumbest thing you can do. You take a mother smoking crack, you take her $800 a month payment from her. You save $10,000 in tax dollars a year. But her two children end up in foster care, which costs $80,000 a year in tax dollars—per child. So, you save $10,000 and spend $160,000. And with those two kids in foster care, there's a 380 percent chance they're going to end up in the criminal justice system! Not 10 percent, not 20, but a 380 percent chance. So the cost, the dollars and cents, don't even compute. I call that a resentment bill.

These politicians resent addicts. And it's weird how that is. But, there are ways to have a resentment bill that's workable. Okay, fine. I'm not going to give the check payment to Mary. I'm going to give it to her mother and let her mother pay the rent for her. That way, we can keep her in her house and her kids together and hopefully it all works out.

WOMAN IN GROUP. I don't believe they believe in the recovery system. I don't think they believe that an addict can truly recover. I think that's the bottom line of the problem.

JOHN. You know what, you are so right. There are so many of them who don't believe it. If we were to be the faces and voices of recovery and tell our story every chance we got to everybody we came in contact with, we could reverse at least 50 percent of those people and make believers out of them. We're not going to get everybody to believe. That will never happen, but by golly, we'll be turning half of them around. You go further back in history, those same people did not believe a woman should vote. Those same people didn't believe a black should vote, or be a citizen, or a President. So, history is on our side. History will show one day who and what we are. So I say we make history. That's what I say.

It's a pretty good guess John has read Bill White. He is doing his best to bring about change through advocacy, and especially through his daily work of reaching out at the grassroots level and affecting lives one person, one successful recovery, at a time.

And how about those brave people in the recovery advocacy you just heard? I sensed they were all keenly aware of the importance of sharing their stories and showing their success. They seemed to know, and rightly so, that as a group, they could make a difference.

We met so many people close to John and his work—members of his staff, McShin's physician, the pastor of the church, board members, clients who were volunteering time—and we talked with them all. Many of their interviews remain among the collected gems on the cutting room floor, but make no mistake they all contributed indispensably to our understanding and appreciation of the daily work of recovery. I vow that these people's stories will some day see the light of day, but for now, you must hear from the light of John's life, the other half of McShin: Carol McDaid.

CAROL McDAID

"Today, the addiction recovery community is recognized as a constituency of consequence because we have figured out how to mobilize people willing to be a face and voice in recovery."

Carol McDaid has already made history—and is a continuing part of it. Within the walls and halls of Congress, and under the direction of the two recovering legislators who authored the bill, Patrick Kennedy and Jim Ramstad, Carol led the Parity NOW Coalition behind passage of the 2008 Paul Wellstone and Pete Domenici Mental Health Parity and Addiction Equity Act. This landmark legislation requires insurers to treat addiction, mental, and physical health problems equally. As a registered lobbyist, Carol worked to coordinate over 300 addiction and mental health provider and consumer organizations, plus criminal justice, child welfare, recovery community organizations, and other groups to advocate for this bill. The Parity NOW Coalition was a model for how to successfully advocate for policy change and to include addiction and mental health benefits in healthcare reform legislation.

Carol is a person in long-term recovery from alcohol and other drugs, and it was her first-hand experience with insurance discrimination that motivated her commitment to level the playing field for people suffering from mental health and addiction issues. When she sought care for her own addiction in the eighties and nineties, she had difficulty accessing benefits for treatment under her employer's health plan. ". . . Nor hell a fury like a woman scorned," the playwright Congreve wrote, before he could possibly know the passion and determination this woman had to right the injustice. She worked for more than ten years on the issue and never gave up until the parity bill was passed.

When you meet Carol, it is hard to imagine she possesses such a bulldog personality. Her warmth, charm, and good humor stand out and would seem antithetical to the down and dirty, dogged perseverance required of the stereotypical lobbyist trying to get a bill through Congress. Truth is, more than likely it was her good qualities that helped sustain the fight and earn the victory.

It was easy to keep perspective on her lobbying work as she spoke to us in her Washington, DC office with a close and thrilling view of the Capitol directly behind her. She gave us fascinating insight into the Machiavellian machinations lawmakers and lobbyists devise to create legislation. It was our rare privilege to look inside the powerhouse and see at least one way that history is made.

GREG. What happened to you that set you on your path to work so long and hard for parity?

CAROL. In 1989, I was working as a legislative analyst at this big international accounting firm, and my addiction was getting so bad, my family and boss did an intervention on me. It was ironic, because I worked in the employee benefits department and they weren't even aware that the health benefits they promised their employees were not actually accessible. We had a nice employer plan, it said that it covered up to thirty days of residential addiction treatment, but when we tried to access those benefits for me, they said that I had to have failed at outpatient twice. My boss said, "Carol has been an outpatient before." And they said, "Well, she missed two appointments during her last term of outpatient, and the clock starts over then." So there are clearly terms that insurers manipulate sometimes, and people don't understand that. When people are in addiction, they oftentimes get to that brink where there's a crisis and you need to be able to access those benefits right there and then, when they need help.

The second time I went to rehab, I had started working in our field, and I made it my personal passion to seek reimbursement from my health plan. By that time, I had gotten the benefit of being involved in this parity issue. It took me three years and seven appeals, but one day, three years after I started the appeal process, a check for half of my treatment just wafted in through the mail. No explanation, no nothing, and so it can be done, but other people don't have the resources. I was a lobbyist for Blue Cross-Blue Shield myself; I know the game. People shouldn't have to have the resources of somebody who's an insurance expert in order to get benefits their employer has already paid for.

G. What are some of the ways insurance companies make it difficult for people to access benefits?

C. One of the first reasons it's so difficult is that it's not transparent to the consumer. Everybody gets a plan booklet when you go to work for a new employer, and it says you have all these benefits. But what's not listed is what they call "medical management criteria," which are techniques that plans use to manage the cost of the insurance they are providing you. There are medical criteria in our field that says this type of patient belongs at this level of care. And even if you meet that, they still say, well, you didn't fail at outpatient twice, even if you've already been in rehab two times, or you've been in six outpatient programs, which was the case with me. So it's not transparent to people, it's not written in their plan booklet. The health plan is in charge of it; they don't listen to the physician or the clinician directing the care. It's basically the fox guarding the henhouse. They can change their criteria whenever they want, without informing their plan participants, so it's really a stacked deal against the consumer.

G. What are the criteria policymakers should look at to make them uniform?

C. There are uniform patient placement criteria that have been developed by the American Society of Addiction Medicine [ASAM], the trade association that's been around for about fifty-sixty years for addiction physicians. It allows health plans to match a patient to the right level of care based on the chronicity of their illness.

G. Within the essential health benefit of the Affordable Care Act [ACA], it is mandated that substance abuse is part of the insurance benefit. How important is that?

C. This has been the moment I was waiting for my whole career! If the law gets fully implemented, it will be the biggest expansion of addiction coverage in a generation. We wanted to get parity passed first, and parity simply means that if you cover addiction, you've got to cover it on par with any other medical benefit you cover. What we got in the ACA that's so tremendous is that addiction will, for the first time, be required to be covered as one of ten essential benefits, and, it will be required with the new Medicaid expansion population. In many states, addiction coverage under Medicaid is really lousy, so this will be a huge advance for people who need help.

G. Tell us the story of the Mental Health Parity Act. You called it the first step toward fair and just health insurance policy, but it was a huge first step. You worked ten, twelve years to help get it passed. How did you get involved and how did it happen?

C. I'd love to tell you I had this grand plan that I sat down and wrote out. But, like a lot of things in recovery, synchronicity and grace played a big role. I had come to Washington to work. I was still actively using alcohol and other drugs at the time. I thought I was going to go to law school at night here—this was in the early eighties—and I got a job as a paralegal at a law firm. A senator was retiring from the Hill and opened one of the early lobbying practices within a law firm in Washington. My job, with the antitrust litigation department, was to stamp a five-digit number on the right hand corner of 300,000 documents. Months and months and months, it was chi-cha, chi-cha, chi-cha, and this senator would walk by. I think he felt sorry for me. And he was a character. He looked like a caricature of what you think a lobbyist is, with the cigar smoking and the gray hair. I think he took pity on me and said, "Hey little lady, run over to the Hill and back." In those days you had to get a hard copy of bills. He said, "Jump on the Metro!" I had no idea how to ride the subway, but I played it off like I did. I started reading the bills on the way back and he would quiz me. I remember when I called my parents and said, "You know that deposit you made to George Washington for law school? Well, I'm not going to go there this fall. I'm going to become a lobbyist." And my mother, who's from South Carolina and very southern, said, "A lobbyist? Carol Ann that's similar to a street walker!" Back in those days, women worked for lobbyists, but not many were registered lobbyists themselves. So that's how I got my start.

G. How did you get involved in working on addiction policy issues?

C. It was in 1993 when Bill and Hillary Clinton were doing the first big health reform law and healthcare lobbyists were in great demand. A man from a lobbying firm called me, asked me for an interview and said, "Here's a list of our clients, do you know anything about this one?" pointing to Hazelden. I had gone to rehab at Hazelden and I thought, this is a conspiracy—he knows I went there, and this is his way of teasing it out in an interview—when actually he had no idea. I got the job. I'll never forget, he said, "You've gotta fly to Minnesota and figure out what these people want 'cause they're bothering me to death. I have no idea what they do, and they hug all the time instead of handshakes, and honestly I can't take it."

Right before we went out there, I decided I'd better tell him I'd been a Hazelden patient. I went into his office, and he had one of those palatial offices with the high ceilings and the big fireplaces and everything, and I said, "I went to Hazelden." He said, "What did you go there for, a conference or something?" And I said, "No, I was a patient there." There was just this long sigh. He asked, "Do you have an alcohol problem?" And I said, "Yeah, and drugs." He said, "You? You look so sweet and innocent. You couldn't have a drug problem." And he leaned forward and said, "Does everybody on the Hill know that?" and I said, "Some do, but only the ones who used with me." He started laughing and he paced back and forth, and I'm thinking, *Oh, God, I just sent all these announcements about how I'd become a vice president at this lobbying firm and I'm going to have to call everyone and tell them I got canned.* He turned to me and said, "McDaid, they're going to think I'm a genius." "Here's the plan. We're going to go to Hazelden and tell them I hired you just to service their account, and you're going to become *the* addiction lobbyist in Washington. I can see it now. We'll get Hazelden, then we'll get Betty Ford." He laid out my career plan that day.

G. What was it like in those early days being a lobbyist and being public about your recovery?

C. I'm a public advocate; I'm a face and voice of recovery now here in Washington and everywhere I go, but at that time, even my employer who had been so supportive of me representing Hazelden told me, "It's fine if you want to talk about your experience with addiction and recovery with them, but not all of our clients will appreciate it." So I had to keep it under wraps that I was a recovering addict.

In 1996, we were in the heat of the battle on what was then the Mental Health Parity Act and we were on the Senate floor. The senator from New Mexico, Senator Domenici, offered an amendment to strike addiction from the bill because at that time, in his view, addiction was not a disease, it was a moral failing. We worked closely at the time with Senator Paul Wellstone, from Minnesota, and both he and Senator Domenici had this issue in their family, both mental health and addiction. We were scrambling on the floor trying to make sure the amendment didn't pass. A senator from Maryland whom over the years I had developed a relationship with, took me aside and said, "I'd love to help you out with this, but this addiction stuff, it's not a great issue. No one cares about it. And let's be frank, Carol, addicts don't vote."

It was heartbreaking to me. I knew right then I wasn't going to drop the issue; my challenge was to make sure we became a constituency of consequence, that we played the game in state capitols, and in Washington, and in other places, so we can do what's necessary to have an elected official say, "I have to be with addiction advocates because I will suffer political pain if I'm not."

It took a long while, but I will say that today the addiction recovery community is recognized as a constituency of consequence in large part because we have figured out how to mobilize people like me, like others who are willing to be a face and voice in recovery, share their personal experiences and triumphs. My story is a story of triumph. I'm a fifth generation Irish person who had alcoholism and addiction all through her family. And, it stops with me. Now I've been able to give back and help, so that hopefully, it'll stop with other families.

G. You made it your big battle through all those years to get addiction parity back up for a vote, didn't you?

C. I did with the help of devoted legislators and other advocates. I was lucky enough to have clients for many years who financed this effort, but clients get tired of financing unsuccessful advocacy campaigns. Five years go by, seven years go by, nine years . . . there were some years where I pretended I had clients and kept working on it. For many years though, the addiction treatment industry helped finance this, along with addiction medicine, and others. But—and this isn't a partisan comment, this is just a statement of fact—we could not even get a hearing at health committees in the House on addiction and mental health parity in the early nineties when Republicans were in charge. But timing is everything in life, and it really is in politics, and so in 2008, when we saw that both houses had gone Democrat, and it looked like we were going to have a Democratic President, this was like lightening striking twice. We knew that was our moment to move this legislation. So, literally, on election night, I was calling other advocates, like Legal Action, who work with me on this issue. We were calling Patrick Kennedy and Jim Ramstad, saying, "This is our time; let's go!" We worked on drafting legislation all during Thanksgiving, all during Christmas, and when Congress came back in session, we were ready to rock. In fact, we did. Finally the law passed in 2008 with bipartisan majorities, and President Bush signed it into law.

G. What's the inside story on the passage of the bill? What were some things that happened behind the scenes to make it happen?

C. We left so much shoe leather in the halls; our coalition went and saw 535 members in the Congress over a series of years when we were working on this. I had incredible colleagues who were crucial in scheduling Hill meetings and keeping the troops marching. And we were able to motivate and mobilize people in recovery to call their members of Congress. We had one call-in day when everyone calls a 1-800 number to ask for a bill to be put on the House floor, and we had 10,000 phone calls go into Nancy Pelosi's office, who was Speaker of the House at the time. That was really a tipping point. When that happened, they knew we were a constituency of consequence.

They scheduled the vote on the House floor in March of that year and it was one of the few bills that had bi-partisan support.

G. You mentioned the call-in day as a tipping point in getting the parity bill to a vote. How were you able to mobilize the recovery community to own this issue, to mobilize and respond in such numbers?

C. The great thing about parity is that it's easy to explain; it's about fairness. We want to be treated like anybody else. It's insurance discrimination; it's the next big civil rights frontier. We put the information out about how to dial-in during those September recovery month events all over the country. When we got 10,000 calls that one day, I knew it was because the recovery community had been mobilized in a way that we had not been able to touch them and activate them before.

G. Describe the day when President Bush signed the law, who was in the room, the press conference. What was it like actually seeing the parity bill become law?

C. There were mixed feelings about it because it was attached to the bailout bill. That was controversial, and both the administration and Congress wanted to play that down. They only had a ceremony for the four bill sponsors with President Bush—Ted Kennedy, Senator Domenici, and House co-sponsors Patrick Kennedy and Jim Ramstad. But we had a massive celebration here in town, and it's probably one of the only times as a lobbyist I have not had trouble raising money. Everybody wanted to be one of the sponsors of the parity party. It was a very festive day, but in the back of the room, shouting because of all the music, another lobbyist and I were plotting what we were going to do to get the regulations done. Getting a law passed, that's all great and everybody can celebrate, but people who work inside government know that's just half the battle. The harder battle is to get regulations done that implement the law.

G. So during the parity party, you were plotting your next move?

C. I was celebrating, but I knew the regulations are where the action is, to move a law from a book that sits on a bookshelf, to operationalize it into people getting access to the care they need and they want. So another lobbyist, Al Guida and I pulled out cocktail napkins, and we were sketching out what we needed to do to start a regulatory campaign, much in the same way we had had a legislative campaign. And we followed the playbook. We've run the plays; it's taken a long time—it does in Washington—but we're getting there.

G. The process of policy change seems so long and often frustrating, to say the least. How do you keep on keeping on?

C. I have staff who are smarter than I am. One of the ways I kept the cynicism at bay was that I worked out a lot in the gym at the bottom of this building. I would picture the bill signing and I would listen to certain old Stevie Wonder songs about people being discriminated against, and people rising up, to motivate me to keep fighting. Working in this town is not easy, and it's gotten even more difficult to get things done. It's a tough business. It's like the last man standing; if you stay in the ring and you keep fighting, you got a shot to win. Part of it was the mental thing to stay in there, no matter what, and keep fighting.

G. And the reward for you, personally, for all your work, was . . . ?

C. I was gratified by the trade associations and organizations that presented me with plaques and awards. But the most meaningful thing to me was when I would get calls from people who would say, "My insurance paid for my care." That's where the rubber meets the road in this work. Because you can lose your mind in this town, waiting for them to act. What's really satisfying is to get the call from someone that they got the care they needed and deserved.

G. Assuming we can get all these robust addiction health benefits implemented, who gains?

C. Providing effective and quality addiction and mental health benefits benefits everybody. The first beneficiaries, and probably the largest, are the federal and state governments. For years, private health insurance and employer-based insurance have been cost-shifting the cost of addiction and mental healthcare onto the federal government and the state governments. Unlike any other condition, 70 to 80 percent of addiction care is currently provided in the public sector. That needs to be right-sized. The public sector has a great stake in making sure that the private sector picks up their fair cost of the care, which they've been pushing onto the public sector. And obviously individuals and families benefit.

G. Please explain what "cost-shifting" is.

C. Take my case. If I hadn't had a family that was willing to pay out-of-pocket when I first needed rehab in 1989, I might have lost my job as a result of not performing and not getting help, as a condition of my employment. What oftentimes happens is that people lose their jobs, and then they become the public sector's problem. The public sector has to pick up the cost of their care, which is not right. It pays to pay for it to begin with. I know when I returned from rehab, my productivity shot out the roof. In fact, it was so powerful, a part of my recovery within my office was that I had to tell some of the other accounting firm offices what my story was, to show that this investment makes sense for employers.

G. That's why this is really not a partisan issue.

C. Right. Because in the end it's dollars and cents, baby, dollars and cents.

G. It makes dollars and cents to invest in addiction services.

C. Not only that, for employers, we know 70 percent of people with addiction are employed. Employers have as much invested in the game in getting their employees well as the public sector does. We know the costs associated with untreated addiction are huge—absenteeism, lost productivity, etc. It's the number one reason why people go on disability. The costs associated with not doing anything have become so high, it is one of the reasons we were able to get addiction included as a mandated benefit in the healthcare law, relatively easily. Each year they delayed, the cost kept getting more staggering and more compelling.

G. People on the Hill know you well now, but when you meet a new senator or client and you talk about your recovery, what kind of response do you get from people?

C. The first reaction I get, often, is congratulations. I think people are much more respectful, and they pat you on the back and say, "This is a tough business to be in. How do you do it?" Because there's a lot of alcohol involved in the government relations business. On the other hand, I had an article come out in *Congressional Quarterly*, which is one of the magazines of the government relations community, and they asked for my story. I shared with them what drugs I had used and, lo and behold, I get a magazine story with my photo, and it said I shot heroin at sixteen. Instead of the focus on parity and on the mobilization of the recovery community, which is what I'd hoped they would cover, the story got to be that this little Southern girl shot dope when she was sixteen. Occasionally, I have had a competitor pitching business say, you might want to look at this article—her real love is in this area. I've had my knocks along the way about how to tell my story and what to tell, but I haven't looked back. This is my life's work. By and large, it has helped me more than it's hurt me, at least in the advocacy work in the Washington community. And I think the temperature of America has changed. People are warming up to the fact that people have personal adversities, and they have recovered, and go on to triumph in their life. Americans love a good redemption story, and recovery's a great one to tell.

G. But there are still many false perceptions the public has about addiction. What is your take on that and what we can do about it?

C. Unfortunately, we live in a society that likes to have the darkest, scariest, most intense stories. We've seen far too much in the media about the horrors of addiction and far too little about the triumphs of recovery. And part of that is that recovery's not as sexy. You know, I don't have a war story to tell you. I've got nothing but incredible stories of resilience and recovery, and family, and success at business, and passion in my personal life. In the media that doesn't sell right now. Our challenge is to make that salient in today's world, to get the right sound bites, to get the right young people involved, and to unlock the key. You don't give up.

"You don't give up." Is there anything more basic to recovery? Or to life?

In Carol, we see the integration of that idea in the whole of her being. Again, it is that power of recovery that infuses and informs all she is and does. As we observed Carol and John in action, doing their daily details of living and advocacy, the concept of "you don't give up" became real. It is something most of us do not usually think about unless we are faced with a definable, difficult challenge. With Carol and John, it is in their every moment, and it is not just about themselves. Yes, they do not give up in their recovery, but even more importantly, they do not give up on others. In the halls of McShin, in the halls of the county jail, and in the halls of Congress, they change people because they don't give up. In change you see the active manifestation of their creed.

We saw some of the most dramatic examples of this when we met John's friend and colleague, Michael Wade, Sheriff of Henrico County, Virginia. Here's a lawman who doesn't lock 'em up and throw away the key. By not giving up on his inmates, he has helped change the culture of prison life in the jails under his jurisdiction and influenced others throughout the country. Henrico County jails are widely recognized for their state-of-the-art facilities and services, but especially for their unique jail-based addictive behaviors treatment programs for both male and female inmates. Over half of the inmate population participates in Recovery In a Secure Environment (RISE), a positive four-phase drug rehab and life-reflection program that ultimately results in self-sustaining peer-to-peer recovery support among inmates. In 2007, at John's suggestion, Sheriff Wade also started a weekly open NA meeting in the lobby of Jail West. The Saturday night meeting we attended attracted about 120 inmates, family members, and community friends. With innovative programs such as these, which rehabilitate and teach, rather than just warehouse, Sheriff Wade says his operating costs are down and so is recidivism. It is hope that is on the rise.

Here's Bernard, an inmate with whom we spoke just moments after he received his graduation certificate from the Recovery Program in the Richmond city jail. This is a hardcore jail and a scary place. Inevitably, you see a lot of darkness in the wary eyes that appraise you from behind the bars of bleak cells as you walk past. But, as Bernard stepped out into the hallway to meet us, freely, there was an undeniable light of optimism in his eyes.

GREG. First of all, congratulations on earning your certificate.

BERNARD. Thank you.

G. How long have you been in and out of jail?

B. Since I was twenty-one. I've been here sixteen months.

G. What was the recovery program like that you just went through?

B. It was a behavior modification and recovery-coaching program. I had a behavior problem and I also had a drug problem. I've learned I can't get high anymore. They teach you how to control your behavior, the Twelve Steps, and ways to think differently, things like that.

G. What is recovery for you?

B. Recovery is different. It's something I never tried before in the years I was getting high—twenty-seven years. I like it. I have to face life on life's terms now. Can't hide my feelings.

G. Do you think you would have grabbed on to the recovery program, if they had one, back when you were twenty-one?

B. I wish they had this when I was twenty-one. I don't think I would be here now. My first time in jail was drug-related. If I had been introduced to recovery then, my life would have been different. At least, I would have known about it and it would have given me something to work toward.

G. What do you mean you think your life could have been different?

B. My life was centered around drugs. I never thought about treatment. I never thought about recovery. I thought everybody got high. In my neighborhood, that's what everybody does. I just thought it was a way of life. And now I know it's not.

G. And now, you not only have your own recovery, but you are qualified to help others, aren't you?

B. Yes. I went through sixteen weeks of recovery coach training in the McShin program. So, I'm going to be able to help others who need recovery. I think I can share my experience with them and show them using drugs is not the way of life. If you face life on life's terms, open up, be honest, and share your feelings, things will be all right.

That's what hope can do for recovery—and what recovery can do for hope. But hope doesn't come easily; nor is it meaningful if it is empty. You have to create solid reasons to have it. Peers can give it to you. Personal, incremental successes can build it. Advocates for change can inspire it. And national policy can institutionalize it and make it real.

In August of 2013 came a high-profile announcement from the Attorney General of the United States, Eric H. Holder, Jr. that raised some real hope. Mr. Holder told prosecutors that when writing indictments in certain low-level federal drug cases, they may not indicate the specific quantity of drugs possessed by the defendants. This major policy change will give prosecutors and judges more discretion in setting sentences by sidestepping laws that automatically impose stiff mandatory minimum sentences for drug-related offences. The purpose is to correct unfairness in the justice system, reduce America's large prison population, and save related costs.

In making the announcement, Mr. Holder said that "widespread incarceration at the federal, state, and local levels is both ineffective and unsustainable," and that the current system "imposes a significant economic burden—totaling $80 billion in 2010 alone—and it comes with human and moral costs that are impossible to calculate."

But that wasn't all. He also called for applying more alternatives to incarceration, including increasing the use of drug-treatment programs.

What brought about all this enlightened thinking at the federal level, do you suppose?

A little dose of hard reality helps. Since that catchy "War on Drugs" campaign, begun during the Nixon Administration and ramped up in the eighties to become more accurately a war on people, the incarceration rate in the United States increased about 800 percent. According to Holder, nearly half of the inmates in federal prisons are there for drug-related offences, putting prisons at nearly 40 percent over capacity.

Bring in the politicians with their bean counters who pander to the electorate by promising to cut taxes and spending. One way to save money, they say, is to downsize the prison industrial complex. No need to build more prisons if you are going to have fewer inmates. Polls show that the heightened public fear of drug-related crime that once pervaded this country has subsided, making "tough on crime" political candidates less relevant. Now, many proponents of justice system reform are coming from politically conservative groups. It is not so surprising when you accept that saving money and shifting power to the states are traditional conservative values. In places like Texas, Arkansas, and Florida—typically "red states"—there have been innovative changes in justice system policies that have, by some accounts, saved hundreds of millions of dollars. These states have taken the pressure off their prison systems by giving low-level drug offenders shorter sentences, providing more treatment programs, creating early-release programs, and enhancing community re-entry and job opportunities.

These successes obviously caught the attention of the Obama Administration. As Mr. Holder said in his speech,

> "While the federal prison system has continued to slowly expand, significant state-level reductions have led to three consecutive years of decline in America's overall prison population including, in 2012, the largest drop ever experienced in a single year. They've attracted overwhelming, bipartisan support in 'red states' as well as 'blue states.' And it's past time for others to take notice."

Now we're getting somewhere. This is news that gives reason for hope. But, again, how did the Feds notice this? They saw it work in the states. But then, how did the states know it would work? What motivated this strange meld of progressive and conservative ideas to be considered, implemented, and proven at the local level?

These revolutionary ideas came from you! Recovery advocates. Recovery ambassadors. And from enlightened people who simply recognize the power of recovery. The validation for new policy comes from individual people taking small steps—one person at a time, one meeting at a time, one day at a time, one success at a time—never giving up and proving that recovery works. You met many of these heroes, big and small, in this book and saw them in Greg's film. They are saving lives. Saving money. And raising hopes. People notice these things.

People also notice the celebration of these things and what better time to raise awareness than during National Recovery Month every September. In cities and towns all across this nation, and throughout the world, people in recovery and their supporters hold public rallies. They march through the streets, they gather in parks, in concert venues, in government halls, churches, parking lots, or anywhere else they can be seen and heard. These events are not just to raise community awareness, they are important to the participants, as well. It is a time for people in recovery to affirm, to bond, to inspire and, most of all, to celebrate themselves and each other. To be sure, people in recovery, whether it's been thirty-five days or thirty-five years, have reason to celebrate. Can you imagine the exhilaration standing shoulder to shoulder in the light of day, in a public place, with your brothers and sisters in recovery, with people from all walks of life, drawing strength from each other, feeling proud, and having all the work and hope that is your daily recovery and come out in a great explosion of joy? "Recovery Works!" Spontaneously it bursts out of one person's heart and jolts the surrounding crowd, which takes up the chant for all the world to hear, "Recovery Works!" It is a thrilling moment to witness.

We couldn't wait, Craig and I. Greg knew. He knew what was in store for us when we finally had the opportunity to film a Recovery Rally. For the previous ten months, we had been on the road learning about the new recovery advocacy movement, meeting individuals and small groups, gaining intense, but limited understanding of the movement. We heard about it in historical contexts, in policy discussions, and in academic circles. We saw it at work locally, in recovery centers, in community activism, in institutional systems. But what was the big picture? And how would we depict it? Greg would talk about this during our long hours on the road, pointing us toward September, where, in the rallies scheduled during that commemorative month, he promised we would find some of the most literal and powerful images of the movement.

If Greg had had his way, our cameras would have been in every state, every city, and every hamlet that had a rally. Clearly, it was impossible to attend every one, but I knew, in the back of his mind, Greg was trying to conjure up a way to get some kind of coverage and recognition for all these celebrations. Why? Because as everyone in recovery knows, every individual in recovery is important, so, in that sense, no one rally was more important than another. I'll say this, Greg gave it a shot. We went to recovery events in Massachusetts, New York, New Jersey, Pennsylvania, Virginia, North Carolina (at the DNC Recovery Caucus), Georgia, and one other. It was the one that, for me, was the watershed experience in our long journey.

DETROIT: A METAPHOR FOR ADDICTION AND RECOVERY

When Henry Ford brought the auto industry to Detroit it was the start of a heady time. Fords, then Packards, Chryslers, and Chevrolets rolled off the assembly lines. Let the good times roll! Detroit partied. The city—and we—became addicted to the culture of the automobile, a sexy, streamlined, powertrain, petro-chemical dependence. At first, it felt good. Fun. Cool. A new escape. But before long, we became slaves to it. Whether we wanted it or not, we needed it. The addiction spread and then so did the suppliers. The dealer went global. And Detroit declined, slid into darkness. The face of Detroit went vacant, its complexion pockmarked with poverty and decay. You can see it in the burned out shells of buildings, empty now, where once the working class was high. Left are the ravages—crime, prostitution, the homeless, the hustle. Detroit literally went bankrupt. Hit rock bottom.

But rock bottom, as every sufferer knows, is just what you see. It is how addiction at the lowest point feels. Yet, rock bottom is just a place, not what you are. It's your state, not your soul. Detroit today looks lost, but the soul of the city can be found in its people, and the people know there is a better community inside and a better way forward. The soul wants out, eager for treatment, redemption, and recovery. There is life beneath all the rot, looking for some fertile soil in which to re-grow. If you look, if you care, under the injured surface are resources not immediately apparent, but persistent nevertheless, and places where the soul can go to be nourished and healed. It might be found in a local church or a mosque or it could be in the work of the Detroit Recovery Project and similar organizations. These are places where healing happens one individual at a time, one day at a time, and new life begins for the whole community. Where, in spite of darkness all around, sparks of light burst through the cracks and with rays of hope erase the epidemic shadows of a decaying neighborhood. Hope for one person today. Hope for a community tomorrow. Hope for a whole city, long-term. And hope for us all.

Detroit may never be exactly what it once was, but it will get better. It will cast off its tattered old habit and renew itself. Isn't that what recovery is all about?

Our visit to Detroit changed my whole perspective on the issue of recovery. In a flash, I saw Detroit as a microcosm of what recovery means to our larger society and to each of us who are a part of it. The revelation shocked me because suddenly, I felt a personal connection to the issue of addiction and recovery in a way I hadn't felt before.

I confess; I had friends and extended family members who suffered to one degree or another with addiction to alcohol and/or other drugs. But we never talked about it much. I never gave it much thought because whatever pain they may have been going through rarely reached my eyes or ears, never entered my consciousness, nor my conscience. It was either hidden, or I was in denial of it. It is not something Norman Rockwell would have painted. It was not my life. If awareness of responsibility for the plight of any one individual in the throes of addiction, or concern for a larger segment of suffering humanity ever entered my mind, it was mostly piqued by those lurid, pervasive media reports of celebrity burnouts. What a shame, I thought, reading of Whitney's death. Or LiLo's latest drama. Miss USA? What a waste. Can't understand how that could happen. A moment's pang of compassion, then turn the page. Let's see how the Yankees did last night. Escape reality.

On our journey with Greg, as I gradually learned, my empathy grew. You would think the scale of the problem alone—two-thirds of Americans are affected by addiction, so say the experts—would be enough to at least open one's eyes. But unless you see those effects first-hand, the number doesn't mean much beyond having an intellectual appreciation of the problem. True understanding comes with experiencing. Our intimate expedition into this world of addiction and recovery gave us a revelatory, sensitizing experience. One thing began to stand out and, for me, started to fan a small ember of insight: I saw that people who were committed to their recovery were also simultaneously committed to the recovery of others. For Phil Valentine, it was neighborhood to neighborhood throughout Connecticut. For John Shinholser, it was to special populations, especially in Virginia prisons. For Roger Oser it was to high-schoolers. For Jim Ramstad, it was to a nation. So many others. Remarkable things were happening everywhere.

With their stories of redemption and continuing success, I saw them give strength and hope to individuals who were still struggling. And I said to myself, only a person in recovery can do that. You had to have been there yourself, down in zombie hell, to be able to relate to some brother or sister trying to escape, to help that suffering person climb out, clean up, and be free.

But, in all of that good work done in the service of others, by people of like mind and experience, I noticed an important motive—a not entirely selfless reason for helping others. In the film, Dr. Robert DuPont, former head of the White House Office of National Drug Control Policy (ONDCP), alluded to it in his interview when he referred to AA cofounder Bill Wilson's belief that the secret to recovery is to help someone else recover. Is that why people in recovery were so passionate about helping others? Because helping others gave them the strength to sustain their own recoveries? No doubt that is part of it. But what I soon found out, the truth is much bigger. And not self-centered at all.

In Detroit, we met two stars, Andre Johnson and Dr. Calvin Trent, who shined a light on this question and what recovery can mean, not just to those suffering from addiction, but to the millions like me who are more or less oblivious to the issue.

What Johnson and Trent revealed was a reality bigger than any one person, bigger even than a neighborhood, a community, or a city. It was about the connection between something inside each of us to the world-at-large and how one individual affects many. Michael Askew, that compelling leader of the Bridgeport Community Center, referred to it in the film as the rock-in-the-pond ripple effect. The way Johnson and Trent put it sparked me to think that the effect could go further than the pond. Maybe we were seeing something that was more akin to Edward Lorenz's theory of the "butterfly effect," wherein a butterfly in a remote place flaps its wings and, by calculable consequences, produces a hurricane in another part of the world. Had I been looking a little more closely during our journey through American recovery, I could have seen the potential energy that recovery advocacy contains and how it has the power to unleash, widely. Everyone we met along the way, who was connected with the recovery movement, was already feeling, thinking, doing something positive that could affect us all. Some were acting privately, even, yes, anonymously. Others were influencing great numbers of people with their advocacy, changing minds and policy. But all of them started with a personal story, and small as it seemed, each was beautiful, like the beat of a butterfly wing. Add them up and something was definitely blowing in the wind.

It wasn't until I listened to Andre Johnson and Dr. Calvin Trent that I got it. It was in their voices, literally. We sat down for their interviews, first Andre, then an hour later, we re-set the scene for Dr. Trent. For each man, I did the usual—hid a lavalier mic in his clothing and set a boom mic close overhead just out of Craig's camera frame. I put my SONY earphones snug over my ears, blotting out all sounds except the input of the mics. Craig rolled camera and Greg started his questioning. I was sitting maybe ten feet away at the mixer adjusting the sound levels and listening for technical flaws. I closed my eyes to listen intently to their voices, the close placement of the microphones picking up every breath, every swallow, so intimate I could almost hear their heartbeats. The clear, unfiltered sound of their voices went into my ears and reverberated in my brain as if they were originating there. The technical artificiality of the interview set disappeared. These men were no longer sitting under lights answering questions from Greg Williams; they became a physical presence inside my consciousness, reaching for my conscience. After a time, I could almost anticipate what they were going to say. Their words became my own thoughts and I began to formulate an understanding of the connections they, in fact, had made long ago and were now trying to communicate to us. I saw the idea as soon as they spoke it:

> "The connection between recovery for one individual and recovery for society is: One. Thing. Recovery is profound, elemental, and involves us all, singly and collectively."

What these gentlemen are saying—the practical implications of their responses are no less than revolutionary. First, Andre Johnson, CEO of the Detroit Recovery Project, followed by his mentor, Dr. Calvin Trent.

ANDRE JOHNSON

"Recovery . . . it's like a light shining inside of people."

We were in Andre Johnson's office at the Detroit Recovery Project on the East Side of the city. His building is one of two large recovery drop-in centers he runs in Detroit. This one, on "Six Mile Road" (two miles south of Eminem's famed "Eight Mile") is just off the noisy Chrysler Freeway and in the middle of one of the city's highest concentrations of crime and addiction. It was raining that day, and besides the traffic noise, there was a constant splat of raindrops outside the office window. These intrusive sounds were going to make it impossible to record a "clean" audio track for Greg's interview with Andre. I was feeling rather cranky. Then, Andre walked in and greeted us. Talk about a shining light. You know when Andre Johnson has entered your space; he fills a room—first, with his physical presence. He's a large, strong-looking man with a spotlight smile and a splendid sheaf of long dreadlocks, which he wears neatly tied back. Even more striking though, is the positive energy that radiates from him, dissipating any negativity in the room and seemingly, all unwanted distractions. Outside, as if on cue, the sun broke through, the rain stopped, and, incredibly, the roar of passing trucks subsided. So did my crankiness. I happily shook Andre's hand and mic-ed him up.

I suspect the glow of light Andre Johnson brings to any situation has been one of the key ingredients to his success. All the more impressive when you consider the darkness from which he emerged twenty-four years ago.

GREG. **If you don't mind, and to get a little personal, tell us about your journey that led you to where you are today.**

ANDRE. My journey of recovery started right here in the city of Detroit. I was eighteen years old. I entered a drug-treatment program with my ass in my hands asking, "What can I do?" I was a high school dropout. I was a parolee. I committed a crime. I was a fugitive and on the run, because I ran off with three different dope man's drugs that I was supposed to have been distributing and selling. So I ran into the drug-treatment center trying to escape the streets of Detroit for fear of harm or possibly death. I found people who were passionate, people who spent a lot of time and energy to say, "Let me help this boy find recovery." At first, I said, "After thirty days of treatment, I'll just smoke a little weed and drink a little alcohol and leave the crack-cocaine alone." But after thirty days turned into sixty days, I started to feel something. I started to feel good about myself. I started to feel worthy. My self-esteem started to build. My skin started to change. People started complimenting me. People were loving me, Greg. I had a group of people say, "We're going to love you until you learn how to love yourself." Eventually, I continued to stay clean. I continued to be committed to the recovery community. So when I entered and ran into that drug-treatment center, I found recovery.

G. How did you maintain your recovery?

A. I started doing service work. I had a mentor, Allen Bray, who was the CEO of that treatment program. He spent a lot of time talking to me. I spent 120 days in drug treatment. I spent two years in a transition house, and I went back to school, got my GED. Went to Morehouse College, the historic black university in Atlanta, Georgia, and with completion of a bachelor's degree in psychology, I returned to Detroit. I had ten years of recovery and was committed to continuously working in this field. At that time, I got hired by my next mentor, Dr. Calvin Trent. Dr. Calvin Trent is a clinical psychologist, so I'm continually getting treatment from him. I was getting recovery support from my peers, but I was also getting motivated about how important it is for younger people like myself to be committed to work in this field. I've been clean for over twenty-four years. I live, I breathe this recovery stuff. This recovery work is not a job; it's a calling. It's something you have to want to do in your heart.

G. What was key for you in finally understanding what was in your heart?

A. Having mentors like Dr. Trent and Allen Bray. I'm talking about passionate guys who love helping somebody else. And when you find people like that who coach you and give you solid advice, it helps you with your maturation. Simultaneously, I had been charged and challenged to work with the recovery community on behalf of the City of Detroit Health Department. I got clean in the city of Detroit in 1988 and made more meetings than anybody I know. I can go to a meeting and I can expect to feel some love. I can expect to feel a connection with a group of people who love me, man. I didn't have that kind of love in my home. I grew up in an environment where my mother worked twelve hours a day. Only time I saw her was when she was going to bed or getting up going to work in the morning. And my stepfather was shooting dope or smoking crack. That's the kind of love I was getting as a teenager. But then I got introduced to people in recovery who inspired me—love that Dr. Trent showed to me, a young man who never had his biological father growing up. So it's a number of variables and factors that have influenced my life personally and professionally. Recovery has given me the hope that I can do anything, and anything is possible. As I mentioned earlier, I was a high school dropout, now I'm two and half years from finishing my doctorate degree in psychology. Someday I'll get back in school, but I'm having so much fun working with the recovery community. I'm having so much fun watching people in recovery maturing, becoming responsible members in our community.

G. **The reluctance to talk publicly about one's own recovery has been a stumbling block for the recovery movement. How did you figure it out and navigate the idea of anonymity for yourself and how does it apply to the larger movement?**

A. Well, again, I think first of all being in the city of Detroit and having a mentor who would call me out. He would say, what's wrong with you all? You scared to say who you are? He would challenge us. We started a radio show entitled, *Beating the Odds.* It was a live show and I would say, "Hey, this is Andre Johnson. I'm a brother in recovery. Can we hear from some other brothers in recovery?" The next thing you know, you hear, "This is Lawrence K. I've been in recovery twenty years." Or "This is Mike T. I've been in recovery ten years." Or "This is Cynthia, and I've been in recovery nine months." That was a channel, an avenue that allowed people to self-disclose. Detroit has a cable commission, and we would facilitate a monthly meeting inside the Detroit City Council chambers and we would talk about recovery openly on public access TV. We had these vehicles, TV and radio, we were able to capitalize on. And now, the shame has gone away. Bill White talks about it in *Slaying the Dragon* when he gives that historical perspective how it wasn't positive to say you were a drunkard or you're an addict. But now, you can get respect in some venues. We work with Detroit Public Schools. We work with many churches. And people, when we self-disclose say, "Thank you so much. You've given me hope. I've been praying for my son, my daughter who's been on that stuff for ten years." Or "Can you help my son or my daughter?" Or "Can you help my husband?" Or the judge says, "I've been smoking a little weed too, I need some help." There are so many benefits to self-disclosing and not self-promoting. People have to learn how to carry a solid message of recovery. Sometimes it doesn't sound so hot to say, "I'm a grateful long-term, recovering drug addict." Because people think, "What does that mean? You're still using?" But when you say, "I'm a person in long-term recovery, and that means I have not used drugs in this period of time," then that's a cleaner message, a little smoother, hipper. Faces & Voices of Recovery and the entire movement around the country have been diligent around a certain message of recovery that can be universal, that can be shared with the media, that can be shared with politicians, and that can be shared with non-recovering folks in a dignified manner.

G. **Tell us a little bit about the Detroit Recovery Project.**

A. Detroit Recovery Project is a 501(c)3 nonprofit organization that was created in 2001 to assist people in sustaining their long-term recovery in the city of Detroit. We're here as a safety net. We're here to help people make that transition from treatment—residential outpatient, methadone maintenance treatment—to long-term recovery.

G. **Did it start as an advocacy organization or a service organization? What's the evolution been?**

A. Initially, I was the Director of the Coalition Partnership for a Drug-Free Detroit, and my supervisor, Dr. Calvin Trent at the time, charged me to develop recovery programming and for us to start doing some advocacy in the city of Detroit. We recognized that we had a large group of people who were exiting treatment and relapsing within the first ninety days. On average, the drug-treatment programs in Detroit service about 13,000 people a year, and at that time, we discovered that over 50 percent of those people come back needing treatment. So we were charged to create programs to help people sustain their recovery, maintain that transformation back into the community. We applied for a federal grant from SAMHSA, and we were awarded $325,000 for four years. We started the Detroit Recovery Project [DRP]. Initially, the DRP was a concept of how we could impact the community recovery in Detroit. Then we found that we had a cadre of people in recovery who had co-occurring issues, mental health disorders, as well as substance abuse. We also found that a number of people who we worked with were recently released from prison or the local jails. A lot of it was substance abuse related, so we began to work with those special populations and develop the same programs that we had developed initially for people in recovery who were leaving treatment. In 2007, we got another federal grant, as well as local funding from our City of Detroit Bureau of Substance Abuse Prevention, Treatment and Recovery, and the Detroit-Wayne County Community Mental Health Agency.

The crux of how we were built was all about recovery support services, but we had to wake up and say, "If we're going to be a player in this game, we need to look at providing prevention services, providing treatment services, but not lose touch of recovery." Recovery is the most important thing. Fast-forwarding, our agency skyrocketed, just blossomed really fast. This past July marked our seventh year of being in business.

G. What goes on at this Detroit Recovery Project location; what specific services do you provide?

A. This is our recovery drop-in center. This is the place where people in recovery come to hang out, to talk to each other, to support. It's a lot of gut relating, as we say. We say: "A problem shared is a problem cut in half."

Our program is peer-led, peer-run, and peer-driven. That means that 90 percent of our employees are individuals in recovery.

We have midnight meetings six days a week, from Monday to Saturday, midnight to two. Most cases, they end up lasting until four or five o'clock in the morning, so if you can't sleep, come by at midnight, because a lot of people in recovery have problems sleeping. Friday and Saturday nights were prime time, at least for me. It was action time; people need places to go. One of the plusses of our organization is that we've always designed programs beyond traditional work hours of nine to five. We have relapse-prevention workshops, didactics that we do on Tuesday nights. We develop support groups for people in long-term recovery who have secondary illnesses—cancer survivors, HIV-positive, kidney transplants, people in recovery still needing a special kind of support group. We don't discriminate against a person's race, creed, religion, lack of religion, sexual orientation, or age. In fact, over the last couple years, we have developed more programs aimed toward youth. We have cognitive behavioral therapy support groups at this location. We have a team of recovery coaches.

G. **Wow, Detroit Recovery Project has a big role to fill throughout Detroit.**

A. That's right. Recovery is everywhere. Recovery is next door. People in recovery are throughout this city. This is our East Side location; our West Side location is where there's a huge Hispanic community, a lot of gangs, a lot of drugs. We're in the heart and that facility is about 20,000 square feet. We have regular recovery dances, where people in recovery DJ, where people come to party and have fun. We provide rapid HIV testing at all our locations. We have three transition homes in Detroit, where we provide housing for the men and women who are in recovery for a minimum of one to two years. That gives people the opportunity to build a relationship, to live in a safe, drug-free, recovery-oriented environment and build that foundation—whether you're going to school, whether you're trying to find a job, whether you're just trying to get your life back in order.

G. It's great you received all these federal and local grants. But why do you think the government is granting money and why are people investing in recovery?

A. America needs recovery right now. Our community is recovering from the auto industry collapse. Our community is recovering from the exodus that drugs caused. It's impacted the quality of life in our city of Detroit. I think the government realizes it's cost-effective, and the benefits are long-term, and it's worth it in many ways. What I mean by that is once we invest in a person, a person's recovery—then that person becomes a productive, tax-paying citizen. That person becomes an asset to the community versus locking up that person. We work with the local drug courts. We have one of the nationally recognized best drug-court programs right here, 36th District Court, where we have judges who are allies with the recovery community. They believe in helping people who have suffered from addiction. We've worked diligently with local law enforcement, our county sheriff's department, our Detroit Police Department, our Detroit DEA, a number of judges, a number of community organizations, a number of churches and faith-based organizations. We all function as allies and we realize we are more together than we are apart. And so, we say around here: "I can't. We can."

G. What does it do for the city of Detroit to put a face and a voice on recovery?

A. When we were created, our task was how do we raise consciousness in our community? My recovery foundation was built on the twelve-step model, and the twelve-step model was anonymous: Don't tell people that we're in recovery because people will judge us. But we began to get involved with organizations like Faces & Voices of Recovery, and we began to say, "Let's take a step forward. Let's step out of our box and tell folks in Detroit we are in recovery, and that recovery is possible and treatment works." We've given more people hope in this community, and we've worked to reduce the stigma that's associated with addiction. That stigma, I would say, has begun to decline. The beauty of Detroit today [September 14, 2012], is seen by its acting as a national recovery hub for this marching rally that's going to start on Saturday, where thousands of people are coming together to walk for recovery on one of the biggest islands in the United States right here in the city, one of Detroit's jewels. People of all nationalities are walking and rallying and celebrating this national movement as part of National Recovery Month. People will feel the energy in Detroit. People are enthusiastic. I'm getting excited just thinking about it. I might jump out of this chair in a minute!

G. **Looking to the future, where do you see the Detroit Recovery Project and your work headed?**

A. Our goal is to have recovery drop-in centers throughout our country where people in recovery can expect to be greeted by people in recovery and treated with dignity. Where people are treated with respect. Where people are given that second chance. Many people are not given an opportunity to work, to be employed because of their past records. My goal is to create a national center where we set standards to help people create recovery community organizations throughout the country. We've had some experiences helping to build a recovery community organization in East Africa, in Tanzania. And people have nowhere near the material or the financial resources we have here in the states. But you have a group who are some of the humblest people I've ever met on this earth who don't have much, but their spirits are strong. You can feel the spirit of that person yearning for recovery. You can feel the spirit of that person who's sick and tired of being sick and tired. You can feel that person who's tired of being miserable. And you can feel that same spirit when people have internalized and embraced this whole recovery program. It's something. It's like a light shining inside of people. Our agency wants to continue to be that beacon of light in the city of Detroit and southeastern Michigan. We are the trailblazers in this region who have brought this paradigm shift to our community and we're still a young organization, still in its early maturation period.

G. When a whole village or a community is recovery-friendly, what are the possibilities? How does that concept, realized, affect the quality of life?

A. Here in Detroit, our two biggest challenges for people in recovery are adequate living arrangements and employment. If we can address those two aspects, we have begun to solve the problems in our community, as well as the problems of the world, so to speak. We've been talking about building a recovery village in our community for at least five or six years.

We recently acquired a home next door to this West Side location. It's going to be a home for women in recovery. Next door is vacant land, and right behind is vacant land. Our goal is to take those vacant lots and build recovery houses. We'll have living arrangements that are recovery friendly, and then the recovery center, where you get all your recovery support. So we'll have a continuum of care.

There's another building across the street. Our goal is to acquire that property. That will be our employment center. That's going to be a hub to generate revenue that can support our organization, so we ultimately don't have to depend on grant funding 100 percent. We want to provide a variety of training and other options—electrician, plumbing, carpet cleaning, cosmetology, a whole pool of opportunities for people who have the desire to work—either for somebody or as an entrepreneur. So instead of asking people for jobs, we want to create our own jobs. Why not? People have done it before us. People will do it after us. We want to create, to learn how to do videography, and create a camera crew like Greg Williams. If you can do this, why can't we?

G. You've been one of the pioneers of this emerging recovery movement since the summit in St. Paul in 2001. Tell me about connecting with people from all across the country who are trying to unite this movement and to bring something national forward to the country.

A. I think the one thing I've found in working with people around the country is that we all have a passion. Leaders, people who are dynamic, people who have been committed to this recovery process. I've sat down with Phil Valentine out of Connecticut, Joe Powell out of Dallas. What's my buddy in Texas? Ben Bass. Anita Bertram out of Ohio. David Whiters out of Atlanta. Tim Cheney from Maine. I had heard these names before I met them, but when I met them it was an honor and a privilege. I've probably been one of the youngest guys who has been a part of this movement. Back in the day, way before you came along, Greg—we were still praying for you at that time. I've got to plug that in because that's how they used to do me when I was young. We're people in long-term recovery leading successful organizations throughout the country. We were part of this initial funding from SAMHSA. And just to have some federal funding to help people in recovery, it's a huge blessing.

G. So getting the funding, networking in the movement . . . in what other ways did your exposure to organizing nationally prove relevant to your work?

A. Dr. Trent and I started to spend more time traveling to Washington, DC. We started traveling throughout the country to see what other programs were doing, to see what we could bring back to Detroit because all those programs were the first. They were our predecessors in terms of establishing recovery community centers. This is nothing we've created per se; we try not to reinvent the wheel. We see what other people are doing and how we can apply it to our community. And we found something that has worked. We have a wireless computer laboratory at all our facilities, new Mac computers teaching people basic Internet skills, teaching people how to connect online. We keep our pulse on the recovery community and the recovery community keeps their pulse on the Detroit Recovery Project.

G. That's an effective way to unite and grow. One last big question. As this new recovery advocacy movement grows, and the paradigm

shifts to recovery in a big way, what are the possibilities, not just in the city of Detroit, but what happens to America, and even the world?

A. I think what happens is when the world can embrace the recovery movement, the world will support it better. It can be financial, it can be in-kind, it can be resources, it can be improving the mindsets of people in recovery, or inspiring people who are not in recovery. It's about long-term, increasing public awareness. And having people accept us more. We need to make sure, not only locally, but also nationally, that recovery is readily available for everybody. How do we do that? We make sure we have resources. We make sure we understand that to suffer from this illness is not to suffer from lack of morality. It doesn't care about your economic condition; it doesn't care about your race, ethnicity, or religion. We have to educate our community. Ultimately, I'm hoping this dynamic documentary you guys are working on will raise awareness, raise consciousness locally and nationally, and let folks know that recovery is possible. Treatment does work and we've got to support this. When we support people in recovery, we're supporting our community, and we're supporting our country.

Thanks to Andre's passion, I was beginning to see beyond the cliché and deeper into the fresh truth of an old idea: one-to-one is one-for-all. I got it in the following interview with Dr. Trent—like a swift kick in the seat of my pants.

CALVIN TRENT, PHD

"The next step for us is to not see this as a recovery thing just for addicts, but to see it as a way of building community for all of us."

Dr. Trent is *not* a person in recovery, that is, he never suffered from addiction and never personally experienced its horror, and so, in that sense, he is not a bona fide member of the recovery club. Nevertheless, he is fully immersed in its support and learning activities. Dr. Trent is a psychologist by trade who found his calling helping individuals and communities deal with addiction and all its associated psychological and social problems. He is retired from the City of Detroit Health Department, where he served as Director of the Bureau of Substance Abuse, providing prevention, treatment, and recovery services for individuals in the city. He was also Director of Special Populations Health Services, in which he served a similar function, which included HIV services. He later became Director of the Health Department and the Health Officer for the City of Detroit. Currently, he leads Real Michigan, a nonprofit organization he founded that is dedicated to promoting a policy agenda around recovery and the recovery community.

As you read his words, I hope you can hear his voice—calm, measured, thoughtful, and graced with warmth and humor. Serenity envelops this wise man. When you are in the presence of someone who has followed his or her bliss, like Dr. Trent, you tend to listen intently because they are likely on to something, a truth you would be blessed to understand.

GREG. Andre talked about how you mentored him and how important it was to have someone like you with the passion and skills to help him along. What did you see in Andre and how did your leadership assist in his growth as a leader?

CALVIN. Andre was working at another community organization, Grandparents Taking Care of Grandkids, and they were doing work with seniors. And it ended up that 80 percent of the kids who were being taken care of were the children of addicts. Andre, coincidentally, was a person in recovery, so I hired him to head the Partnership for a Drug Free Detroit. That was a prevention coalition, really, because the recovery paradigm really wasn't formed at that time. When I hired Andre, actually, he was not very good at what I had hired him to do, but I noticed that he was very personable and there was always a group of people around him, very involved in this whole thing called recovery. As a psychologist, I was very interested in recovery. I had worked in addiction, as a counselor, and that was my passion. I found that as long as people were in a treatment environment they did fine, but once they left, a huge number returned to their previous activities. That was always very discouraging. It was fascinating to me that Andre had maybe ten years of recovery and this cadre of people around him were also in long-term recovery, and I was curious about what it was that worked for him and those others that did not work for so many of the other people.

G. How did you get the Detroit Recovery Project started and get Andre involved?

C. Interestingly, a grant came out under the Bush Administration called the Recovery Community Support Program Grant, and it was to promote people coming together to advocate for recovery. So, Andre and I went to Washington to investigate if we could get the grant. We applied for the grant. We didn't get it the first round, but because I was a director of the Bureau and we did have some money to build coalitions, I was able to allocate $100,000 to the young people interested in being a visible voice for recovery within the community. I asked Andre to get together a group of these people. We did some surveys, and we took their experiences and created a recovery community group and he provided leadership for that. In the next round offered on the grant, we applied and we were successful—$325,000 for four years. Being in city government, I understood that grants were good as long as they lasted, but when the grant went out, we closed the program down. I didn't want to see that happen, so we thought of establishing a community-based organization for sustainability, Detroit Recovery Project, which would work on recovery before the money was spent, and transfer the grant to that organization. Then I got Andre to become the head of Detroit Recovery Project.

G. Could you ever have imagined what the Detroit Recovery Project has become today?

C. Actually, I can. I saw the power in the recovery community. But these people in recovery, they were anonymous. I was able to see that most of the people who go to meetings were all right, but the people who didn't go were not. I knew there was a kernel of something about this relationship they were forming, either with the twelve-step program or with individuals there. In many ways they were doing the majority work of sustaining people in recovery. I was taken aback that, as psychologists and professionals, we didn't include these people in our work or thinking about the utility of it. It was like, why can't we grow this and pay them for doing the work? Because they are keeping people sober. That's the beginning of it, but it has grown into something much more for me.

G. You've actually taken the Detroit Recovery Project model of public recovery to a global level, haven't you? Talk a little about your work in Africa, for example.

C. In Detroit we're able to say that treatment is not the center of the work we should be doing. Recovery is the center and treatment is a part of it. We were successful here, and other people heard about the projects we're doing and said, "For the first time in Africa, we can do a substance abuse project to help prevent HIV and AIDS; could you guys come and help us with our program?" It was perfect for me when I got there because I found out that, in the whole of East Africa, there was only one treatment facility, and it was in Mombasa, Kenya. What do you do when you have no treatment? What you do is recovery. So we found about thirty people in recovery, brought them together, trained them on the twelve-step program, and helped their recovery community bloom. They began to establish meetings and a recovery drop-in center. They had no funding. Our project was advisory; it did not give them any organizational funding, no capital funding to build a recovery center or anything like that. But they were able to grab onto the principles of recovery outlined by the Twelve Steps and worked that recovery within their community. The community that we did our work in is 95 percent Muslim and I thought, how are we going to do a twelve-step there? This is kind of a Christian thing, isn't it? Wouldn't they reject it? No, they adapted it to their belief system and they worked the program in the mosques. So it is more than about recovery.

They still have no treatment programs, but they have twelve sober houses with probably twenty people in each, and they have a sober house for women. Everybody in Zanzibar and most people in Tanzania are trying to send their young people to these sober houses, which are self-sufficient in a community that has no means, you know, is very poor. But even in the poorest place, they are so devastated by the issue of addiction that they'll take even their last few cents to help their child find some way to get out of this. It's tremendously successful.

G. **Your experience in Africa seems to be an affirmation that recovery can work in any community. What did you learn from your experience . . . anything surprise you?**

C. I am surprised at the amount of drug addiction that is pervasive throughout the world. You don't go to a country no matter how poor or how rich without finding this issue, and it's a growing issue. We don't recognize how pervasive it is, but I believe the drug culture informs everything that we do. Our kids are caught up in the reliance on things outside themselves and outside their fellows. If you have a headache, your mood is not good, you're bored—you take a pill or you take a drink. We don't find the quality in each other. We're losing so many of our young people. This recovery process is the way to gain back those kids.

G. **What did you mean a moment ago when you said, "It is more than about recovery"?**

C. I don't like to separate community because these things are happening everywhere. People desire and crave for people. I believe what my life is directed toward now is a better understanding of what community is and how important community is to people and their development. What to me was curative about this recovery piece is the idea of being included in a community and being loved by people in that community. That force helps people believe they can achieve things. In the recovery community people talk to each other, people meet, and they associate. When you get into this group, who's the most important person in the recovery group? It's the newest person in there. They have a sense of giving back and they have an understanding that it's not all about "me." It is about a connectedness not only to each other, but also to some spiritual essence.

As I look around me, I don't see that in my Detroit neighborhoods. I see people in the general neighborhood where they don't really interact. We are social people, but somehow our lives now are taking us out of that social realm. People don't talk to their neighbors. This sense of disconnectedness is all around us.

My hope for recovery is that it will inform the broader communities, the broader neighborhoods, about how we get back to community. How do we get back to needing each other, caring for each other, not for a monetary gain and all these things, but like what happens within the recovery community? People have distress. They call each other up. They're friends. They hug each other. They hug newcomers. How does this inform us in our lives now, in the digital age of texting? I think that this has something to give us all in terms of how we should be responding to each other. So, I expect it to grow, but I expect it to go to another level, where it begins to inform the larger community about how to really be community.

G. You seem to be saying that recovery can apply to more than just addiction problems in a community, that it can have relevance to our larger society.

C. I think this process of recovery has a lot to offer our community as a whole, our city as a whole, and the country as a whole. There is something about human nature and human aspiration and human potential that is involved in how this recovery piece works. I'm not in recovery. I never had a drug issue, but I am so attracted to the togetherness, to the sense of community that people in recovery have, that I'm, you know, a recovery groupie. I want everybody to have what they have. I hope the next step for us is to not see this as a thing just for addicts, but to see it as a way of building community for all of us. We need to go to places where we see each other more. We need to associate with people more. I've discovered and become part of a field of study and research around community and what that means— fascinating work on how we don't go to church anymore, how we don't have organizations anymore, how we don't have dinner with our friends anymore, how we don't have dinner with our kids. All this is about how we associate. The recovery movement re-teaches us, in our real existence, not only how to associate again, but how important it is for us to be feeling loved together. There's a curative thing about being in community and that's what we're building. We're building a recovery community.

The voices of Andre Johnson and Dr. Calvin Trent. Their words clanged around inside my head, ringing and mingling with the faces and voices of literally thousands of others we encountered on our journey through recovery land. The sounds and images we had collected were beginning to coalesce. Like catalysts, Andre Johnson and Dr. Trent brought together the disparate ingredients of our experience to produce a new idea about recovery that was even bigger than recovery from addiction to substances.

I'm getting to it. Do you see it yet? It may not be obvious at first. Look inside. Or, look in the mirror.

While you're doing that . . . two more things happened in Detroit to heighten the epiphany.

At dawn the next day, we headed for Belle Isle, a great island park in the middle of the Detroit River, the Motor City on one side, Canada's mainland on the other. We drove east across the MacArthur Bridge blinded by a brilliant sunrise, which boded fair weather for the Worldwide Rally for Recovery scheduled to begin in the park at 11:00 A.M. Given the distinction and importance of this event, Greg blew the budget and hired an additional camera crew with a thirty-foot crane to capture the full size and spirit of the event. When we saw that prized piece of cinematic hardware arrive and assembled, we cheered, "Oh man, we are going to make a movie today!" We worked the early morning hours planning and setting up shots along the march route and in the central stage area on a large athletic field. There, preparations were already underway for the music, speakers, food, and vendors, all of which would welcome the march's end and help celebrate the day.

The crisp autumn air seemed to crackle with anticipation of the event, as organizers scurried about warming themselves with hot coffee. Bob Lindsay, President and CEO of NCADD came all the way from New York and joined us in the parking lot as we unloaded. He brought us hot coffee, too, and asked, "How can I help?" He was the first of several giving folks who would show up throughout the day to assist us, including one enterprising volunteer, who drove us around in a golf cart, so we and our equipment could stay ahead of the march.

This was the first recovery march I had been to and I wasn't sure what the mood would be like. Certainly, the McShin Foundation event in Richmond that we had attended the previous weekend was public and festive, attracting thousands, but it was tucked away in the rear parking area of a church, barely visible to passersby. Detroit's event was about as wide open as you could find one—and in view of two countries! It could have been a subdued affair, actually, with the heavy force of a serious cause motivating earnest, but reticent people, somewhat shy of exposing their recovery in such a public way. Stigma is a powerful inhibitor. I just didn't know what to expect.

It didn't take long to find out. By 9:00 A.M., buses started to arrive and participants spilled out into the staging area. When these crusaders hopped off their buses, smiles and hoots of joy would break out, as if each were taking the first step on the surface of the moon. One small step for a person, one giant leap for recovery. They wore the colors of their cause and their organizations, and carried a confusion of placards, banners, and balloons. Immediately, the temperature began to rise. The feeling of excitement, camaraderie, and focus among the celebrants was palpable. The day was transformed. It was like a second dawn lighting up the place with new life energy.

There was no shame evident, just pride. And unrestrained happiness. The area filled with thousands in no time, people mingling, hugging, and greeting friends they knew from other places. There was laughter and tears, singing and chanting. This was a celebration for all the world to see, hear, and embrace. Even I burst out with a laugh when I turned to see the door of a bus open, and out bounded John Shinholser from Virginia.

Besides the emotional surge one felt witnessing this eager gathering of faces and voices in recovery, there was something else to recognize, thanks to the insights of Andre Johnson and Dr. Trent. This was clearly a community of people. No matter where they came from, they were and felt connected to one another. Of course, there was a common cause to unite them, and it is not uncommon for any convention of people with a purpose to feel a bond. But the connection here went beyond the cause. It was illustrative of the power of nurtured interpersonal connections—the distinctive attribute of people in recovery—to create and strengthen a community, and simultaneously, strengthen one's self.

I realized: You do not have to be in recovery from addiction to apply this to your life.

As if to fertilize the growth of this insight, we were invited to attend a spiritual service of recovery that evening. Late afternoon, we wrapped the park site, buoyant with the success of the rally and our filming, and by seven o'clock, we found ourselves in the middle of one of Detroit's many downtrodden neighborhoods. As we turned the corner at East State Fair, just six blocks off Interstate 75, we noticed a stream of well-dressed people—couples, children, seniors, most of them African-American—entering a single-story, painted brick building that might have once housed a machine shop. Whatever. It was now a house of God. We were at the church of the True Oracles of God Ministries, Pastor Reverend Germany E. Bennett officiating. Or I should say "celebrating."

Talk about a point of light in the darkness. Here was a critical mass of people, many in recovery, or touched by addiction in their families, generating so much energy in testimony, song, and spirit, I thought their radiation would blow the roof off. It might have bathed the whole city in white light.

We jockeyed for fly-on-the-wall camera positions in the crowded sanctuary, but there was no way we could not feel part of the service. The decibels were high in this bright, colorful room; the walls, the pews, the pulpit, and parishioners, alike, all pulsated with exuberant rejoicing. We were inside a nuclear reactor where people, like molecules, were fusing, exploding, and creating chain reactions. The congregation was connecting to their higher power, in unison and in harmony with each other. These connections, with one another and with their God, were giving them strength, and it was clear that when they left this gospel service, they would be radiating light and spreading strength out into their communities.

This joyous service of praise and affirmation was a cathartic experience. It didn't have to be about addiction recovery to see the light.

The following day, we did an early interview with the twenty-year President and CEO of the National Association for Children of Alcoholics (NACoA), Sis Wenger, in whose home we stayed for the three days we were in Detroit. Then, we made a beeline for Boston where the next recovery event was to culminate in a rally inside the State House—an assembly of citizens in a place oozing with history. On the long drive, we had plenty of time to contemplate Detroit and exchange ideas among the three of us. Our brains were roiling with experiences, conversations, and observations while each of us tried to find adequate expression in words.

Then, just outside of Youngstown, Ohio, I was at the wheel cruising along on I-80, which I took to mean how fast I could go. The boys were napping. We were out of granola bars, I was feeling a bit hungry and I noticed, too, that the gas tank needed a drink. As we approached one of the major intersections of interstate and local highways, I kept my eye out for signs of eats and fuel. Suddenly before me, a barrage of billboards appeared, all offering indulgent dining experiences—donuts, waffles, pizza, tacos, wings, burgers, chicken, fried this, fried that, and the ever-popular beef & bacon barbecue. A sign for each, many repeating relentlessly.

Point is, the choices were excessive. It was an assault, these highway sirens of caloric temptation: Come ye hither and be satisfied. Then, as I looked and admittedly licked my chops, the words came. Four simple words. I whispered them under my breath.

And I felt like I had just divulged a secret at my first anonymous group meeting.

Chapter Eight

INSIGHTS

We. Are. All. Addicts.

There. I said it again. That word, "addicts." This time, however, I am lumping myself and everyone else into that category.

But wait. Before I go on, I must qualify. By calling us all addicts, I do not mean to diminish the severity of the type of addiction people have who suffer from substance use disorders. There is nothing that compares to that. The devastation that chemical addiction causes to individual and society, simultaneously, is unmatched in its damage and scope. No question, if we focused on solutions to alcohol and other drug use disorders with urgency, as Patrick Kennedy said, "We could change this overnight." But if we could address *all* our addictions, the world would be an even better place.

And this is possible, because no matter what we are addicted to, no matter how trivial seeming or severe, people in addiction recovery have secrets to share— secrets to help us all repair, recover, and redeem our lives.

OUR COMMON PROBLEM

We are all addicted to something. Apart from alcohol and other drugs, some of our manifestations of addiction are quite serious, ultimately with heavy personal and societal costs: nicotine, for example. Some are minor and manageable: chocolate. And some are symptomatic of a greater, insidious malaise that also requires our attention: the Internet, for one, which can have the paradoxical effect of disconnecting us from human interaction.

There are so many others, all with serious consequences. That's why there are so many support groups patterned after AA's twelve-step program, which exist for specific problems and manifestations, not necessarily related to alcohol and/or other drugs. By some accounts, there are upward of 250 groups, many with Anonymous after their name. They run the gamut of troubled behavior and reveal, by their very existence, populations of people who feel they need help: food addicts; gamblers; debtors; neurotics; nicotine; overeaters; online gamers; sexaholics; shopaholics; smokers; workaholics. These and other overindulged activities, whether TV, texting, or even running are commonly acknowledged addictive behaviors that can interfere with normal life. All these things feel good. Until they don't anymore. Until they make you physically or mentally ill. Or affect someone close to you.

As disparate as our "dis-eases" may be, there are enough similarities to justify looking for a common "cure." The disease theory holds that the brain is physically altered by addiction, and the science is clear about how alcohol and other drugs can physically change the neural receptors in the reward center of the brain's circuitry. Changes can be permanent. That is unquestionably a disease model, as surely as cirrhosis changes the architecture of the liver.

The difficulty in painting this disease picture black and white is that there is a concurrent emotional learning going on in the brain as one is getting and feeling high. The resulting emotional memory is comprised not only of the euphoria created by the drug, but also of the context in which it was taken—the place, the people, the ritual, and other external factors. These external stimuli are variable, and the brain, which houses literally quadrillions of synapses, has ample resources to develop new associations and learning pathways that facilitate that memory. So whether you are using heroin or sneaking a Twinkie, your brain is learning a habit that, to a greater or lesser degree, gives you no choice but to seek the reward of it over and over. That's why AA says to avoid the people, places, and things that reinforce your addiction and that your new behavior will help you recover from. Taking the idea further, there are those who therefore believe that addiction can be "unlearned" through aversive therapies; they don't see addiction as a true disease, allowing only that it is *like* a disease.

Personally, this sounds like a semantic argument to me. I find it hard to accept that addiction is not a disease, when it incontrovertibly changes that organ between our ears. But I'll let the lab coats debate that one.

What we can learn from this, though, is that the mechanism of emotional learning—the old region of the mid-brain that signals our likes and dislikes, fears and pleasures—can be tapped and taught to build new connections involving both the reward and reasoning regions of the brain. Under conditions of support and will, we can change our patterns of behavior and belief. Granted, that is a more difficult and potentially lifelong process for those suffering from substance use disorders, than it is for someone trying to quell TV habits or a craving for chips. But the brain's approach to recovery from any manifestation of addiction is similar biologically, one to the other. Healing can happen. And people can get better.

So, if we accept that recovery is possible and is real, what do we work on that is going to help us all overcome our problems? I wrote earlier in this book that I had discovered something about recovery, from people in recovery, that transcends even the healing of addiction to substances. Andre Johnson and Dr. Trent nailed it for me. Recovery is a process; it recognizes and admits the problem, and then takes steps toward elevating the human spirit to a higher plane, and serving a greater good. In short, recovery works for all of us when we see ourselves as a community capable of healing. Dr. Trent said:

> "We are social people, but somehow our lives now are taking us out of that social realm. People don't talk to their neighbors. This sense of disconnectedness is all around us."

That's what I think defines addiction. Feeling—then becoming—disconnected. Whether you are chemically intoxicating yourself, or isolating yourself from others to increase your own peculiar gratification, or numbing yourself from some physical or psychological pain, or insulating yourself from the plight of others, you are disconnecting. We, as a community of people, are headed down that path. Research suggests that the more materialistic our society has become, the more our ties to community have broken apart, and we have become more individualistic, or some would say narcissistic. Robert Putnam, in his extensively researched book, *Bowling Alone: The Collapse and Revival of American Community* (New York: Simon & Schuster, 2000), substantiates how our social capital—the relationships we build in and through our families and out into our communities—has declined. As Putnam observes, more of us are bowling, but there are fewer leagues.

We become addicted to the disconnected state we are in and, like an addict, we are lying to ourselves, telling ourselves we feel better by retreating into the safety of feeling nothing, a place where there seems to be no pain. It's a lie, but we cannot get out of it. We are overwhelmed and even frightened by the world around us as we face what we perceive as threats to our well-being—finances, epidemics, violence near and far, even changing weather. Our old amygdala, deep inside our brain, sends out the fear signal and we react to protect ourselves with boredom, apathy, cynicism, lethargy, and isolation salved by can't-get-enough potato chips, TV, shopping, work, cigarettes, sex, or gambling. Or drugs. Or alcohol. We look for whatever feel-good substitute we can find for the serenity we should be feeling when we are in harmony with the world. When reality sucks, it seems easier to escape inward than change the world outside ourselves.

Yes, we are all addicts; each of us is addicted to something, which makes our larger society addicted, too. Our destructive behaviors erode the quality of the society in which we live, which in turn, is a feedback mechanism for our fears. Our societal body is not unlike the suffering of an individual whose addiction to a substance sucks the life right out of body and soul. As a consequence, we feel even more pain and go deeper into the darkness. It is our common problem.

Before this gets all too depressing, let us re-affirm something. People in successful, long-term recovery have answers. There are lighted pathways out of the darkness. Rest assured, there is hope. People in recovery of another kind showed me that, too—in a place where you might least expect it.

CONNECTIONS

In late 2012, shortly after we came off the road having finished principal filming, the three of us, and more so our patient families, were looking forward to the holiday break to chill with our loved ones in Connecticut after the long and frequent absences of the past year. Then, on December 14, unimaginable tragedy struck our world. In five minutes time, twenty children and six adult teachers and staff were shot dead in the Sandy Hook Elementary School by a lone, mentally ill young man armed with an automatic assault rifle, handgun, and other instruments of destruction. Earlier that morning, he also murdered his mother.

Greg is from Newtown, the municipality that includes Sandy Hook, while Craig and I are just minutes away in neighboring towns. Each of us knew families directly affected by this horrific event. I have found no words in all that has been written and said that adequately describes the aftermath or how we all felt about it. Suffice it to say, the event remains beyond our understanding and beyond our ability to share grief deeply enough, except in tears, hugs, knowing looks, and too feeble acts of sympathy.

There is a sad irony to this story. The official report about the crime describes the shooter as a youth who was so disconnected from normal life that though he lived in the same house as his mother, in the months preceding his rampage he communicated with her only by email. He spent most of his time holed up and isolated in the basement of the house playing violent video games and obsessing over mass murderers.

Then, it all breaks. He goes forth and literally breaks his most fundamental life connections. He murders his mother and then, in some significantly symbolic way, severs his connection with Sandy Hook Elementary School, a place that from all reports represented a good time in his life. Finally, he performed on himself the ultimate disconnection. How much more of an explicit example do we need of one's own personal tragedy causing widespread collateral damage? His killing deeds broke not only his personal connections; it tore apart families, communities, and ripped through the world. In disconnecting himself, he disconnected us. The enormity of the trauma affected us all, to one degree or another. While there was an initial outpouring of sympathy directed to the people of Newtown, we simultaneously withdrew into the perceived safety of our self-protective cocoons and failed to act—as a society—to curb the larger forces tearing at our common bonds.

Physically, emotionally, spiritually, that time was rock bottom for Sandy Hook. How does one find recovery from that? What the small community of Newton did illustrates the power of recovery.

SMALL IS BIG

Newtown is trying to recover and is succeeding in many small, practical, and observable ways. People are connecting anew. One local woman said that when you walk down the aisle of the local supermarket now, people make eye contact and say, "Hi," even when they don't know one another. People seem kinder. Small gestures fill one with a sense of connection with all others in the community. There is a rising sense of responsibility to each other. It grows and pervades the community. That "Hi" in the aisle is a like the gentle flap of a butterfly wing. That's how recovery works. Small. Moment to moment. Daily. It builds into a giant realization that individuals and communities are in recovery together. One can never be healed completely from the wounds of the loss at Sandy Hook, just as no one can erase the horror of addiction from their life. It's part of us forever, but it doesn't have to define us. In a weird way it's a gift, because of what it awakens in people.

One thing that lights up is hope. In the weeks immediately following the tragedy, Greg, Craig, and I made a short film to raise urgently needed support for the Newtown Parent Connection, a local volunteer group that runs programs of education, prevention, healing, and wellness related to mental health, drug, and alcohol problems in the community, all of which were exacerbated by the tragedy. The way the organization goes about its work involves an intimate connection with one person, one family at a time. Can you conceive of anything more difficult than confronting the personal trauma of Sandy Hook? Yet, in the face of fresh pain, Donna DeLuca, cofounder of the Newtown Parent Connection had the perspective to realize, "This is an issue that is much more far-reaching than Newtown; it's more about humanity." Her cofounder, Dorrie

Carolan added, "We will be around long after the cameras are gone and we will be a beacon of hope for the rest of the world."

So how do we find recovery from our personal and societal ills and restore our connections? Just like an addict does: You climb out of your dark hole and into the light of recovery, a little at a time. You start rebuilding your social capital, much like the person coming out of addiction seeks to rely on recovery capital (such as peers and recovery community organizations) for support. Specific, practical steps, not very complicated, will do.

You say "Hi" to a stranger in the supermarket.

You make sure to have more frequent dinners with your family. No smart phones allowed at the table, just smart and silly talk among family.

You invite friends over. Eat together. Play a board game.

Join a bowling league, if you must. But get out into your community, join any group and make connections. Join the PTA. Coach youth soccer. Bring food regularly to a local soup kitchen. Volunteer at a Recovery Community Center. Local volunteerism is a rewarding, infectious activity.

Lest some of these ideas sound trivial, superficial, and inadequate, remember the small, simple things a person in recovery does when facing a weak moment, craving a drink or a drug. He or she calls someone to talk with, goes to a meeting, or listens to a piece of music. Or, goes out to help someone else.

THE GOLDEN RULE

Over 2,500 years ago, someone came up with this basic humanist idea: "Do not do to others what you do not want done to yourself." That was Confucius, of course, and what became known as the Golden Rule has had various reiterations in the centuries since. Its modern interpretation is more positive and exhorts the individual to be proactive, "Do unto others what you would have them do unto you." We all know it, most of us believe in its goodness, but we have forgotten its meaning and intent in the cloud of its cliché. A moment of contemplation, though, about its active benevolence can refresh it, reframe it, and reveal its secret power: "Do good for others and you do good for yourself." Unleash it in your life and it can help build a universal moral system, unencumbered by the trappings of any religion, one that promotes empathy, understanding, and compassion.

COMPASSION AND CHANGE

The secret of people in recovery? They practice the Golden Rule variant every day. Bill Wilson knew that helping someone else was key to recovery. Dr. Trent broadened that to include community. By proactively caring for others, he believes, we can rebuild our communities. We can have a loving community just like the recovery community has. I believe he is right. The recovery community is a healing community, because all its members care for each other. With kindness and love, there is no hesitation to help or to hug. And the miracle is that your own strength grows, even as you are giving it away to others.

Imagine now, 313 million of us variously addicted persons in long-term successful recovery—healing ourselves, then becoming healers and simultaneously becoming productive, caring citizens—connecting and lifting each other up constantly. One individual at a time. One day at a time. That's how communities recover. That's how a whole nation can recover.

The new recovery advocacy movement with its cries for life, freedom, and fairness is relevant to everyone. We should all embrace it, for we are all in this together. Allies. (Thank you, Andre!) Every one of us must surely want what the movement wants: anti-discriminatory health policies, treatment and recovery support services, education, prevention, and criminal justice reforms to name a few, because they are issues that affect us all. We only need to learn to have the compassion that will effect change. Flap those wings and cause a stir.

Can addicts change the world?

Yes.

We can.

Chapter Nine

MORE GEMS

I had a problem writing this book—the same problem Greg had editing his film. There is so much content we both had to leave out. There are, I confess, many more gems still lying on the cutting room floor and in files on my laptop called "outtakes."

With all the hours of compelling interviews, exclusive footage of recovery programs, and privileged experiences with gracious people, our bins overflowed with powerful stories of recovery. In a planned ninety-minute film, there was no way Greg could include anywhere near all of those stories we recorded. The problem is, there is not an insignificant face or voice in the recovery movement. There is not one person whose face and voice should not be in Greg's film, nor in this book; but there was no time in the film for everyone, nor space in this book.

Greg had pointed his Honda Pilot, with his two filmmaker brothers in tow, toward places unknown, with the absolute faith and optimism that we would discover a movement. What we found and filmed constitutes an exhaustive record of our journey through many faces of America—social, economic, political, racial, and religious—where superficial differences are as apparent as topography.

Deeper into that journey and beneath the landscapes that separate us, Greg led us into mysterious and revelatory territory: that of the human spirit. What we recorded transcends all differences in the diversity we observed. Time and again, we witnessed a powerful force of good in people, elemental and unifying. No matter the appearance, no matter the experience, behind the face one common, beautiful voice emerged. Like a song everyone knew by heart, it sang of changing the national conversation from the dark problems of addiction to the illuminated solutions of recovery, of removing the stigma of a condition that is truly a disease, of fighting for social justice, and of advocating for policies of fairness and equality. It was a mixed chorus singing in unison about commitment, hope, and change—truly many faces, one voice.

You should have been there with us. It was a twenty-four/seven deal, encountering one person or group after another in the recovery movement, filling our days and nights on the road with help and inspiration. Each person we met had an amazing story to tell and nearly all were willing to tell it. It kills me not to include or mention everyone. I can't even give you a valid reason for choosing some over others. For those I couldn't fit into this book, over the months to come I will bring their stories to you one at a time through my blog, which you can find on www.ManyFaces1Voice.org.

EPILOGUE

How powerful are people in recovery? How effective is their network?

To date, Greg reports that over one million people have seen *The Anonymous People*. What is remarkable is how they saw it. After all, it was not widely publicized in mainstream media; few documentaries are. And those special niche films that do come into mass-market consciousness are backed by money machines that can pay $70,000 for full-page ads in the *New York Times*. So who marketed *The Anonymous People*? Who got the film into those local theatres in towns and cities across America? The same people who got the film made in the first place: You—people in recovery.

Kickstarter, the grassroots, crowd-sourcing funding platform, propelled the initial production of the film into high gear, making it possible for Greg to film key people and recovery events throughout the country in a timely way and keep our tanks full of gas and Red Bull. Kickstarter was you.

The story leads, the introductions to influential people, and the invitations to events cascaded beyond our ability to cover them all. They came from you.

The hospitality, the hands-on assistance, the paving of the highway that brought us through our journey smoothly—that was your doing.

The momentum of the new recovery advocacy movement is building and moving forward. You are pushing it.

Like bees in a hive, the recovery community transmits messages among themselves in unseen, seemingly instantaneous ways. There was already an audible buzz about *The Anonymous People* even as we arrived in a city for the first time to do some filming. Your networking and communication is far-reaching and powerful.

Greg set out in his film to change the conversation from the problem of addiction to the solution of recovery. The message is explicit in his film and it has been delivered into the recovery community and to the fringes of the general public. What now? Is the word spreading and the conversation changing?

Well, there have been some notable happenings since *The Anonymous People* was released: the film was screened at the US Capitol before members of Congress, administration leaders, and addiction and recovery experts; the film had a traditional theatrical release in New York City and Los Angeles; by the end of 2014, it had been seen in hundreds of local theaters and community centers and became available through popular streaming services, such as Netflix, Amazon, Hulu, and iTunes. There is no question the film, and the buzz around it, is raising awareness. Anecdotal evidence tells us it contributed to the impetus behind creating Canada's first Recovery Day, and the re-birth of the New Hampshire Recovery Movement, and the formation of new Recovery Community Centers in Idaho. Reports from some of recovery's esteemed ambassadors, including Tara Conner, Tom Coderre, and John Shinholser, all suggest that they are in greater demand and more active than ever in the public arena. It compelled one author to write a book about it. So yes, the conversation is changing—and it is growing in intensity.

Greg, Craig, and I have each attended a number of local screenings of the film around the country, where we have appeared on panels to answer questions from the audience about the film. This makes for a wonderful event, which brings the recovery community together alongside regular moviegoers, and helps to raise awareness and sometimes even funds. The film is always well received and often gets a standing ovation. The film inspires a call to action, and inevitably, someone in the audience wants to know, "What can I do now?"

The issues of addiction and recovery are so large and complex, it is easy to be overwhelmed by the size of the problem and the variety of solutions. It is difficult for individuals to know specifically what to do.

The secret, as you have seen, is already known by people in recovery: act small and, collectively, big things can happen. Use the Golden Rule to guide actions to create empathy and spread compassion.

If you are in recovery, tell your story, to one or to many. It doesn't matter. The point is, talking about recovery and showing that it works, at any level, will change people's perception. Start erasing stigma and only good things will happen. You don't have to mention your affiliation, if you are in an anonymous group. That you are proudly succeeding is quite enough. If you are not a person in recovery, become involved just the same. Make sure to listen to the stories of others, and to encourage their sharing with your understanding and support. The contact and the communication of these simple interactions will create connections and build community.

Check out the web for organizations and resources. ManyFaces1Voice.org and FacingAddiction.org, as well as your local recovery organizations are good places to start, not only for support, but to find out about activities in which you can participate or volunteer.

Choose an issue and fight for it. Maybe it is about establishing a local recovery high school or helping to bring a recovery program to a local jail. Maybe you can call your police station to ensure that their officers have Narcan (Naloxone) auto-injection devices to use in saving the lives of victims of opioid overdose. If you like politics, there are always policy initiatives to begin or to support. At the national level, believe it, members of Congress do respond to your voice, as they have with the release of the Comprehensive Addiction and Recovery Act. Write or call your local legislators to advocate—or just to have a conversation that opens your representative's eyes to the power of recovery, and the power of the vote.

Join or organize demonstrations and celebrations for recovery, especially during Recovery Month in September when the high visibility of success can get people thinking and talking about issues. Use social media to fan the flames.

There are many ways to advocate, small and private, or large and public. But pick a path. Because the positive reinforcement you will receive through your advocacy, no matter how small your first step, will make it easier and easier to go forward in your own life, and in the lives of all whom you inspire.

People who have seen Greg's film frequently comment on the history of the movement he presents, not having understood that the tradition of advocacy is deeply rooted and was always expected to grow. Viewers come away with a newfound sense of responsibility to help others. Some now feel strongly that it is a duty to advocate. This can only strengthen the ranks.

When I learned that during October's Breast Cancer Awareness Month in Providence, Rhode Island, supporters raised over $700,000 in sponsorships and donations, and that, nationally, organizations raised $60,000,000 during the year for their cause, I realized what power a community of people can wield. This is for a cause that addresses 30,000 deaths per year caused by breast cancer; another 69,000 survivors are in recovery. These victims and their families deserve all the support we can muster. But need we be reminded that more than 130,000 deaths a year are attributed to alcohol and substance use disorders? Twenty-two million people are at acute risk from addiction. Another twenty-three million are, thankfully, in recovery, but many of them remain vulnerable. And what about their families? Addiction's numbers are staggering, but its public army of recovery advocates and revolutionaries, not so much. Yet. As my father said, "The squeaky wheel gets the grease."

That's why, up until now, silence continues to equal death for those susceptible to addiction.

At the screenings I have attended, a number of people have commented to me that, as a "regular person," it is good and important that I understand this issue and support it. The very fact that I am not a person in recovery somehow gives further validation and strength to the cause. Someone actually said that while the film was great, it preached to the choir and needed, even more urgently, to reach the great unwashed, represented by people like me. There is some truth to that, which is why I wrote this book, actually. Coming from me, an objective "outsider," the ideas and insights I can communicate may add somewhat to the credibility of the cause. I certainly hope it does. But as I said to that gentleman sitting in the dark of the theater, the urgency is not with me at this point in time. It is with the twenty-two million souls in the dark world outside who desperately need these messages. Right now. It is about saving lives. Immediately. Sufferers need to see that recovery is real and it works. They need the hope, then the means, to heal quickly. The best people to communicate that, I suggested, were "The Choir" who were sitting all around him in that theater. The people who came to the screening were already active and interested participants in the movement—just by being there. But, there are millions out there who are not yet part of the choir. The problem is they don't even know that there is a choir, what the choir looks like, or how to sing its song. So, I'll be out there trying to help write some of the music, but it is up to the choir to start singing. Loud.

Finally, someone asked me what my dreams were for the recovery movement. That was a startling question because it is one Greg asked of nearly every person we interviewed. As a person with no direct experience with addiction, I hardly felt qualified to answer. But I'll try here.

I have a radical dream. I join others who say they would love to see the day when anonymous groups are no longer needed. After all, wouldn't that be the logical, ideal conclusion to the erasure of all stigma associated with addiction? Without stigma, there would be no shame. Without shame, why the need to be anonymous? Naively idealistic, you say? If the recovery movement can get everybody to start talking so that everybody starts listening—really listening with a compassionate purpose—why can't we erase stigma? That's the whole point. No stigma. No shame. No discrimination. No prejudice and no injustice. No fears. Say "so long" to anonymity.

The reality is, of course, there will always be a need for anonymous groups, though I wish we could drop the negative connotation of secrecy. They will always serve the important purpose of offering safe haven to those who seek support for their recovery in private and provide an equal spiritual footing for their members. But privacy is different than secrecy. I don't have to know the personal details of your condition or with whom you share them for support;

that's private. But why would you keep your condition and the fact that you are getting help secret—especially if you are in recovery? That's great news! I feel good when you tell me you are well.

Overstated though it may be, obviating the need for secrecy of one's recovery status would be symbolic of a great moral and societal change marked by reconnecting with each other and accepting everyone for who they are, no matter their problems. No need to hide in secret, if we're all in this together. To come out of the Dark Ages and into a Renaissance of Recovery is a welcomed progression of human understanding and common purpose. We're not there yet, but I think that growth is inevitable. If the recovery movement can light the way, the conversation will change, and if all the rest of us will listen with open ears and minds we will, as Stacia Murphy said, embrace each other with open arms and hearts.

Don't get me wrong, folks. I'm not posing as the wise one, here. You have heard these thoughts over and over again in the conversations recorded in this book. The wisdom is older than Confucius. My words are merely reflections and observations, born of an insightful experience with a singular filmmaker and advocate, Greg Williams. He and his band of brothers and sisters in successful recovery know the secrets and carry the wisdom and the light of redemption in the fulfilling of their selfless responsibilities toward others. By sharing their secrets openly, they are leading a movement of recovery for us all.

What I am is a follower, a disciple, and a groupie, like Dr. Calvin Trent, happy to join your ranks and lend support. I can do my small part, whether it is delivering the hope of recovery to one person through these words or delivering groceries to my ninety-year-old neighbor. It is the small things that count, that add up to the big things, and that help the movement grow.

"Be wary of great leaders," Pete Seeger told the *Associated Press* two days after a 2011 Manhattan Occupy march. "Hope that there are many, many small leaders."

Whether foot soldiers or generals, proletarian or policymaker, we can all be recovery revolutionaries. Individually and collectively, we have the power to change the world through small, positive, compassionate actions.

As Bill White says, you are the "recovery carriers." Let us not inoculate ourselves against the contagion, but rather, let us catch a case of that post-addiction condition called recovery and go out into the world and spread a germ or two.

To your continued and blessed health, people in recovery. And ours along with yours.

ACKNOWLEDGMENTS

This is Greg's book. It could not have been written without him. Just as *The Anonymous People* is Greg's film, this book about the film belongs to him because he is the extraordinary force behind all the information and inspiration in it that has been let loose by his irresistible advocacy for recovery.

Speaking of being let loose, I've lived life locked up. Naive really. Then *The Anonymous People* came along to illuminate for me a new world and give me the opportunity to write this book. The privilege to do so was made possible by many who gave their support, personally sacrificed something, and allowed me the freedom to try expressing what had become so important in my life.

First and foremost, thanks to Greg Williams who opened my eyes, so I could look outside of my cage and see a world I had never seen before.

Thanks to artist Steve Alpert who rattled the bars to wake me from procrastination. And to filmmaker Meryl Joseph who replaced the light bulb once when it blew out.

There are three couples, my dearest friends in the world, more like family really, whose love, spirit, and generosity gave me the freedom of time and space to write this book:

Thanks to Drs. George and Christine Burns, who brought gold keys to my cage, dropped them before me, and said, "They are yours whenever you need them."

Thanks to Wayne and Ronnie Marquoit, who lubricated the lock of my cage with love and support when it became seriously stuck.

And thanks to Dr. John and Nancy Lunt, who at a crucial time inserted the keys into the lock and set me free. They even fed me from time to time.

To my real family I must give more than thanks. I give them everything I am.

Tom Nigolian, who translated his blood love for me into moral and material support of such generous amounts, there isn't enough lahmajoun in the world to repay him.

Craig Mikhitarian, my brother and business partner. He was my best man at my wedding and remains so in my life. Besides lending his constructive editorial eye to this book, he held down the fort at our company while I disappeared for long stretches of time into the tower to write. Craig, my constant star, makes me greater and better than I really am.

Michele and Kara, my daughters, smarter than me by a long shot. The love I have for them and my hopes for their future were constant inspirations behind every word I wrote.

Most of all, Brenda Renfroe, my wife, whose love, understanding, patience, sacrifice, and ideas sustained me throughout a process that she endured with saintly patience. Such sustenance as she gave in the face of my self-absorbed writing task is the manifestation of the deepest kind of love, and I am blessed with the marriage of our souls.

There's another family, too, who helped put these words on the page in ways I couldn't possibly have imagined—those dedicated people at Central Recovery Press (CRP). Executive Editor Nancy Schenck and Managing Editor Valerie Killeen are somehow capable of balancing great passion with smart discipline, and turned my unbridled ramblings into an organized and readable book. Patrick Hughes, whose industry knowledge and insights are deep, instilled confidence in me every step of the way. I am very grateful to all at CRP for their commitment to this book, and for all their work to support recovery in its many forms throughout the world.

Finally, the recovery community. Greg's film, so wide in scope and limited by time, simply couldn't include all the inspiring people we met throughout our filmmaking journey. I hope this written record of our journey helps to bring a small sampling of these wonderful faces and voices of recovery to life, and with that, you will have an even greater appreciation of *The Anonymous People*. In some cases, our encounters were only with faces or voices. I never found out all their names. Many of them were there for just an instant in our journey, just to say "Hi" or lend a hand when we needed, like the young man in Georgia whose name I don't know, who sat silent in the back of one of the recovery groups we filmed and later, without being asked, helped us load the heavy equipment cases back into our vehicle, before disappearing into the night never giving us a chance to thank him. Sometimes, almost eerily, someone would suddenly appear on the side of the road waiting for our production vehicle to arrive so he or she could direct us to the correct turn or proper place to park. They were there to help, then they were gone and we wouldn't see them again. People in recovery can be magical. Thank you to all and to the miracles you make.

Now I'm standing here, finally out of my cage, feeling pretty naked and quite humbled. I look around and there are all these amazing people in recovery beckoning me to join them and change the world. Thanks to all of you for showing that recovery works. For you. For me. For everyone.

Now, as William L. White said, "Let's go make some history." (Thanks to you, too, Mr. White.)